ZAP ZAP ZAP

Unidentified Flying Bovine spotted flying over Shinjuku while shooting laser beams from its eyes and spinning at high speed!

I'm still in a daze from all the things that have happened to me one after another since I became a published manga artist. It's all happening so quickly! It's the unexpected events that make life thrilling.

—Hiromu Arakawa, 2001

Born in Hokkaido (northern Japan), Hiromu Arakawa first attracted national attention in 1999 with her award-winning manga *Stray Dog*. Her series *Fullmetal Alchemist* debuted in 2001 in Square Enix's monthly manga anthology *Shonen Gangan*.

D0035359

FULLMETAL ALCHEMIST
VOL. 7

Story and Art by Hiromu Arakawa

Translation/Akira Watanabe
English Adaptation/Jake Forbes
Touch-up Art & Lettering/Wayne Truman
Design/Amy Martin
Editor/Jason Thompson

VP, Production/Alvin Lu
VP, Publishing Licensing/Rika Inouye
VP, Sales & Product Marketing/Gonzalo Ferreyra
VP, Creative/Linda Espinosa
Publisher/Hyoe Narita

Hagane no RenkinJutsushi vol. 7 © 2004 Hiromu Arakawa/SQUARE ENIX. First published in Japan in 2004 by SQUARE ENIX CO., LTD. English translation rights arranged with SQUARE ENIX CO., LTD. and VIZ Media, LLC. The stories, characters and incidents mentioned in this publication are entirely fictional.

Printed in the U.S.A.

Published by VIZ Media, LLC
P.O. Box 77010
San Francisco, CA 94107

10 9 8 7 6 5 4 3
First printing, May 2006
Third printing, February 2009

VIZ
MEDIA
www.viz.com

store.viz.com

鋼の錬金術師

FULLMETAL ALCHEMIST

HIROMU ARAKAWA 荒川弘

7

■ アルフォンス・エルリック

Alphonse Elric

■ エドワード・エルリック

Edward Elric

■ アレックス・ルイ・アームストロング

Alex Louis Armstrong

■ ロイ・マスタング

Roy Mustang

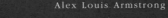

OUTLINE
FULLMETAL ALCHEMIST

Using a forbidden alchemical ritual, the Elric brothers attempted to bring their dead mother back to life. But the ritual went wrong, consuming Edward Elric's leg and Alphonse Elric's entire body. At the cost of his arm, Edward was able to graft his brother's soul into a suit of armor. Equipped with mechanical "auto-mail" to replace his missing limbs, Edward becomes a state alchemist, serving the military on deadly missions. Now, the two brothers roam the world in search of a way to regain what they have lost…

The Elric brothers return to their old alchemy teacher, Izumi Curtis, who also once attempted the abhorred practice of human transmutation. Ed, Al and Izumi have all paid for their sin with a part of themselves but despite losing his entire body, Al has no memory of "the truth" which the others glimpsed when they were "taken." Now Izumi looks for a way to unlock that memory, which may be the key to restoring the boys' bodies. Meanwhile, far away, the assassin Scar recovers from his wounds in a refugee camp…

鋼の錬金術師
FULLMETAL ALCHEMIST

CHARACTERS
FULLMETAL ALCHEMIST

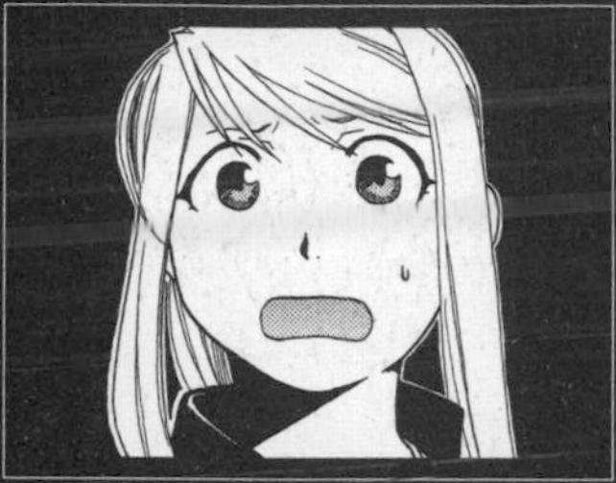

ウィンリィ・ロックベル

Winry Rockbell

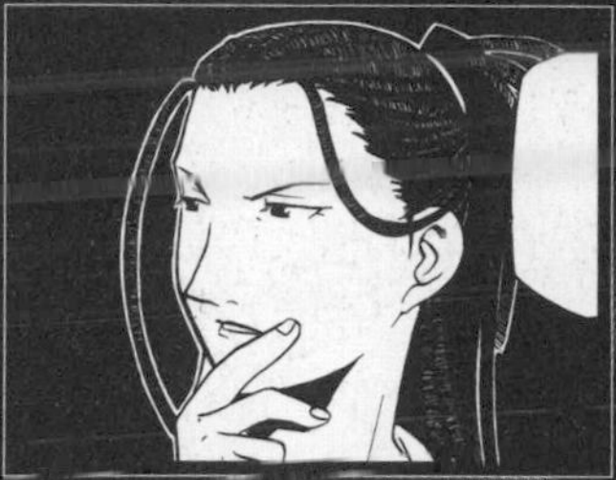

イズミ・カーティス

Izumi Curtis

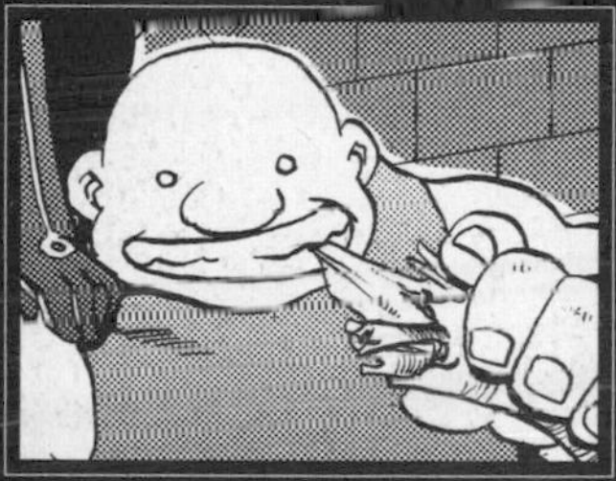

グラトニー

Gluttony

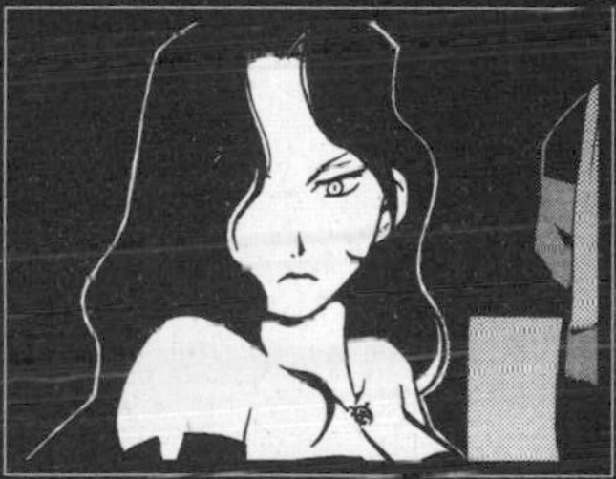

ラスト

Lust

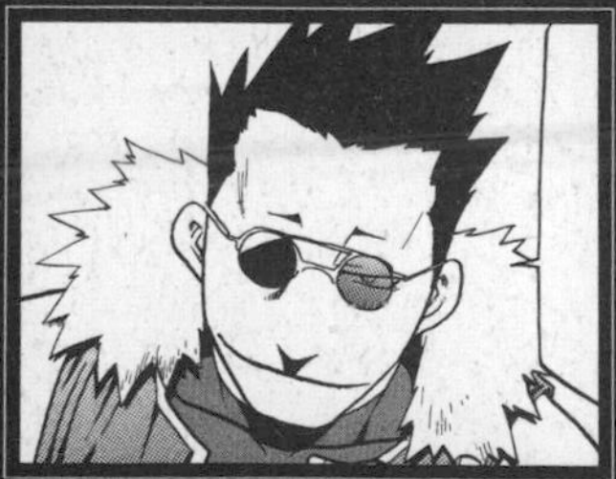

グリード

Greed

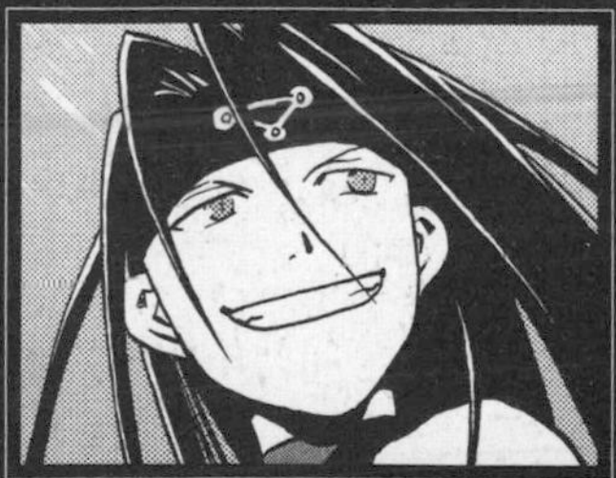

エンヴィー

Envy

CONTENTS

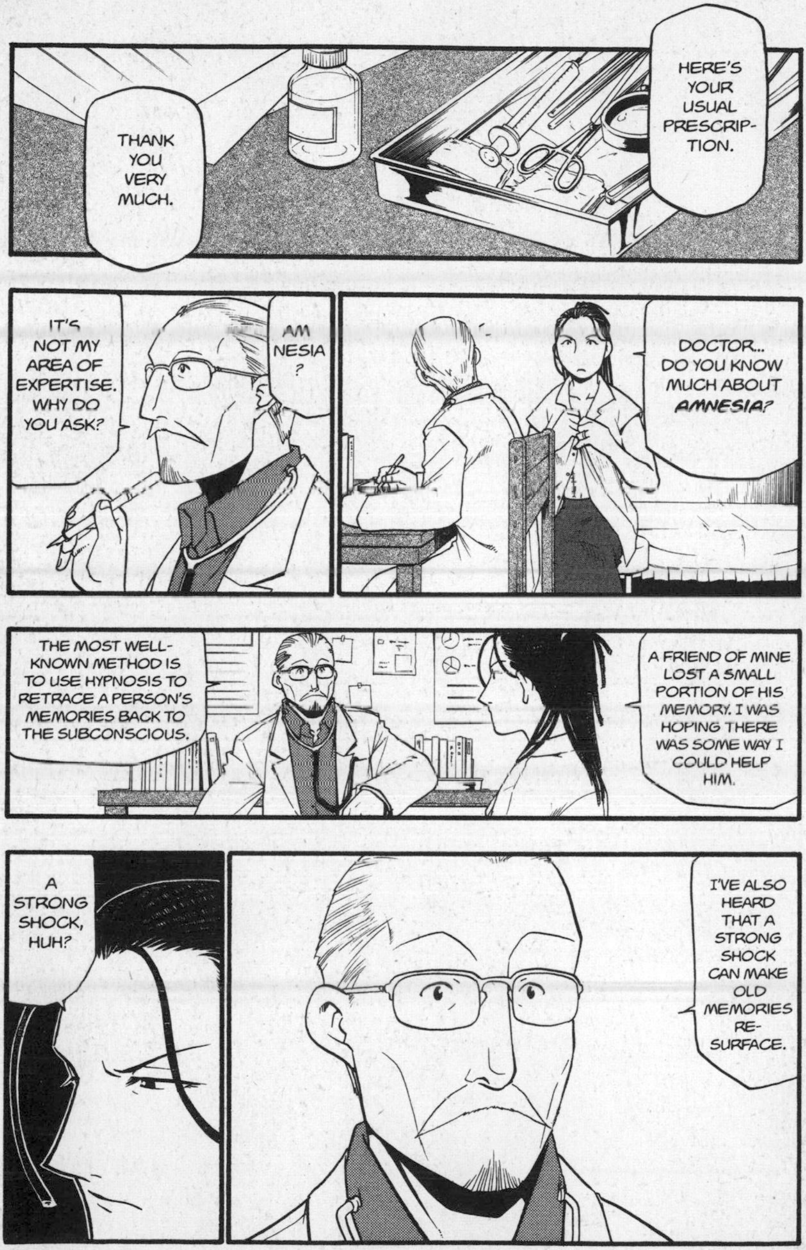
HERE'S YOUR USUAL PRESCRIP-TION.
THANK YOU VERY MUCH.
DOCTOR... DO YOU KNOW MUCH ABOUT AMNESIA?
AM NESIA?
IT'S NOT MY AREA OF EXPERTISE. WHY DO YOU ASK?
A FRIEND OF MINE LOST A SMALL PORTION OF HIS MEMORY. I WAS HOPING THERE WAS SOME WAY I COULD HELP HIM.
THE MOST WELL-KNOWN METHOD IS TO USE HYPNOSIS TO RETRACE A PERSON'S MEMORIES BACK TO THE SUBCONSCIOUS.
I'VE ALSO HEARD THAT A STRONG SHOCK CAN MAKE OLD MEMORIES RE-SURFACE.
A STRONG SHOCK, HUH?

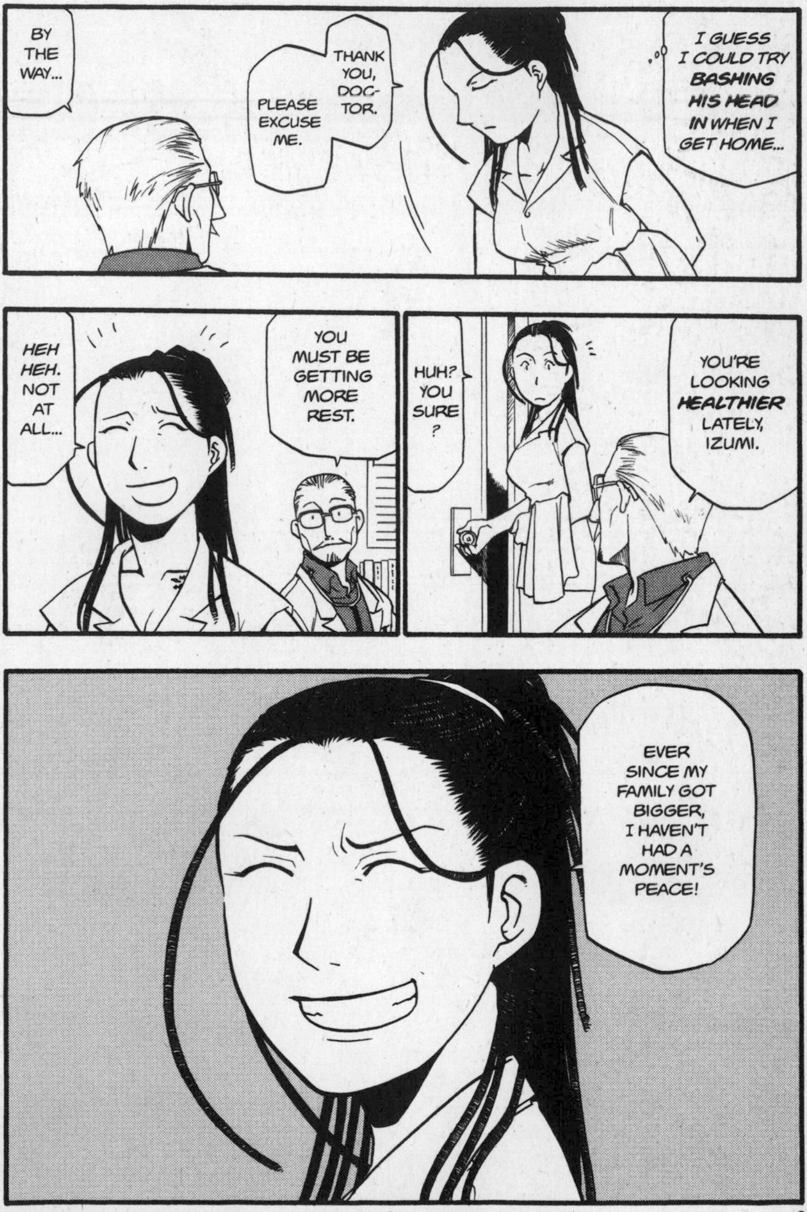
I GUESS I COULD TRY **BASHING HIS HEAD** IN WHEN I GET HOME...
THANK YOU, DOCTOR.
PLEASE EXCUSE ME.
BY THE WAY...
YOU'RE LOOKING **HEALTHIER** LATELY, IZUMI.
HUH? YOU SURE?
YOU MUST BE GETTING MORE REST.
HEH HEH. NOT AT ALL...
EVER SINCE MY FAMILY GOT BIGGER, I HAVEN'T HAD A MOMENT'S PEACE!

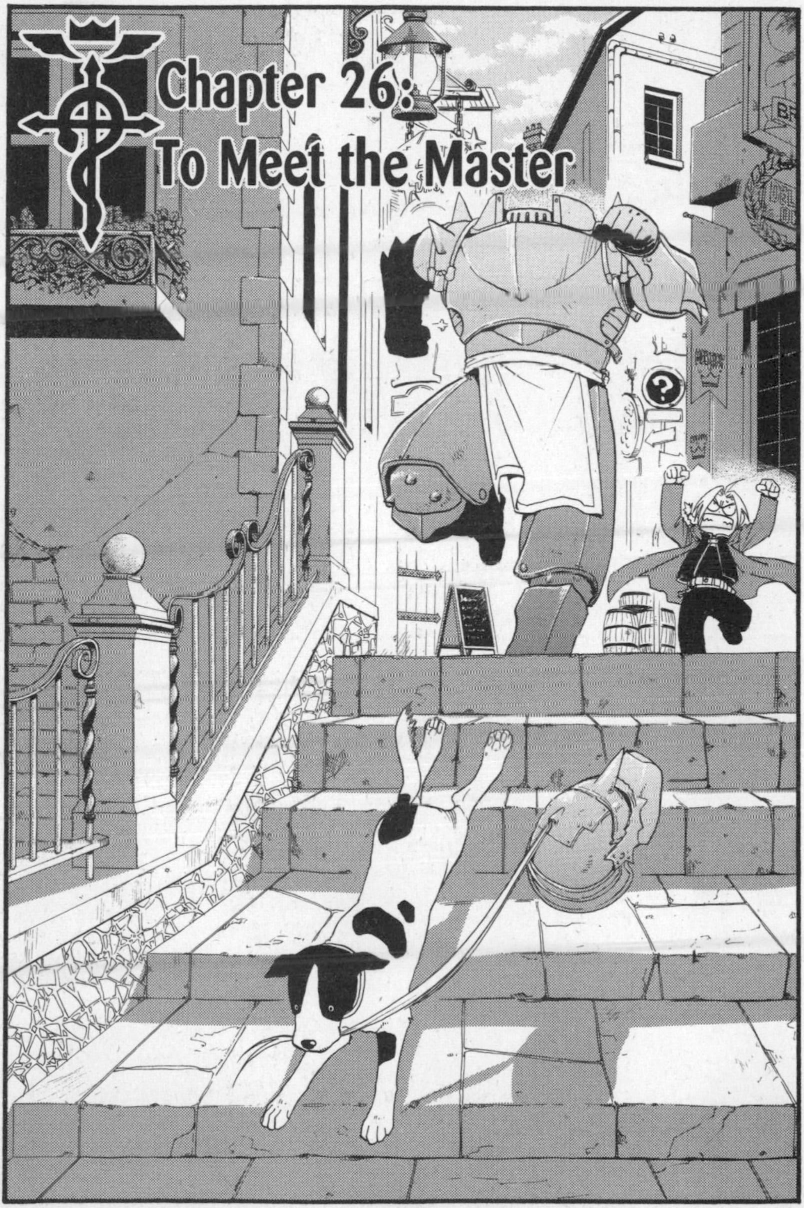

Chapter 26:
To Meet the Master

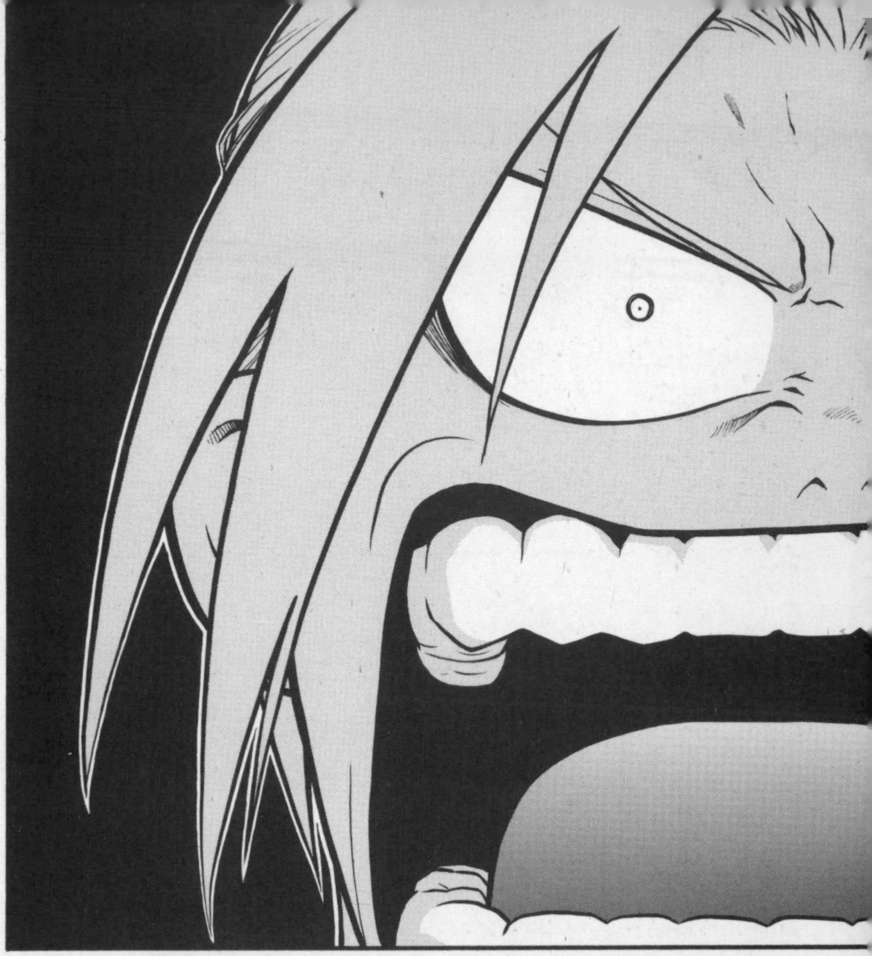
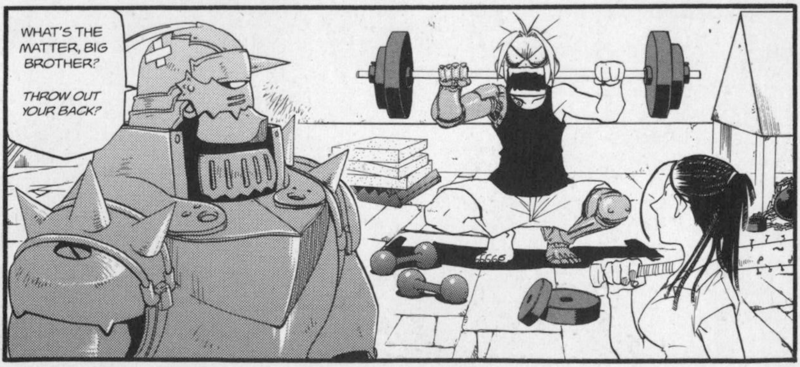
WHAT'S THE MATTER, BIG BROTHER?
THROW OUT YOUR BACK?

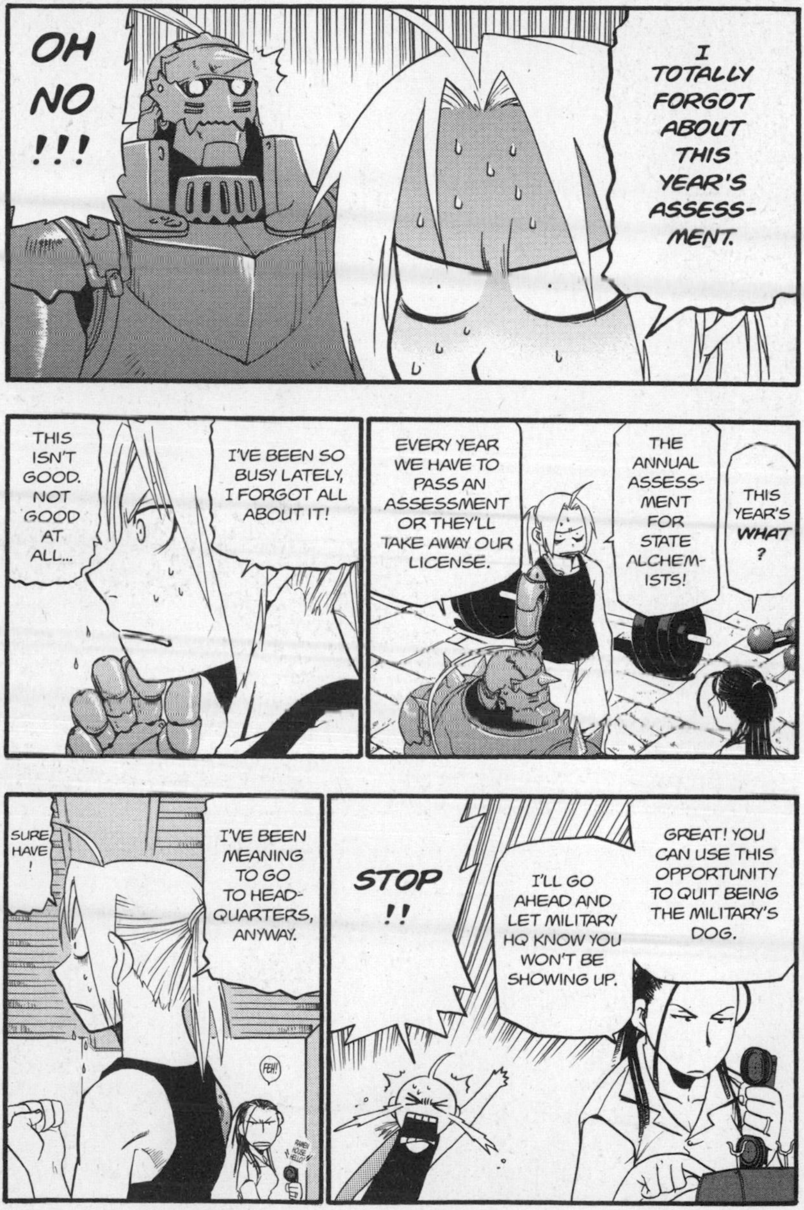
I TOTALLY FORGOT ABOUT THIS YEAR'S ASSESSMENT.
OH NO!!!
THIS YEAR'S WHAT?
THE ANNUAL ASSESSMENT FOR STATE ALCHEMISTS!
EVERY YEAR WE HAVE TO PASS AN ASSESSMENT OR THEY'LL TAKE AWAY OUR LICENSE.
I'VE BEEN SO BUSY LATELY, I FORGOT ALL ABOUT IT!
THIS ISN'T GOOD. NOT GOOD AT ALL...
GREAT! YOU CAN USE THIS OPPORTUNITY TO QUIT BEING THE MILITARY'S DOG.
I'LL GO AHEAD AND LET MILITARY HQ KNOW YOU WON'T BE SHOWING UP.
STOP!!
I'VE BEEN MEANING TO GO TO HEADQUARTERS, ANYWAY.
SURE HAVE!
FEH!
RAMEN HOUSE HELLO?

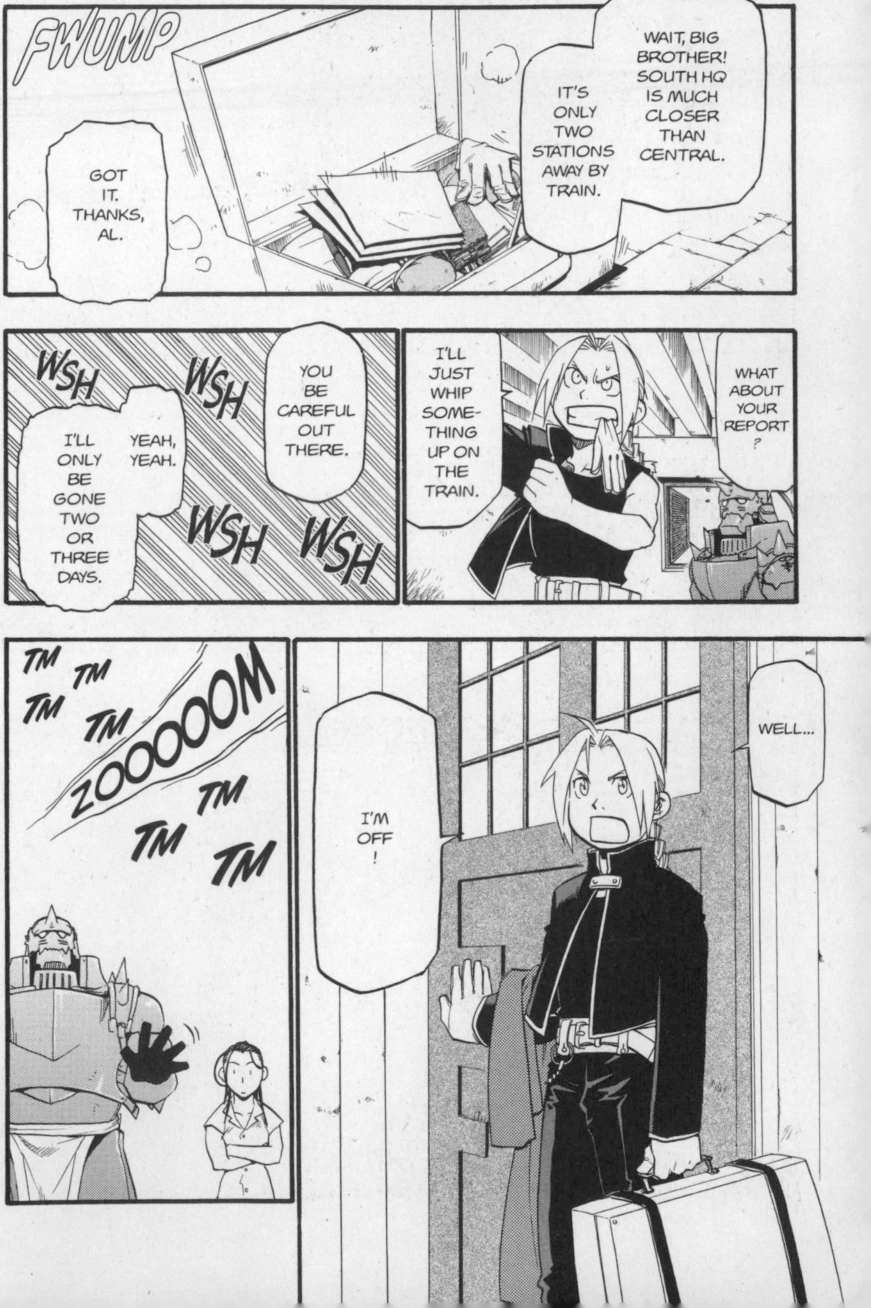
WAIT, BIG BROTHER! SOUTH HQ IS MUCH CLOSER THAN CENTRAL.
IT'S ONLY TWO STATIONS AWAY BY TRAIN.
FWUMP
GOT IT. THANKS, AL.
WHAT ABOUT YOUR REPORT ?
I'LL JUST WHIP SOME-THING UP ON THE TRAIN.
YOU BE CAREFUL OUT THERE.
WSH
WSH
YEAH, YEAH.
I'LL ONLY BE GONE TWO OR THREE DAYS.
WSH
WSH
WELL...
I'M OFF !
TM TM TM TM
ZOOOOOM
TM TM TM

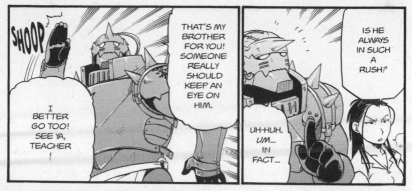

IS HE ALWAYS IN SUCH A RUSH?
UH-HUH. UM... IN FACT...
THAT'S MY BROTHER FOR YOU! SOMEONE REALLY SHOULD KEEP AN EYE ON HIM.
SHOOP
I BETTER GO TOO! SEE YA, TEACHER!
NOT SO FAST. ♡
AIEEE!
YOU'RE GONNA STAY HERE AND SPAR WITH ME. ♡
KRIK KRAK
KLANK

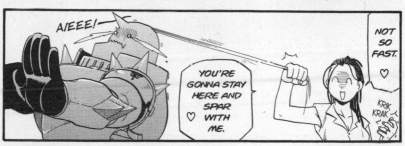

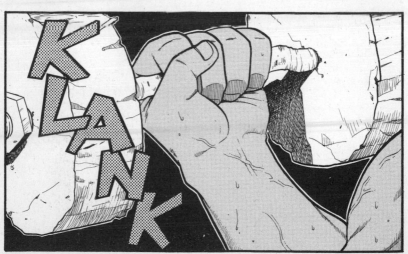

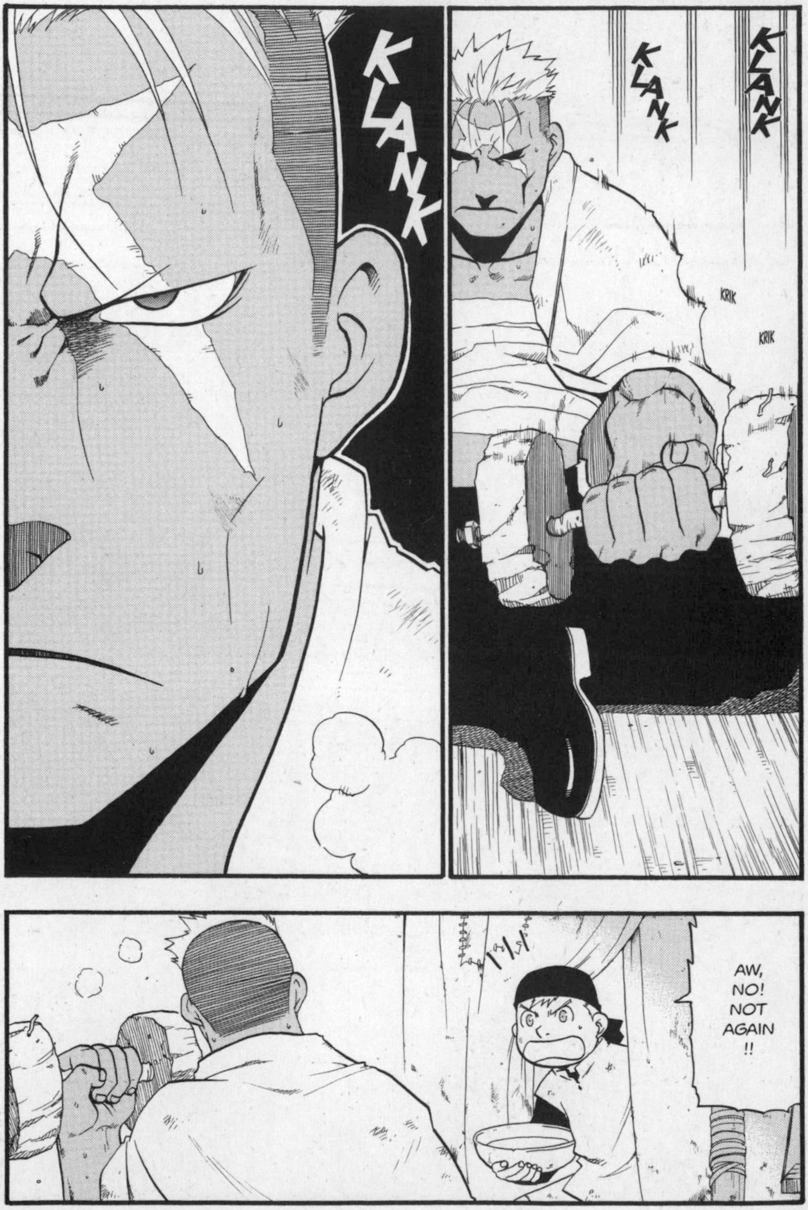
KLANK
KLANK
KRIK
KRIK
KLANK
AW, NO! NOT AGAIN!!

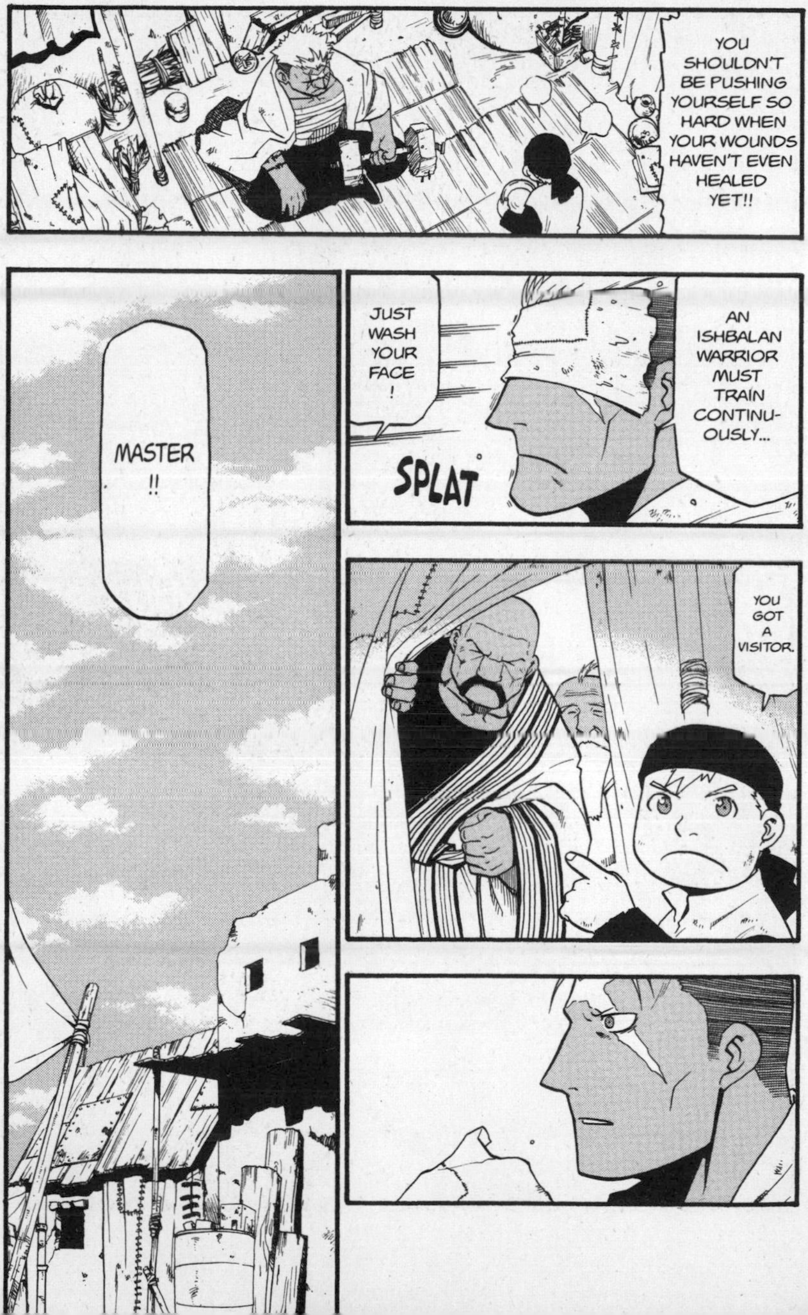
YOU SHOULDN'T BE PUSHING YOURSELF SO HARD WHEN YOUR WOUNDS HAVEN'T EVEN HEALED YET!!
AN ISHBALAN WARRIOR MUST TRAIN CONTINU-OUSLY...
JUST WASH YOUR FACE!
SPLAT
YOU GOT A VISITOR.
MASTER!!

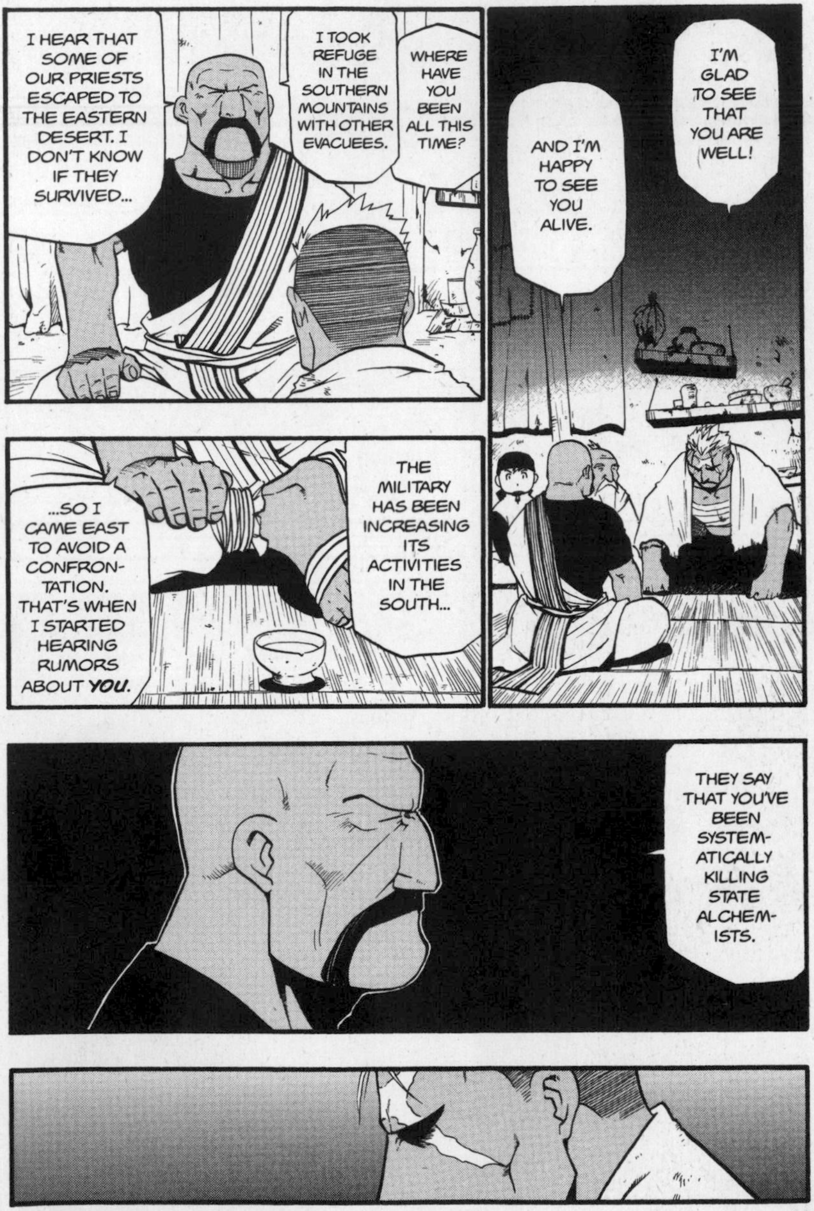
I'M GLAD TO SEE THAT YOU ARE WELL!
AND I'M HAPPY TO SEE YOU ALIVE.
WHERE HAVE YOU BEEN ALL THIS TIME?
I TOOK REFUGE IN THE SOUTHERN MOUNTAINS WITH OTHER EVACUEES.
I HEAR THAT SOME OF OUR PRIESTS ESCAPED TO THE EASTERN DESERT. I DON'T KNOW IF THEY SURVIVED...
THE MILITARY HAS BEEN INCREASING ITS ACTIVITIES IN THE SOUTH...
...SO I CAME EAST TO AVOID A CONFRON-TATION. THAT'S WHEN I STARTED HEARING RUMORS ABOUT *YOU*.
THEY SAY THAT YOU'VE BEEN SYSTEM-ATICALLY KILLING STATE ALCHEM-ISTS.

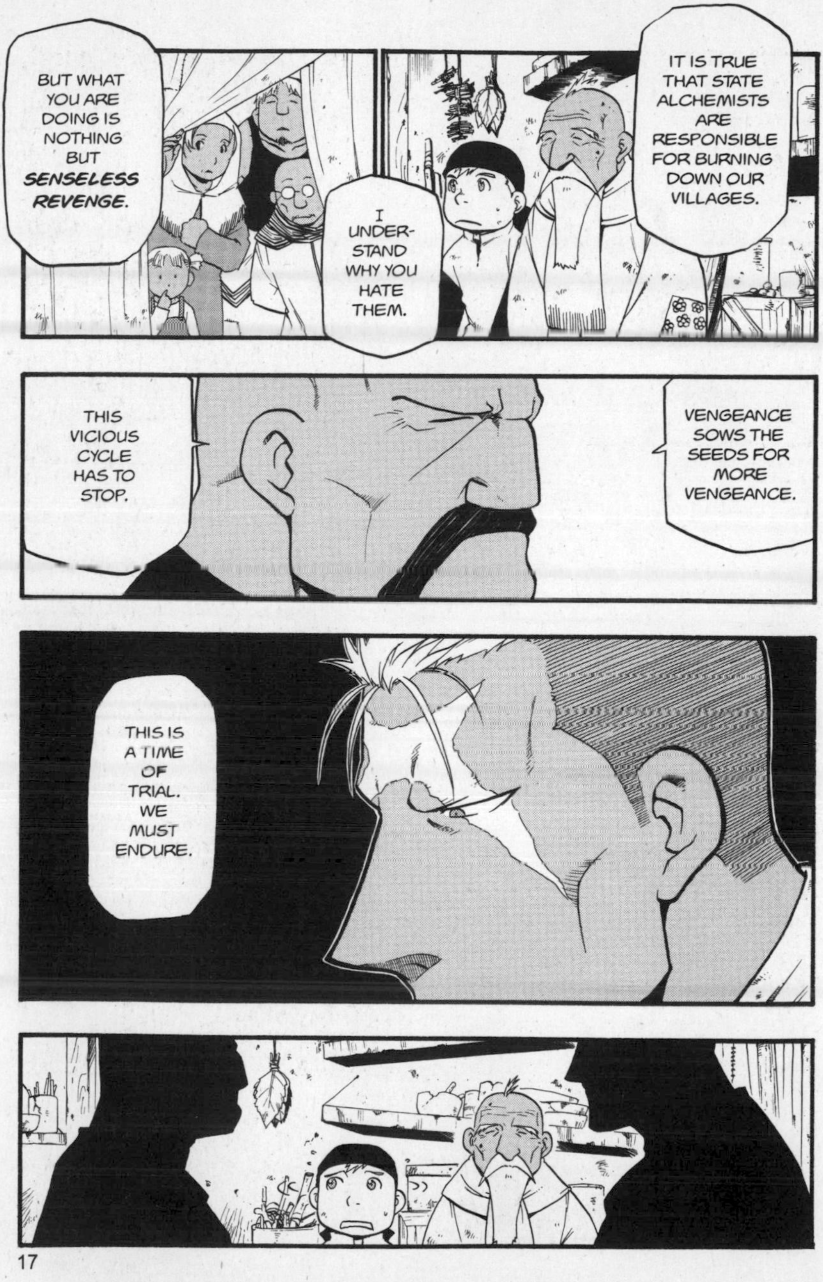
IT IS TRUE THAT STATE ALCHEMISTS ARE RESPONSIBLE FOR BURNING DOWN OUR VILLAGES.
I UNDERSTAND WHY YOU HATE THEM.
BUT WHAT YOU ARE DOING IS NOTHING BUT SENSELESS REVENGE.
VENGEANCE SOWS THE SEEDS FOR MORE VENGEANCE.
THIS VICIOUS CYCLE HAS TO STOP.
THIS IS A TIME OF TRIAL. WE MUST ENDURE.

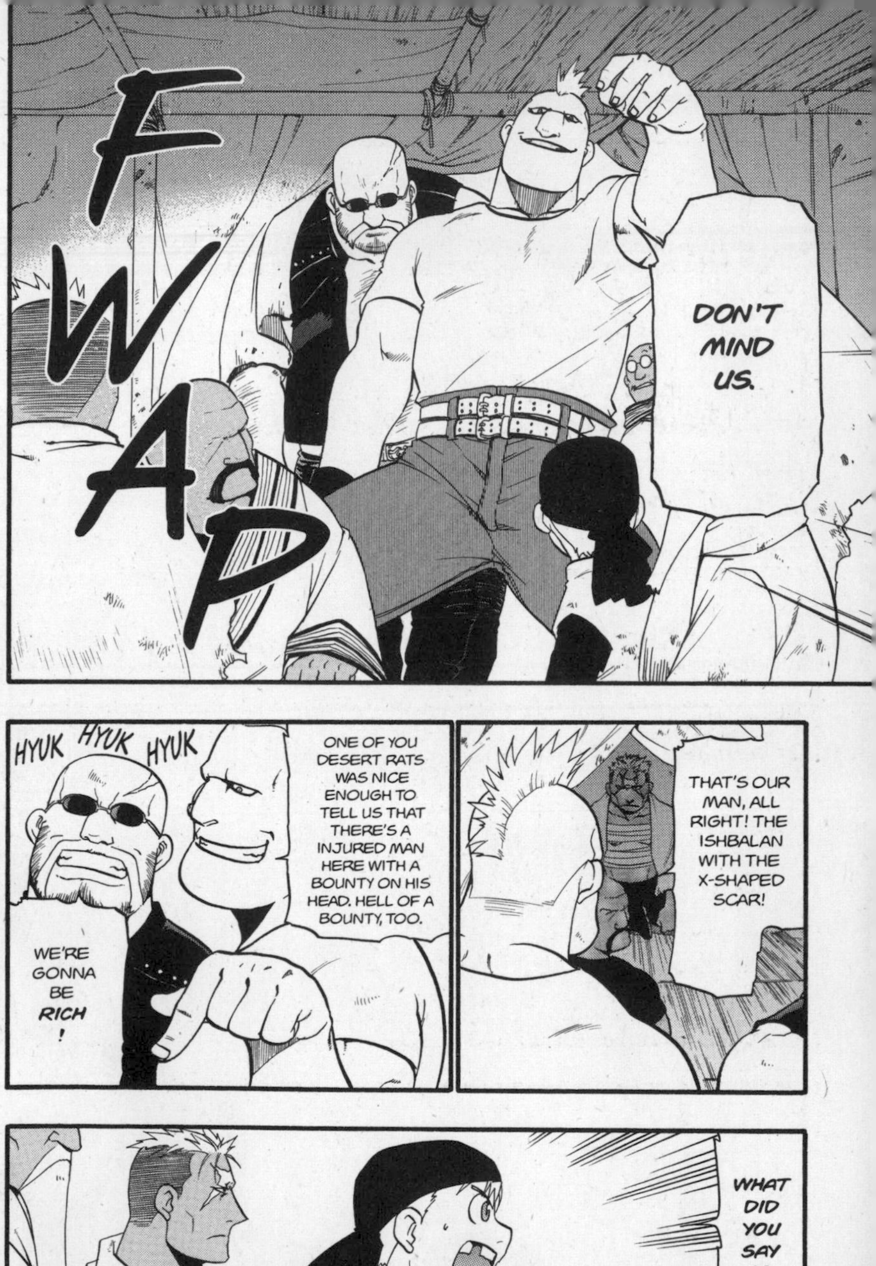
FWAP
DON'T MIND US.
THAT'S OUR MAN, ALL RIGHT! THE ISHBALAN WITH THE X-SHAPED SCAR!
ONE OF YOU DESERT RATS WAS NICE ENOUGH TO TELL US THAT THERE'S A INJURED MAN HERE WITH A BOUNTY ON HIS HEAD. HELL OF A BOUNTY, TOO.
HYUK HYUK HYUK
WE'RE GONNA BE RICH!
WHAT DID YOU SAY!?

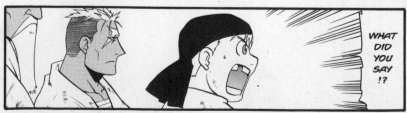

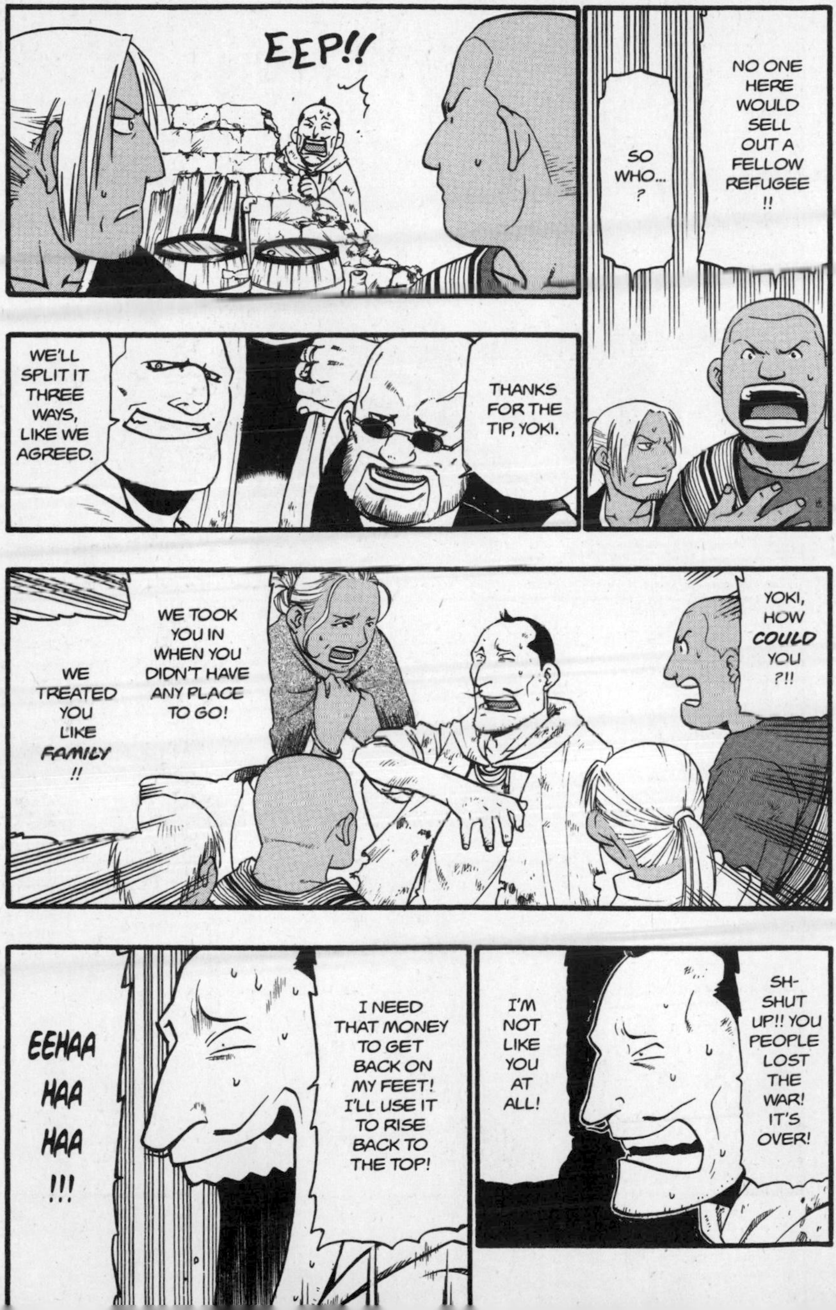
NO ONE HERE WOULD SELL OUT A FELLOW REFUGEE!!
SO WHO...?
EEP!!
THANKS FOR THE TIP, YOKI.
WE'LL SPLIT IT THREE WAYS, LIKE WE AGREED.
YOKI, HOW COULD YOU?!!
WE TOOK YOU IN WHEN YOU DIDN'T HAVE ANY PLACE TO GO!
WE TREATED YOU LIKE FAMILY!!
SH-SHUT UP!! YOU PEOPLE LOST THE WAR! IT'S OVER!
I'M NOT LIKE YOU AT ALL!
I NEED THAT MONEY TO GET BACK ON MY FEET! I'LL USE IT TO RISE BACK TO THE TOP!
EEHAA HAA HAA!!!

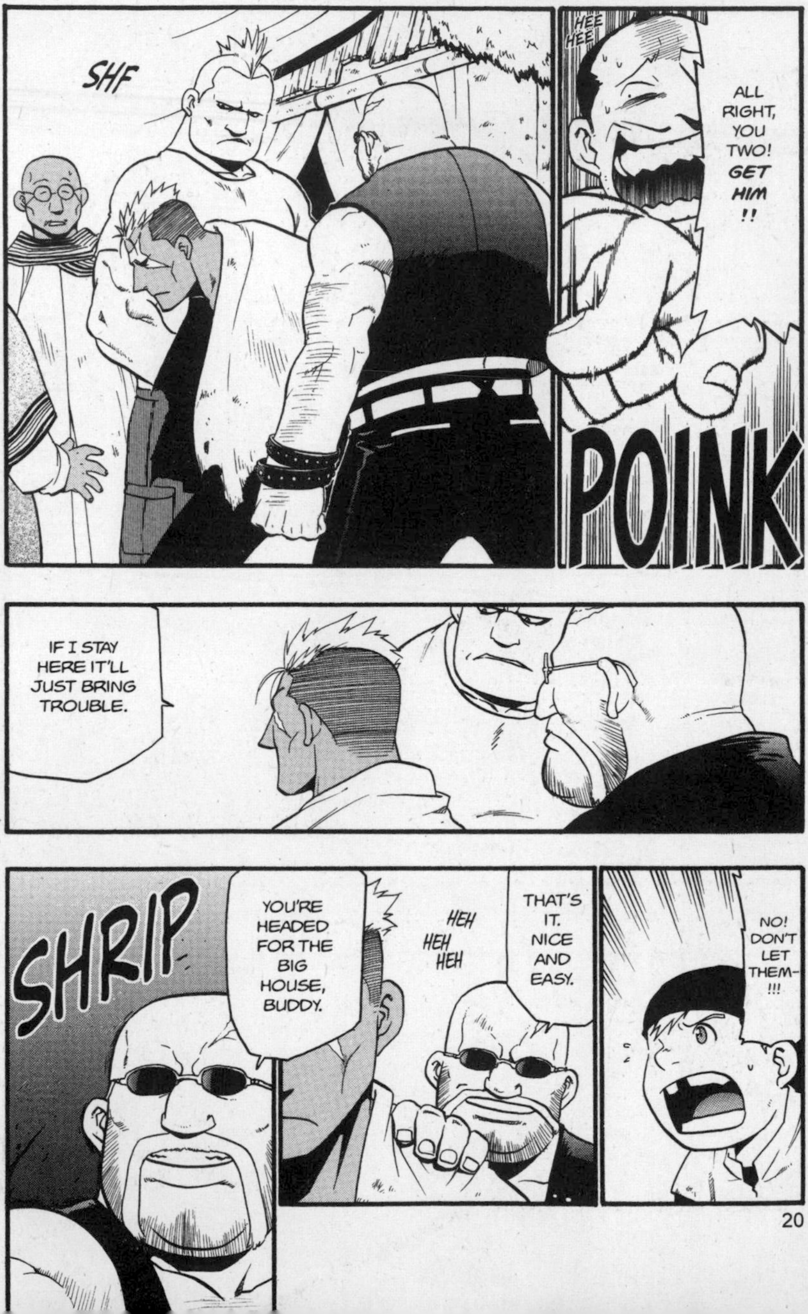
HEE HEE
ALL RIGHT, YOU TWO! GET HIM !!
POINK
SHF
IF I STAY HERE IT'LL JUST BRING TROUBLE.
NO! DON'T LET THEM-!!!
THAT'S IT. NICE AND EASY.
HEH HEH HEH
YOU'RE HEADED FOR THE BIG HOUSE, BUDDY.
SHRIP

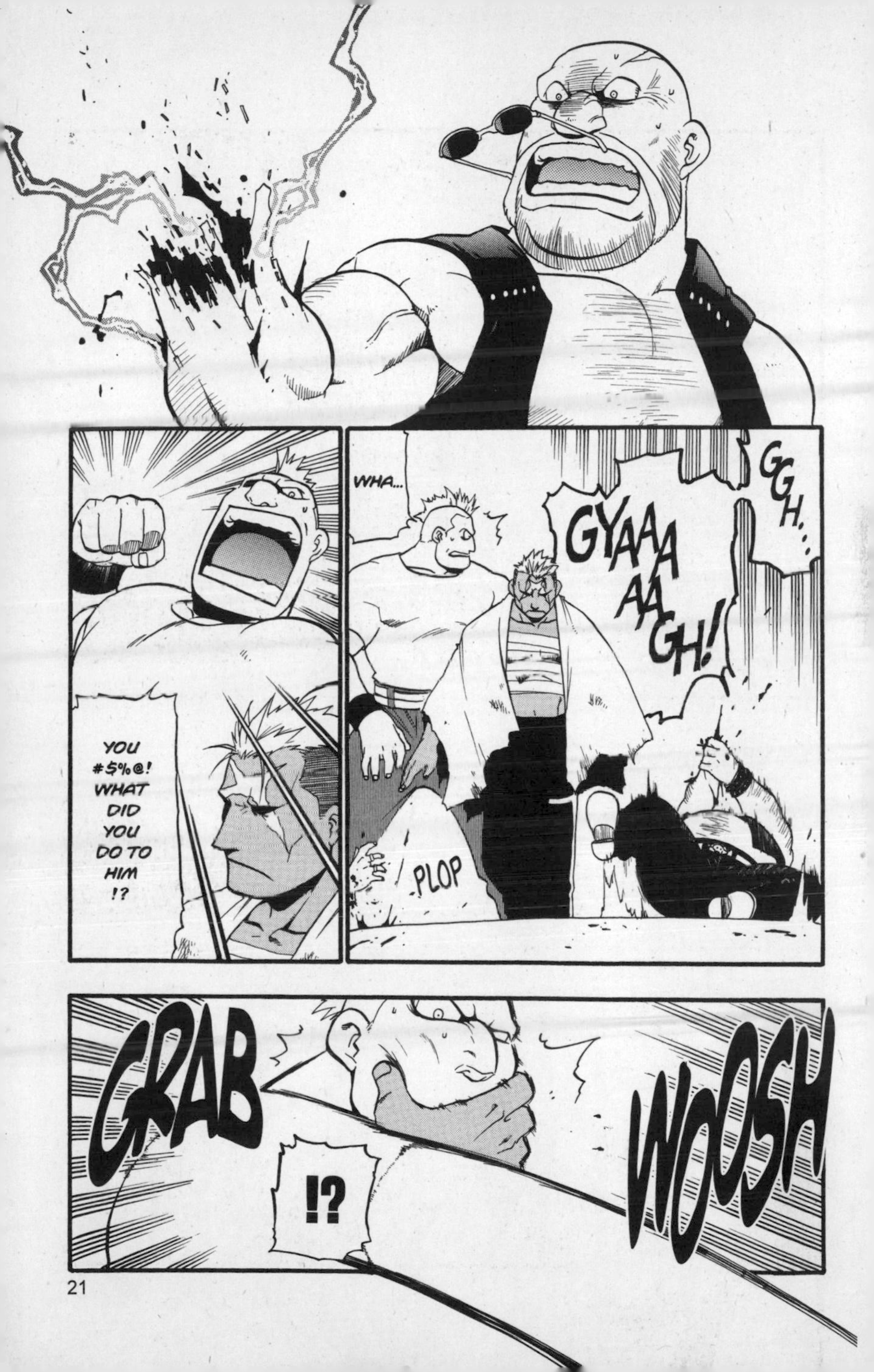
GGH...
GYAAAAAGH!
WHA...
PLOP
YOU #$%@! WHAT DID YOU DO TO HIM !?
WOOSH
!?
GRAB

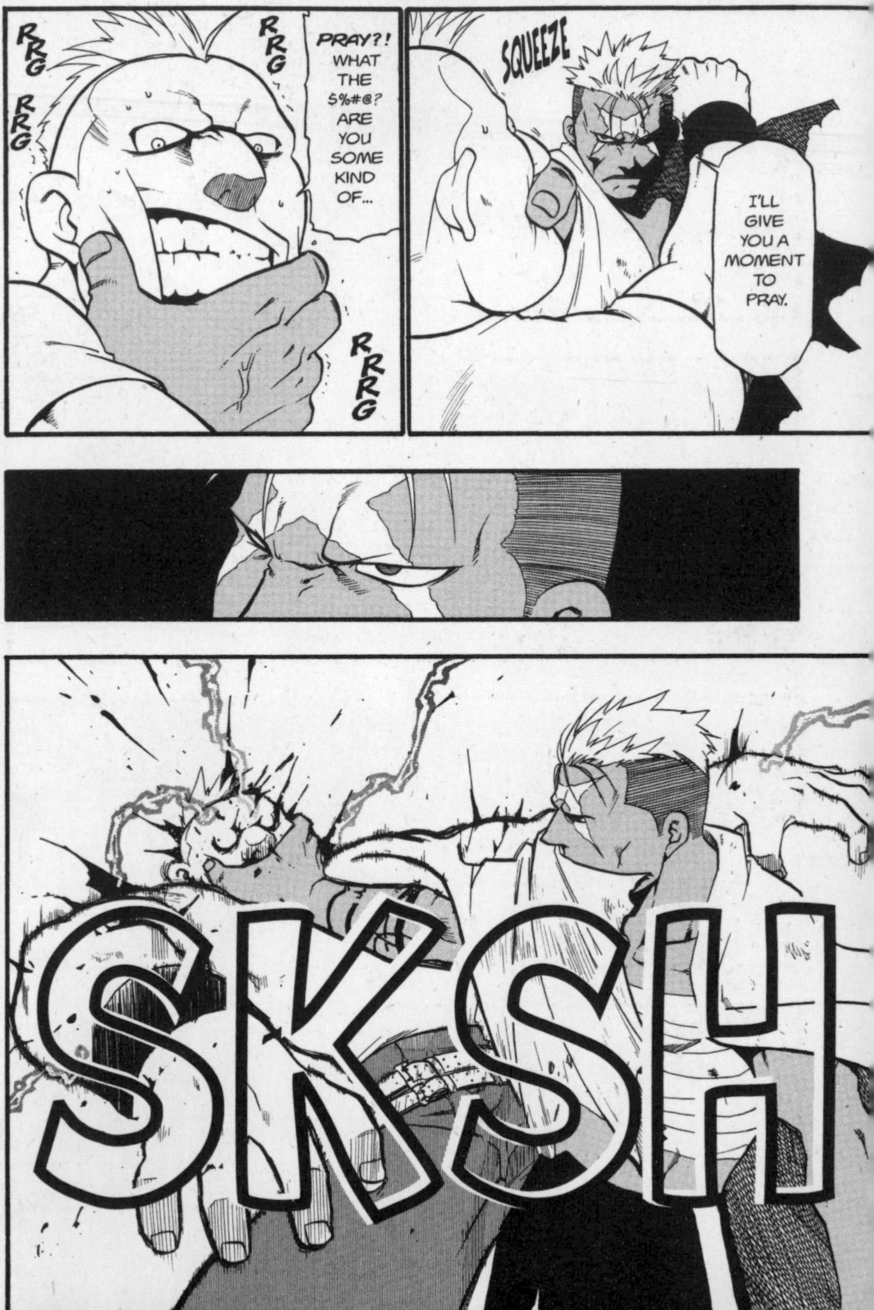
SQUEEZE
I'LL GIVE YOU A MOMENT TO PRAY.
PRAY?! WHAT THE $%#@? ARE YOU SOME KIND OF...
RRG
RRG
RRG
RRRG
SKSH

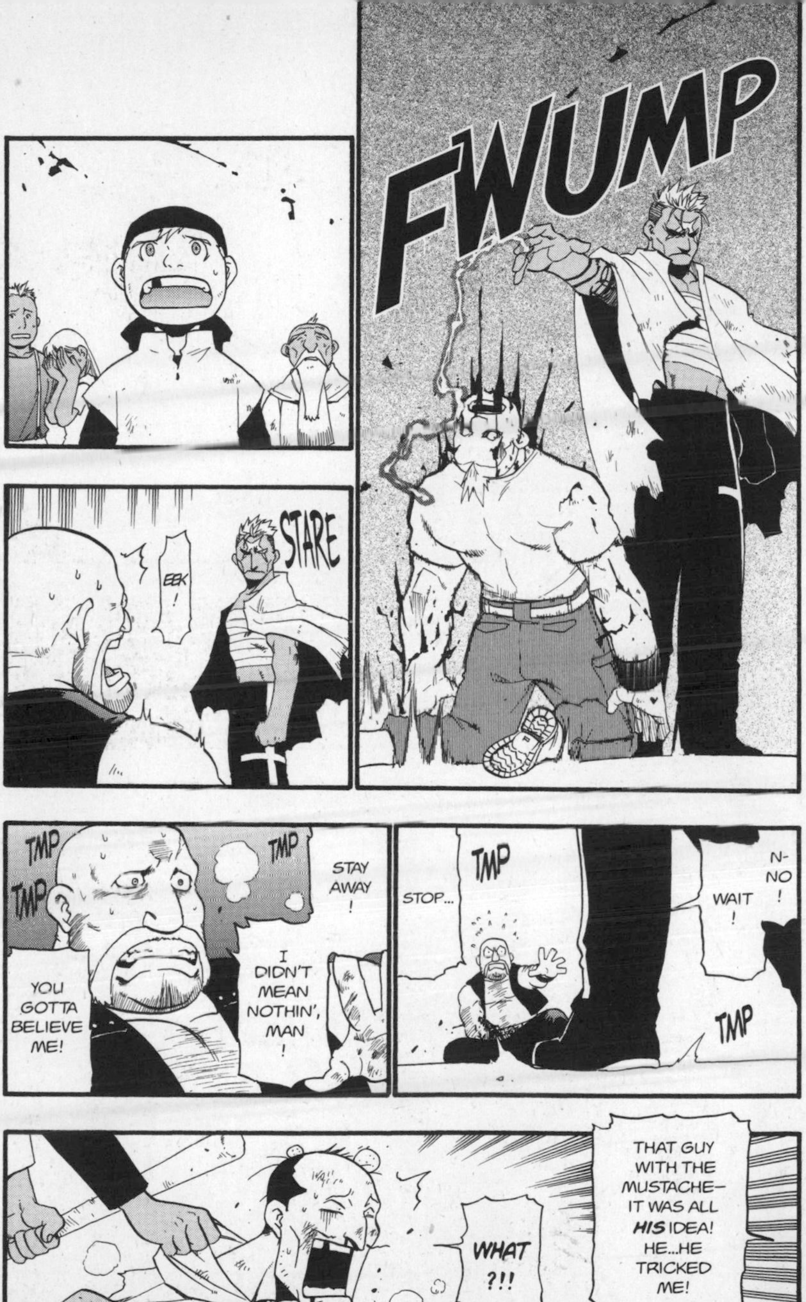
FWUMP
STARE
EEK!
N-NO!
WAIT!
TMP
STOP...
TMP
TMP
STAY AWAY!
TMP
TMP
I DIDN'T MEAN NOTHIN', MAN!
YOU GOTTA BELIEVE ME!
THAT GUY WITH THE MUSTACHE—IT WAS ALL ***HIS*** IDEA! HE...HE TRICKED ME!
WHAT?!!

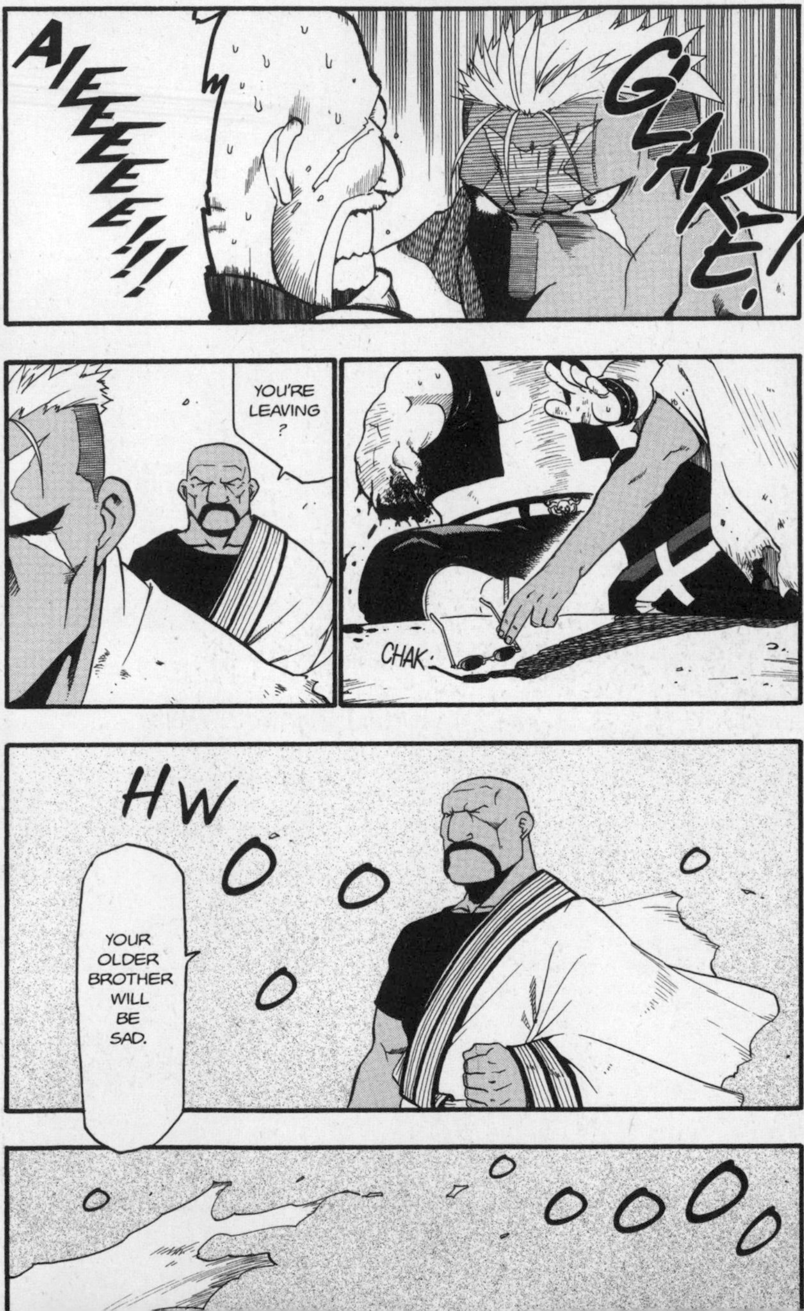
GLARE!
AIEEEEE!!!
CHAK
YOU'RE LEAVING?
HWOOOO
YOUR OLDER BROTHER WILL BE SAD.
OOOOOO

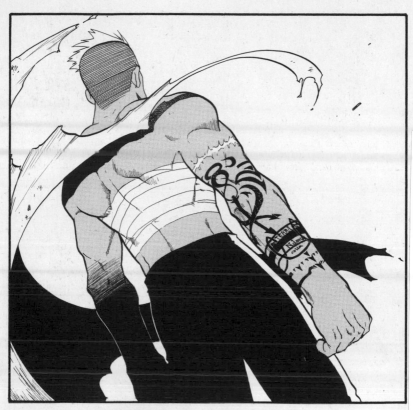

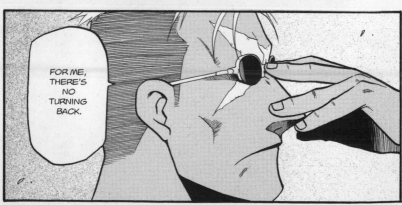

FOR ME, THERE'S NO TURNING BACK.

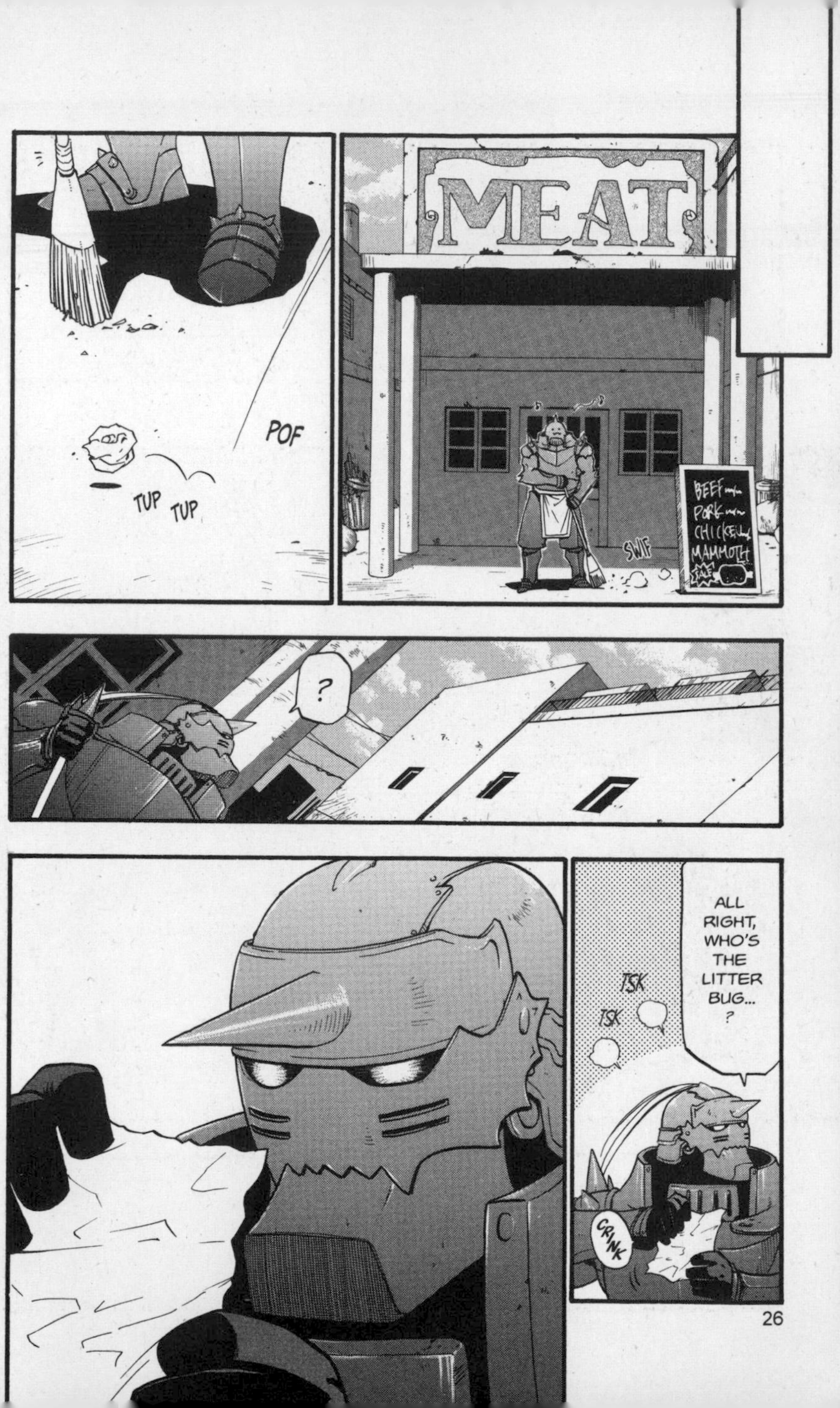
MEAT
BEEF
PORK
CHICKEN
MAMMOTH
SWIF
POF
TUP
TUP
?
ALL RIGHT, WHO'S THE LITTER BUG...?
TSK
TSK
CRINK

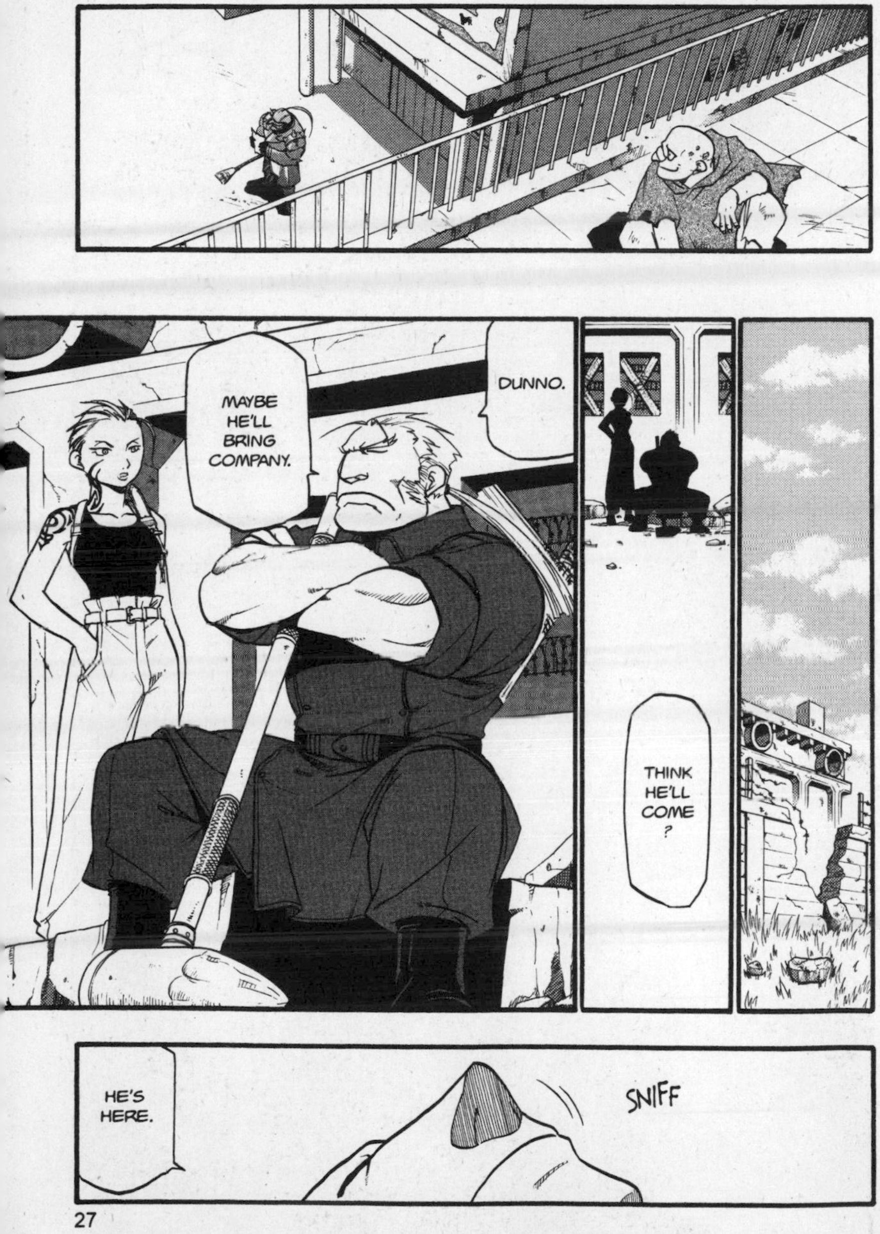
THINK HE'LL COME ?
DUNNO.
MAYBE HE'LL BRING COMPANY.
SNIFF
HE'S HERE.

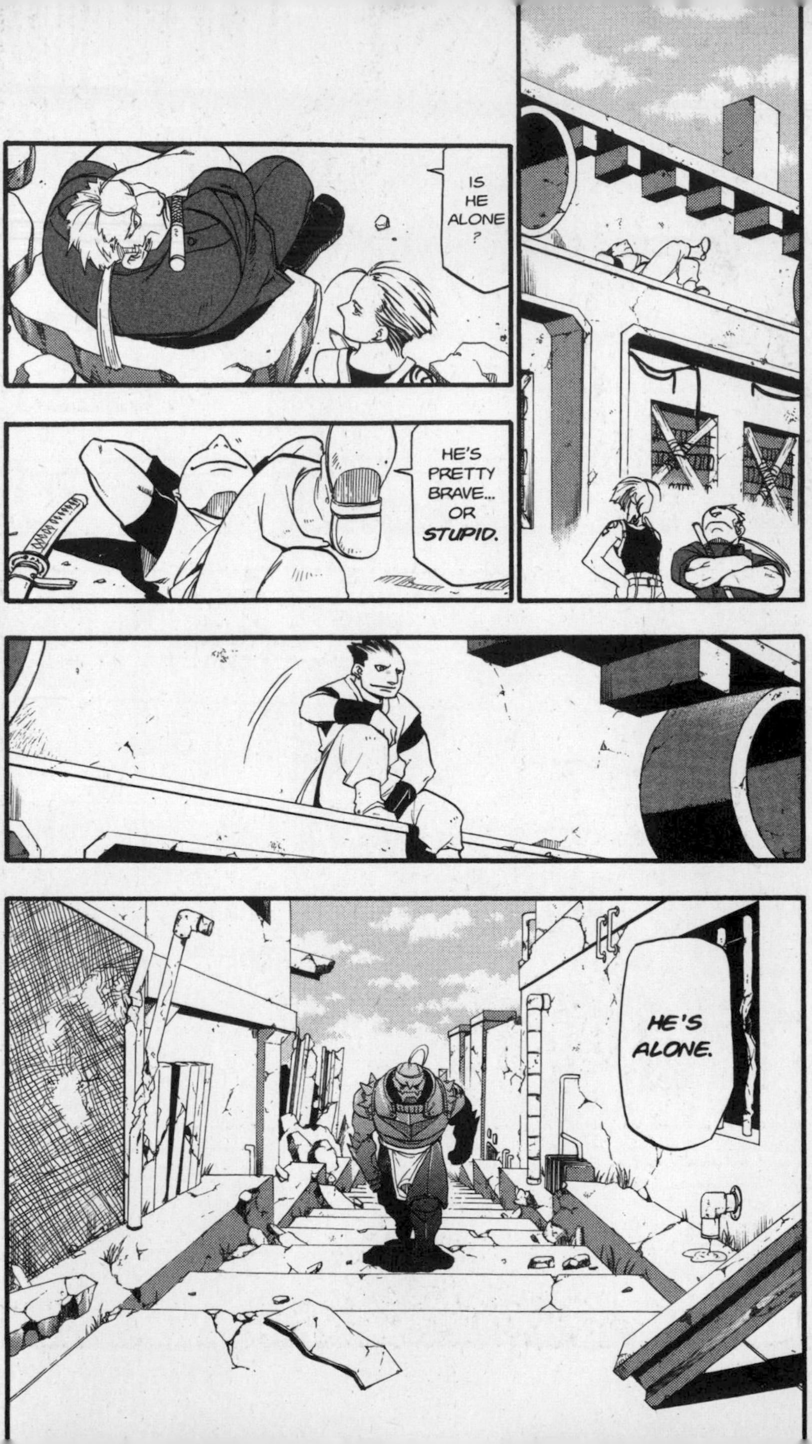
IS HE ALONE?
HE'S PRETTY BRAVE... OR STUPID.
HE'S ALONE.

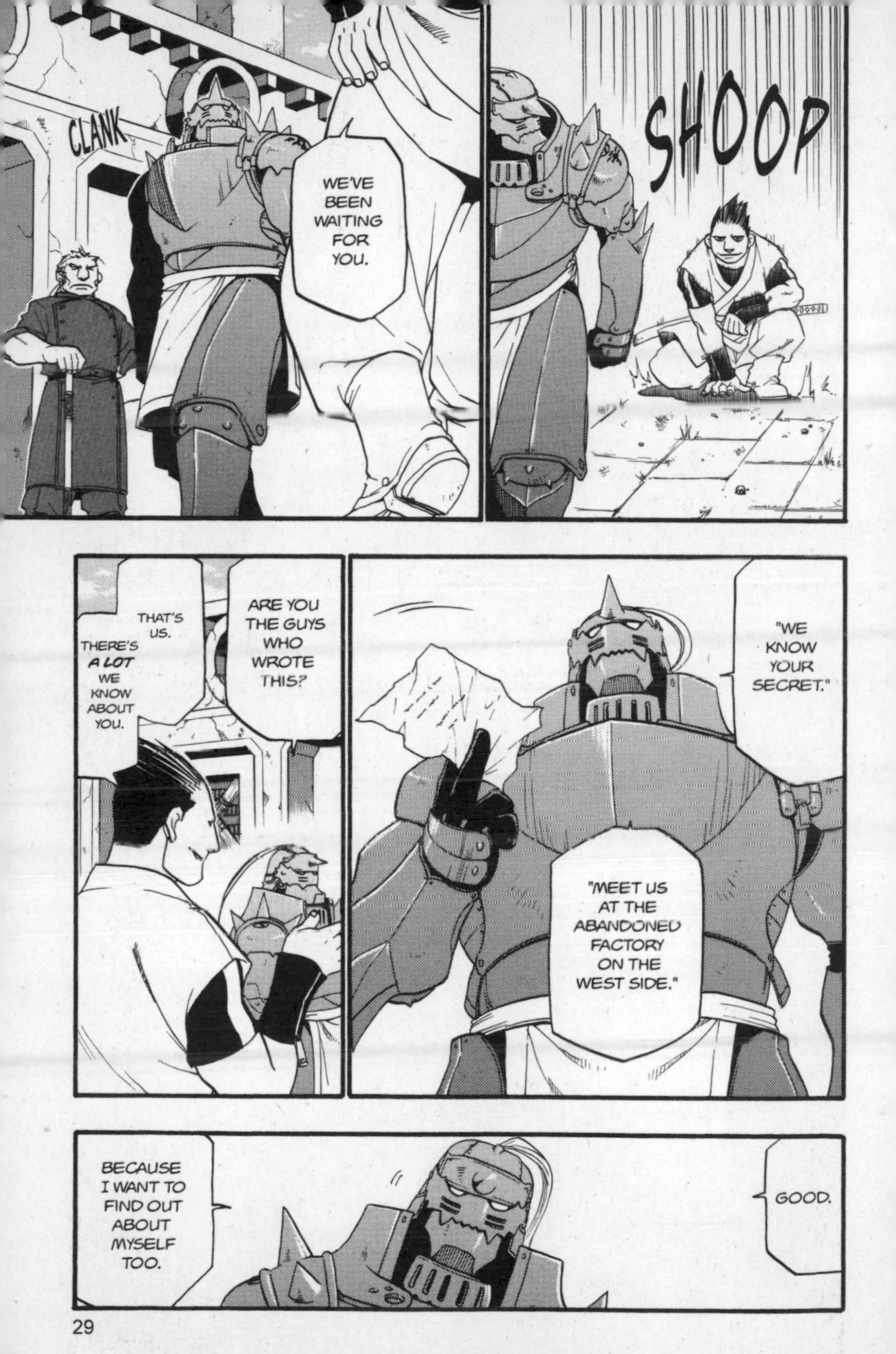
SHOOP
WE'VE BEEN WAITING FOR YOU.
CLANK
"WE KNOW YOUR SECRET."
"MEET US AT THE ABANDONED FACTORY ON THE WEST SIDE."
ARE YOU THE GUYS WHO WROTE THIS?
THAT'S US.
THERE'S *A LOT* WE KNOW ABOUT YOU.
GOOD.
BECAUSE I WANT TO FIND OUT ABOUT MYSELF TOO.

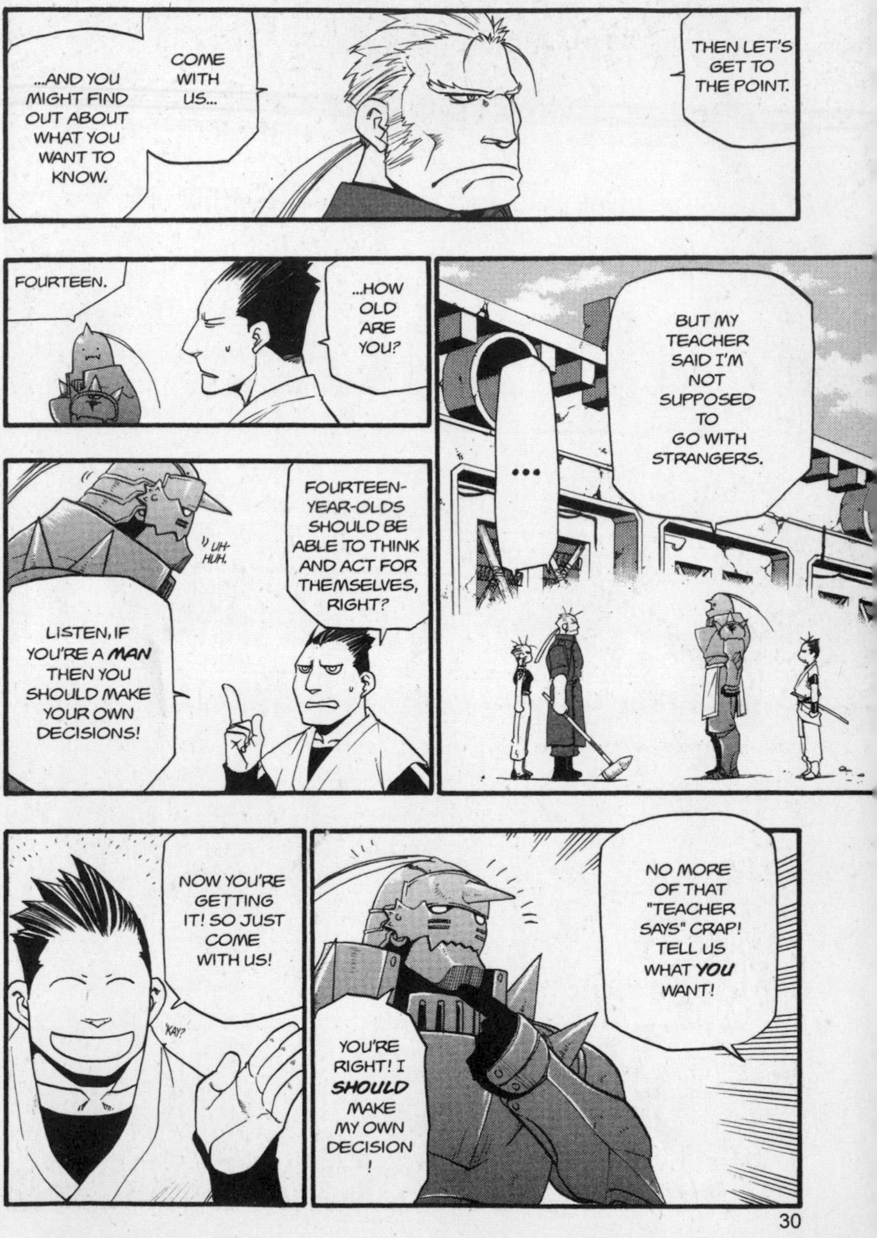
THEN LET'S GET TO THE POINT.
COME WITH US...
...AND YOU MIGHT FIND OUT ABOUT WHAT YOU WANT TO KNOW.
BUT MY TEACHER SAID I'M NOT SUPPOSED TO GO WITH STRANGERS.
...
...HOW OLD ARE YOU?
FOURTEEN.
FOURTEEN-YEAR-OLDS SHOULD BE ABLE TO THINK AND ACT FOR THEMSELVES, RIGHT?
UH-HUH.
LISTEN, IF YOU'RE A MAN THEN YOU SHOULD MAKE YOUR OWN DECISIONS!
NO MORE OF THAT "TEACHER SAYS" CRAP! TELL US WHAT YOU WANT!
YOU'RE RIGHT! I SHOULD MAKE MY OWN DECISION!
NOW YOU'RE GETTING IT! SO JUST COME WITH US!
'KAY?

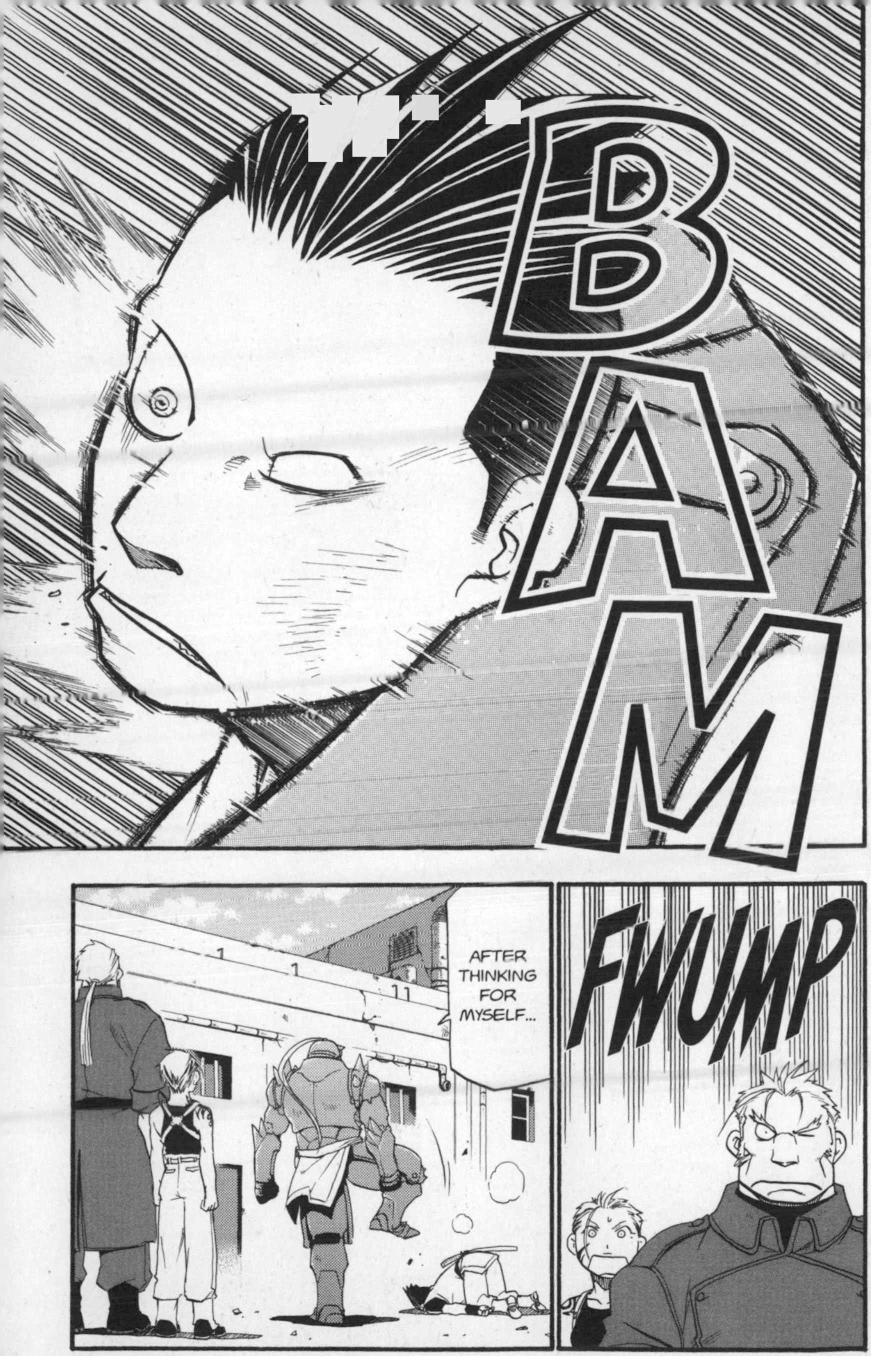
BAM
FWUMP
AFTER THINKING FOR MYSELF...

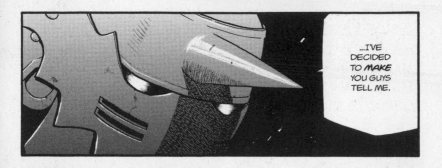

...I'VE DECIDED TO *MAKE* YOU GUYS TELL ME.

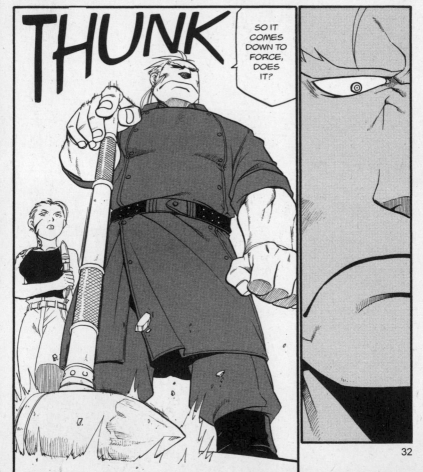

THUNK

SO IT COMES DOWN TO FORCE, DOES IT?

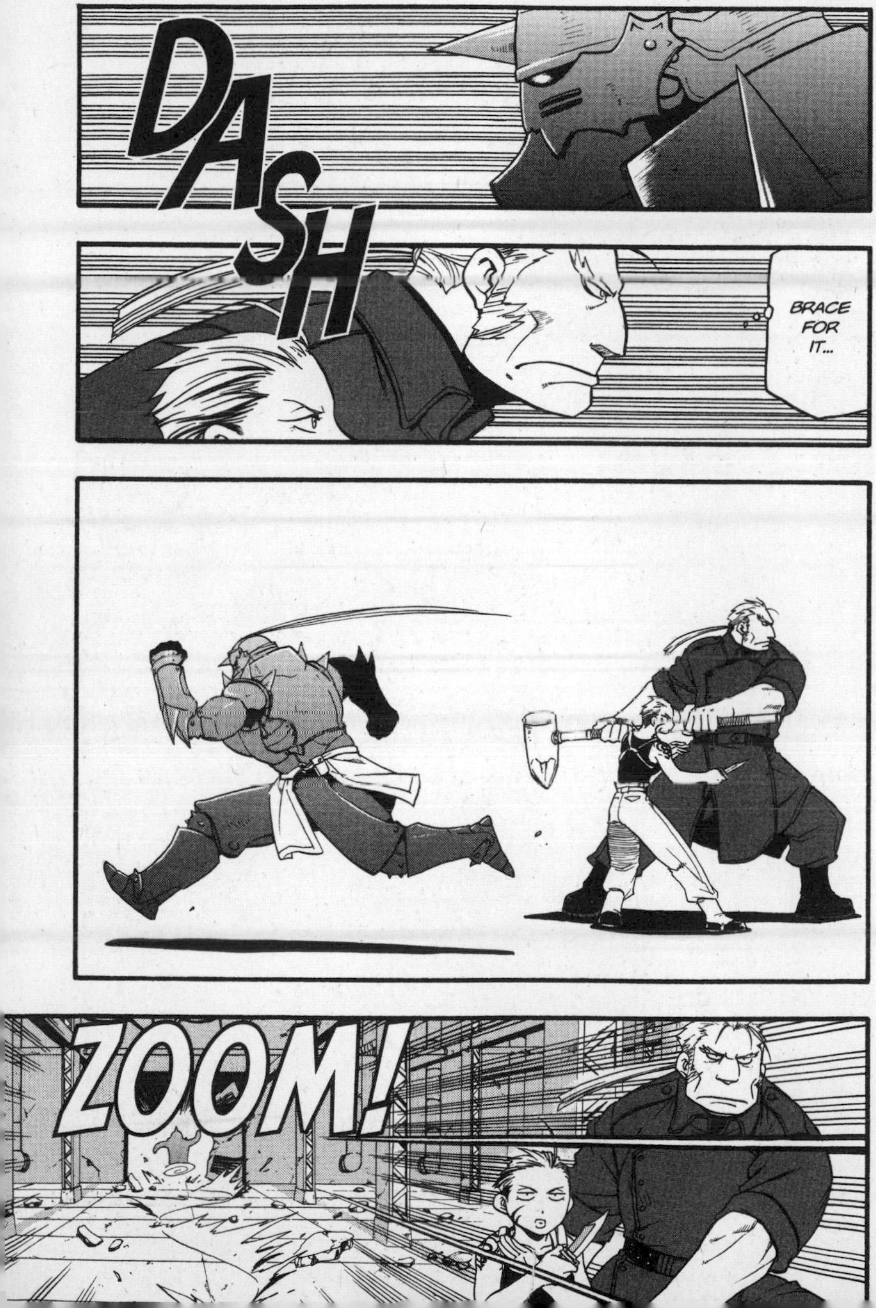
DASH
BRACE FOR IT...
ZOOM!

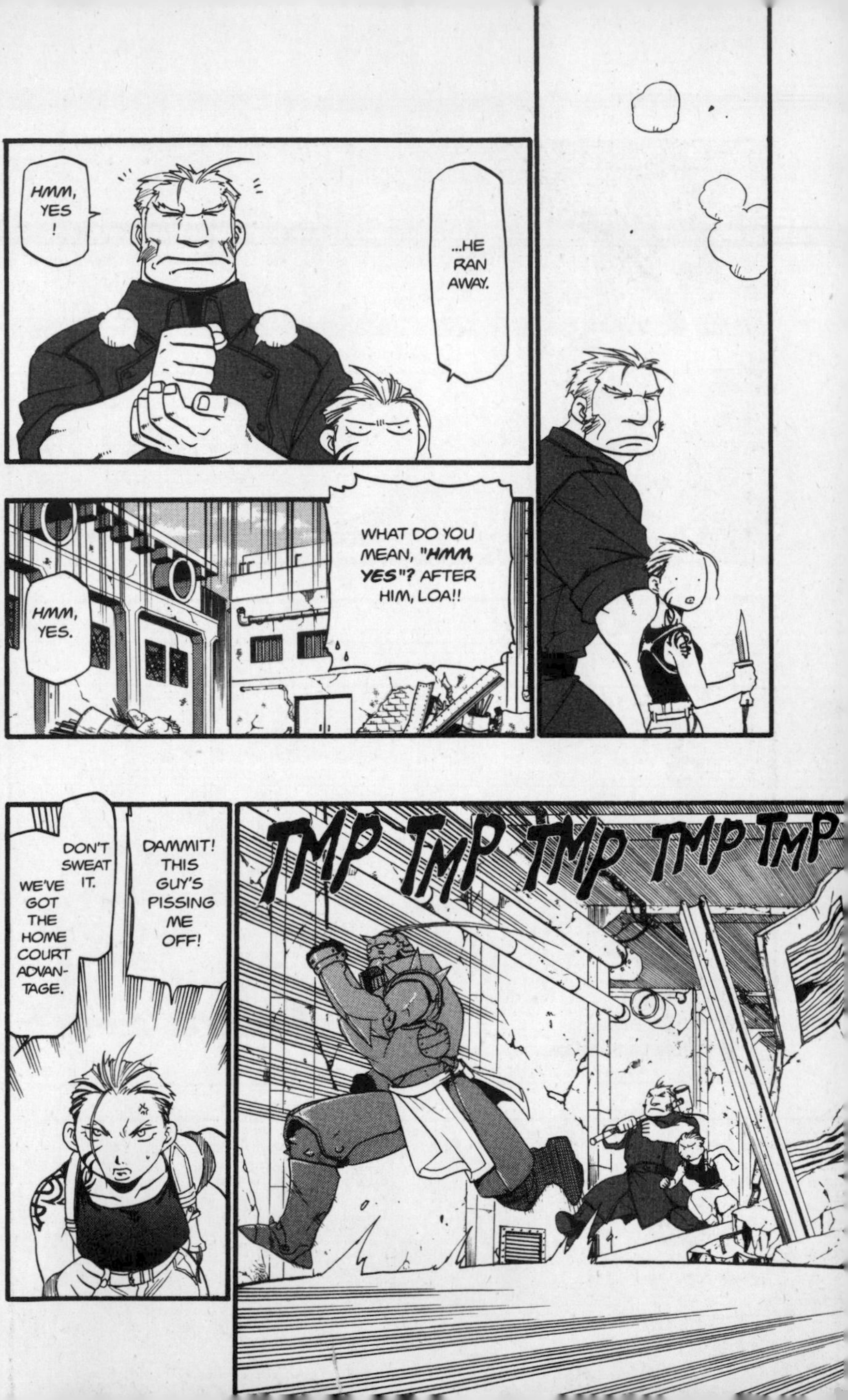
...HE RAN AWAY.
HMM, YES!
WHAT DO YOU MEAN, "HMM, YES"? AFTER HIM, LOA!!
HMM, YES.
TMP TMP TMP TMP TMP
DAMMIT! THIS GUY'S PISSING ME OFF!
DON'T SWEAT IT. WE'VE GOT THE HOME COURT ADVANTAGE.

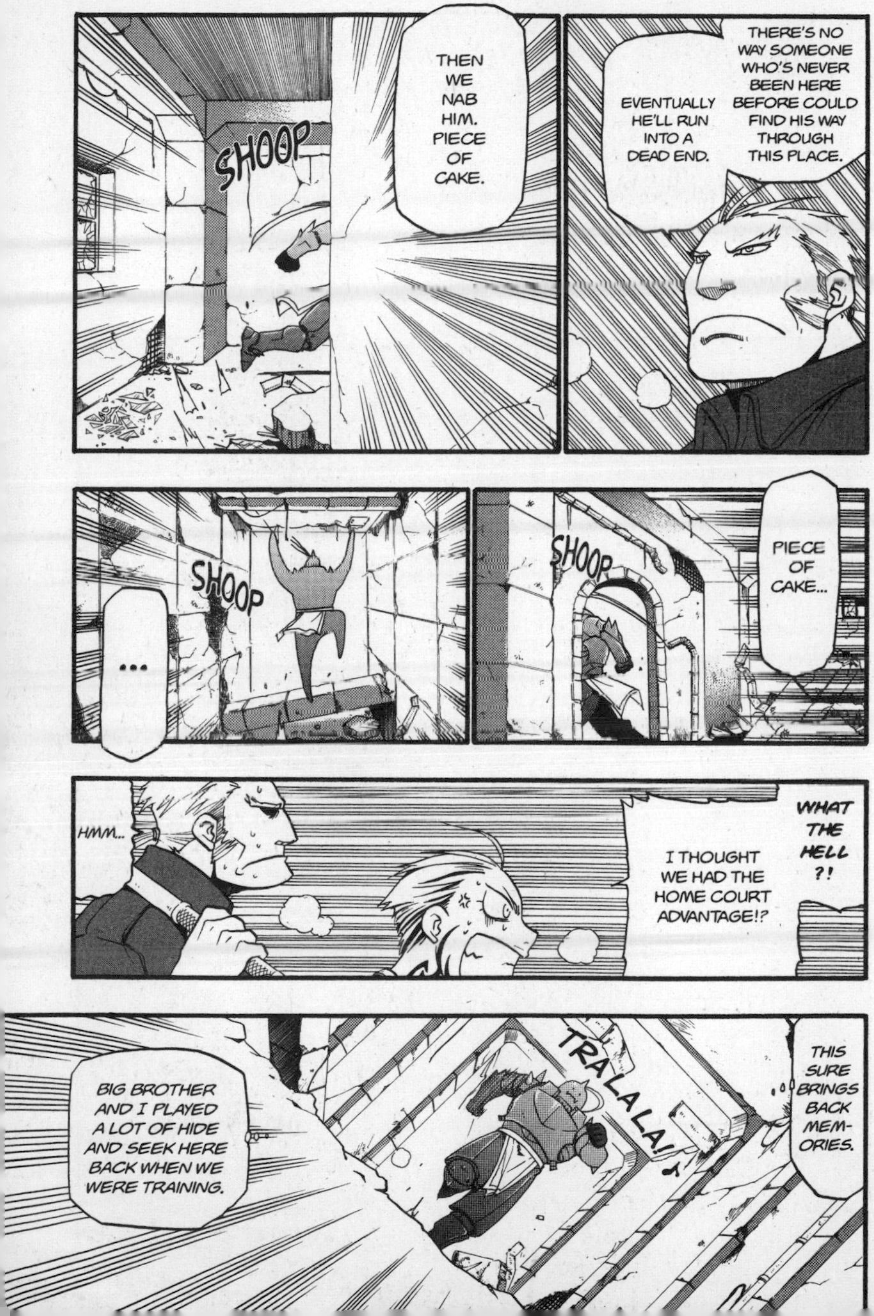
THERE'S NO WAY SOMEONE WHO'S NEVER BEEN HERE BEFORE COULD FIND HIS WAY THROUGH THIS PLACE.
EVENTUALLY HE'LL RUN INTO A DEAD END.
THEN WE NAB HIM. PIECE OF CAKE.
SHOOP
PIECE OF CAKE...
SHOOP
SHOOP
...
WHAT THE HELL ?!
I THOUGHT WE HAD THE HOME COURT ADVANTAGE!?
HMM..
THIS SURE BRINGS BACK MEM-ORIES.
TRA LA LA!
BIG BROTHER AND I PLAYED A LOT OF HIDE AND SEEK HERE BACK WHEN WE WERE TRAINING.

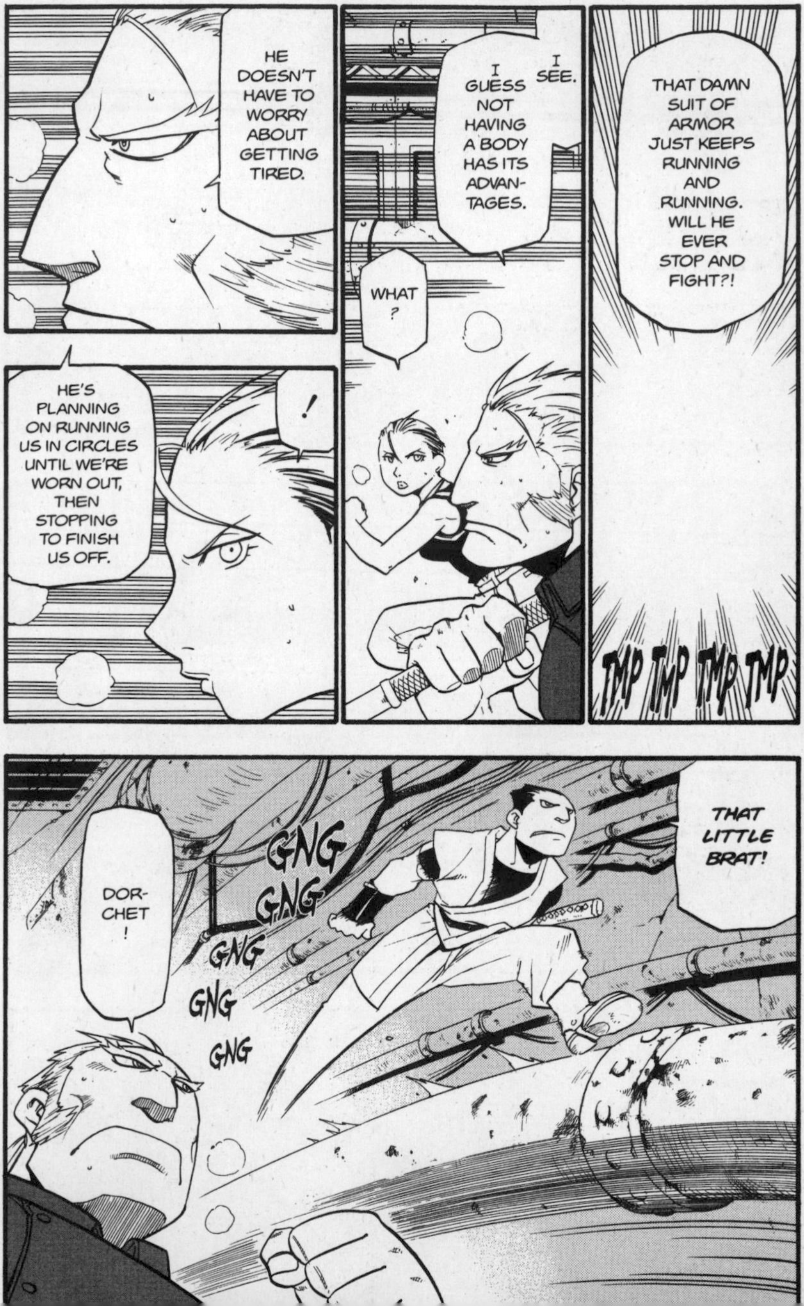
THAT DAMN SUIT OF ARMOR JUST KEEPS RUNNING AND RUNNING. WILL HE EVER STOP AND FIGHT?!
TMP TMP TMP TMP
I SEE.
I GUESS NOT HAVING A BODY HAS ITS ADVANTAGES.
WHAT?
HE DOESN'T HAVE TO WORRY ABOUT GETTING TIRED.
!
HE'S PLANNING ON RUNNING US IN CIRCLES UNTIL WE'RE WORN OUT, THEN STOPPING TO FINISH US OFF.
THAT LITTLE BRAT!
GNG GNG GNG GNG GNG
DOR-CHET!

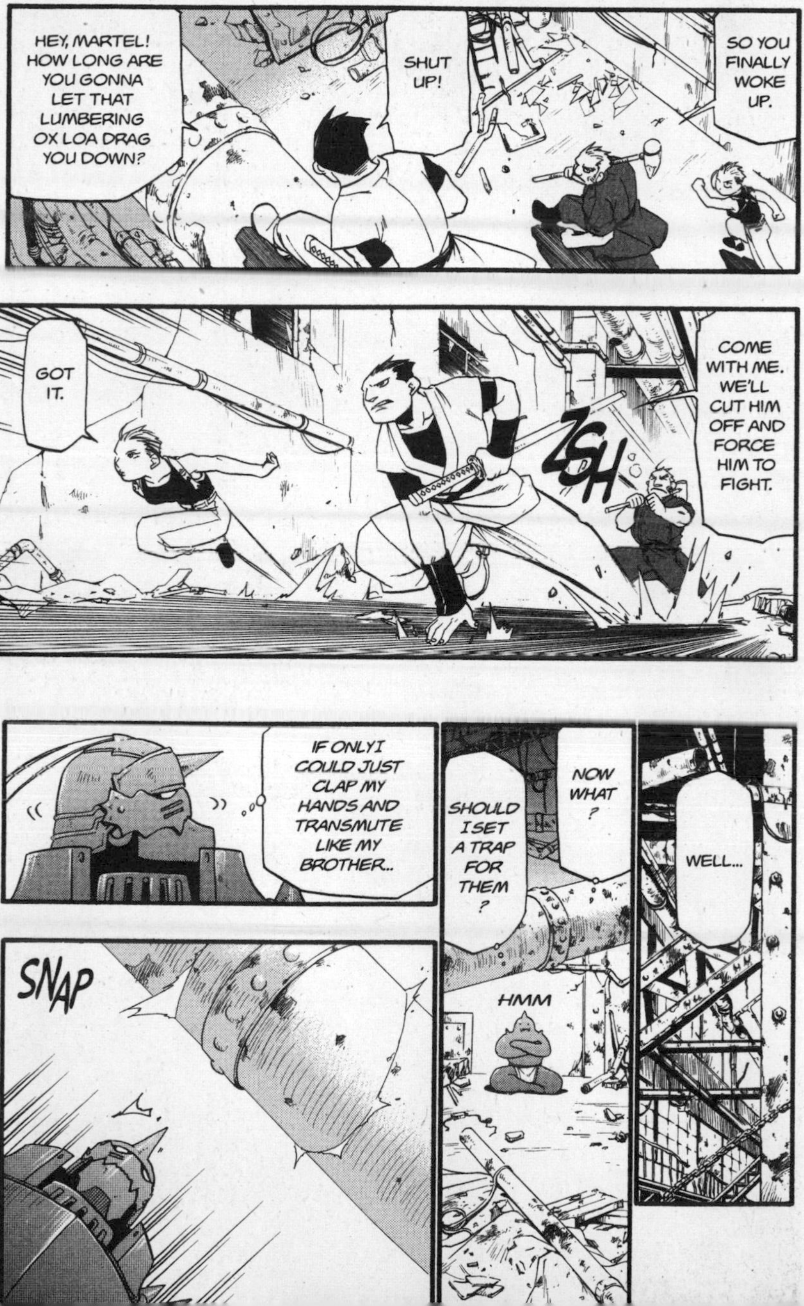
SO YOU FINALLY WOKE UP.
SHUT UP!
HEY, MARTEL! HOW LONG ARE YOU GONNA LET THAT LUMBERING OX LOA DRAG YOU DOWN?
COME WITH ME. WE'LL CUT HIM OFF AND FORCE HIM TO FIGHT.
ZSH
GOT IT.
WELL...
NOW WHAT?
SHOULD I SET A TRAP FOR THEM?
HMM
IF ONLY I COULD JUST CLAP MY HANDS AND TRANSMUTE LIKE MY BROTHER...
SNAP

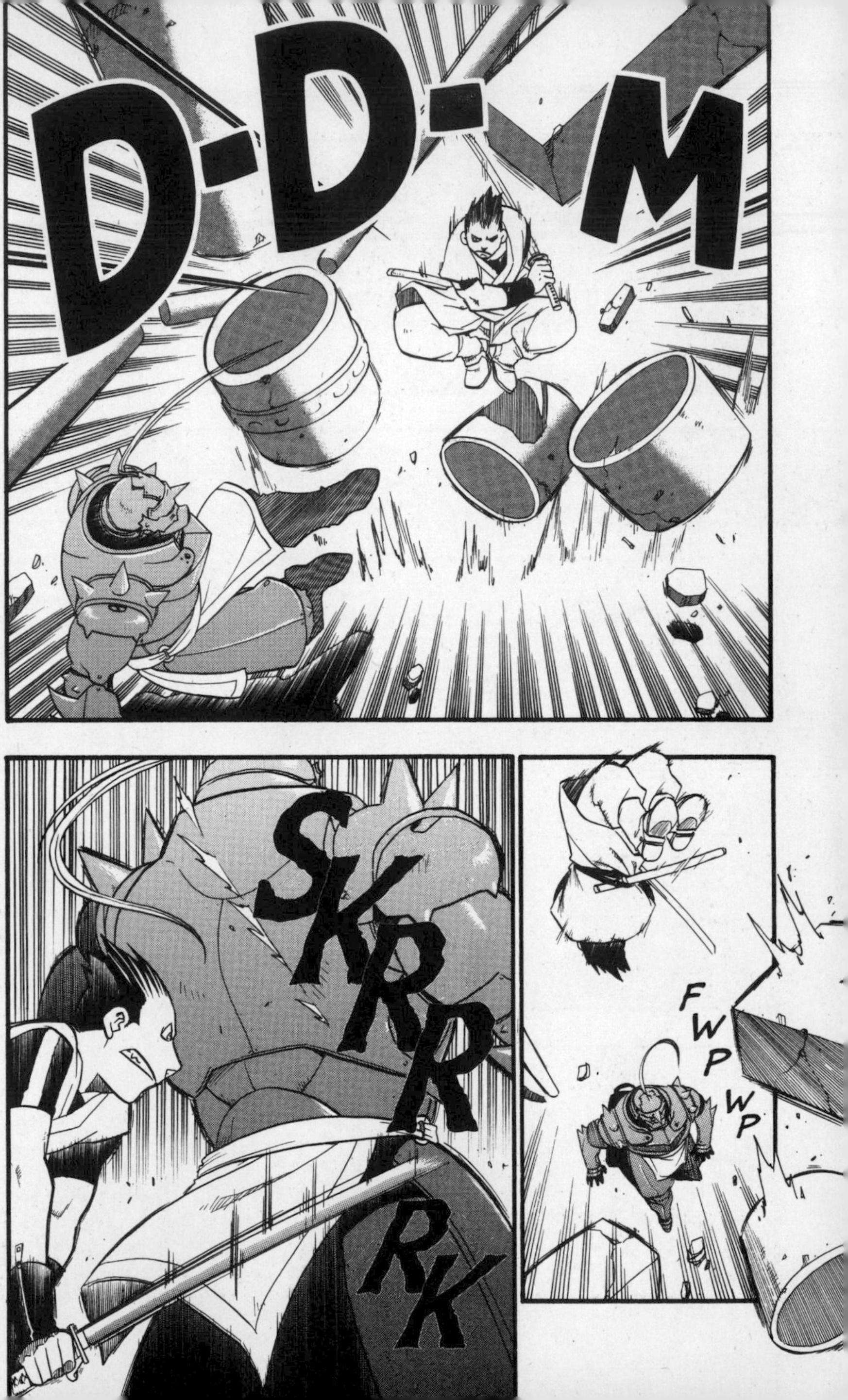
D-D-M
FWP WP
SKRRRK

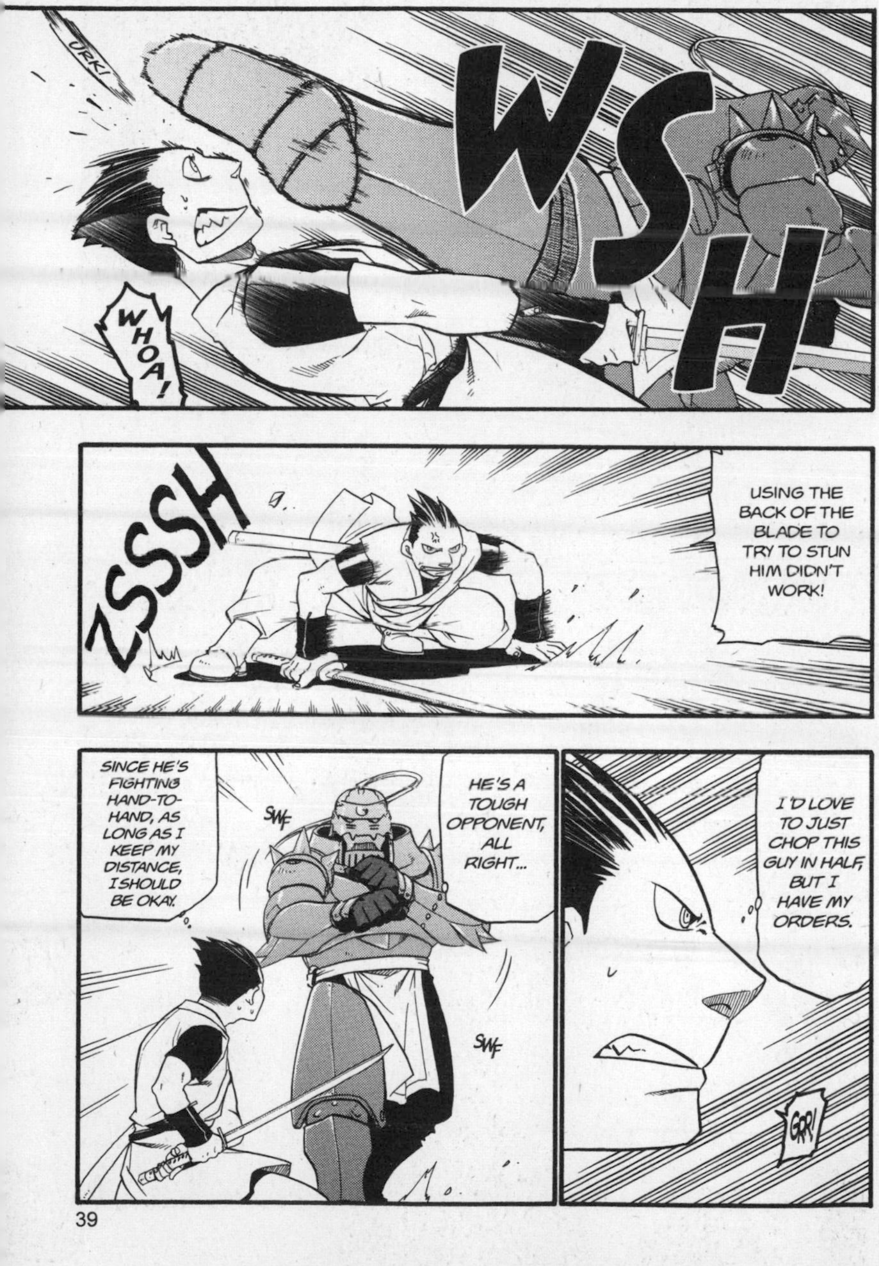
URK!
WSH
WHOA!
USING THE BACK OF THE BLADE TO TRY TO STUN HIM DIDN'T WORK!
ZSSSH
I'D LOVE TO JUST CHOP THIS GUY IN HALF, BUT I HAVE MY ORDERS.
GRR!
HE'S A TOUGH OPPONENT, ALL RIGHT...
SWF
SINCE HE'S FIGHTING HAND-TO-HAND, AS LONG AS I KEEP MY DISTANCE, I SHOULD BE OKAY.
SWF

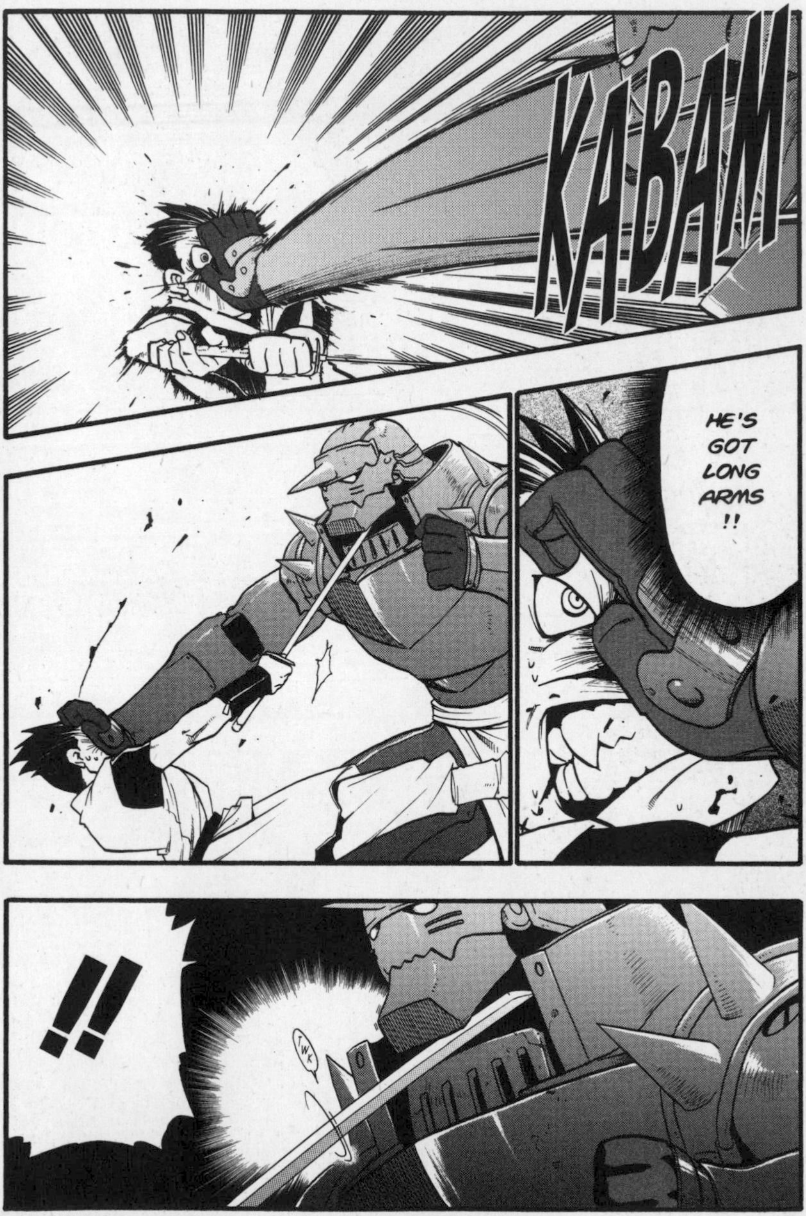
KABAM
HE'S GOT LONG ARMS !!
!!
TWK

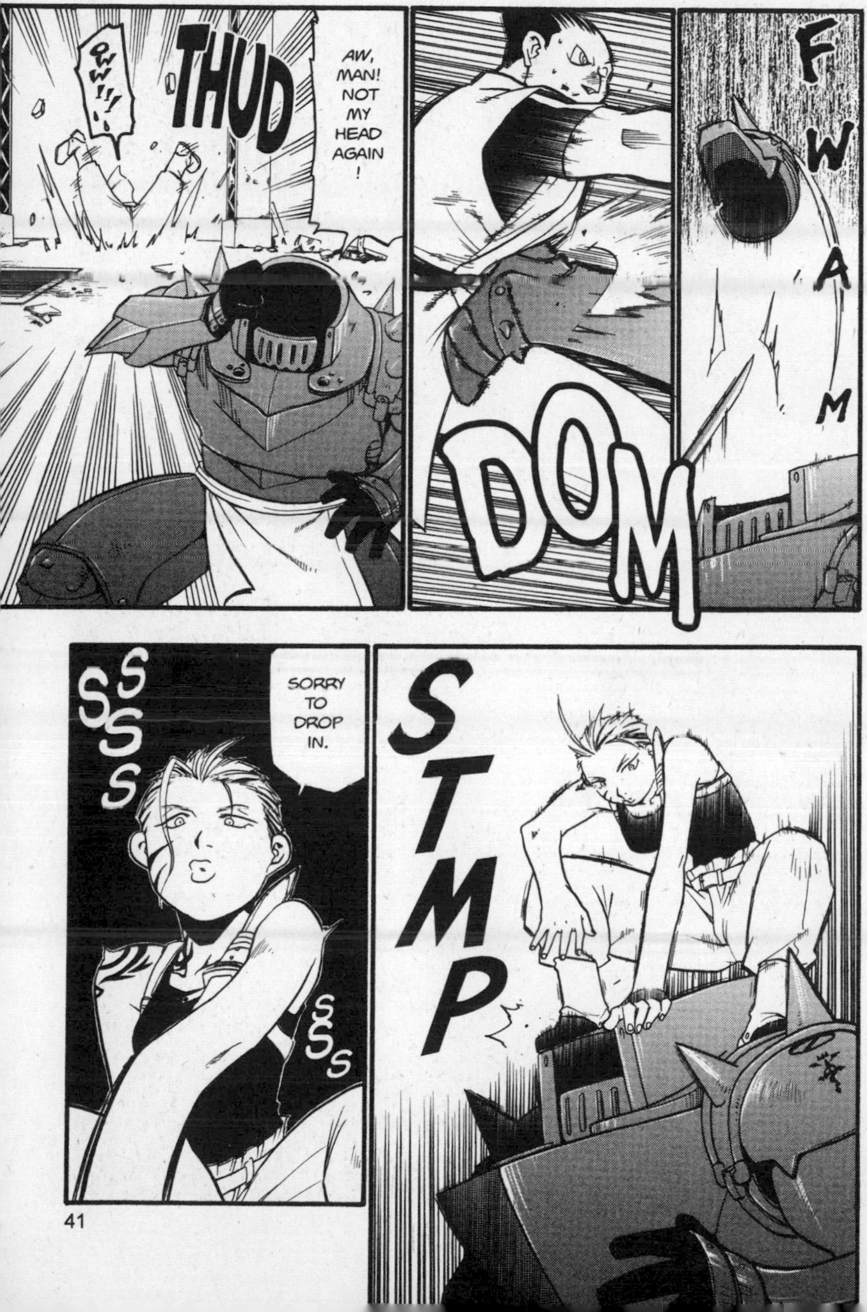
FWAM
DOM
AW, MAN! NOT MY HEAD AGAIN!
THUD
OWW!!
STMP
SORRY TO DROP IN.
SSSSS
SSS

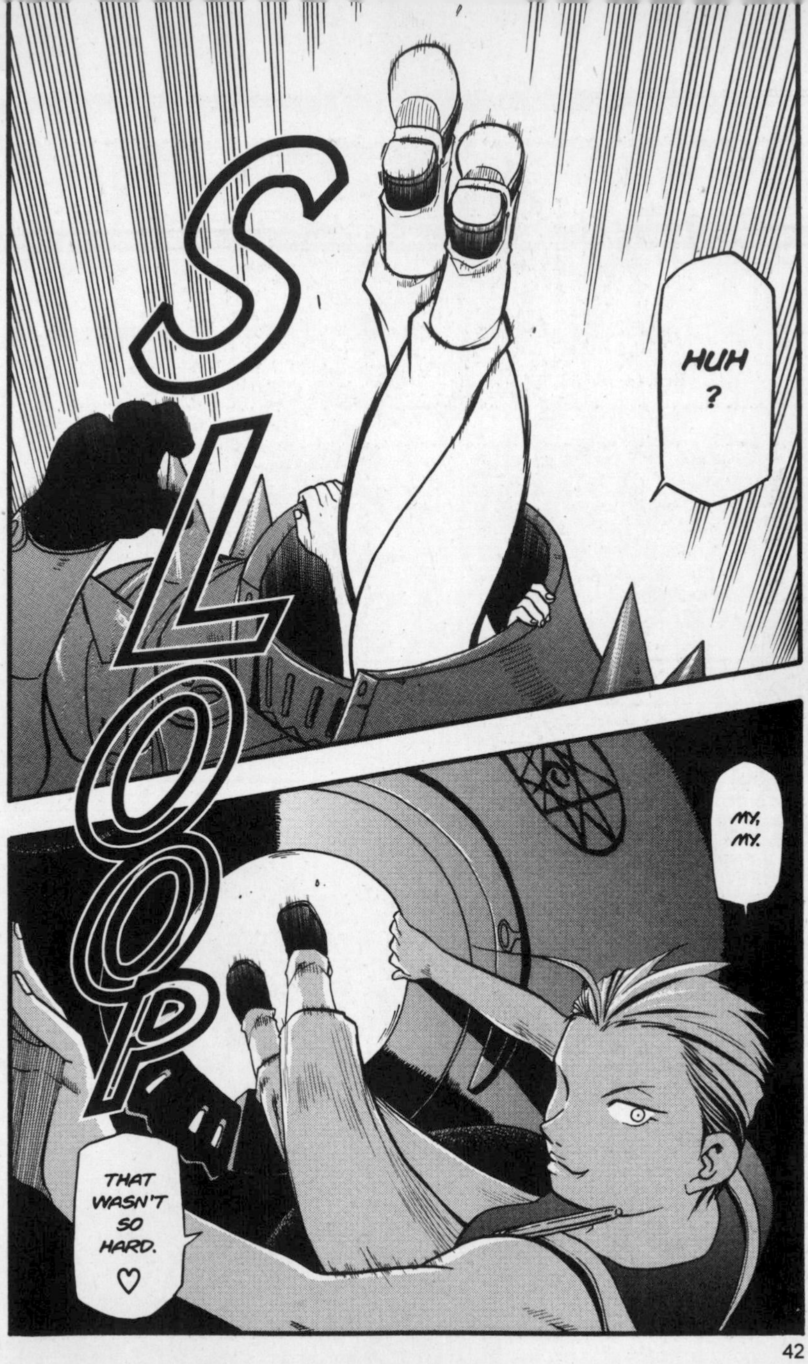
HUH ?
SLOOP
MY, MY.
THAT WASN'T SO HARD. ♡

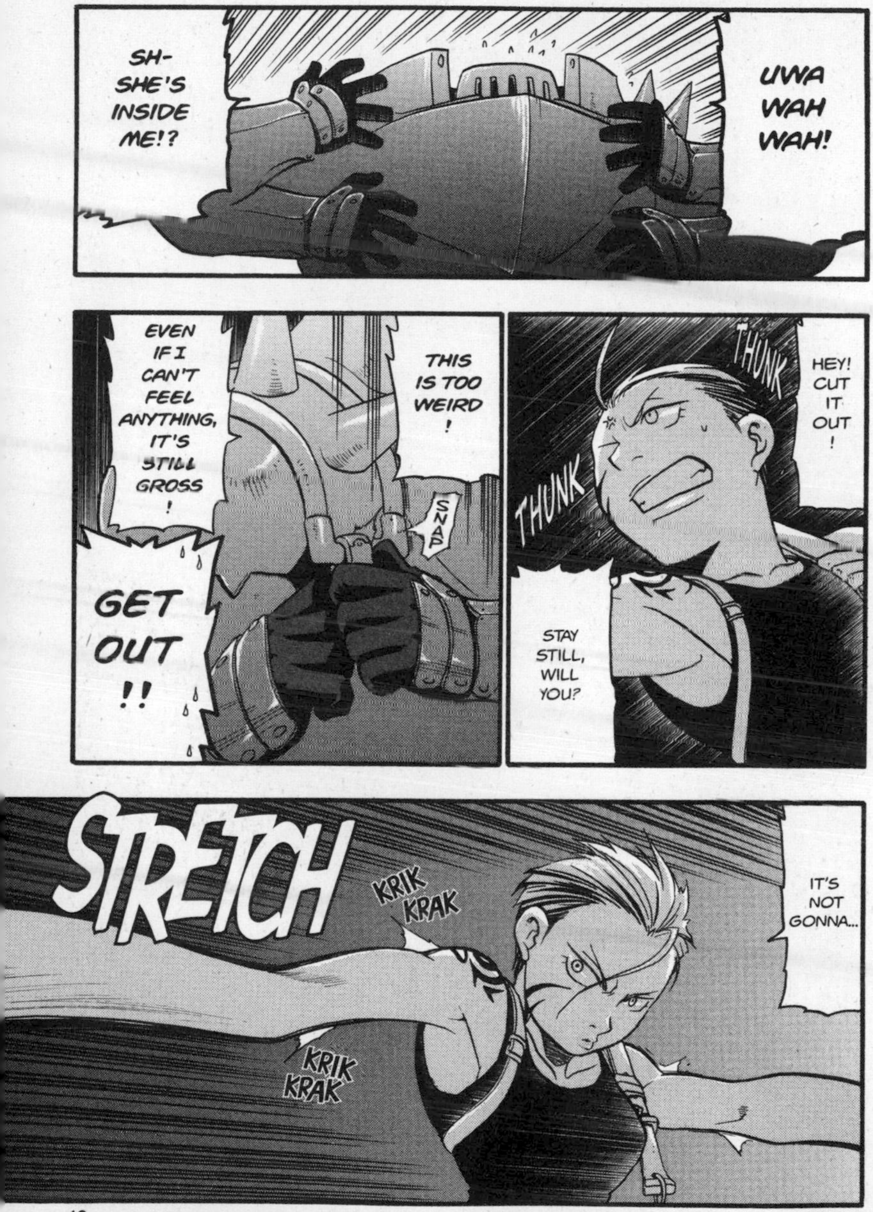
UWA WAH WAH!
SH- SHE'S INSIDE ME!?
THUNK
HEY! CUT IT OUT!
THUNK
STAY STILL, WILL YOU?
THIS IS TOO WEIRD!
EVEN IF I CAN'T FEEL ANYTHING, IT'S STILL GROSS!
SNAP
GET OUT!!
IT'S NOT GONNA...
KRIK KRAK
STRETCH
KRIK KRAK

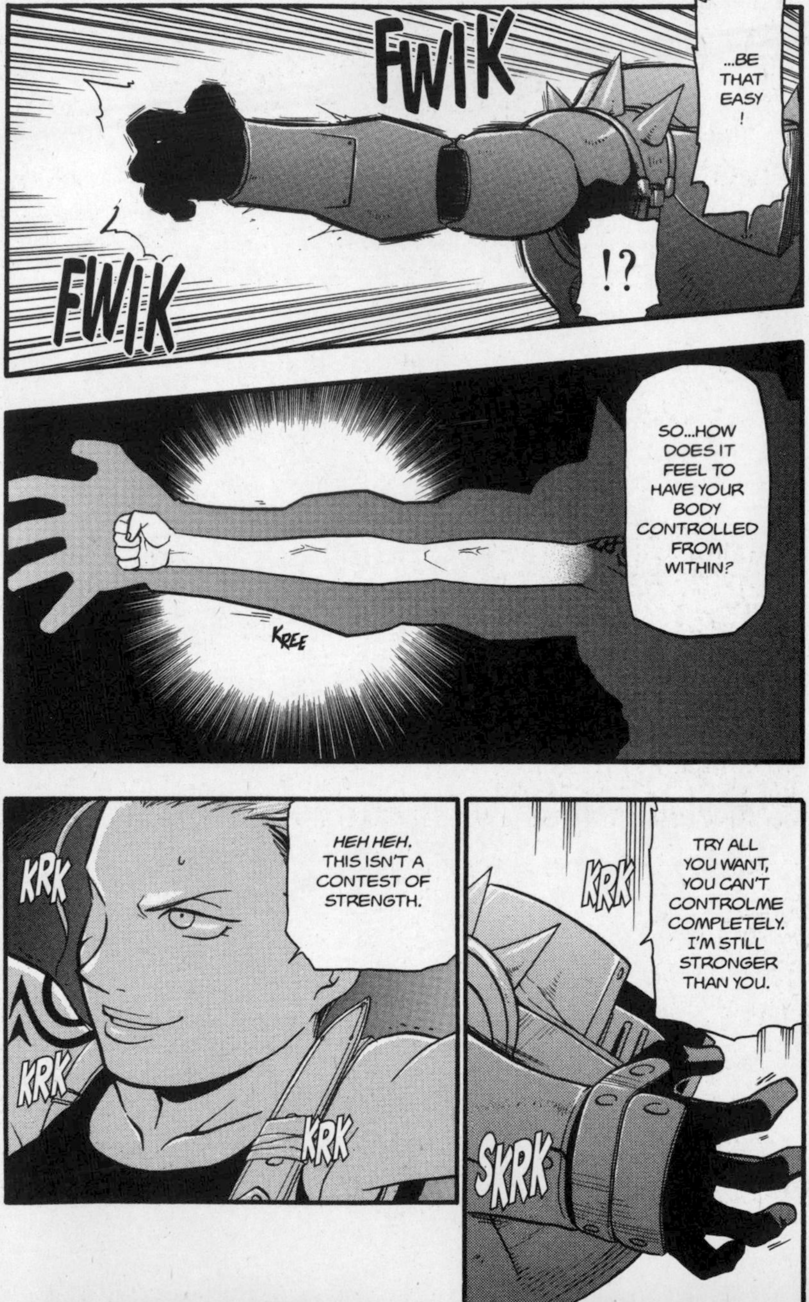
...BE THAT EASY !
FWIK
!?
FWIK
SO...HOW DOES IT FEEL TO HAVE YOUR BODY CONTROLLED FROM WITHIN?
KREE
TRY ALL YOU WANT, YOU CAN'T CONTROLME COMPLETELY. I'M STILL STRONGER THAN YOU.
KRK
SKRK
HEH HEH. THIS ISN'T A CONTEST OF STRENGTH.
KRK
KRK
KRK

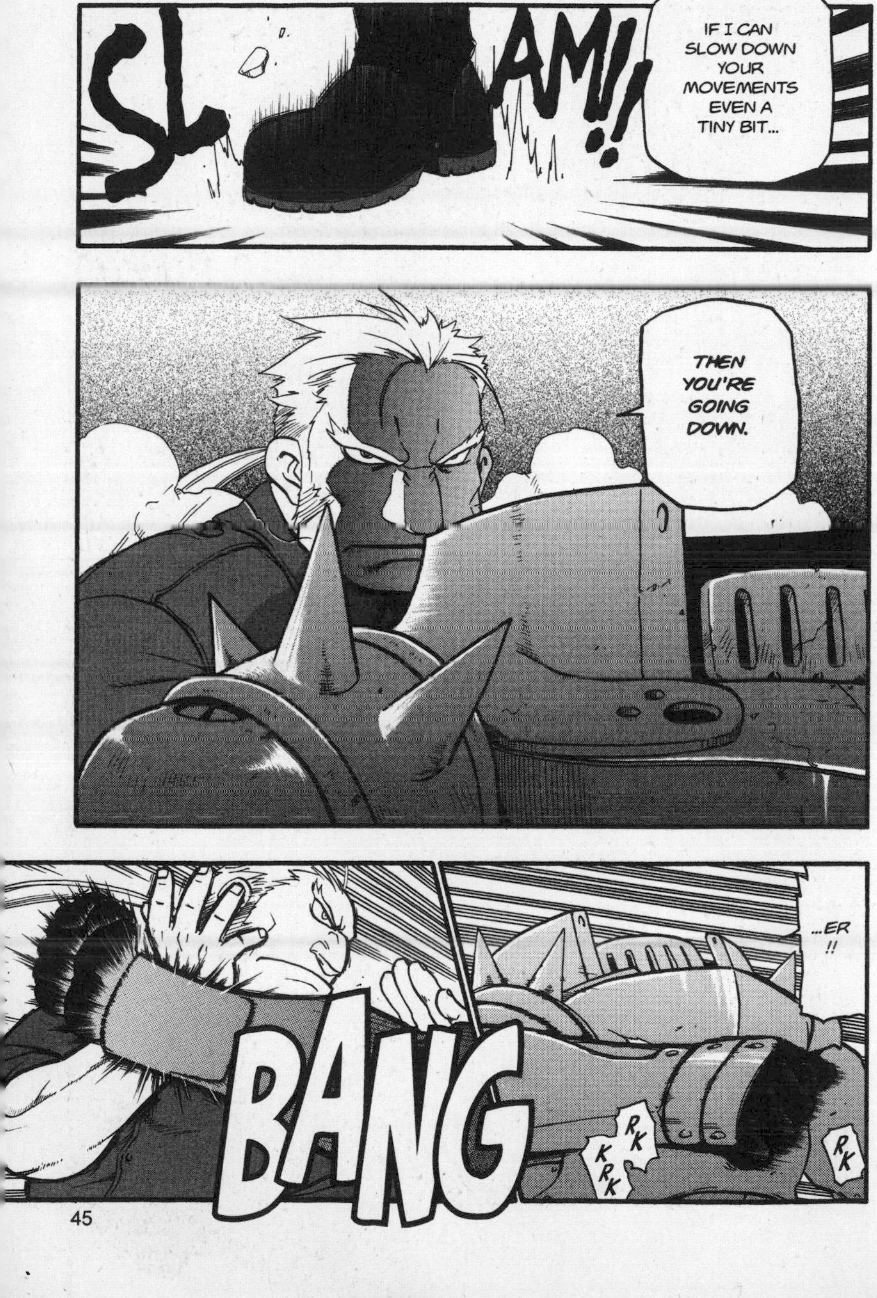
IF I CAN SLOW DOWN YOUR MOVEMENTS EVEN A TINY BIT...
SLAM!!
THEN YOU'RE GOING DOWN.
...ER !!
BANG
RK
RK KRK

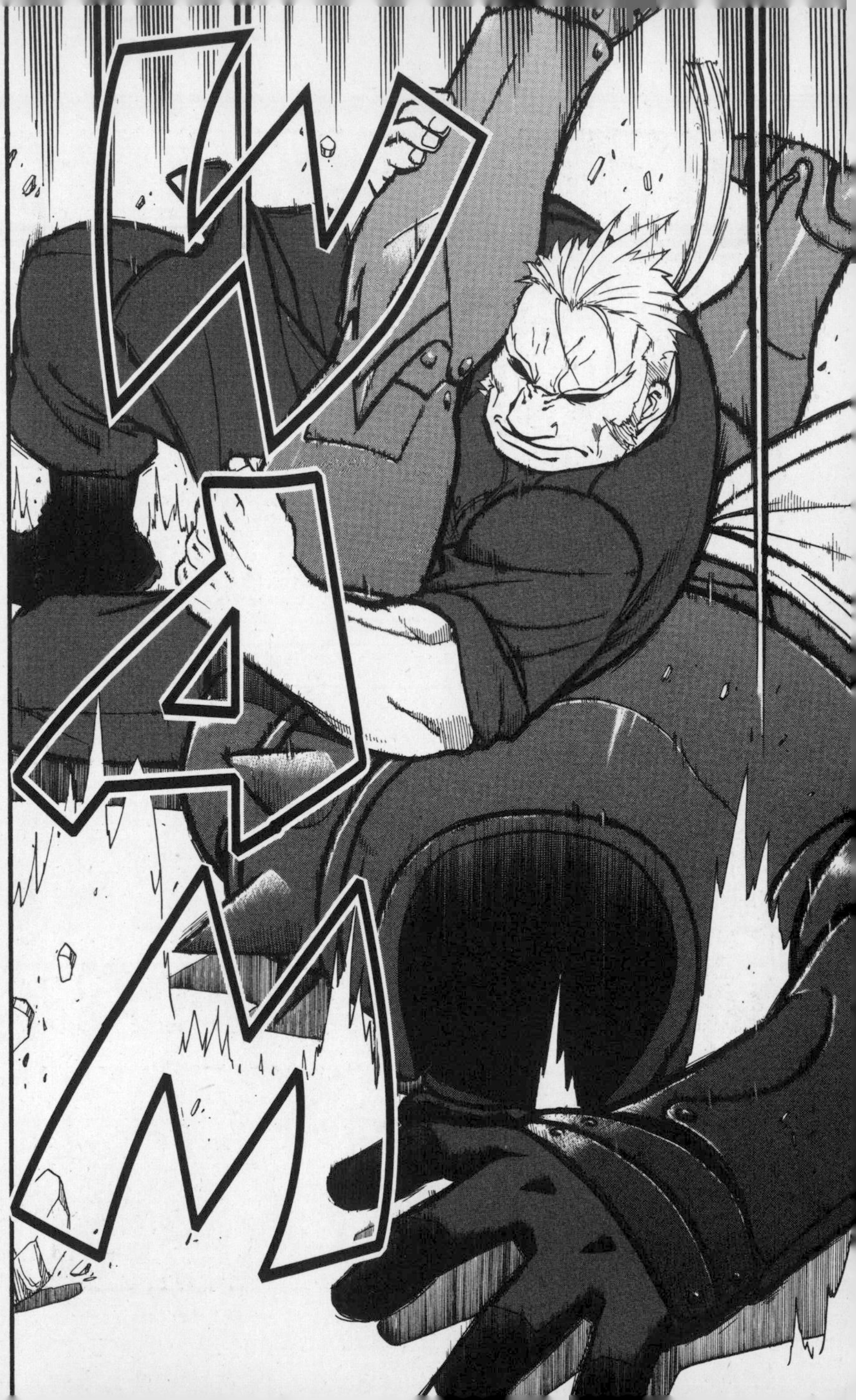

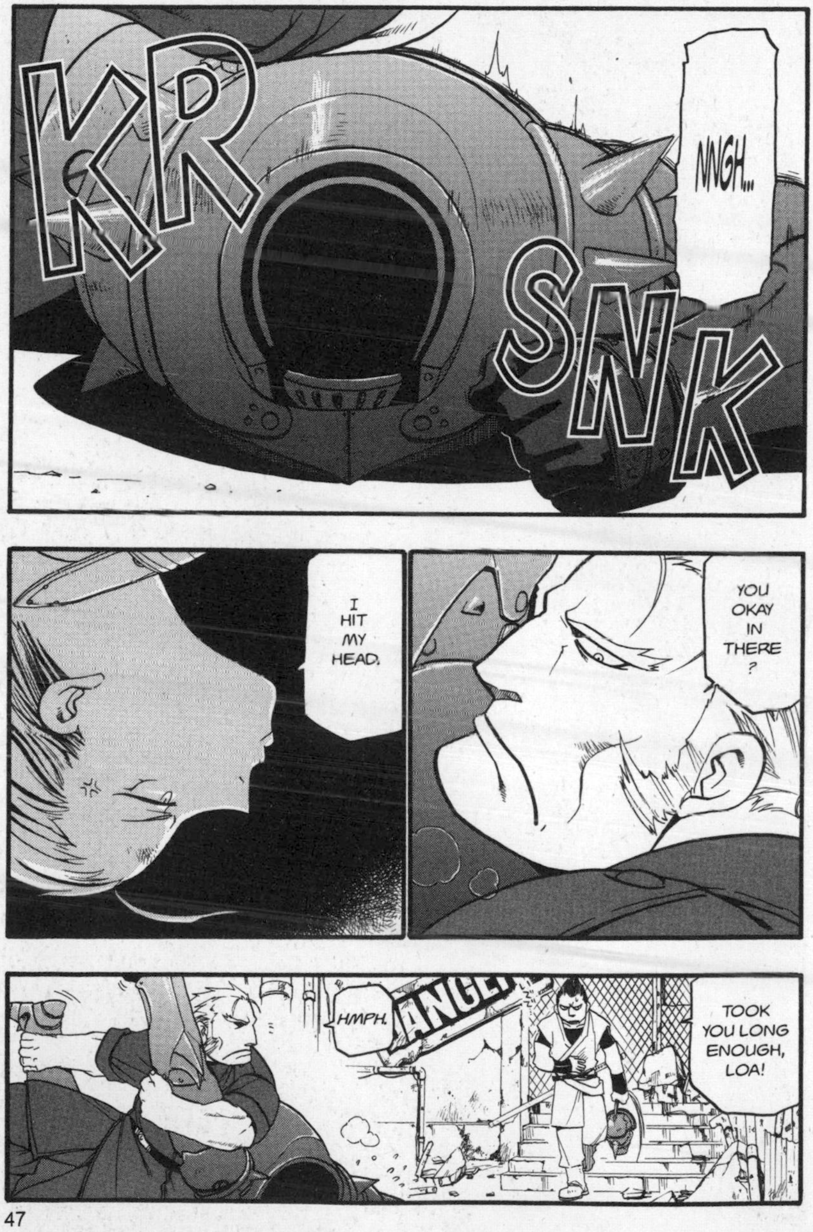
NNGH...
KR
SNK
YOU OKAY IN THERE?
I HIT MY HEAD.
TOOK YOU LONG ENOUGH, LOA!
HMPH.

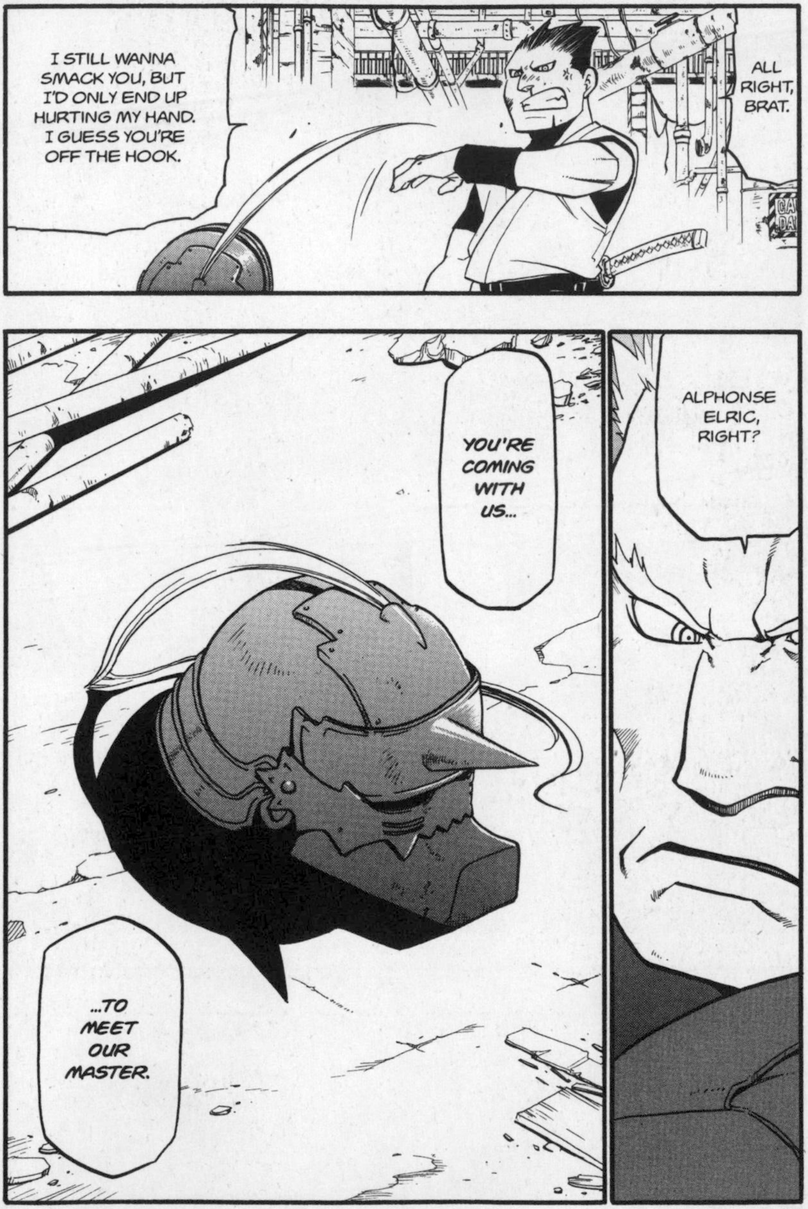
ALL RIGHT, BRAT.
I STILL WANNA SMACK YOU, BUT I'D ONLY END UP HURTING MY HAND. I GUESS YOU'RE OFF THE HOOK.
ALPHONSE ELRIC, RIGHT?
YOU'RE COMING WITH US...
...TO MEET OUR MASTER.

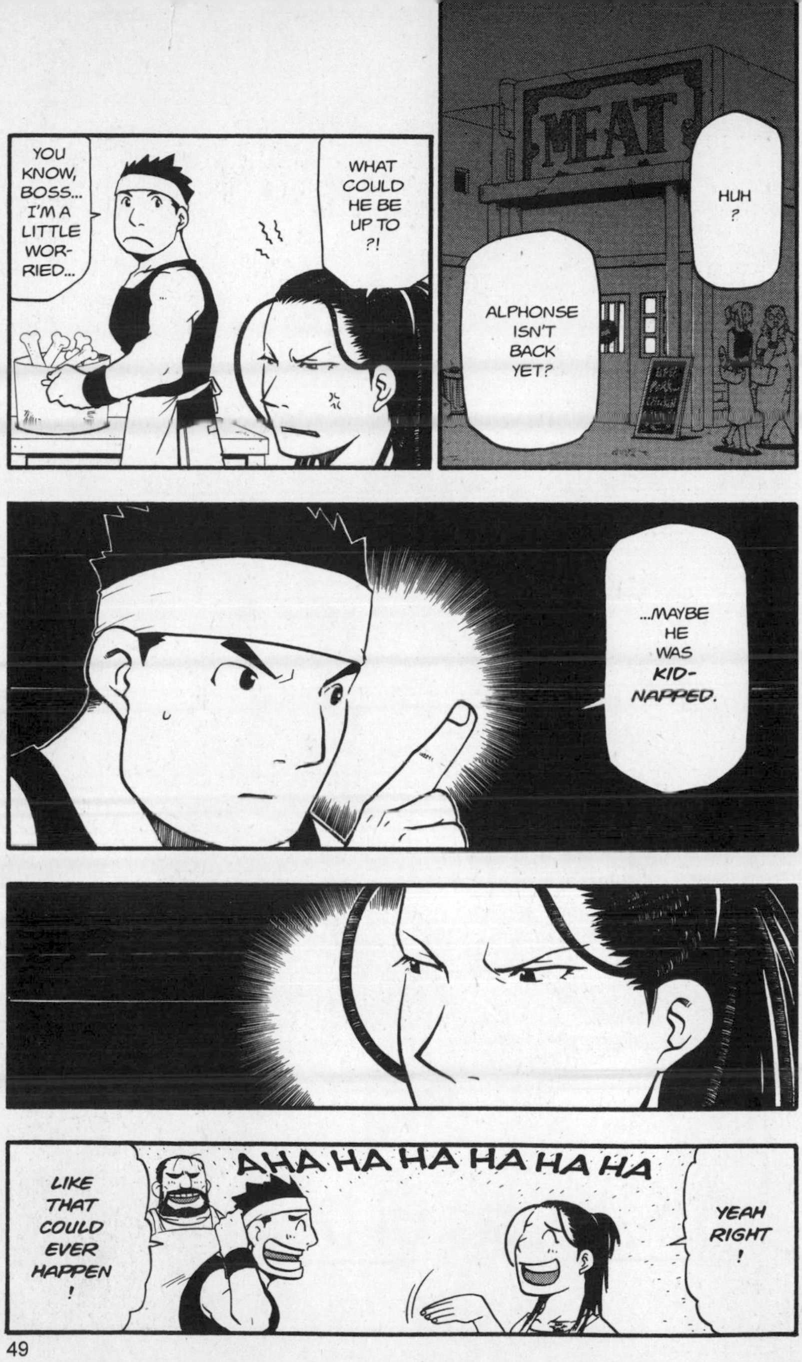
MEAT
HUH?
ALPHONSE ISN'T BACK YET?
WHAT COULD HE BE UP TO ?!
YOU KNOW, BOSS... I'M A LITTLE WORRIED...
...MAYBE HE WAS KIDNAPPED.
AHA HA HA HA HA HA HA
YEAH RIGHT!
LIKE THAT COULD EVER HAPPEN!

Chapter 27:
The Beasts Of Dublith

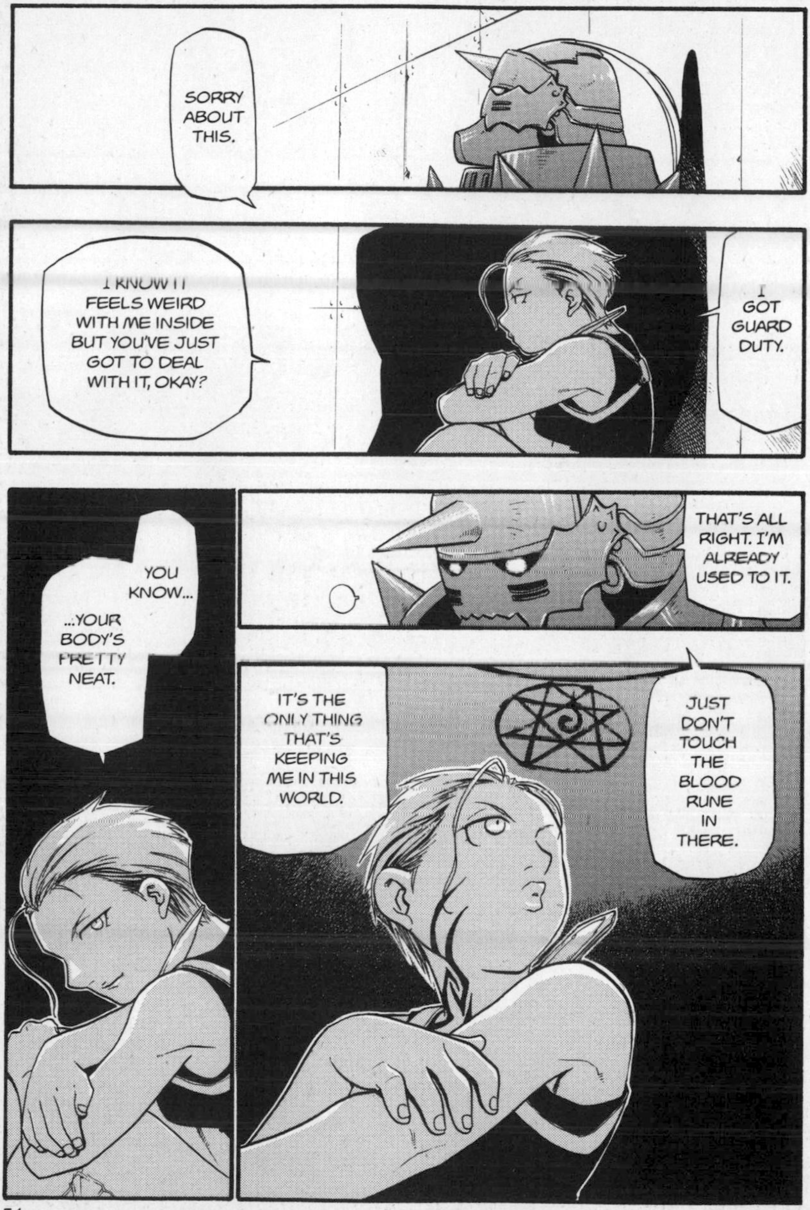

SORRY ABOUT THIS.
I GOT GUARD DUTY.
I KNOW IT FEELS WEIRD WITH ME INSIDE BUT YOU'VE JUST GOT TO DEAL WITH IT, OKAY?
THAT'S ALL RIGHT. I'M ALREADY USED TO IT.
JUST DON'T TOUCH THE BLOOD RUNE IN THERE.
IT'S THE ONLY THING THAT'S KEEPING ME IN THIS WORLD.
YOU KNOW...
...YOUR BODY'S PRETTY NEAT.

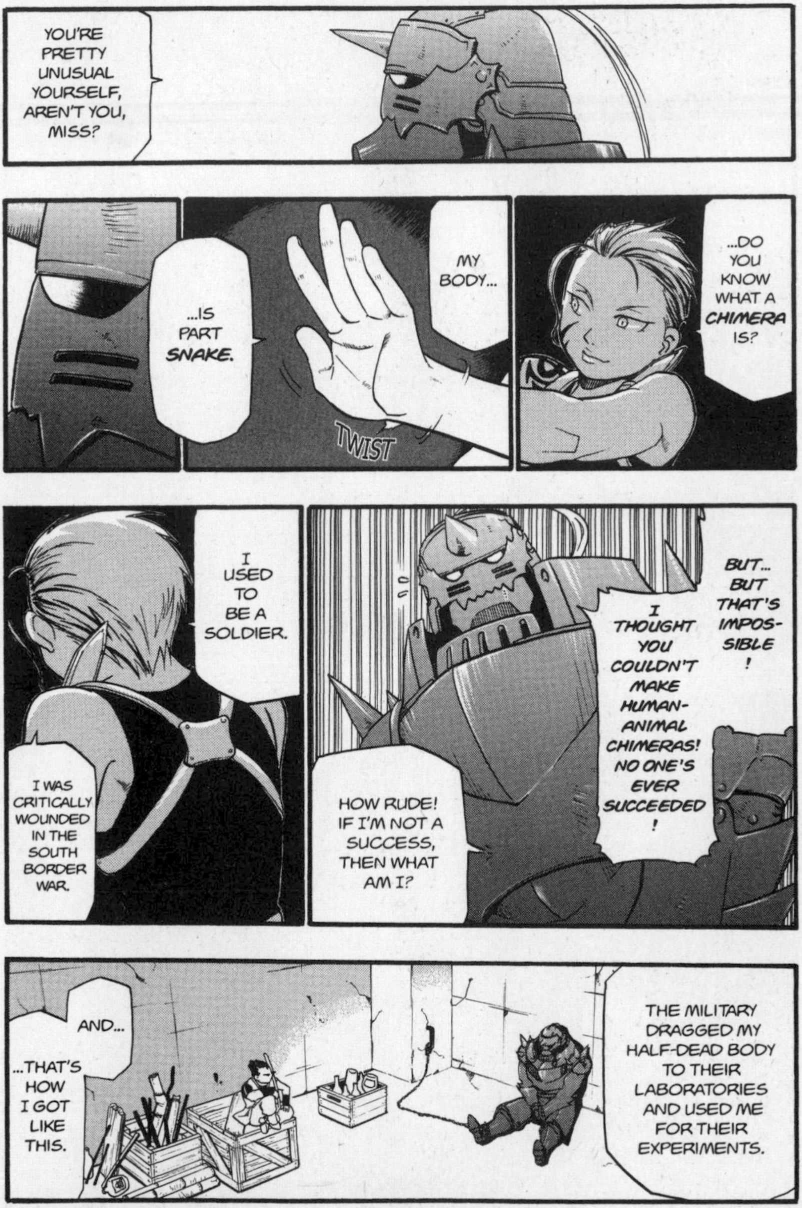
YOU'RE PRETTY UNUSUAL YOURSELF, AREN'T YOU, MISS?
...DO YOU KNOW WHAT A CHIMERA IS?
MY BODY...
TWIST
...IS PART SNAKE.
BUT... BUT THAT'S IMPOSSIBLE!
I THOUGHT YOU COULDN'T MAKE HUMAN-ANIMAL CHIMERAS! NO ONE'S EVER SUCCEEDED!
HOW RUDE! IF I'M NOT A SUCCESS, THEN WHAT AM I?
I USED TO BE A SOLDIER.
I WAS CRITICALLY WOUNDED IN THE SOUTH BORDER WAR.
THE MILITARY DRAGGED MY HALF-DEAD BODY TO THEIR LABORATORIES AND USED ME FOR THEIR EXPERIMENTS.
AND...
...THAT'S HOW I GOT LIKE THIS.

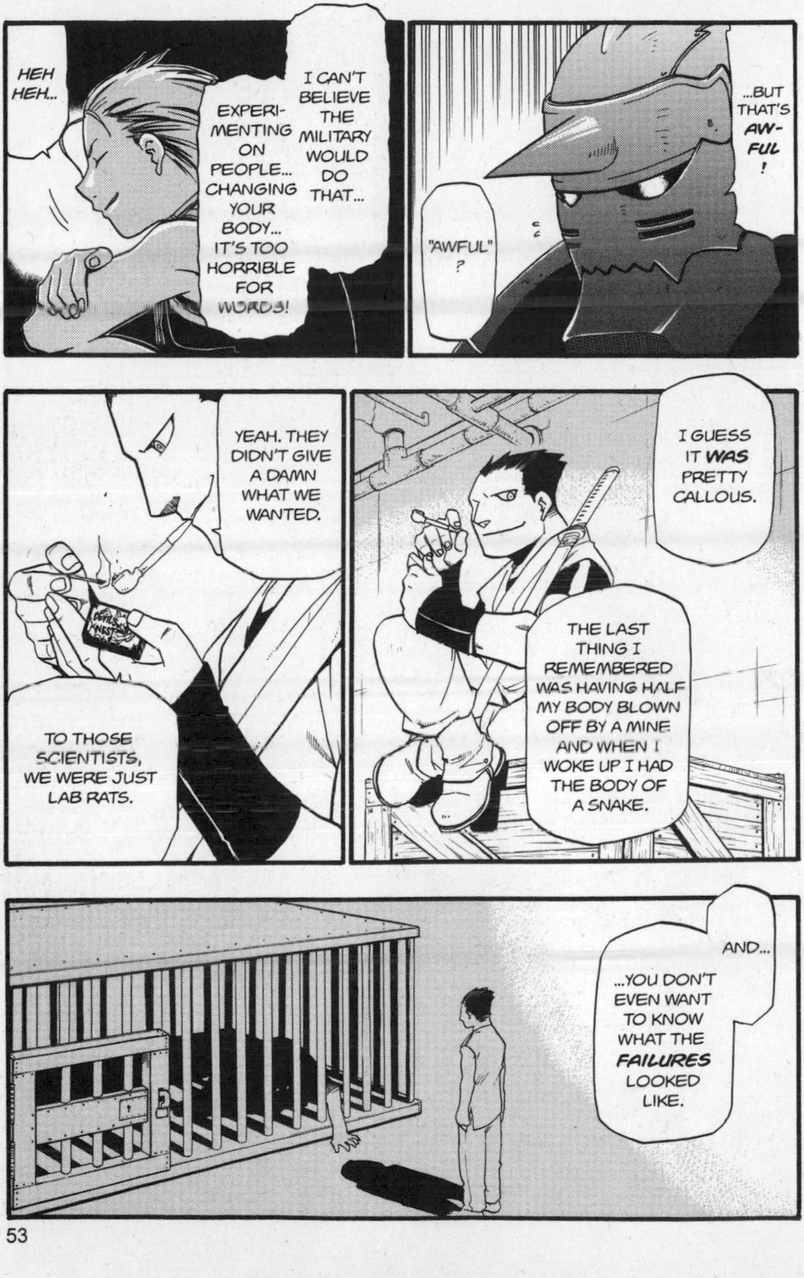
...BUT THAT'S AWFUL!
"AWFUL"?
I CAN'T BELIEVE THE MILITARY WOULD DO THAT...
EXPERIMENTING ON PEOPLE... CHANGING YOUR BODY... IT'S TOO HORRIBLE FOR WORDS!
HEH HEH...
I GUESS IT WAS PRETTY CALLOUS.
THE LAST THING I REMEMBERED WAS HAVING HALF MY BODY BLOWN OFF BY A MINE AND WHEN I WOKE UP I HAD THE BODY OF A SNAKE.
YEAH. THEY DIDN'T GIVE A DAMN WHAT WE WANTED.
TO THOSE SCIENTISTS, WE WERE JUST LAB RATS.
AND...
...YOU DON'T EVEN WANT TO KNOW WHAT THE FAILURES LOOKED LIKE.

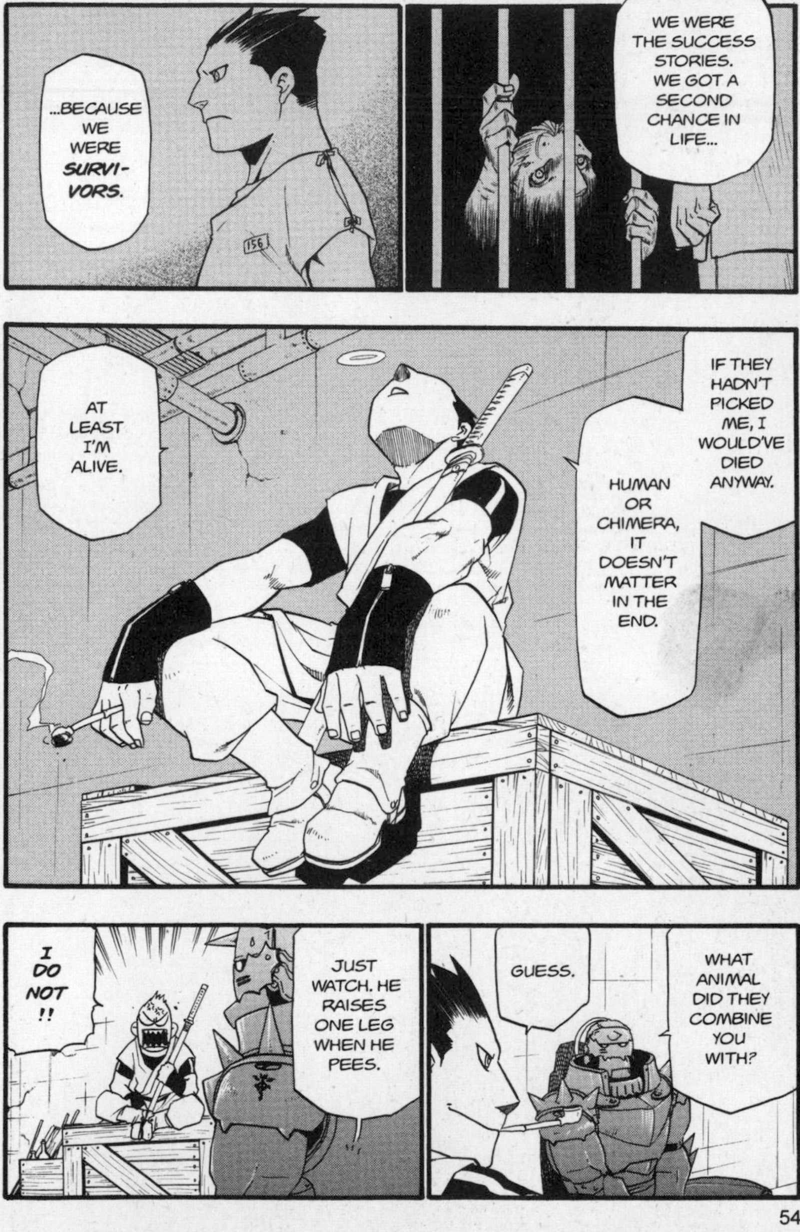
WE WERE THE SUCCESS STORIES. WE GOT A SECOND CHANCE IN LIFE...
...BECAUSE WE WERE ***SURVIVORS.***
IF THEY HADN'T PICKED ME, I WOULD'VE DIED ANYWAY.
HUMAN OR CHIMERA, IT DOESN'T MATTER IN THE END.
AT LEAST I'M ALIVE.
WHAT ANIMAL DID THEY COMBINE YOU WITH?
GUESS.
JUST WATCH. HE RAISES ONE LEG WHEN HE PEES.
I DO NOT!!

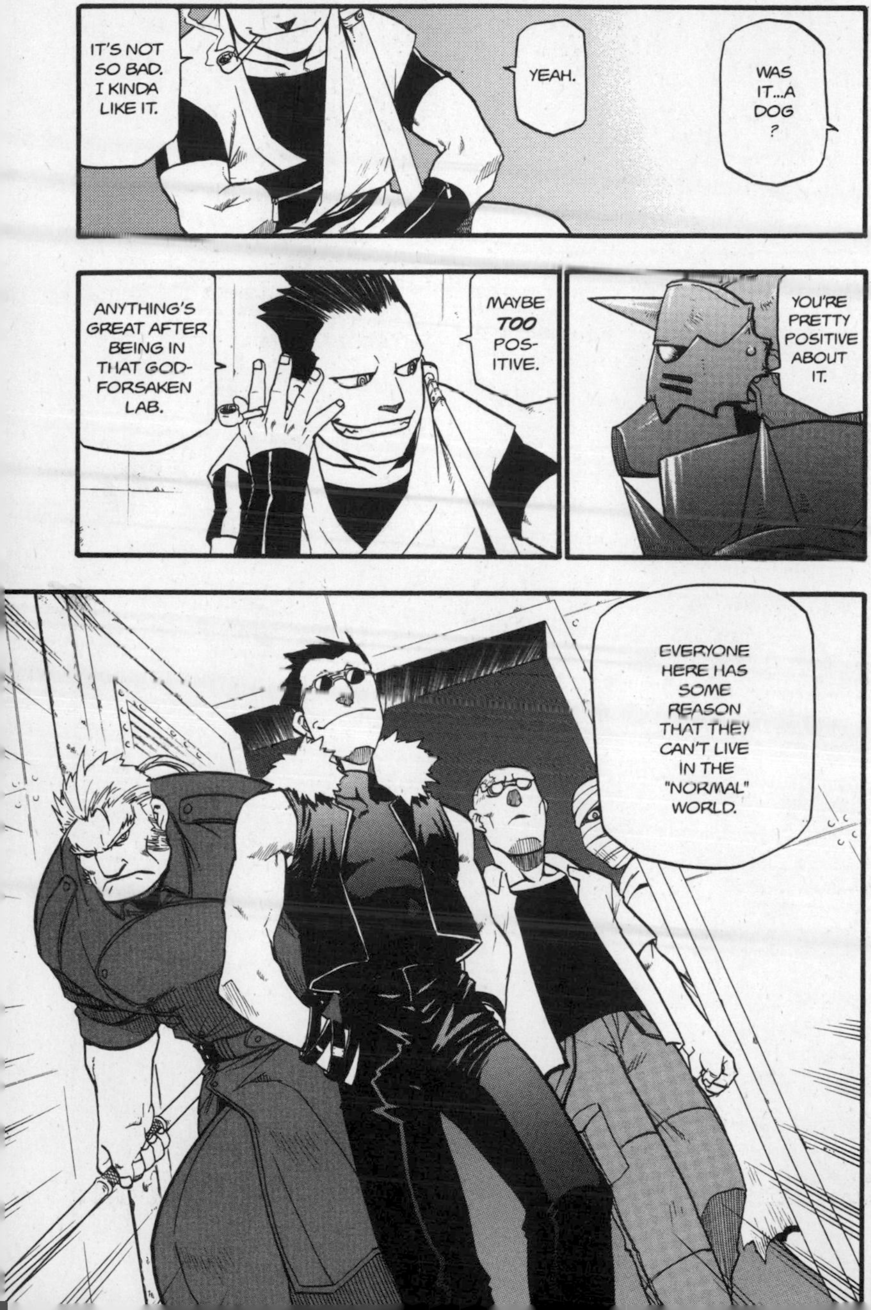
WAS IT...A DOG?
YEAH.
IT'S NOT SO BAD. I KINDA LIKE IT.
YOU'RE PRETTY POSITIVE ABOUT IT.
MAYBE *TOO* POS-ITIVE.
ANYTHING'S GREAT AFTER BEING IN THAT GOD-FORSAKEN LAB.
EVERYONE HERE HAS SOME REASON THAT THEY CAN'T LIVE IN THE "NORMAL" WORLD.

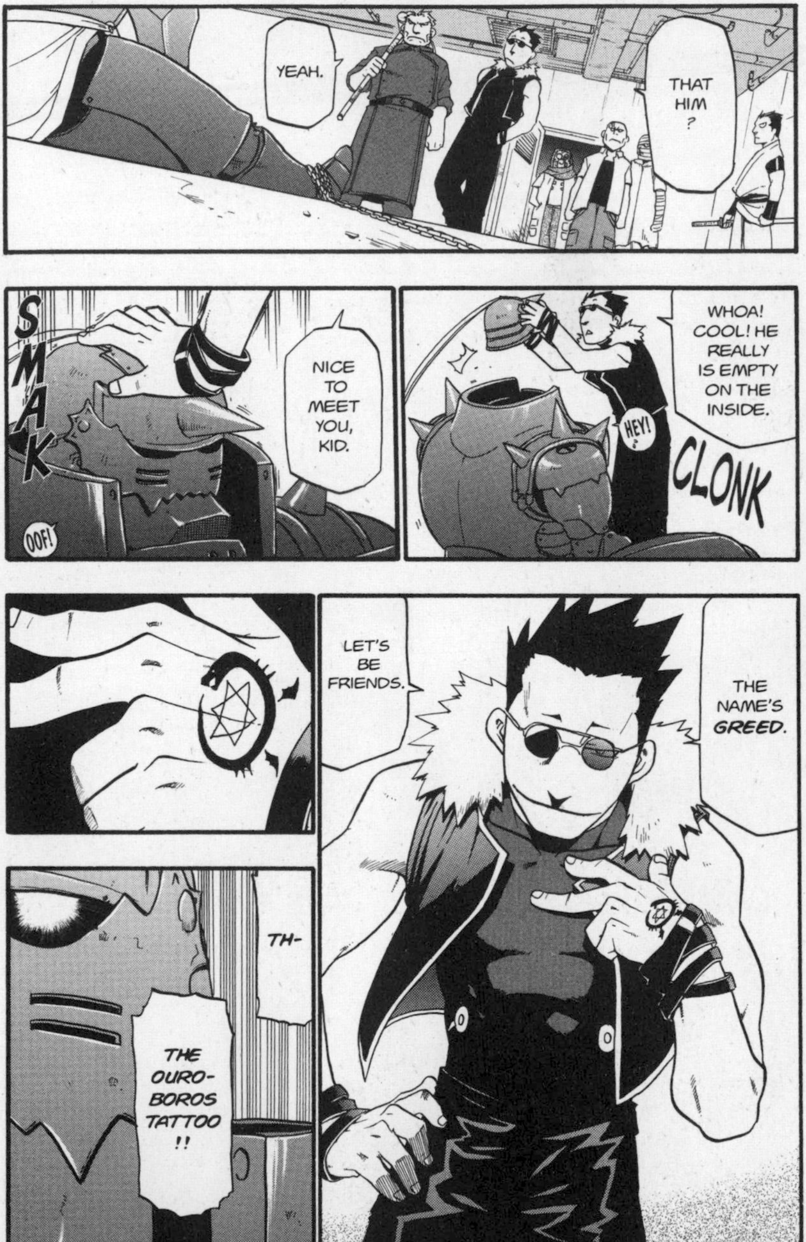
THAT HIM?
YEAH.
WHOA! COOL! HE REALLY IS EMPTY ON THE INSIDE.
HEY!
CLONK
SMAK
NICE TO MEET YOU, KID.
OOF!
THE NAME'S GREED.
LET'S BE FRIENDS.
TH-
THE OURO-BOROS TATTOO!!

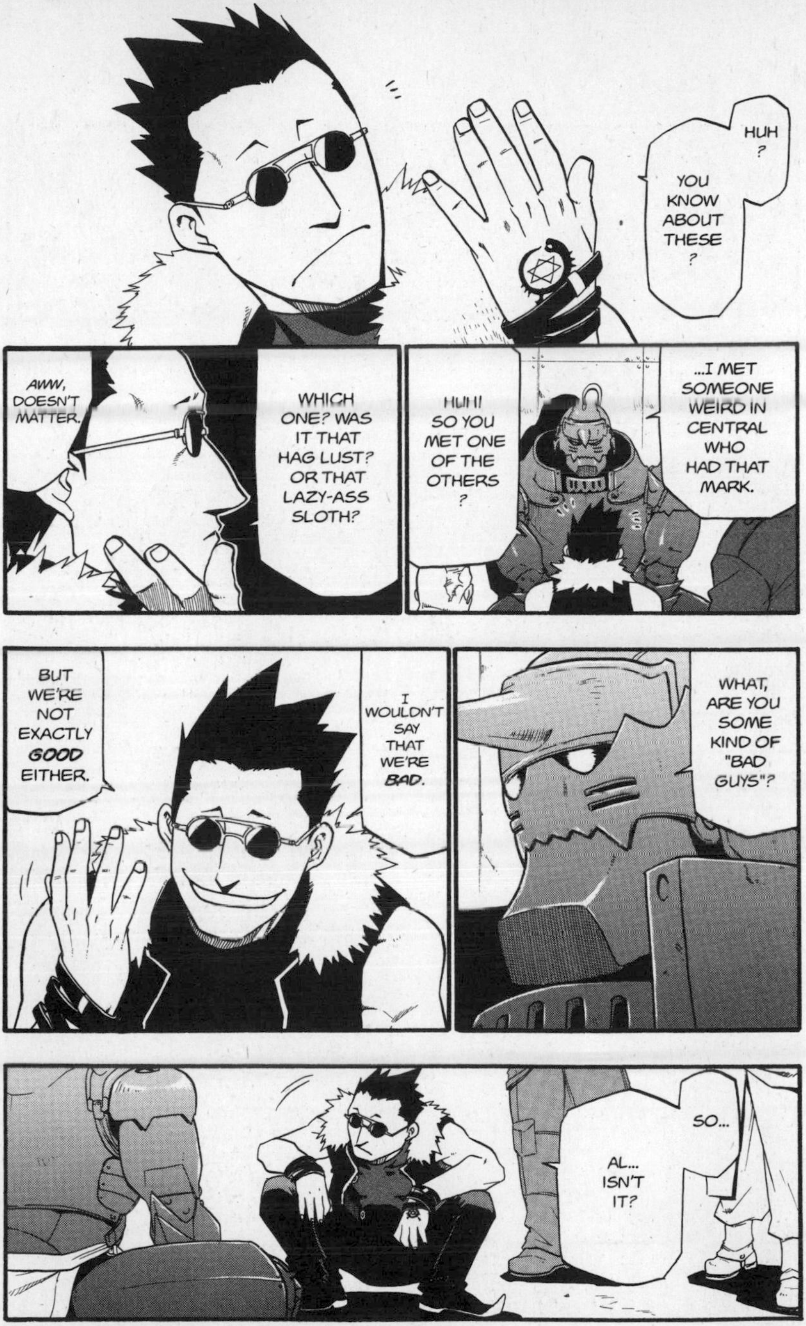
HUH? YOU KNOW ABOUT THESE?
...I MET SOMEONE WEIRD IN CENTRAL WHO HAD THAT MARK.
HUH! SO YOU MET ONE OF THE OTHERS?
WHICH ONE? WAS IT THAT HAG LUST? OR THAT LAZY-ASS SLOTH?
AWW, DOESN'T MATTER.
WHAT, ARE YOU SOME KIND OF "BAD GUYS"?
I WOULDN'T SAY THAT WE'RE BAD.
BUT WE'RE NOT EXACTLY GOOD EITHER.
SO...
AL... ISN'T IT?

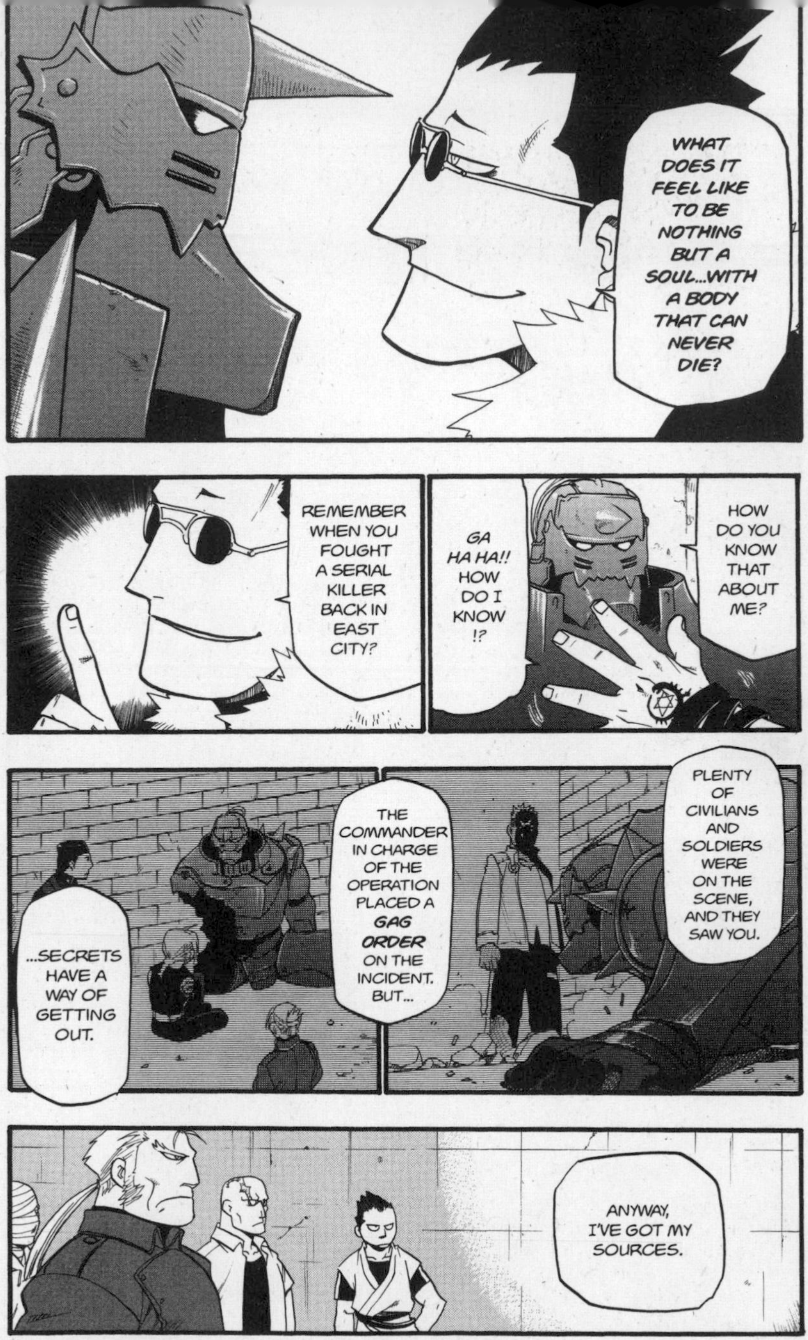
WHAT DOES IT FEEL LIKE TO BE NOTHING BUT A SOUL...WITH A BODY THAT CAN NEVER DIE?
HOW DO YOU KNOW THAT ABOUT ME?
GA HA HA!! HOW DO I KNOW !?
REMEMBER WHEN YOU FOUGHT A SERIAL KILLER BACK IN EAST CITY?
PLENTY OF CIVILIANS AND SOLDIERS WERE ON THE SCENE, AND THEY SAW YOU.
THE COMMANDER IN CHARGE OF THE OPERATION PLACED A GAG ORDER ON THE INCIDENT. BUT...
...SECRETS HAVE A WAY OF GETTING OUT.
ANYWAY, I'VE GOT MY SOURCES.

WHY DID YOU BRING ME HERE?
TRANSMUTING A PERSON'S SOUL AND BINDING IT TO A PHYSICAL OBJECT...
THINK ABOUT IT. IF YOU CAN DO THAT, YOU'VE GOT YOURSELF *ETERNAL LIFE!*
AM I RIGHT?
I WANT IT ALL.
MONEY!! SEX!!
POWER!!
FAME!!
I WANT EVERY-THING IN THE WORLD!

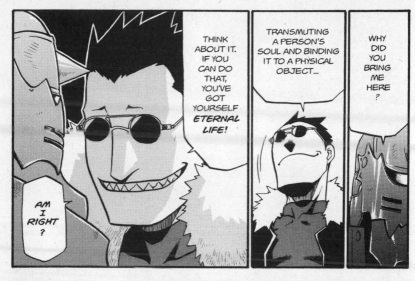

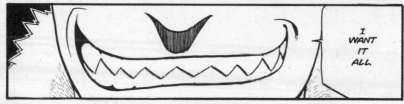

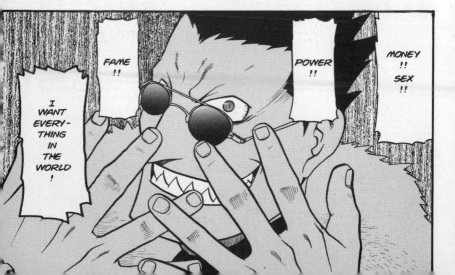

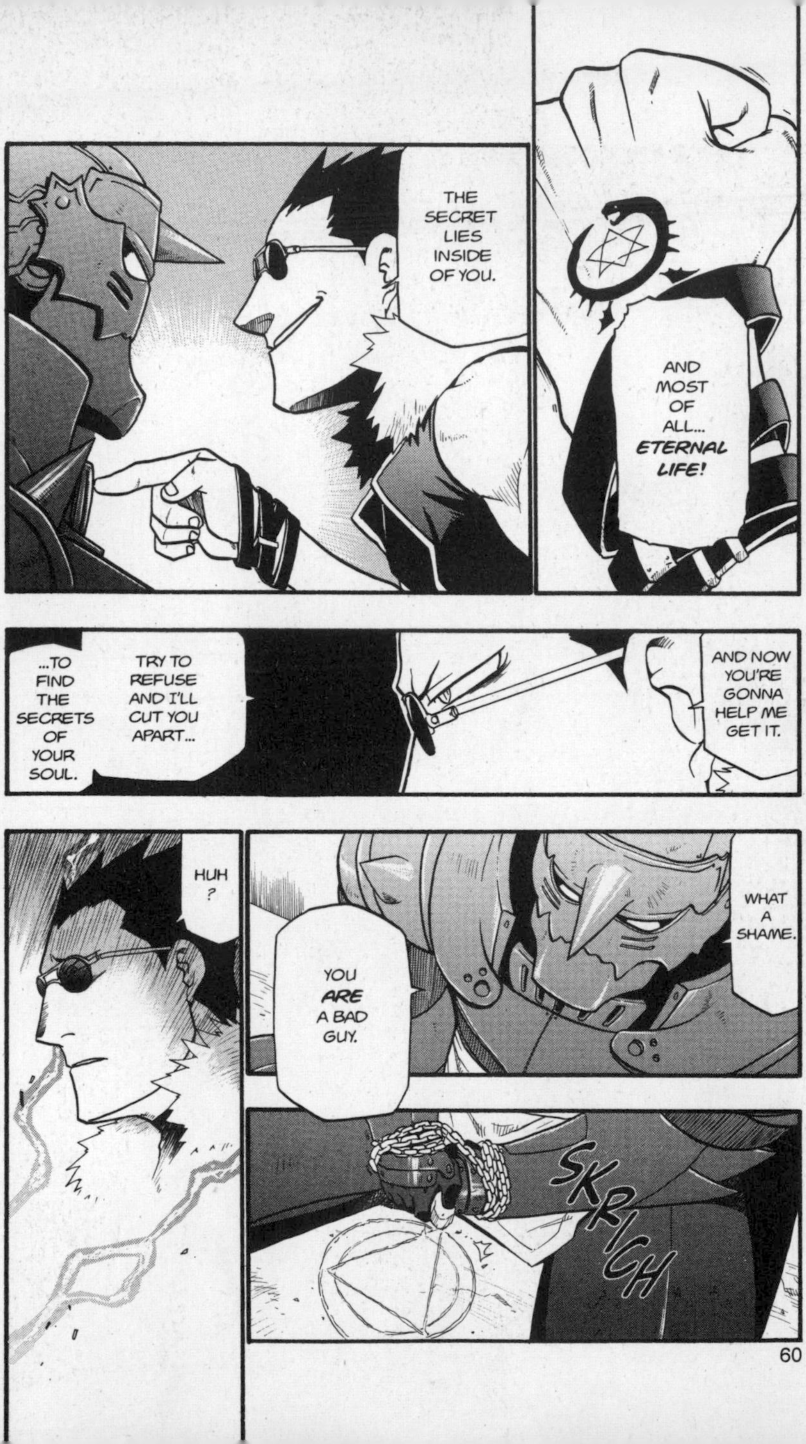
AND MOST OF ALL... ***ETERNAL LIFE!***
THE SECRET LIES INSIDE OF YOU.
AND NOW YOU'RE GONNA HELP ME GET IT.
TRY TO REFUSE AND I'LL CUT YOU APART...
...TO FIND THE SECRETS OF YOUR SOUL.
WHAT A SHAME.
YOU ***ARE*** A BAD GUY.
SKRICH
HUH ?

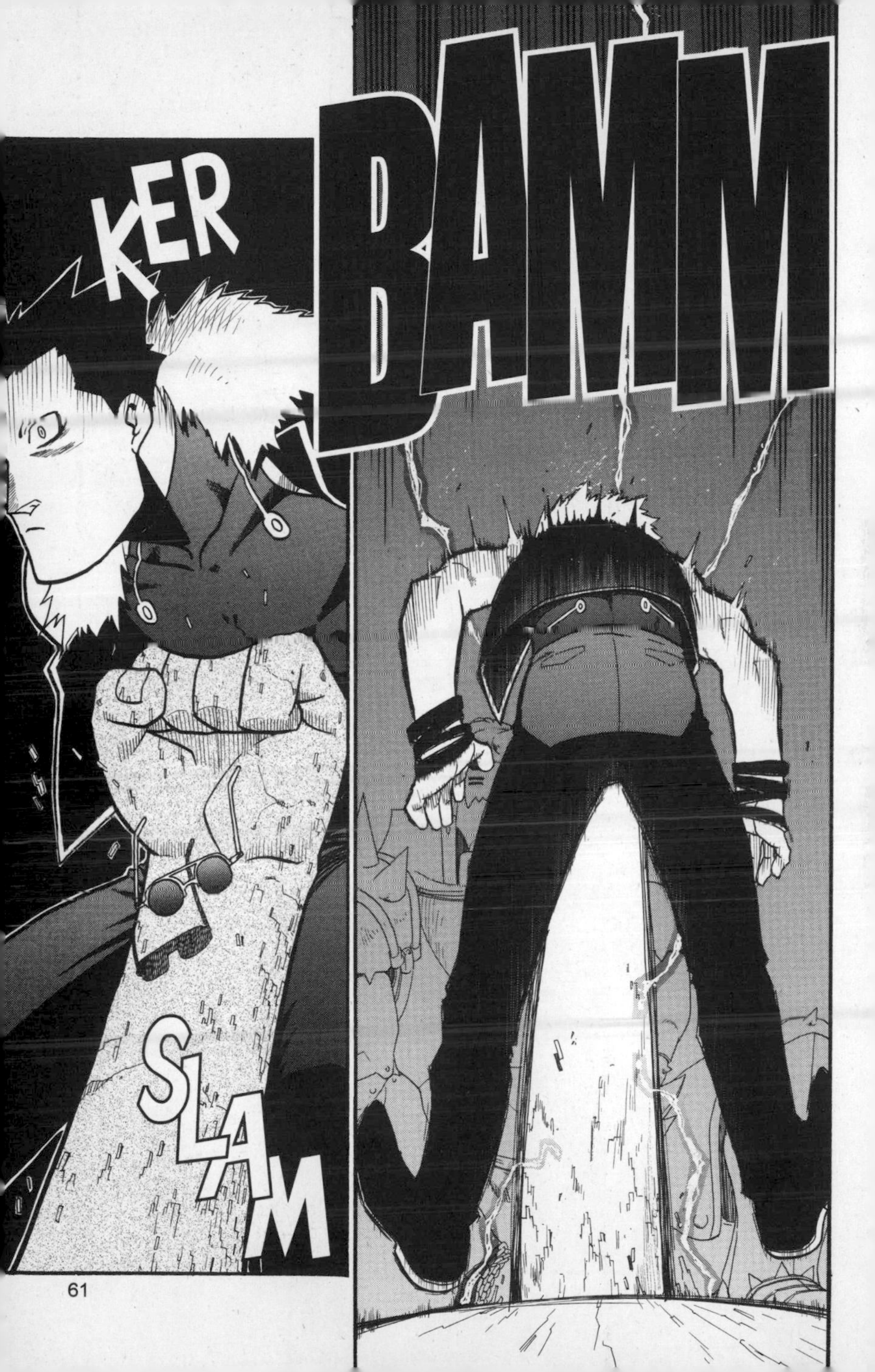
KER BAMM
SLAM

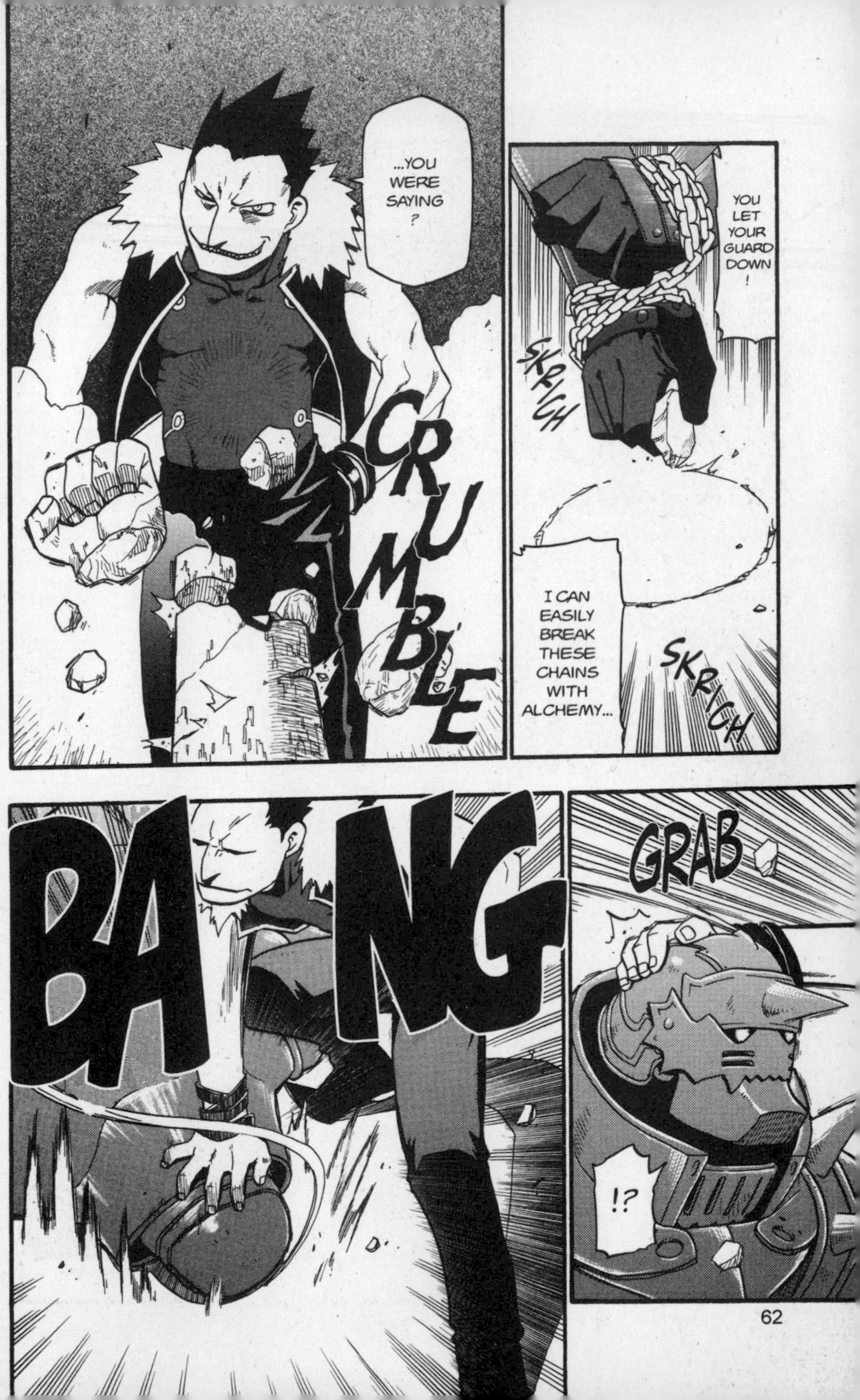
YOU LET YOUR GUARD DOWN!
SKRICH
I CAN EASILY BREAK THESE CHAINS WITH ALCHEMY...
SKRICH
...YOU WERE SAYING?
CRUMBLE
GRAB
!?
BANG

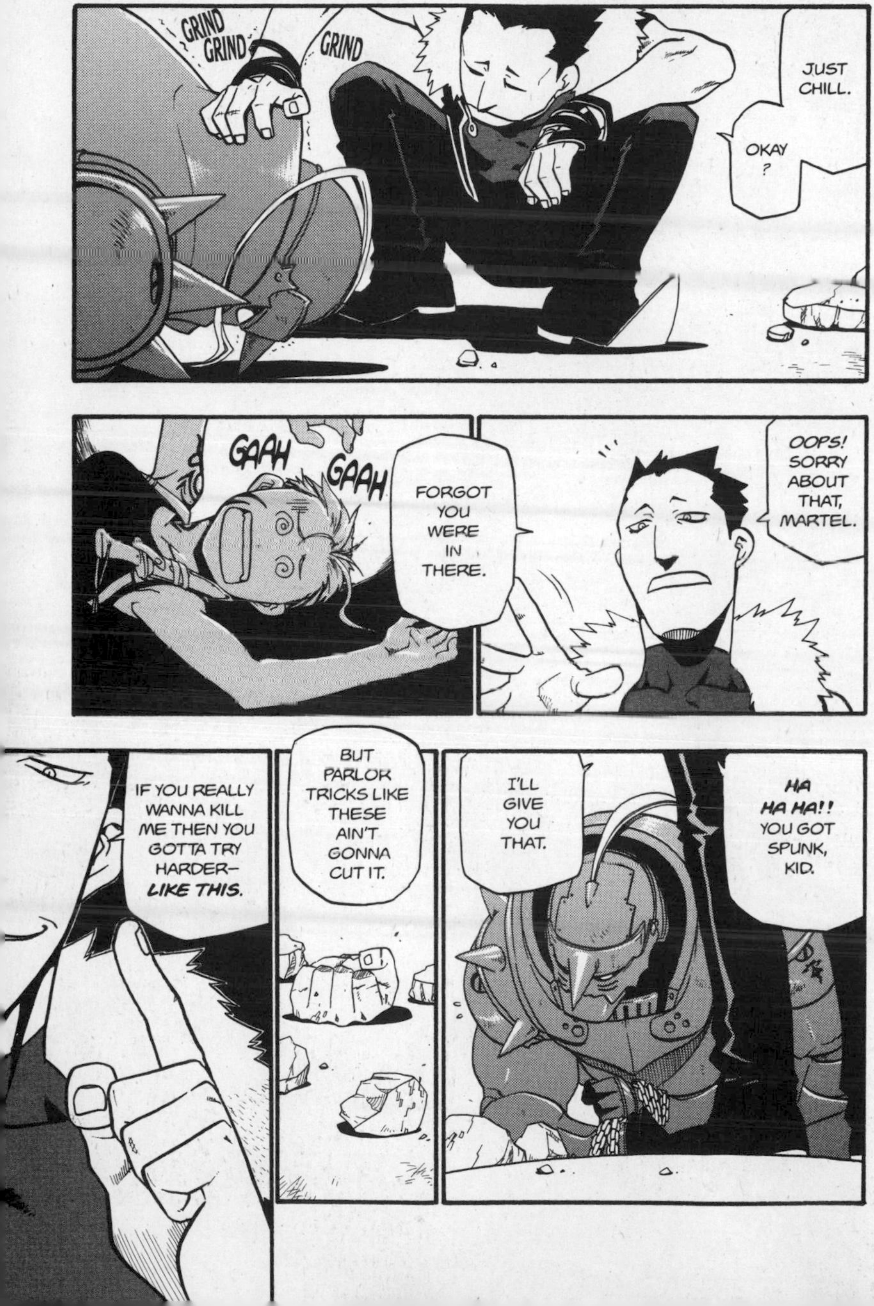
GRIND GRIND
GRIND
JUST CHILL.
OKAY ?
OOPS! SORRY ABOUT THAT, MARTEL.
GAAH
GAAH
FORGOT YOU WERE IN THERE.
HA HA HA!! YOU GOT SPUNK, KID.
I'LL GIVE YOU THAT.
BUT PARLOR TRICKS LIKE THESE AIN'T GONNA CUT IT.
IF YOU REALLY WANNA KILL ME THEN YOU GOTTA TRY HARDER— *LIKE THIS*.

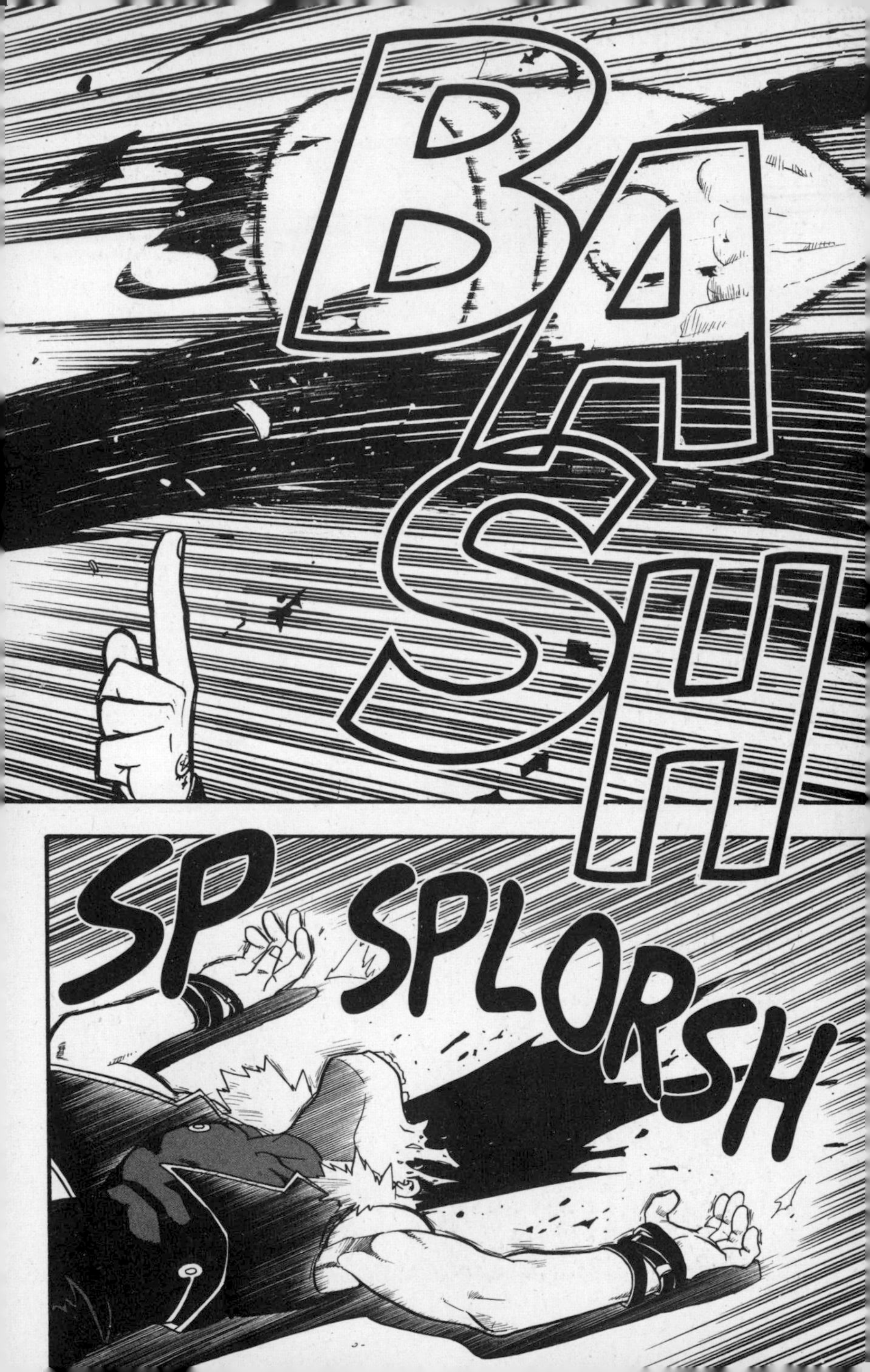
BASH
SP SPLORSH

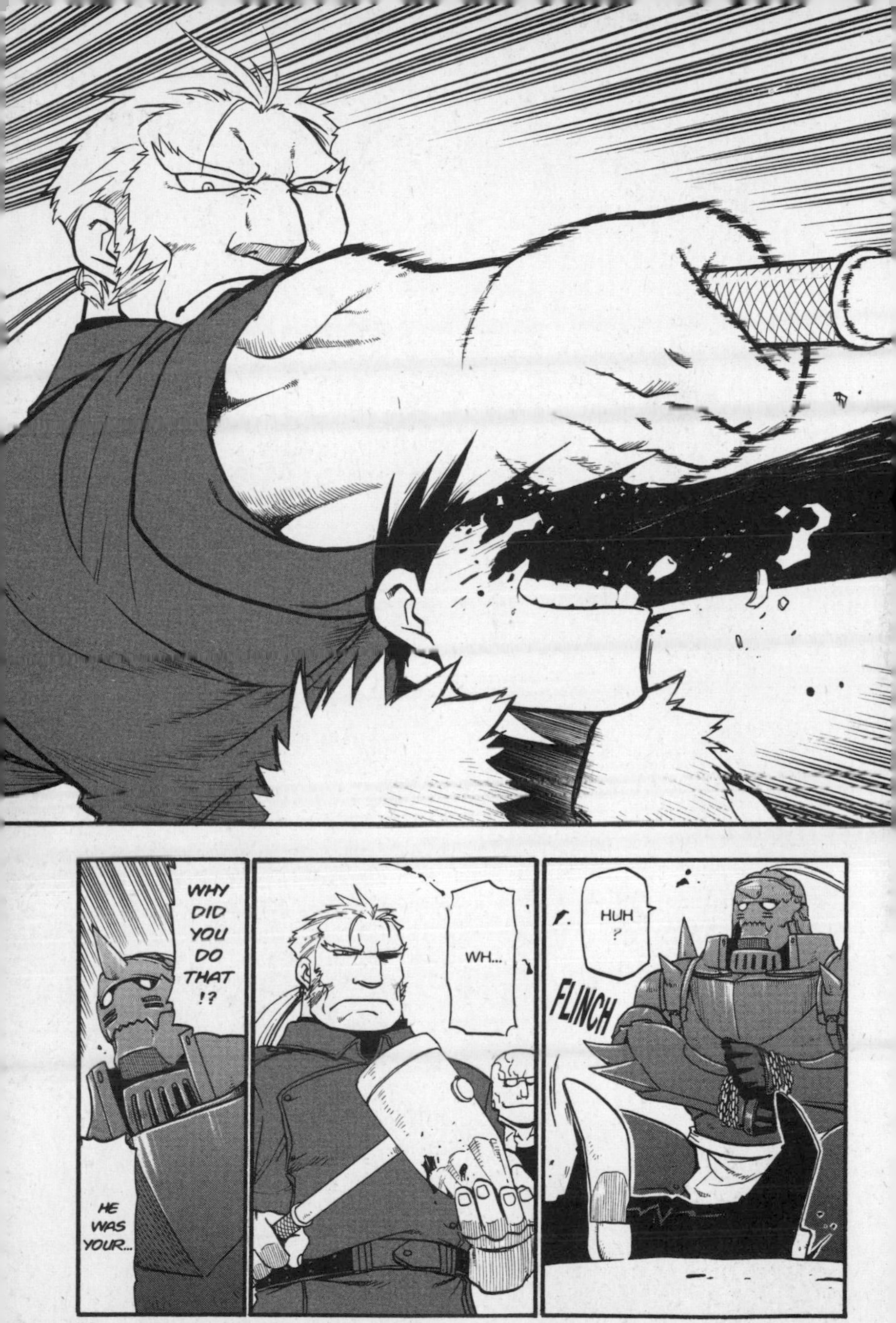
HUH ?
FLINCH
WH...
WHY DID YOU DO THAT !?
HE WAS YOUR...

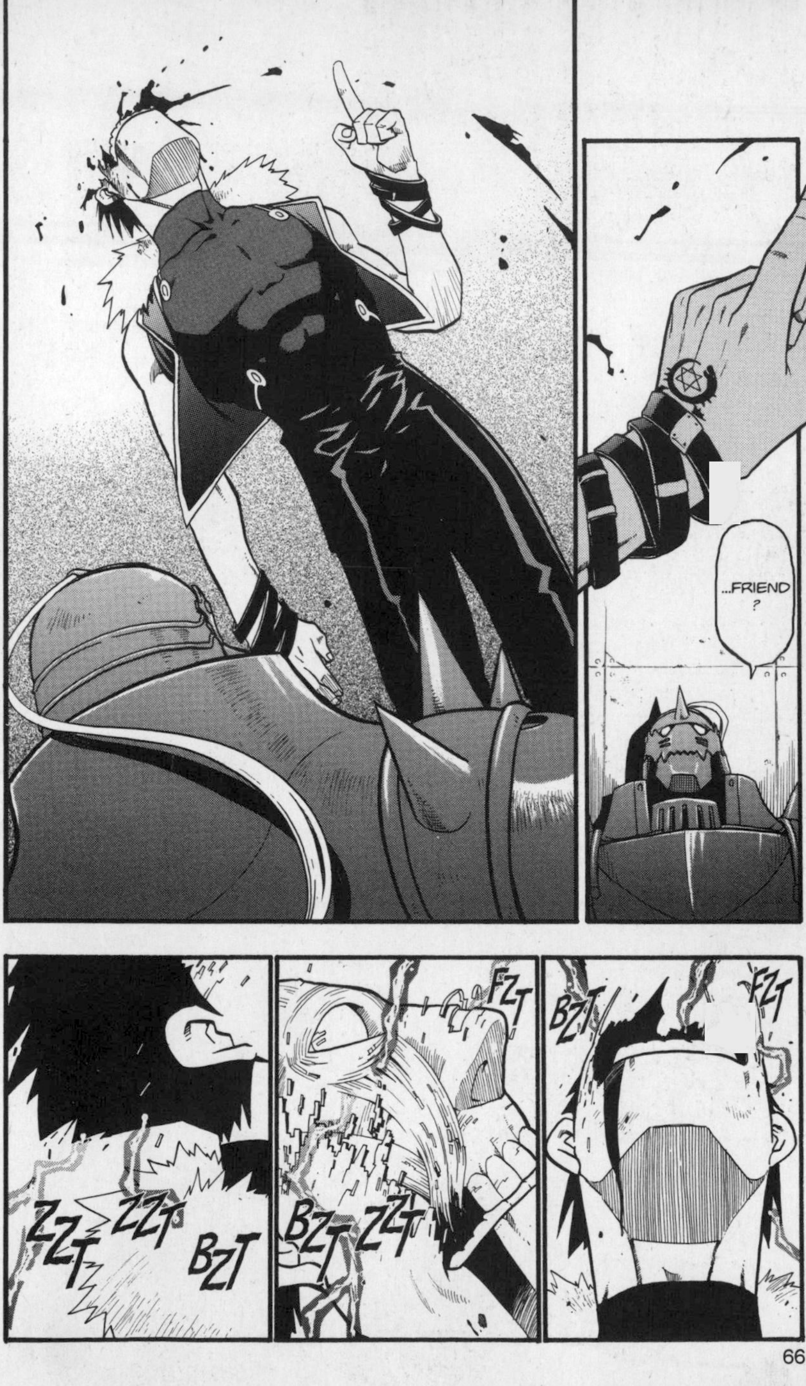
...FRIEND ?
FZT
BZT
FZT
BZT
ZZT
ZZT
ZZT
BZT

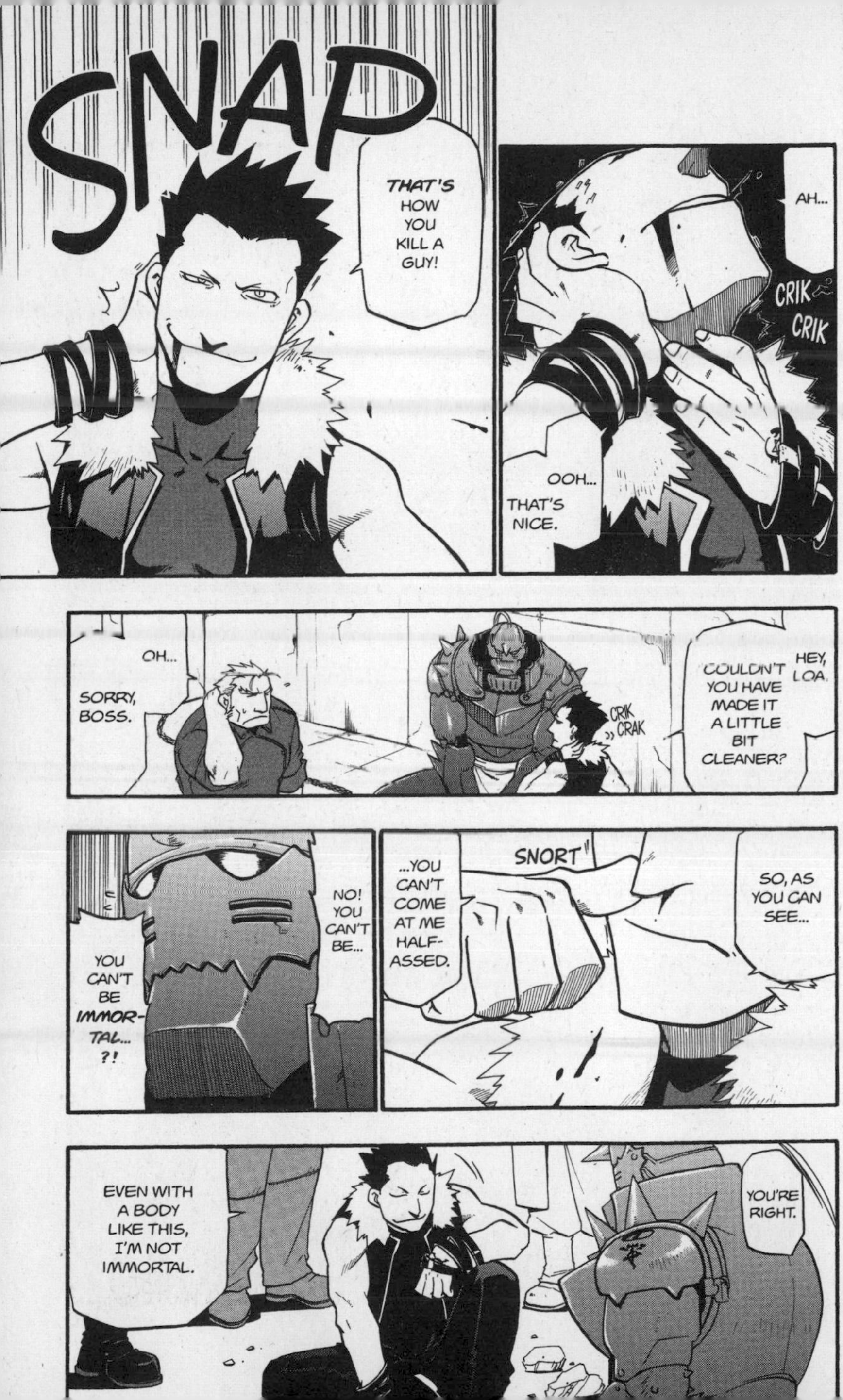
AH...
CRIK CRIK
OOH... THAT'S NICE.
SNAP
THAT'S HOW YOU KILL A GUY!
HEY, LOA.
COULDN'T YOU HAVE MADE IT A LITTLE BIT CLEANER?
CRIK CRAK
OH...
SORRY, BOSS.
SO, AS YOU CAN SEE...
SNORT
...YOU CAN'T COME AT ME HALF-ASSED.
NO! YOU CAN'T BE...
YOU CAN'T BE IMMORTAL...?!
YOU'RE RIGHT.
EVEN WITH A BODY LIKE THIS, I'M NOT IMMORTAL.

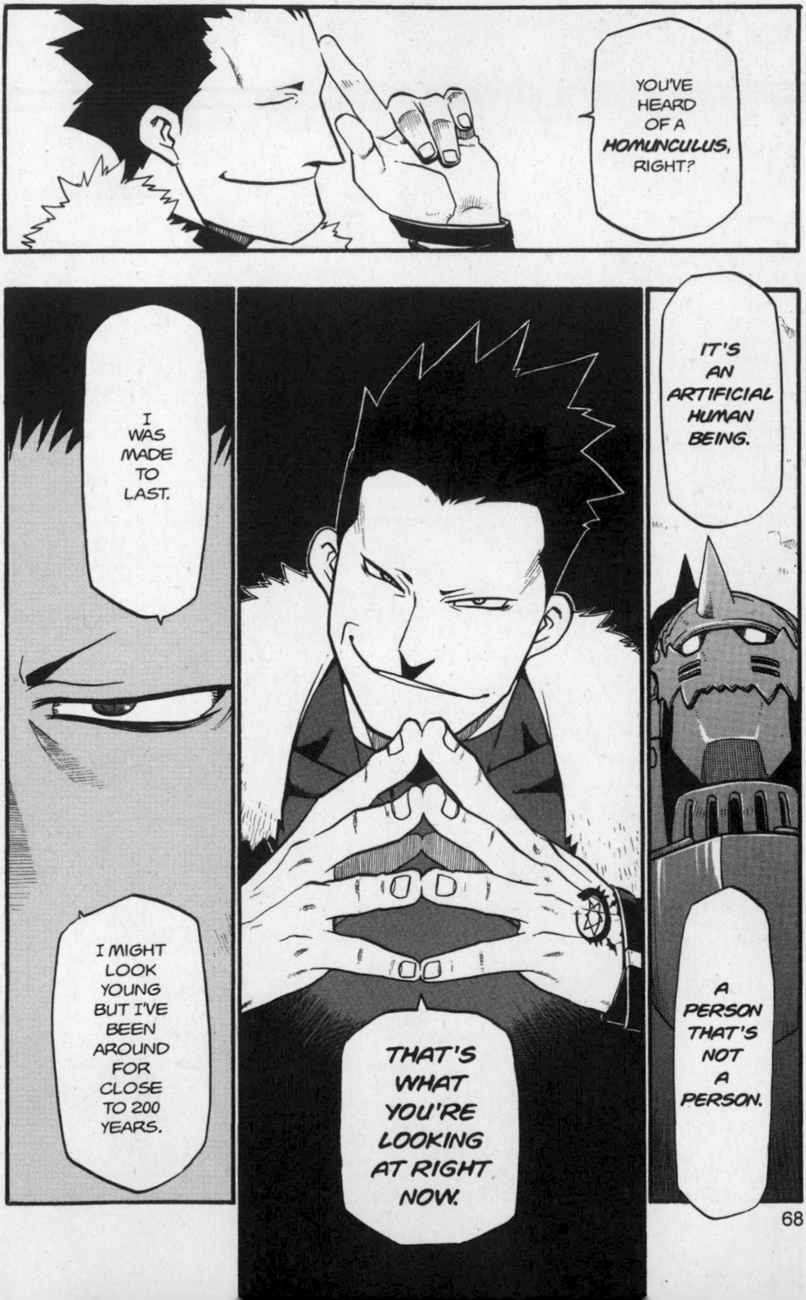
YOU'VE HEARD OF A **HOMUNCULUS,** RIGHT?
IT'S AN ARTIFICIAL HUMAN BEING.
A PERSON THAT'S NOT A PERSON.
THAT'S WHAT YOU'RE LOOKING AT RIGHT NOW.
I WAS MADE TO LAST.
I MIGHT LOOK YOUNG BUT I'VE BEEN AROUND FOR CLOSE TO 200 YEARS.

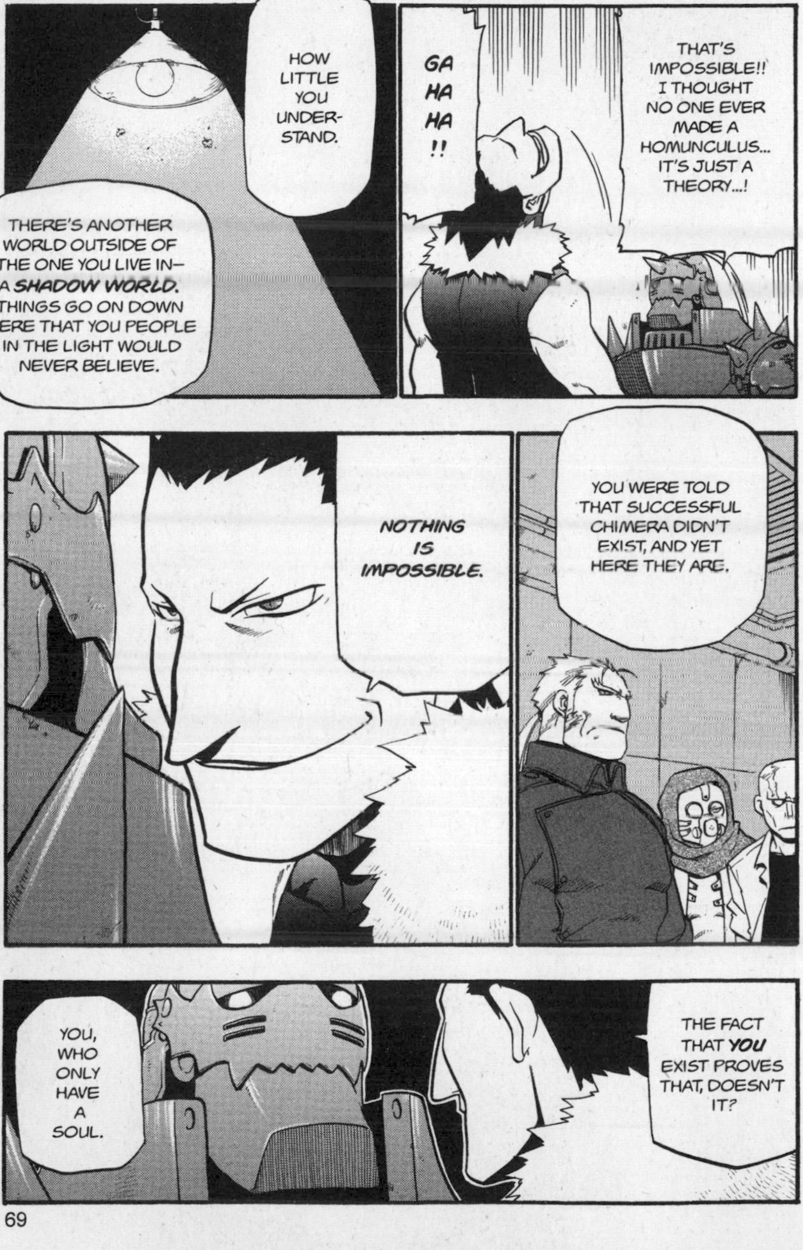
THAT'S IMPOSSIBLE!! I THOUGHT NO ONE EVER MADE A HOMUNCULUS... IT'S JUST A THEORY...!
GA HA HA !!
HOW LITTLE YOU UNDER-STAND.
THERE'S ANOTHER WORLD OUTSIDE OF THE ONE YOU LIVE IN—A SHADOW WORLD. THINGS GO ON DOWN HERE THAT YOU PEOPLE IN THE LIGHT WOULD NEVER BELIEVE.
YOU WERE TOLD THAT SUCCESSFUL CHIMERA DIDN'T EXIST, AND YET HERE THEY ARE.
NOTHING IS IMPOSSIBLE.
THE FACT THAT YOU EXIST PROVES THAT, DOESN'T IT?
YOU, WHO ONLY HAVE A SOUL.

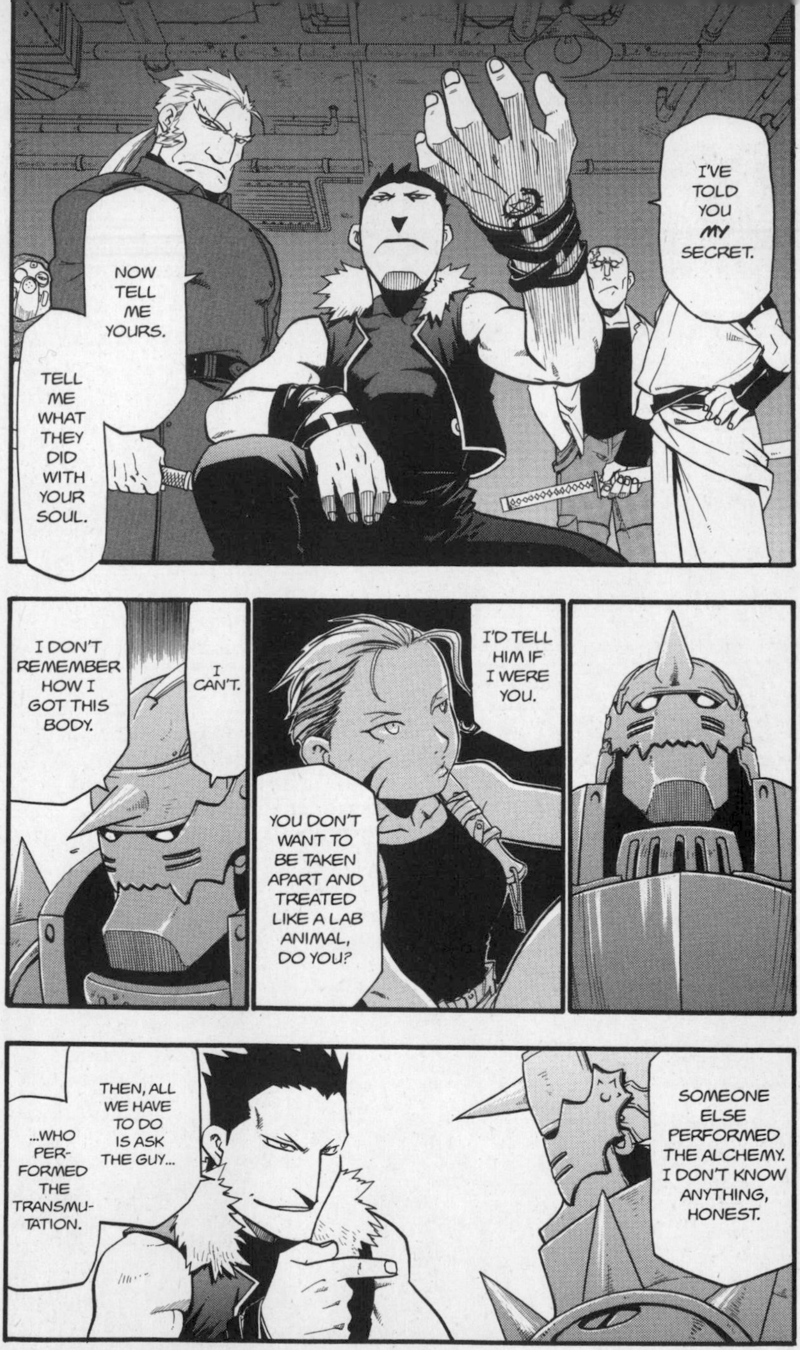
I'VE TOLD YOU MY SECRET.
NOW TELL ME YOURS.
TELL ME WHAT THEY DID WITH YOUR SOUL.
I'D TELL HIM IF I WERE YOU.
YOU DON'T WANT TO BE TAKEN APART AND TREATED LIKE A LAB ANIMAL, DO YOU?
I CAN'T.
I DON'T REMEMBER HOW I GOT THIS BODY.
SOMEONE ELSE PERFORMED THE ALCHEMY. I DON'T KNOW ANYTHING, HONEST.
THEN, ALL WE HAVE TO DO IS ASK THE GUY...
...WHO PER-FORMED THE TRANSMU-TATION.

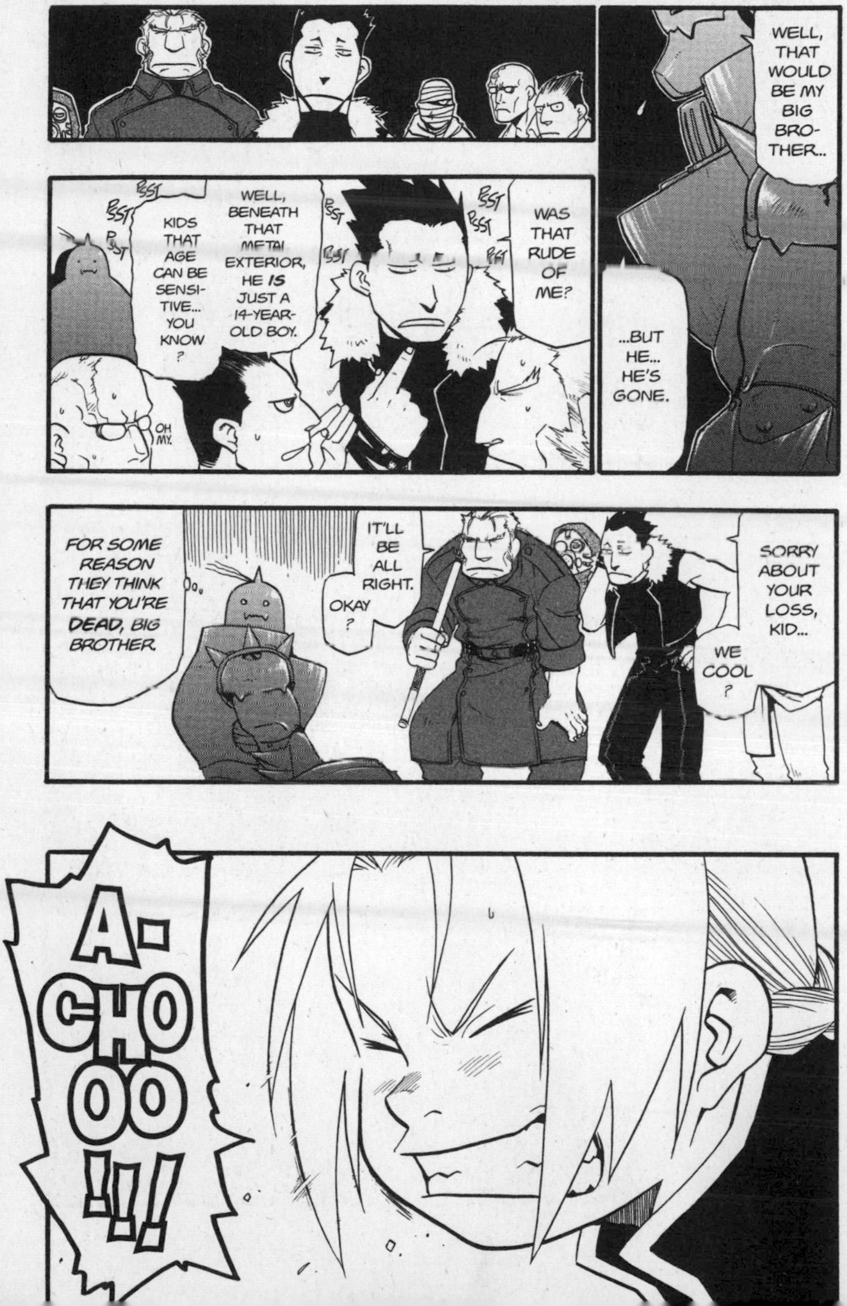
WELL, THAT WOULD BE MY BIG BROTHER...
...BUT HE... HE'S GONE.
WAS THAT RUDE OF ME?
PSST PSST PSST
WELL, BENEATH THAT METAL EXTERIOR, HE IS JUST A 14-YEAR-OLD BOY.
PSST PSST PSST
KIDS THAT AGE CAN BE SENSITIVE... YOU KNOW?
OH MY.
SORRY ABOUT YOUR LOSS, KID...
WE COOL?
IT'LL BE ALL RIGHT.
OKAY?
FOR SOME REASON THEY THINK THAT YOU'RE DEAD, BIG BROTHER.
A-CHOO!!!

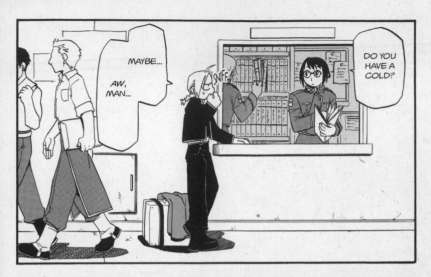

DO YOU HAVE A COLD?
SNIFF
MAYBE...
AW, MAN...
OKAY. TAKE THIS TO THE OFFICE OF TECHNICAL EVALUATION.
THANKS.
YOU MISSED YOUR DEAD-LINE SO IT'S GOING TO TAKE A WHILE TO PROCESS THE PAPER-WORK.
UGH...
THIS IS MY FIRST TIME AT SOUTH HQ...
...AND I AL-READY FEEL LOST.
WHO'S THE KID?
EX-CUSE ME.
I'M LOOKING FOR THE OFFICE OF TECHNICAL EVALUATION. CAN YOU TELL ME...

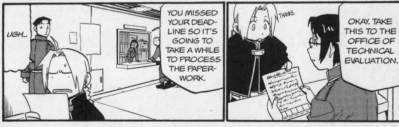

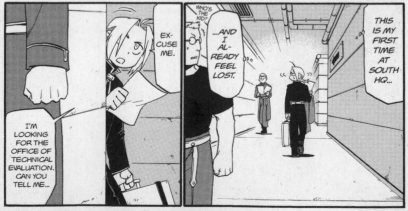

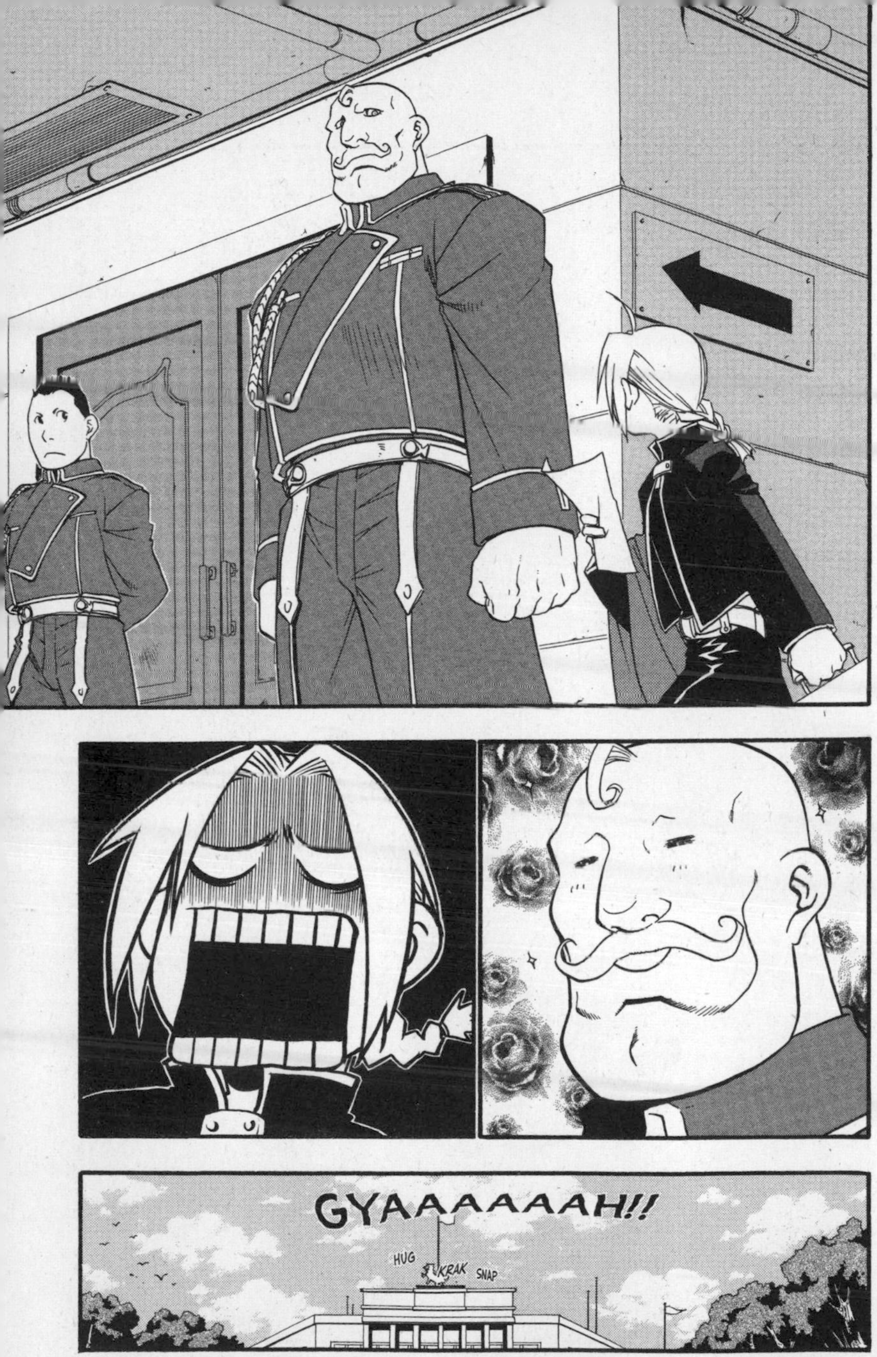
GYAAAAAAH!!
HUG
KRAK
SNAP

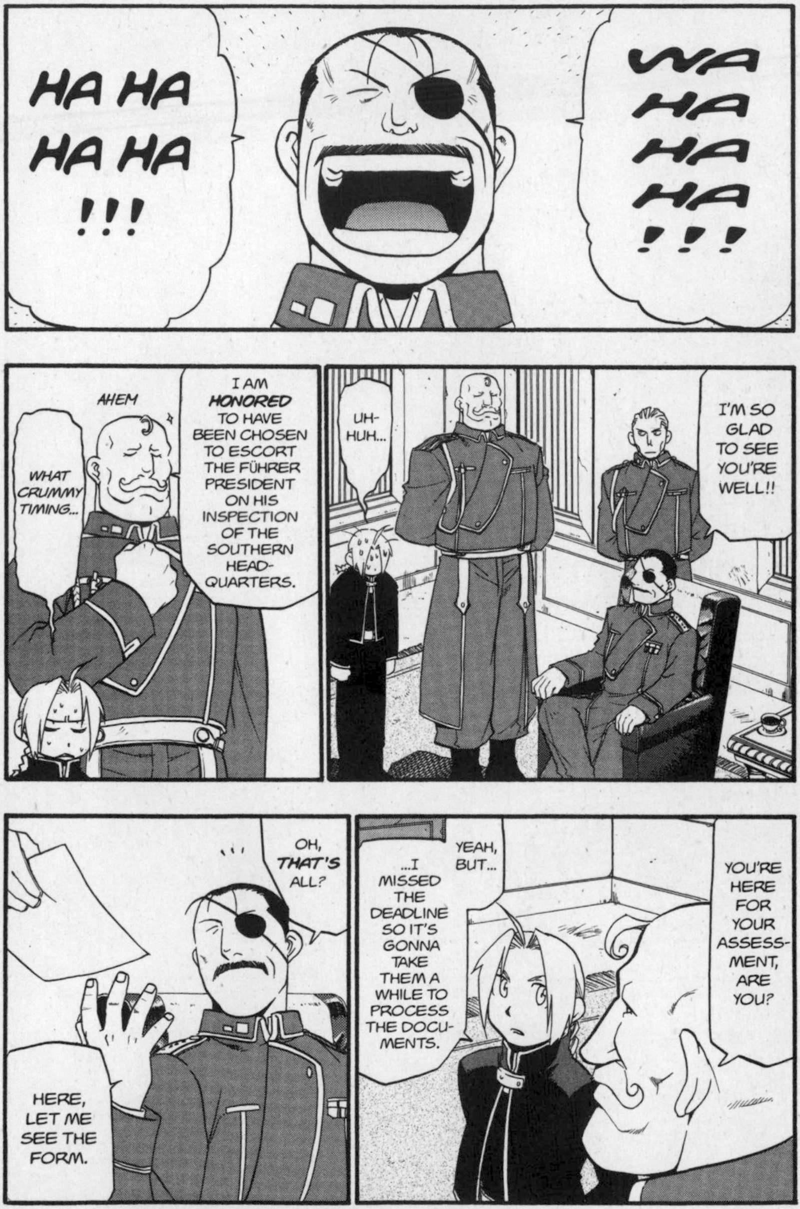
WA HA HA HA!!!
HA HA HA HA!!!
I'M SO GLAD TO SEE YOU'RE WELL!!
UH-HUH...
I AM **HONORED** TO HAVE BEEN CHOSEN TO ESCORT THE FÜHRER PRESIDENT ON HIS INSPECTION OF THE SOUTHERN HEADQUARTERS.
AHEM
WHAT CRUMMY TIMING...
YOU'RE HERE FOR YOUR ASSESSMENT, ARE YOU?
YEAH, BUT...
...I MISSED THE DEADLINE SO IT'S GONNA TAKE THEM A WHILE TO PROCESS THE DOCUMENTS.
OH, ***THAT'S*** ALL?
HERE, LET ME SEE THE FORM.

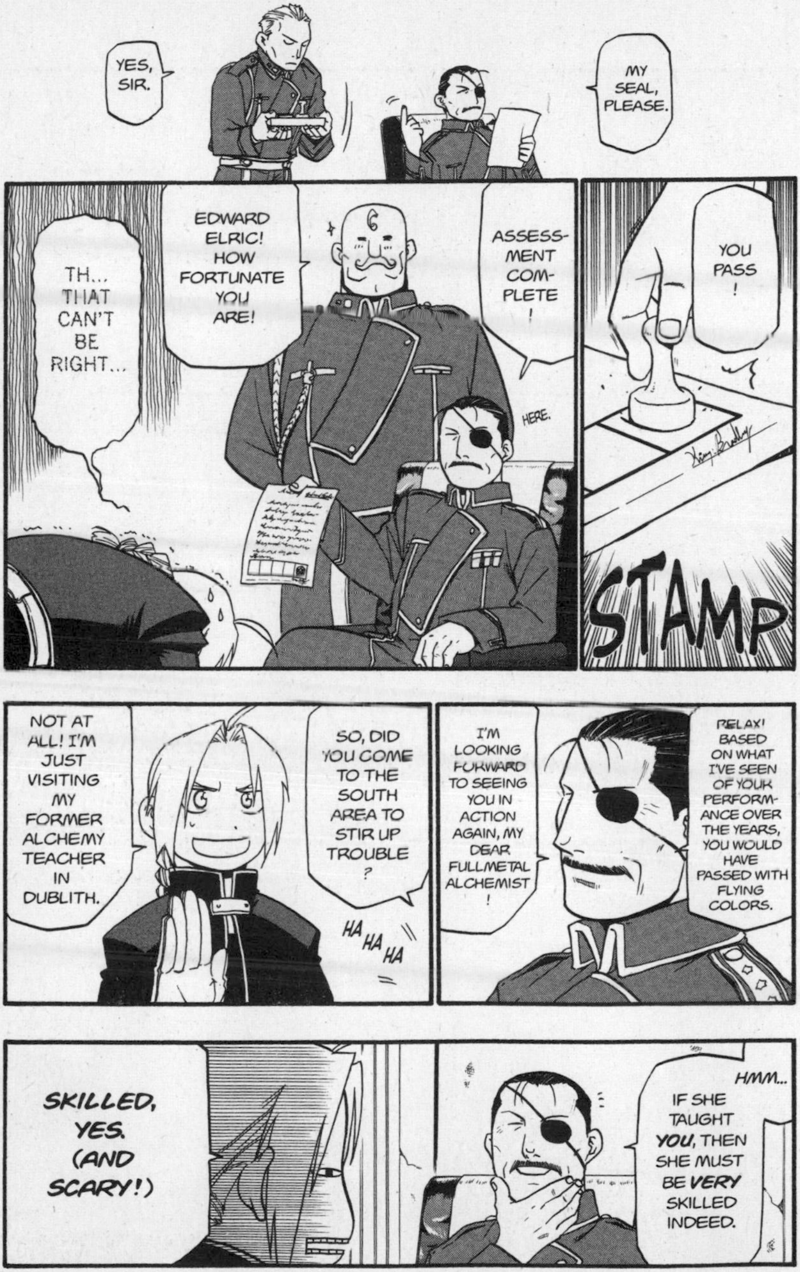
MY SEAL, PLEASE.
YES, SIR.
YOU PASS!
STAMP
ASSESS-MENT COM-PLETE!
HERE.
EDWARD ELRIC! HOW FORTUNATE YOU ARE!
TH... THAT CAN'T BE RIGHT...
RELAX! BASED ON WHAT I'VE SEEN OF YOUR PERFORM-ANCE OVER THE YEARS, YOU WOULD HAVE PASSED WITH FLYING COLORS.
I'M LOOKING FORWARD TO SEEING YOU IN ACTION AGAIN, MY DEAR FULLMETAL ALCHEMIST!
SO, DID YOU COME TO THE SOUTH AREA TO STIR UP TROUBLE?
HA HA HA
NOT AT ALL! I'M JUST VISITING MY FORMER ALCHEMY TEACHER IN DUBLITH.
HMM...
IF SHE TAUGHT YOU, THEN SHE MUST BE VERY SKILLED INDEED.
SKILLED, YES. (AND SCARY!)

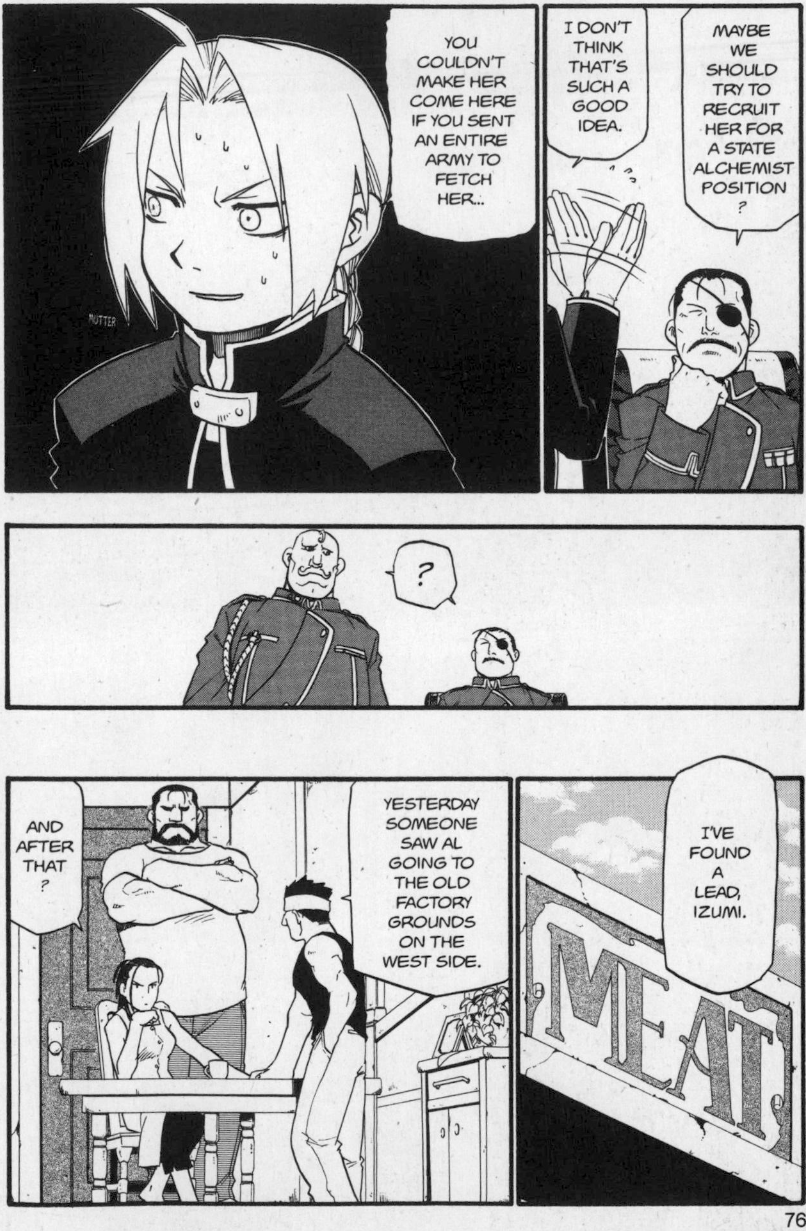
MAYBE WE SHOULD TRY TO RECRUIT HER FOR A STATE ALCHEMIST POSITION?
I DON'T THINK THAT'S SUCH A GOOD IDEA.
YOU COULDN'T MAKE HER COME HERE IF YOU SENT AN ENTIRE ARMY TO FETCH HER...
MUTTER
?
I'VE FOUND A LEAD, IZUMI.
MEAT
YESTERDAY SOMEONE SAW AL GOING TO THE OLD FACTORY GROUNDS ON THE WEST SIDE.
AND AFTER THAT?

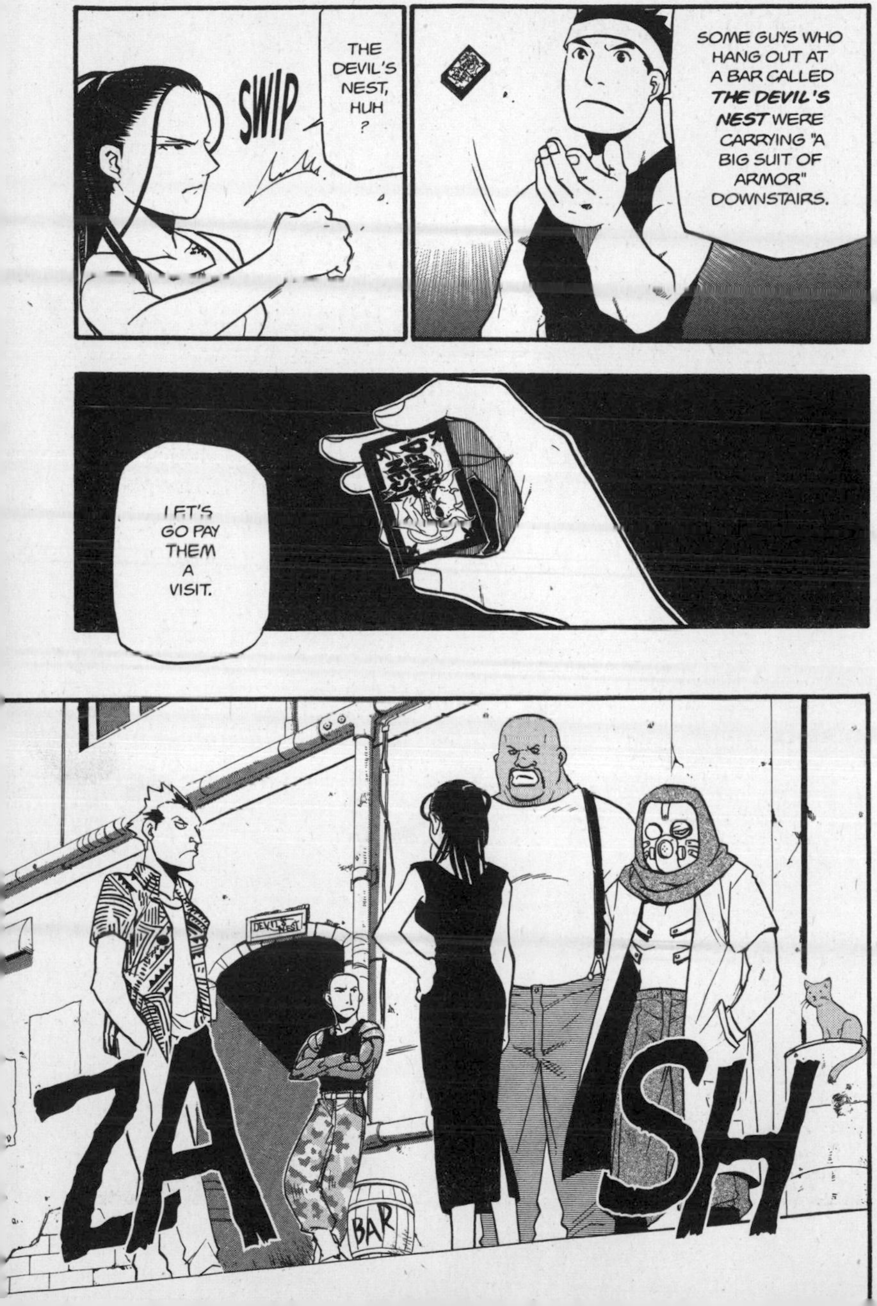
SOME GUYS WHO HANG OUT AT A BAR CALLED **THE DEVIL'S NEST** WERE CARRYING "A BIG SUIT OF ARMOR" DOWNSTAIRS.
SWIP
THE DEVIL'S NEST, HUH?
LET'S GO PAY THEM A VISIT.
DEVIL'S NEST
BAR
ZASH

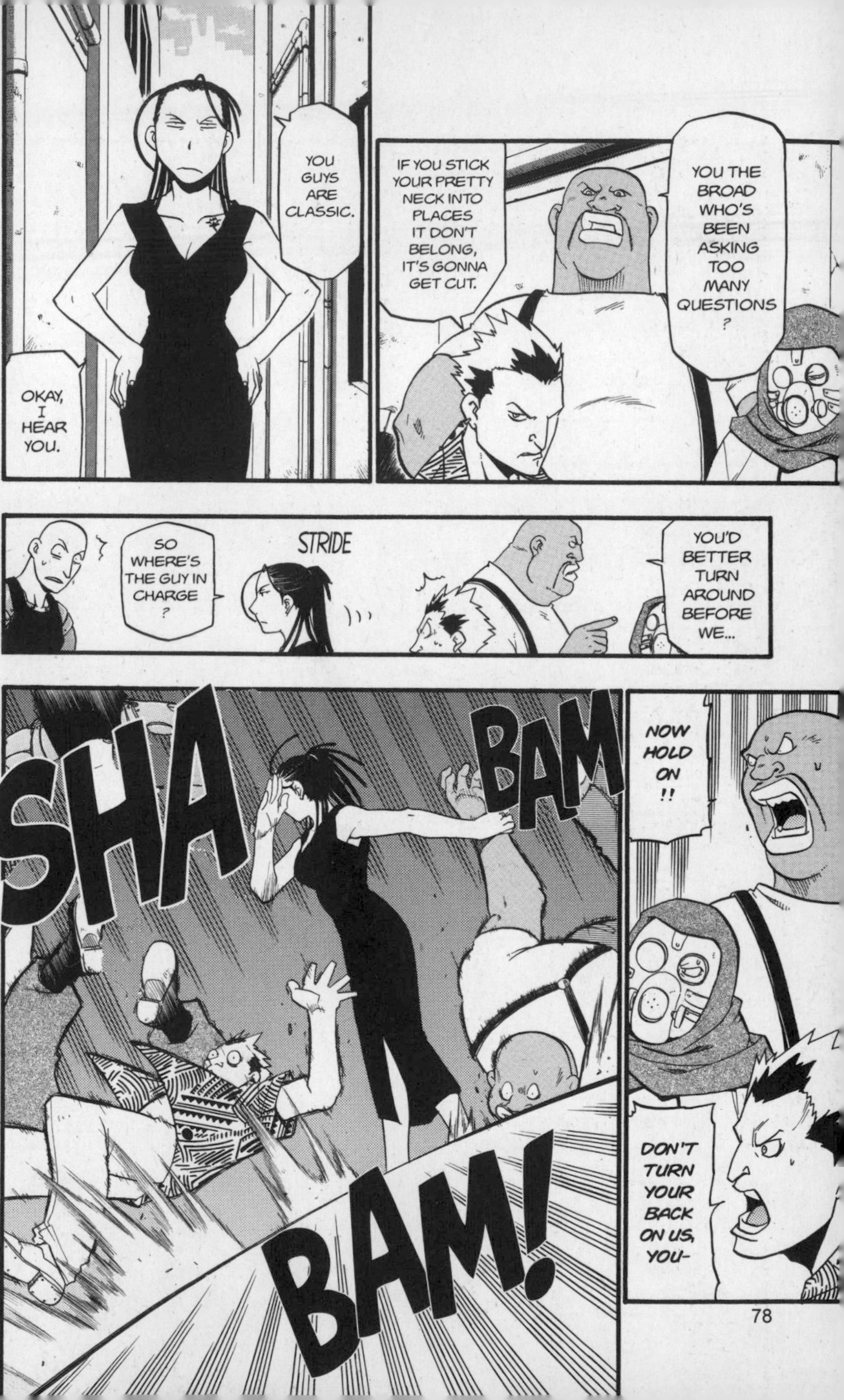
YOU THE BROAD WHO'S BEEN ASKING TOO MANY QUESTIONS?
IF YOU STICK YOUR PRETTY NECK INTO PLACES IT DON'T BELONG, IT'S GONNA GET CUT.
YOU GUYS ARE CLASSIC.
OKAY, I HEAR YOU.
YOU'D BETTER TURN AROUND BEFORE WE...
STRIDE
SO WHERE'S THE GUY IN CHARGE?
NOW HOLD ON!!
DON'T TURN YOUR BACK ON US, YOU-
SHA
BAM
BAM!

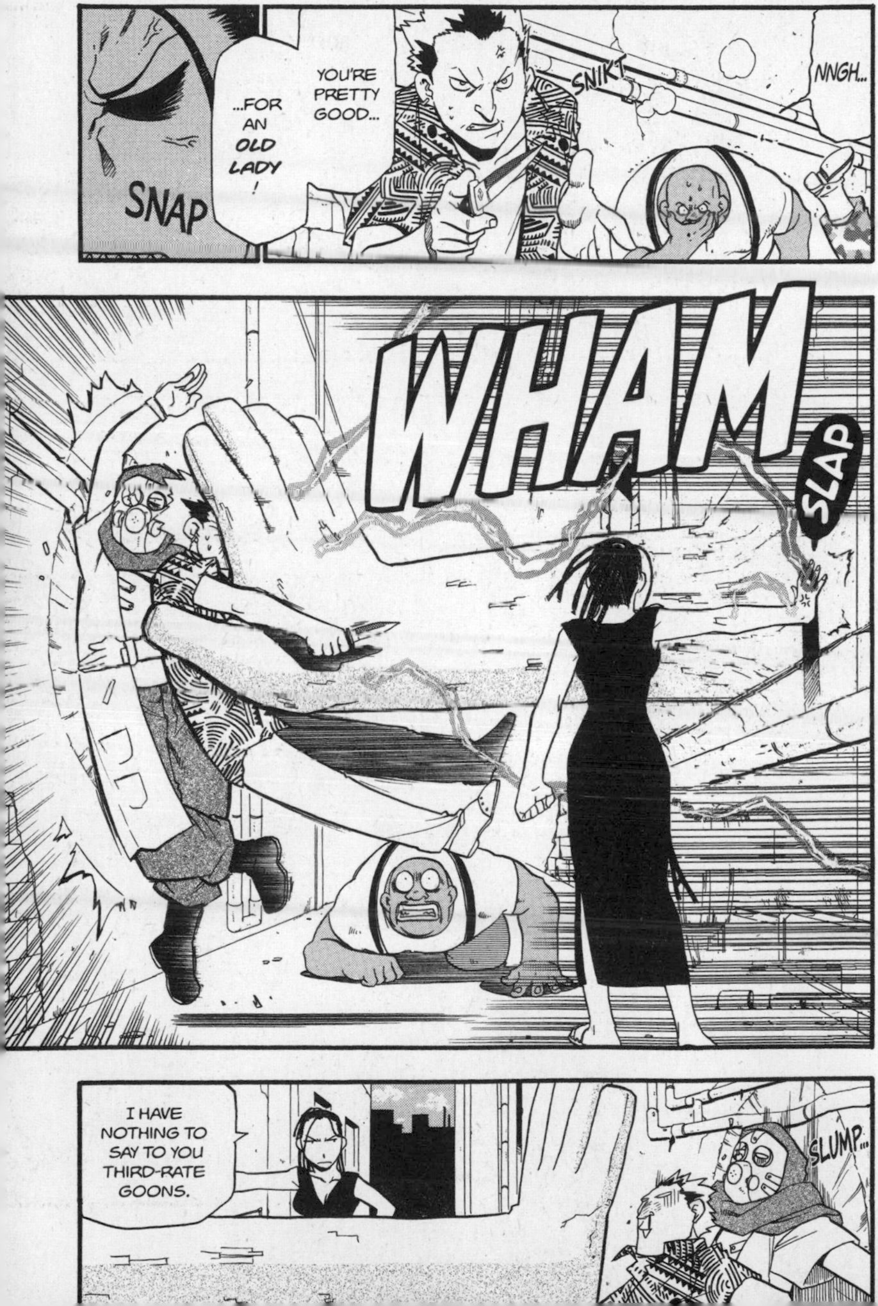
NNGH...
SNIKT
YOU'RE PRETTY GOOD...
...FOR AN OLD LADY!
SNAP
WHAM
SLAP
SLUMP...
I HAVE NOTHING TO SAY TO YOU THIRD-RATE GOONS.

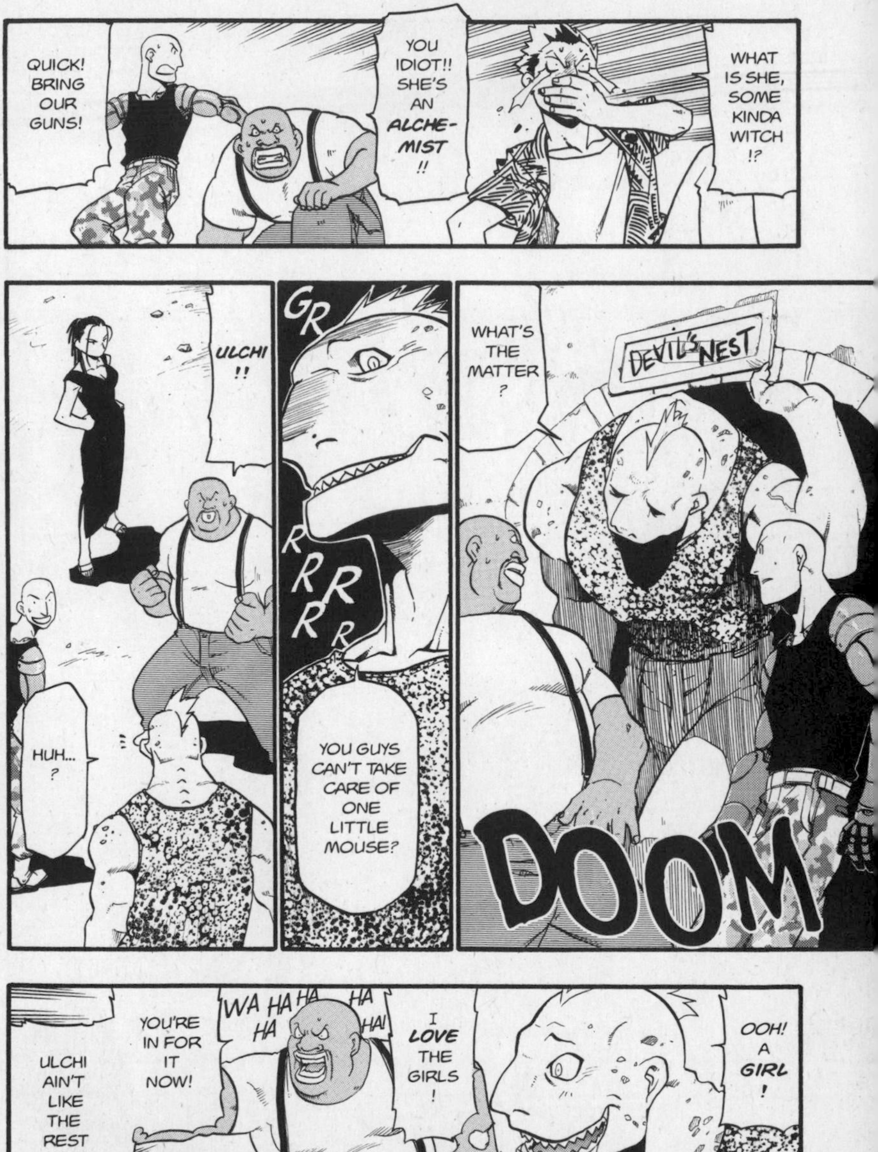
WHAT IS SHE, SOME KINDA WITCH!?
YOU IDIOT!! SHE'S AN ALCHEMIST!!
QUICK! BRING OUR GUNS!
DEVIL'S NEST
WHAT'S THE MATTER?
DOOM
GRRRRRR
YOU GUYS CAN'T TAKE CARE OF ONE LITTLE MOUSE?
ULCHI!!
HUH...?
OOH! A GIRL!
I LOVE THE GIRLS!
WA HA HA HA HA HA HA!
YOU'RE IN FOR IT NOW!
ULCHI AIN'T LIKE THE REST OF US!

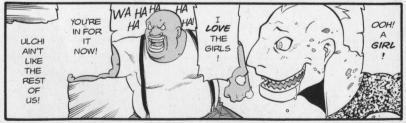

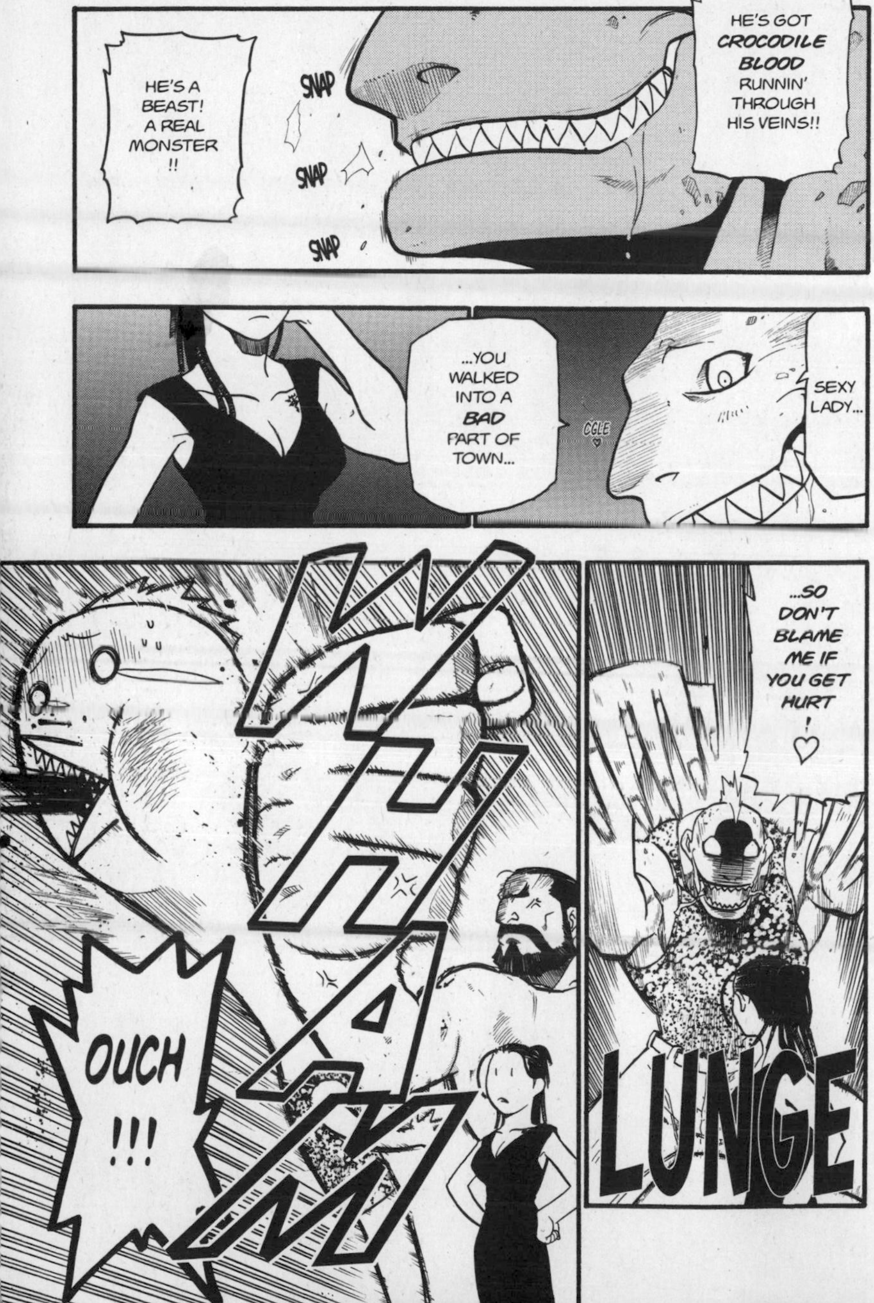
HE'S GOT CROCODILE BLOOD RUNNIN' THROUGH HIS VEINS!!
HE'S A BEAST! A REAL MONSTER!!
SNAP
SNAP
SNAP
SEXY LADY...
CGLE ♥
...YOU WALKED INTO A BAD PART OF TOWN...
...SO DON'T BLAME ME IF YOU GET HURT! ♥
LUNGE
WHAM
OUCH!!!

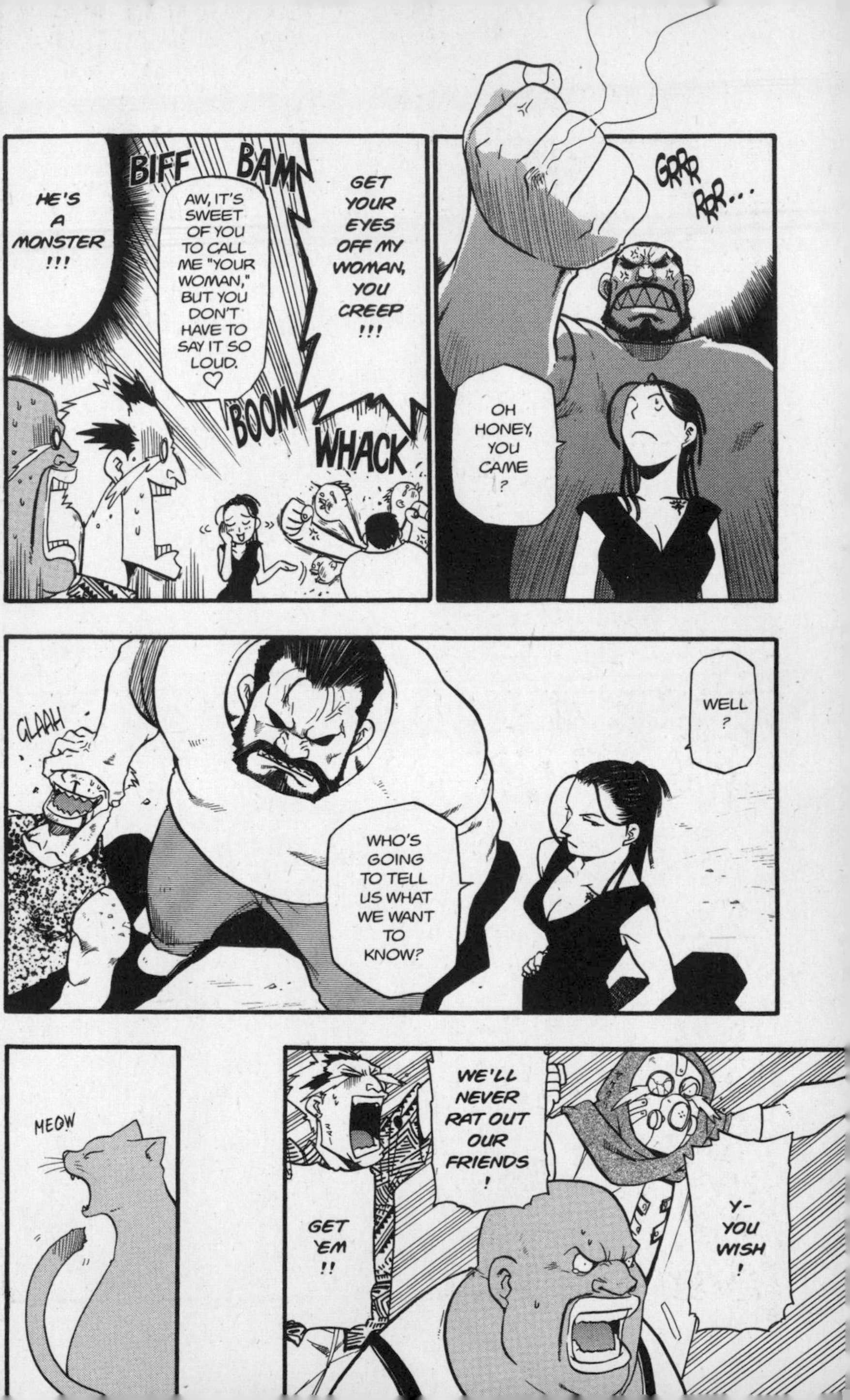
GRRR RRR...
OH HONEY, YOU CAME?
GET YOUR EYES OFF MY WOMAN, YOU CREEP!!!
BAM
BIFF
AW, IT'S SWEET OF YOU TO CALL ME "YOUR WOMAN," BUT YOU DON'T HAVE TO SAY IT SO LOUD. ♡
HE'S A MONSTER!!!
BOOM
WHACK
WELL?
WHO'S GOING TO TELL US WHAT WE WANT TO KNOW?
GLAAH
Y-YOU WISH!
WE'LL NEVER RAT OUT OUR FRIENDS!
GET 'EM!!
MEOW

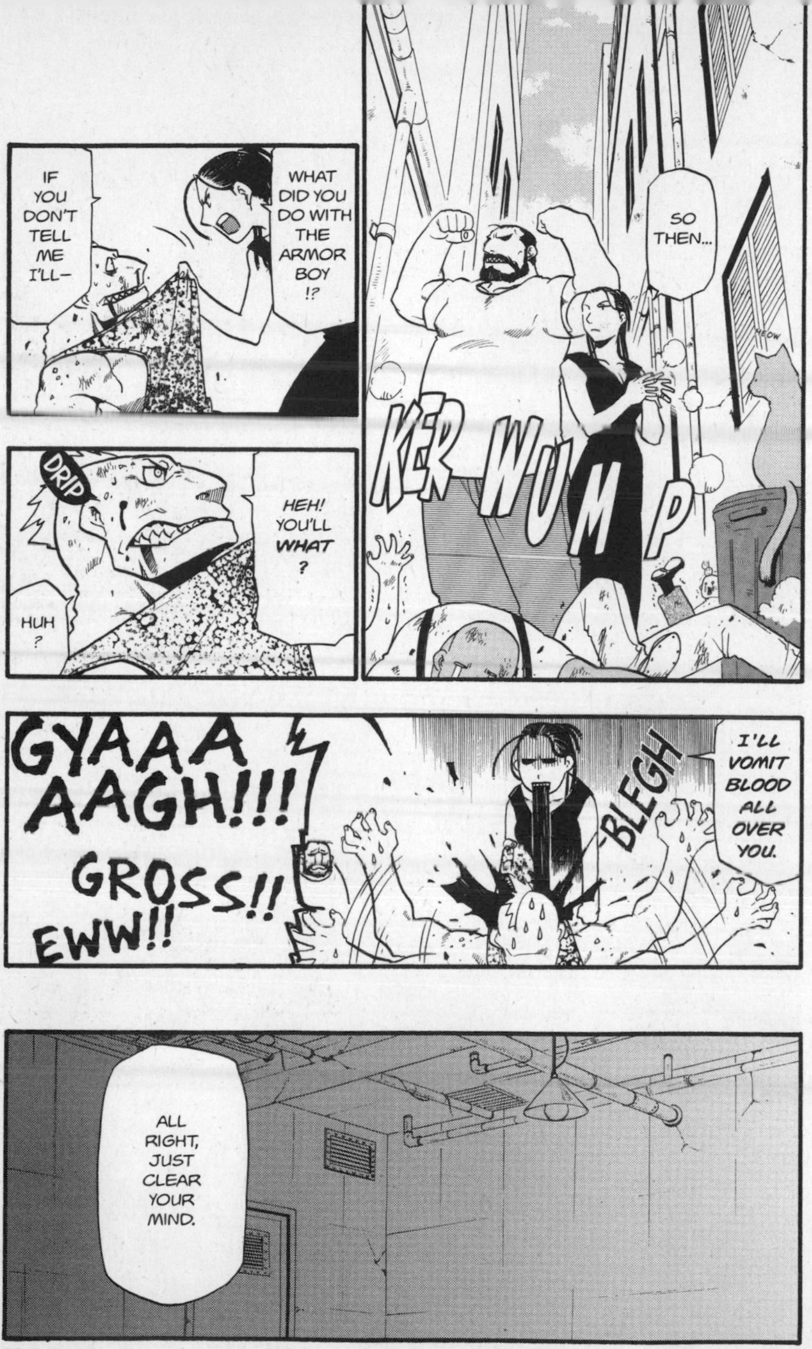
SO THEN...
KER WUMP
MEOW
WHAT DID YOU DO WITH THE ARMOR BOY !?
IF YOU DON'T TELL ME I'LL—
HEH! YOU'LL WHAT ?
DRIP
HUH ?
I'LL VOMIT BLOOD ALL OVER YOU.
BLEGH
GYAAA AAGH!!!
GROSS!!
EWW!!
ALL RIGHT, JUST CLEAR YOUR MIND.

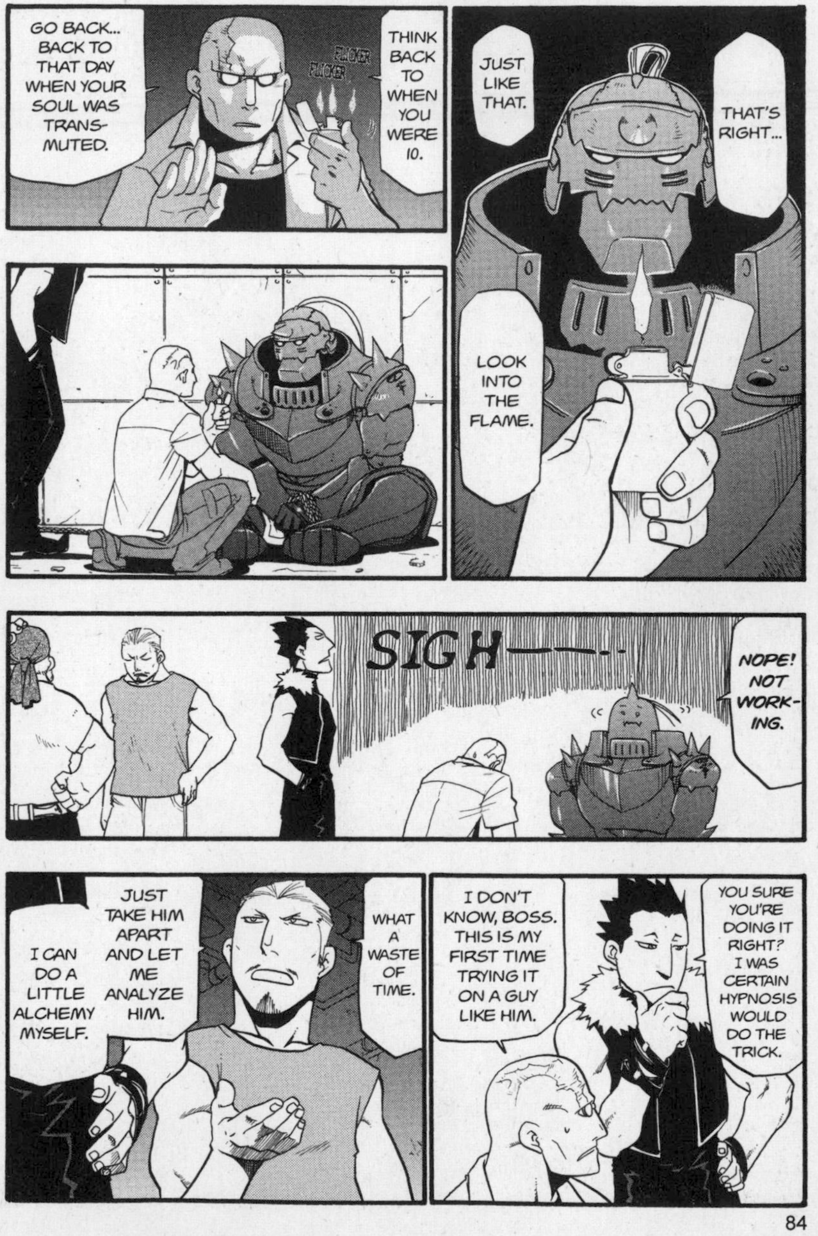
THAT'S RIGHT...
JUST LIKE THAT.
LOOK INTO THE FLAME.
THINK BACK TO WHEN YOU WERE 10.
FLICKER FLICKER
GO BACK... BACK TO THAT DAY WHEN YOUR SOUL WAS TRANSMUTED.
NOPE! NOT WORKING.
SIGH——...
YOU SURE YOU'RE DOING IT RIGHT? I WAS CERTAIN HYPNOSIS WOULD DO THE TRICK.
I DON'T KNOW, BOSS. THIS IS MY FIRST TIME TRYING IT ON A GUY LIKE HIM.
WHAT A WASTE OF TIME.
JUST TAKE HIM APART AND LET ME ANALYZE HIM.
I CAN DO A LITTLE ALCHEMY MYSELF.

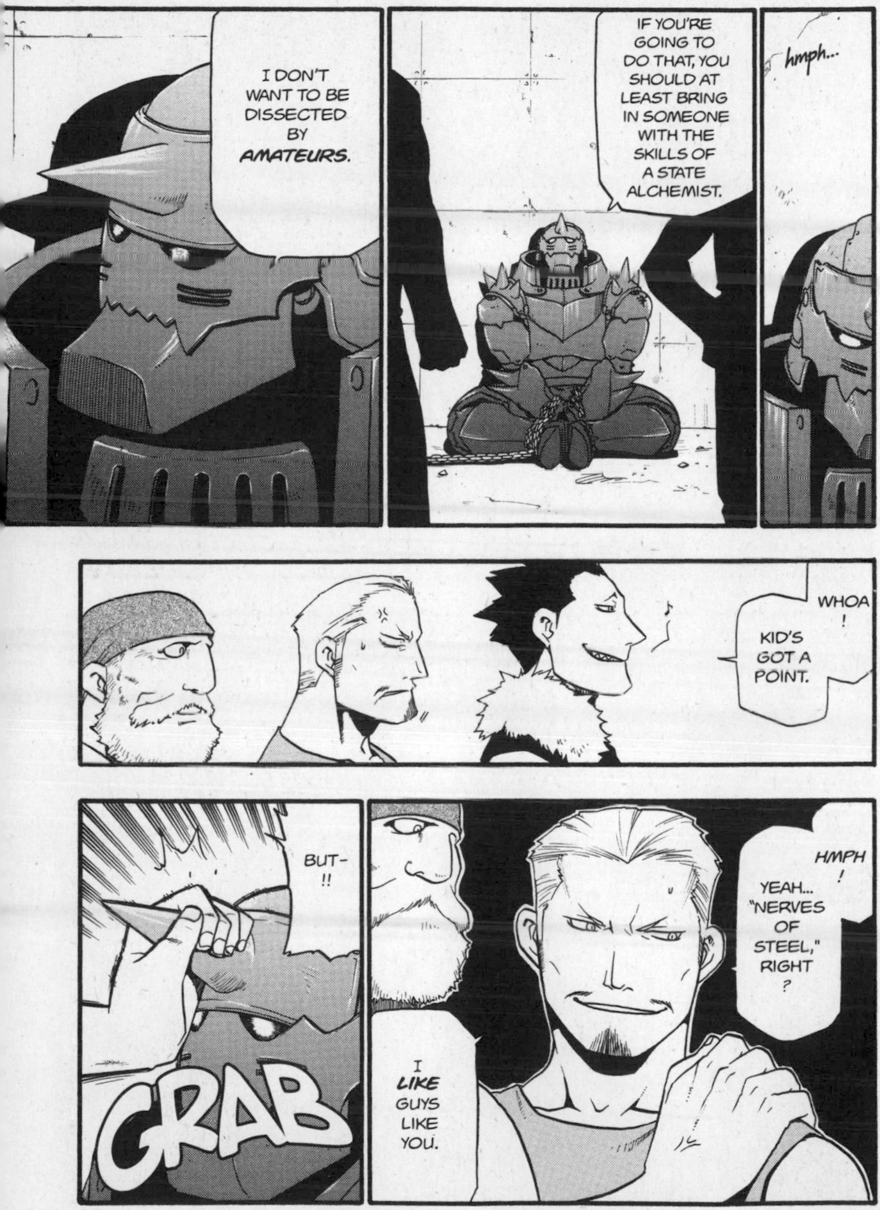
I DON'T WANT TO BE DISSECTED BY AMATEURS.
IF YOU'RE GOING TO DO THAT, YOU SHOULD AT LEAST BRING IN SOMEONE WITH THE SKILLS OF A STATE ALCHEMIST.
hmph...
WHOA! KID'S GOT A POINT.
BUT-!!
GRAB
HMPH! YEAH... "NERVES OF STEEL," RIGHT?
I LIKE GUYS LIKE YOU.

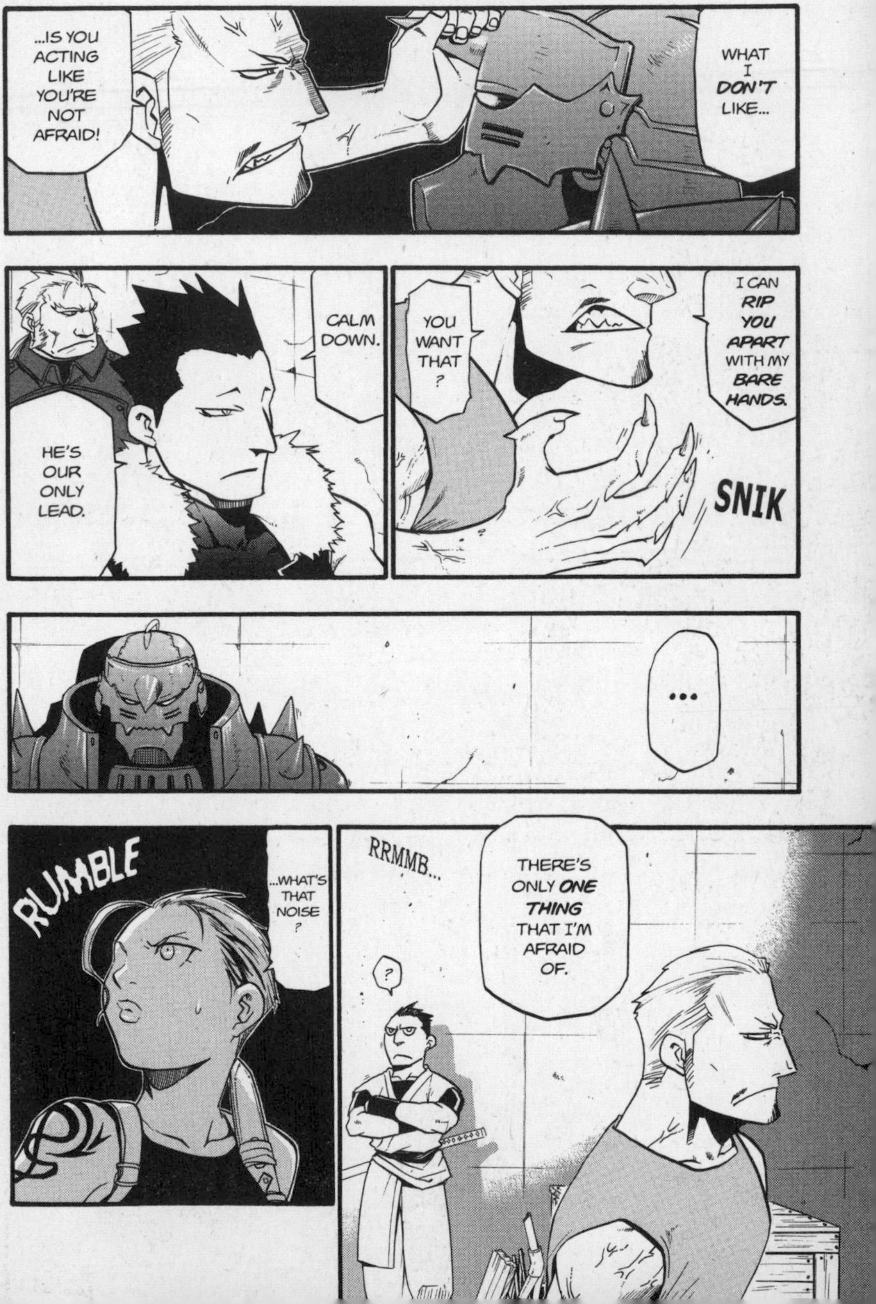
WHAT I DON'T LIKE...
...IS YOU ACTING LIKE YOU'RE NOT AFRAID!
I CAN RIP YOU APART WITH MY BARE HANDS.
SNIK
YOU WANT THAT?
CALM DOWN.
HE'S OUR ONLY LEAD.
...
RRMMB...
THERE'S ONLY ONE THING THAT I'M AFRAID OF.
?
RUMBLE
...WHAT'S THAT NOISE?

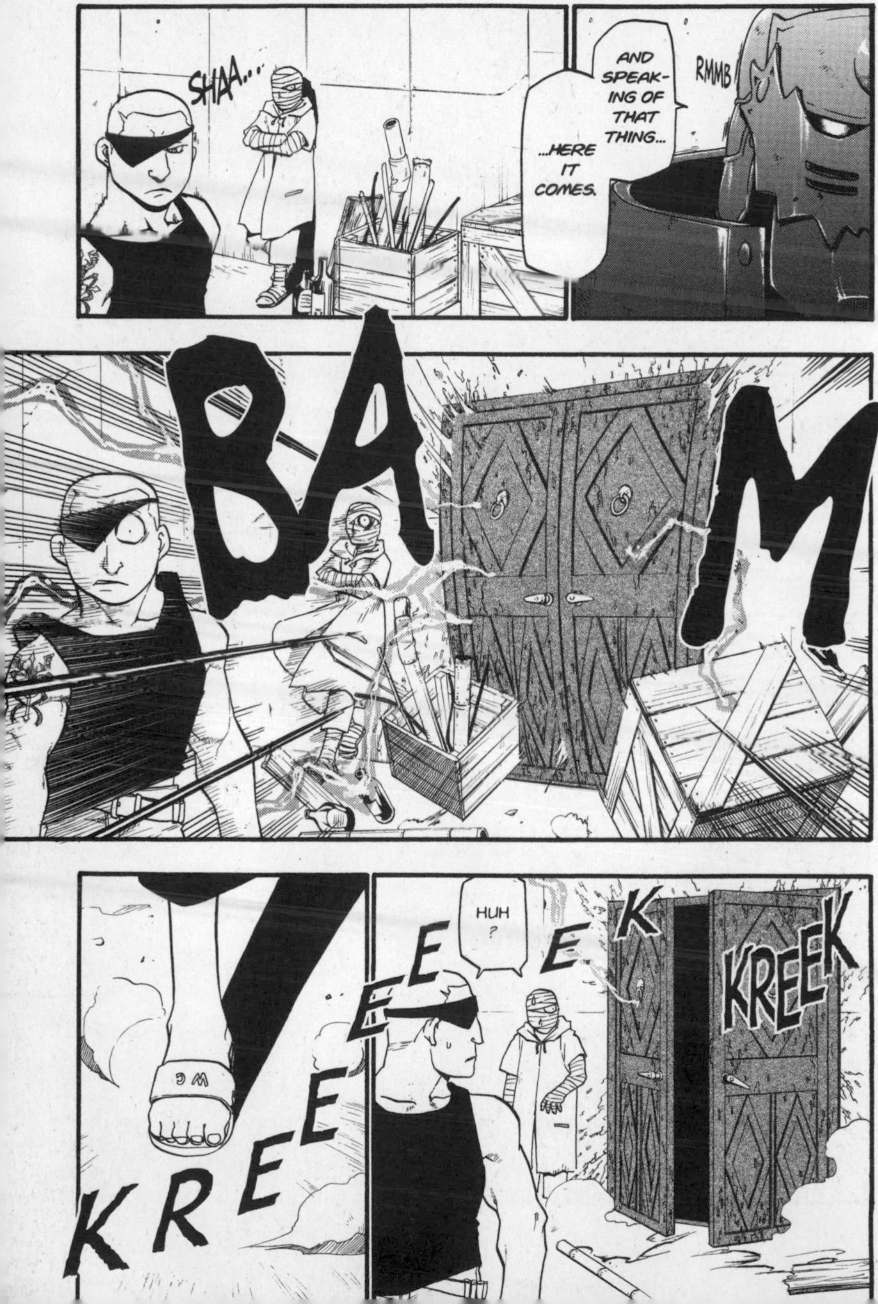
RMMB
AND SPEAKING OF THAT THING...
...HERE IT COMES.
SHAA...
BAM
KREEK
HUH?
KREEEEEEK

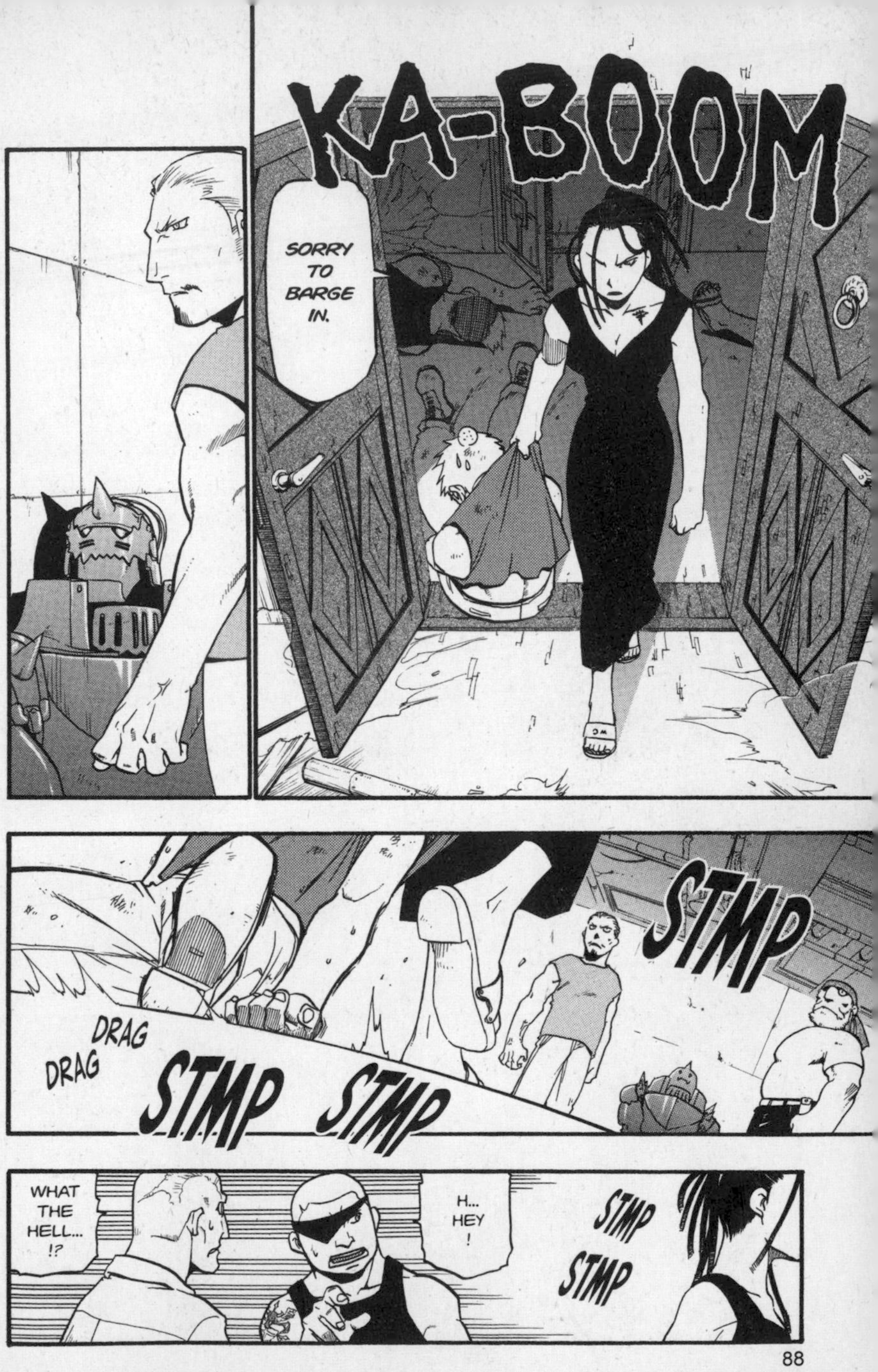
KA-BOOM
SORRY TO BARGE IN.
STMP
STMP
STMP
DRAG
DRAG
STMP
STMP
H... HEY !
WHAT THE HELL... !?

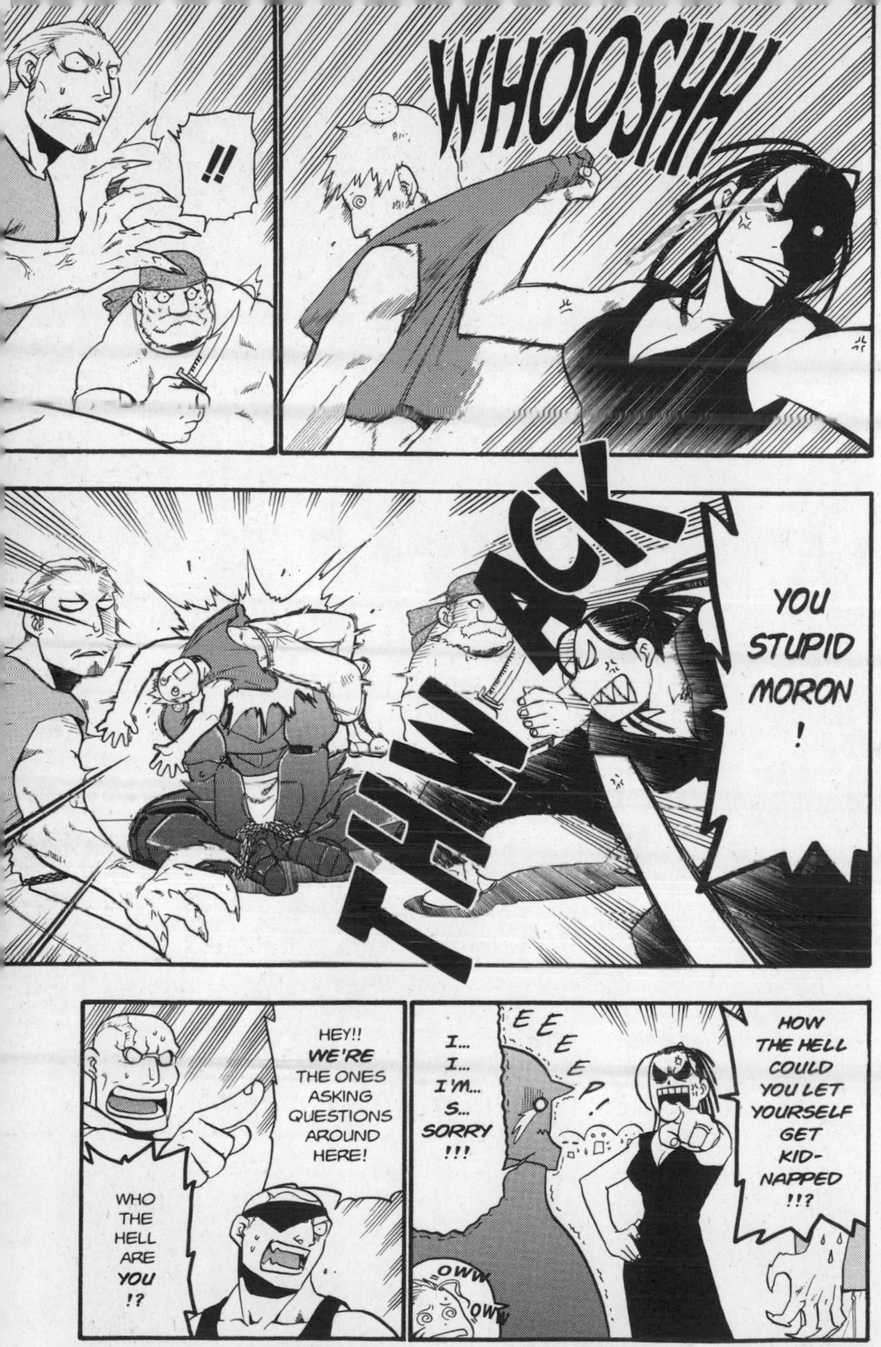
WHOOSHH
!!
THWACK
YOU STUPID MORON!
HOW THE HELL COULD YOU LET YOURSELF GET KID-NAPPED!!?
EEEEP!
I... I... I'M... S... SORRY!!!
OWW OWW
HEY!! WE'RE THE ONES ASKING QUESTIONS AROUND HERE!
WHO THE HELL ARE YOU!?

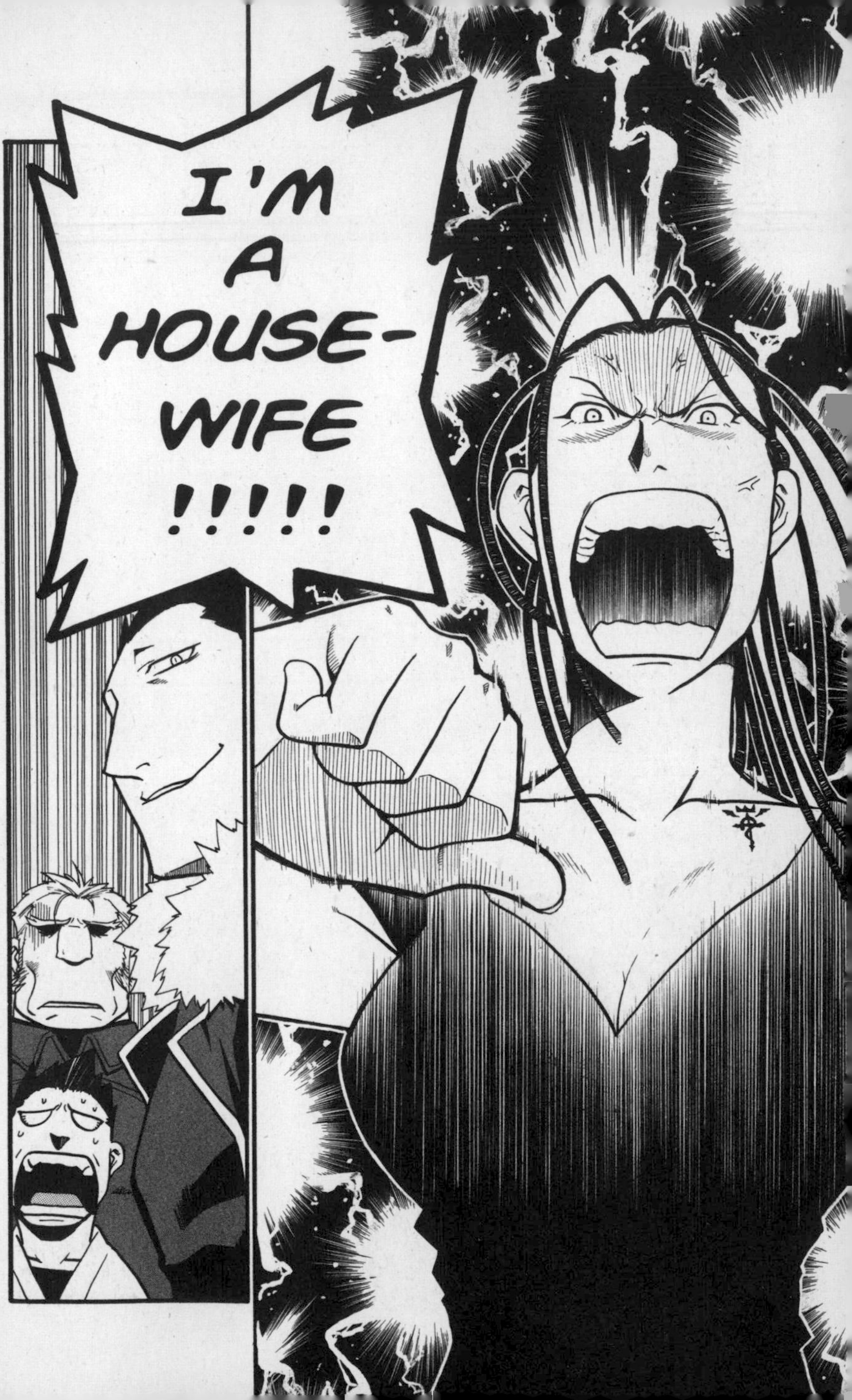
I'M A HOUSE-WIFE !!!!!

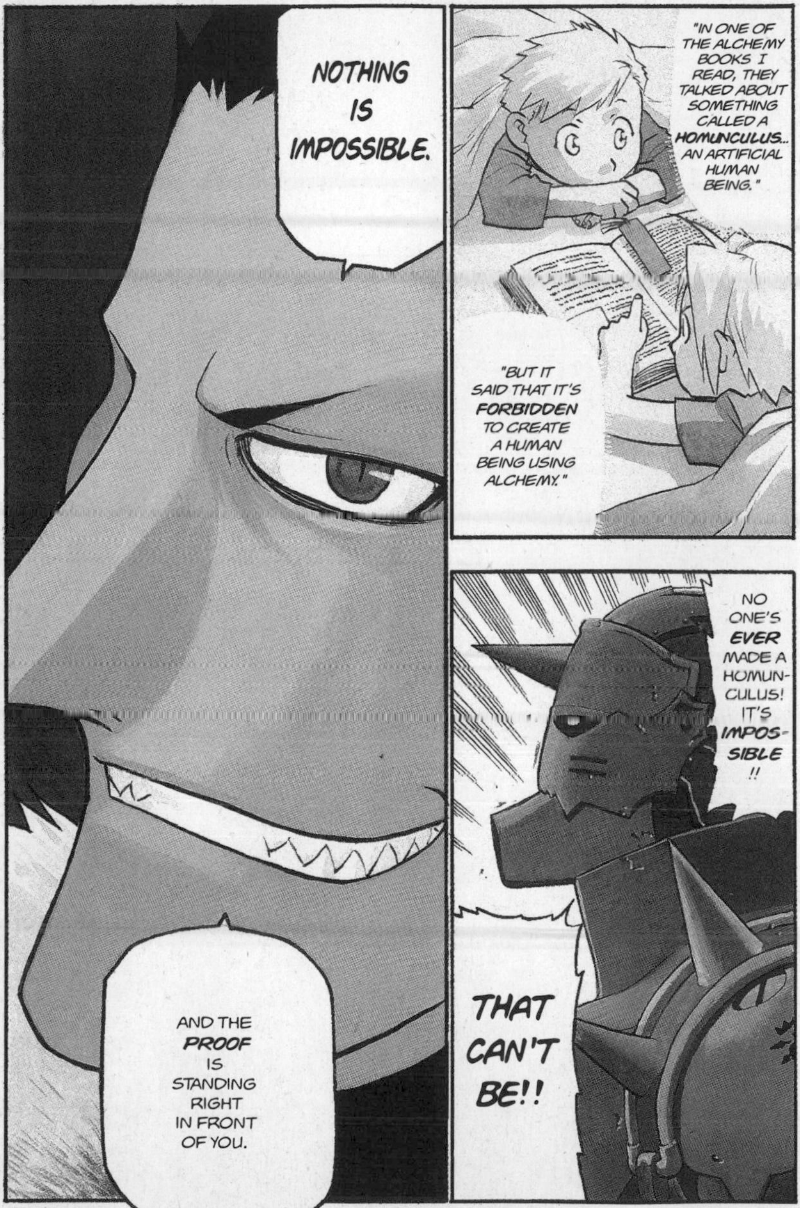
"IN ONE OF THE ALCHEMY BOOKS I READ, THEY TALKED ABOUT SOMETHING CALLED A HOMUNCULUS... AN ARTIFICIAL HUMAN BEING."
"BUT IT SAID THAT IT'S FORBIDDEN TO CREATE A HUMAN BEING USING ALCHEMY."
NO ONE'S EVER MADE A HOMUN-CULUS! IT'S IMPOS-SIBLE!!
THAT CAN'T BE!!
NOTHING IS IMPOSSIBLE.
AND THE PROOF IS STANDING RIGHT IN FRONT OF YOU.

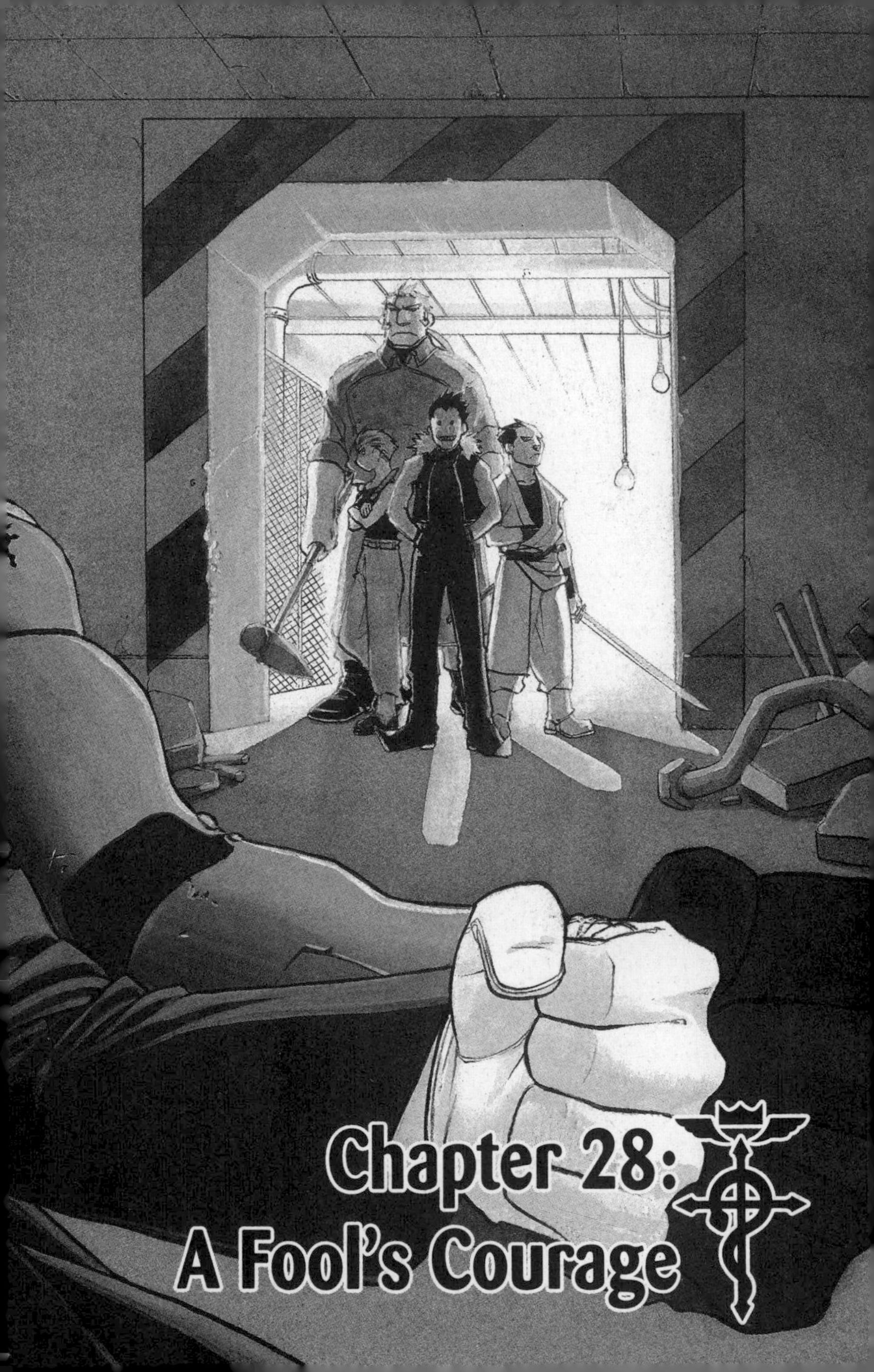
Chapter 28:
A Fool's Courage

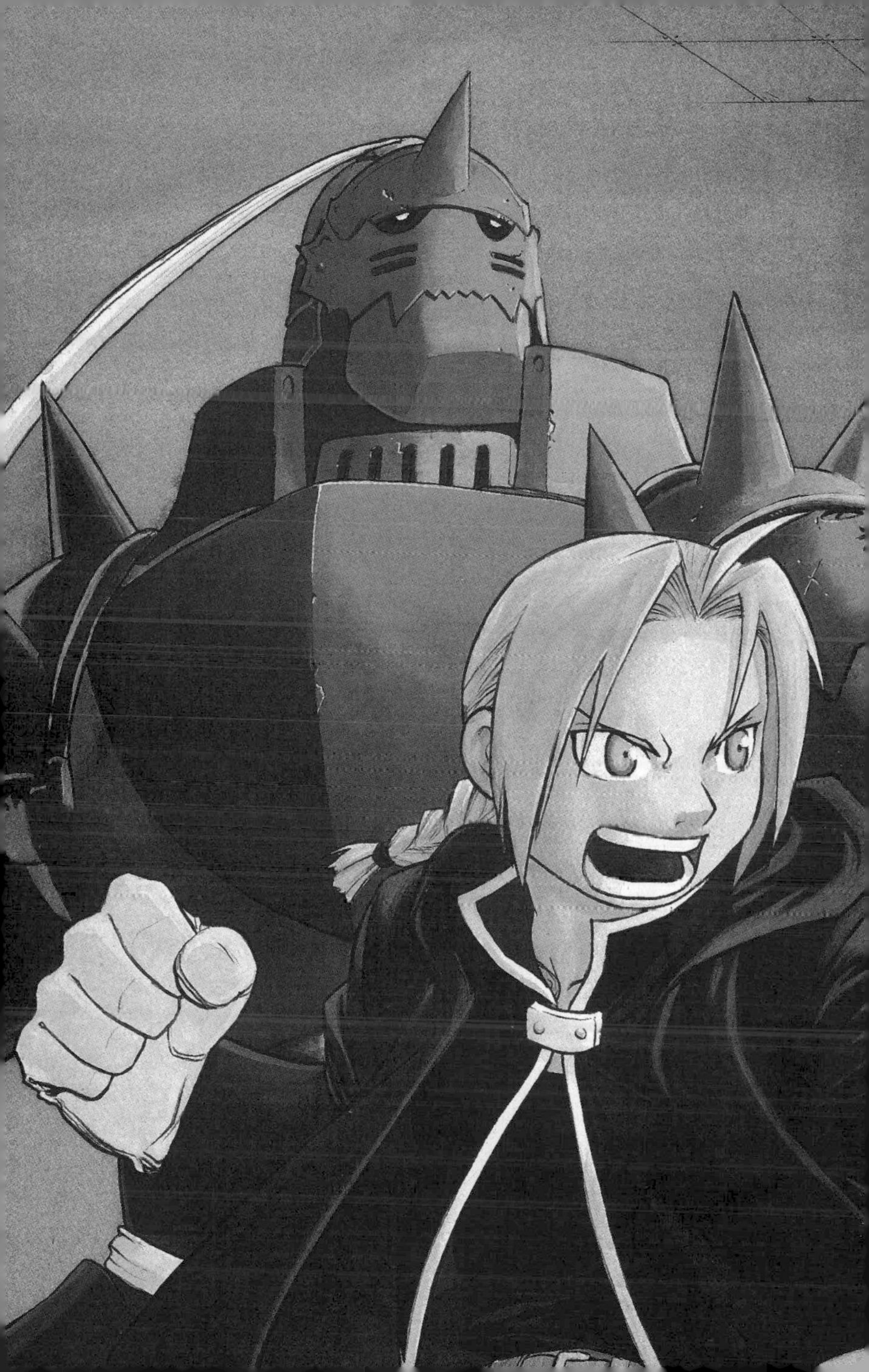

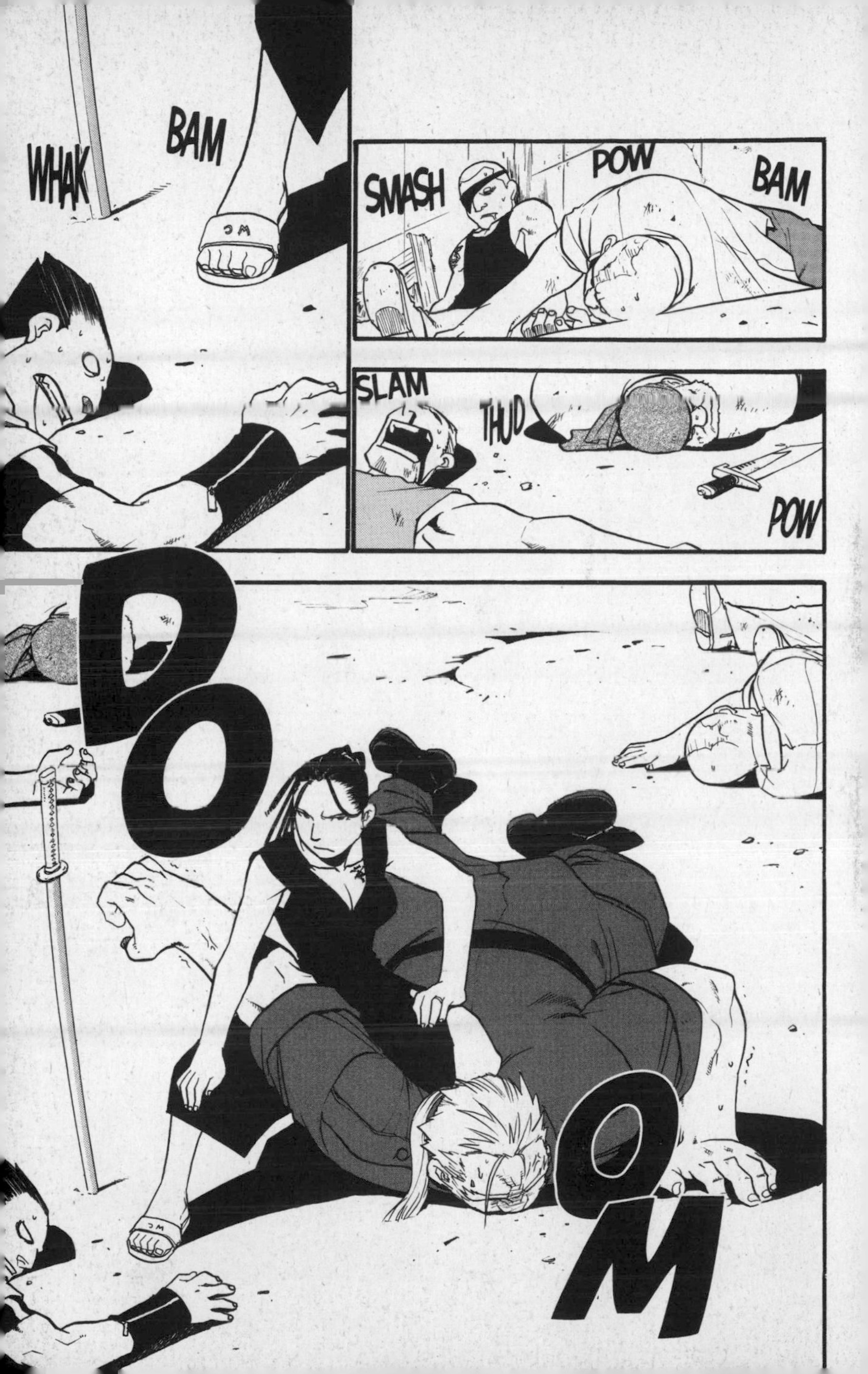
BAM
POW
SMASH
THUD
SLAM
POW
BAM
WHAK
DO
OM

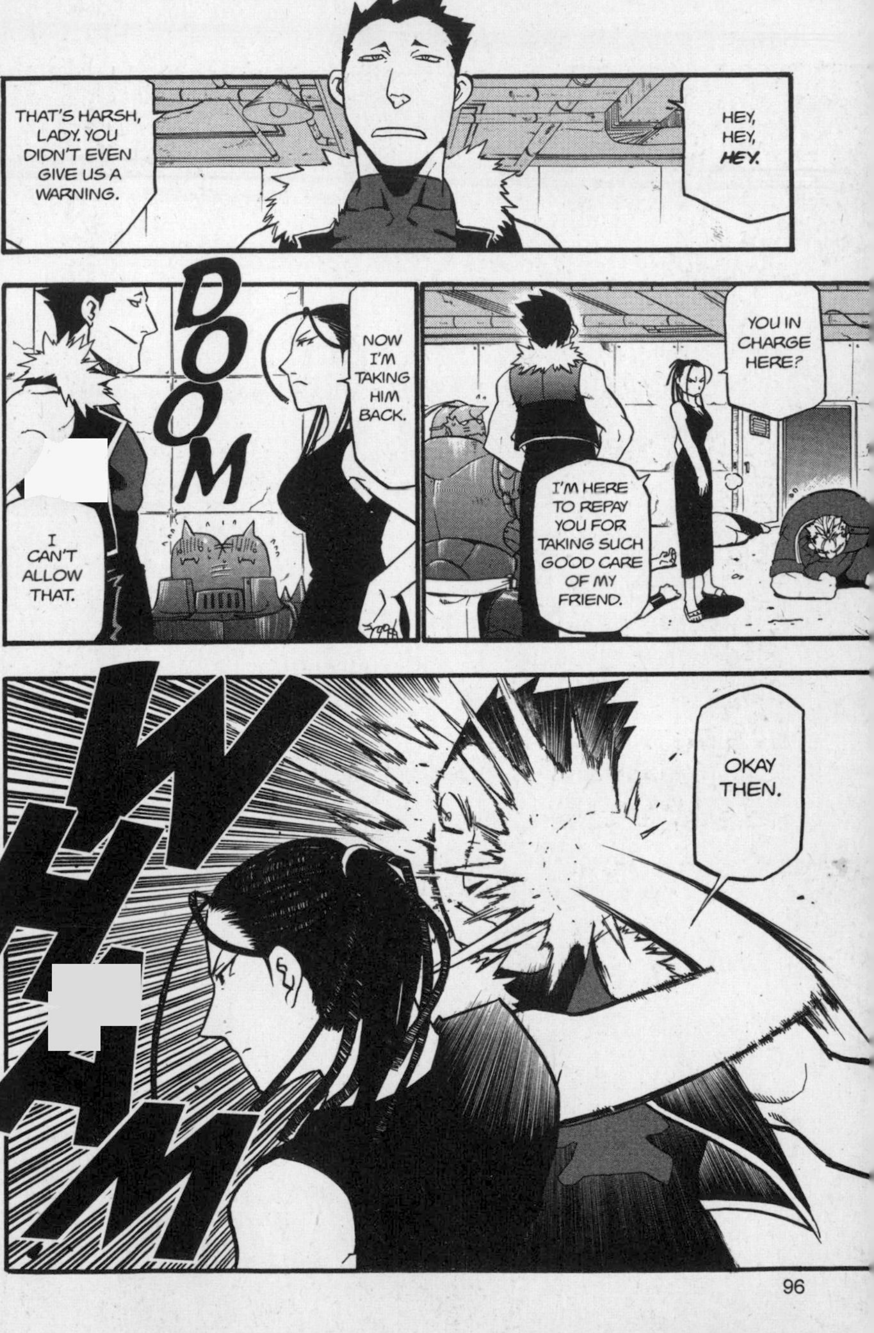
HEY, HEY, HEY.
THAT'S HARSH, LADY. YOU DIDN'T EVEN GIVE US A WARNING.
YOU IN CHARGE HERE?
I'M HERE TO REPAY YOU FOR TAKING SUCH GOOD CARE OF MY FRIEND.
NOW I'M TAKING HIM BACK.
DOOM
I CAN'T ALLOW THAT.
OKAY THEN.

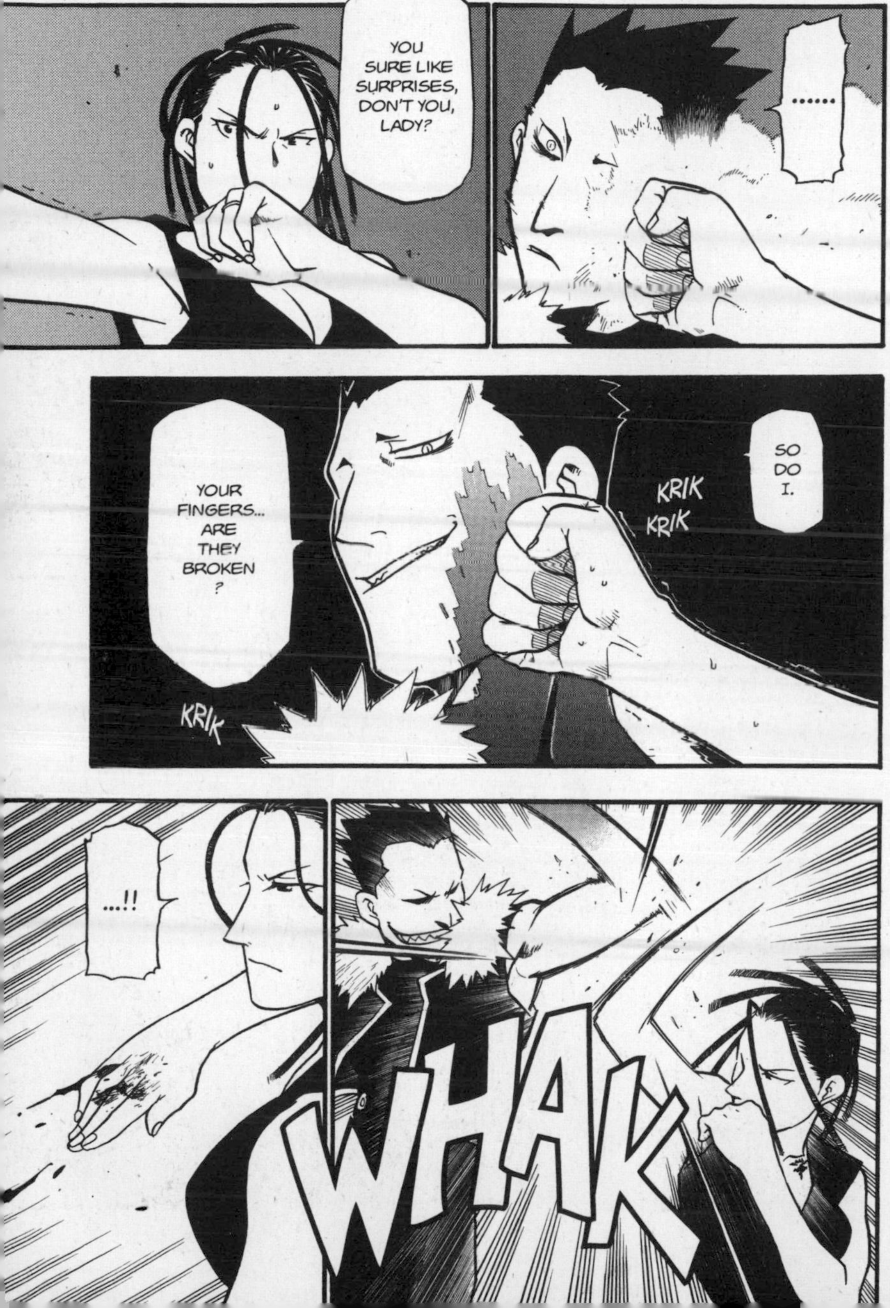
......
YOU SURE LIKE SURPRISES, DON'T YOU, LADY?
SO DO I.
KRIK KRIK
YOUR FINGERS... ARE THEY BROKEN?
KRIK
WHAK
...!!

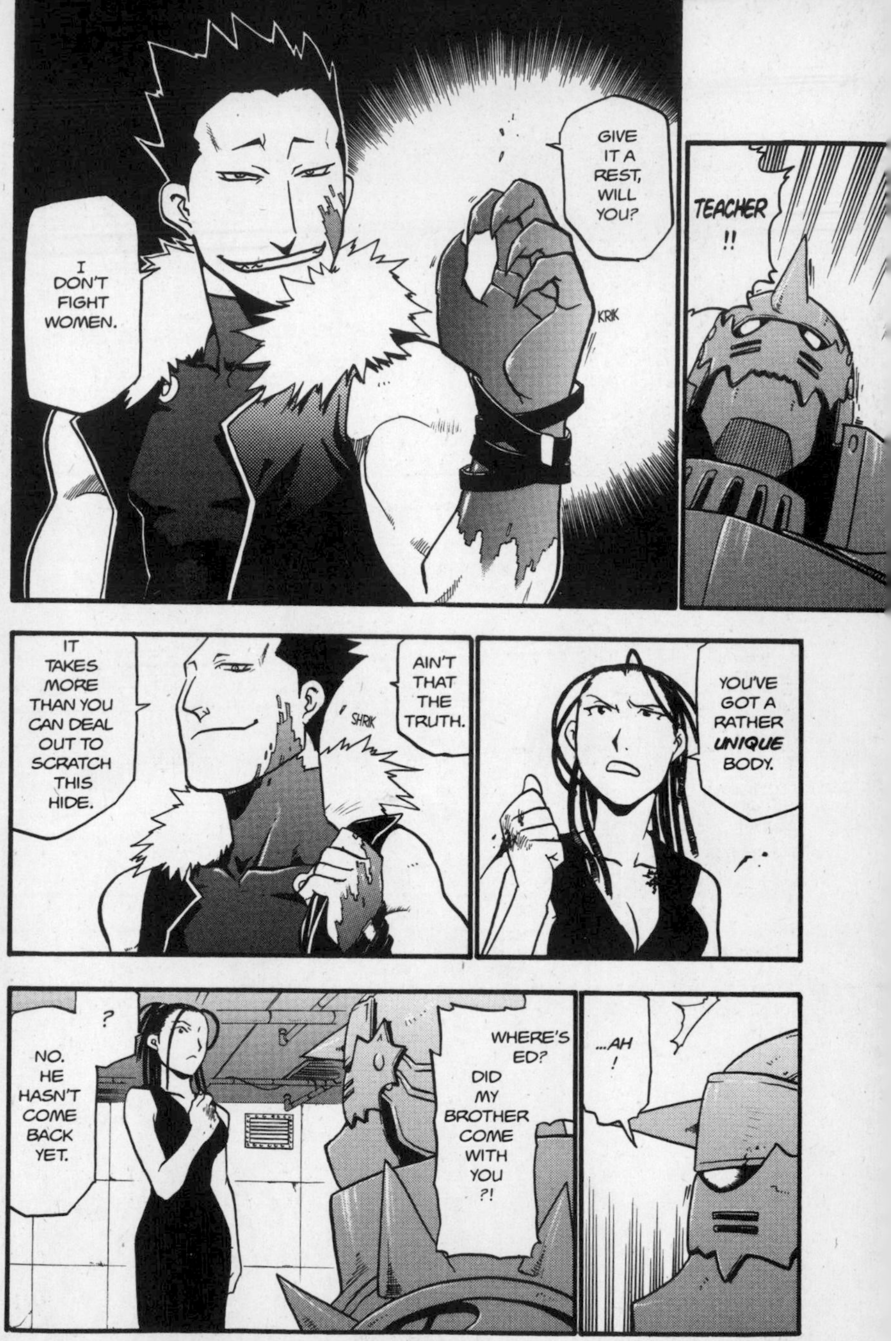
TEACHER !!
GIVE IT A REST, WILL YOU?
I DON'T FIGHT WOMEN.
KRIK
YOU'VE GOT A RATHER UNIQUE BODY.
AIN'T THAT THE TRUTH.
SHRIK
IT TAKES MORE THAN YOU CAN DEAL OUT TO SCRATCH THIS HIDE.
...AH !
WHERE'S ED? DID MY BROTHER COME WITH YOU ?!
?
NO. HE HASN'T COME BACK YET.

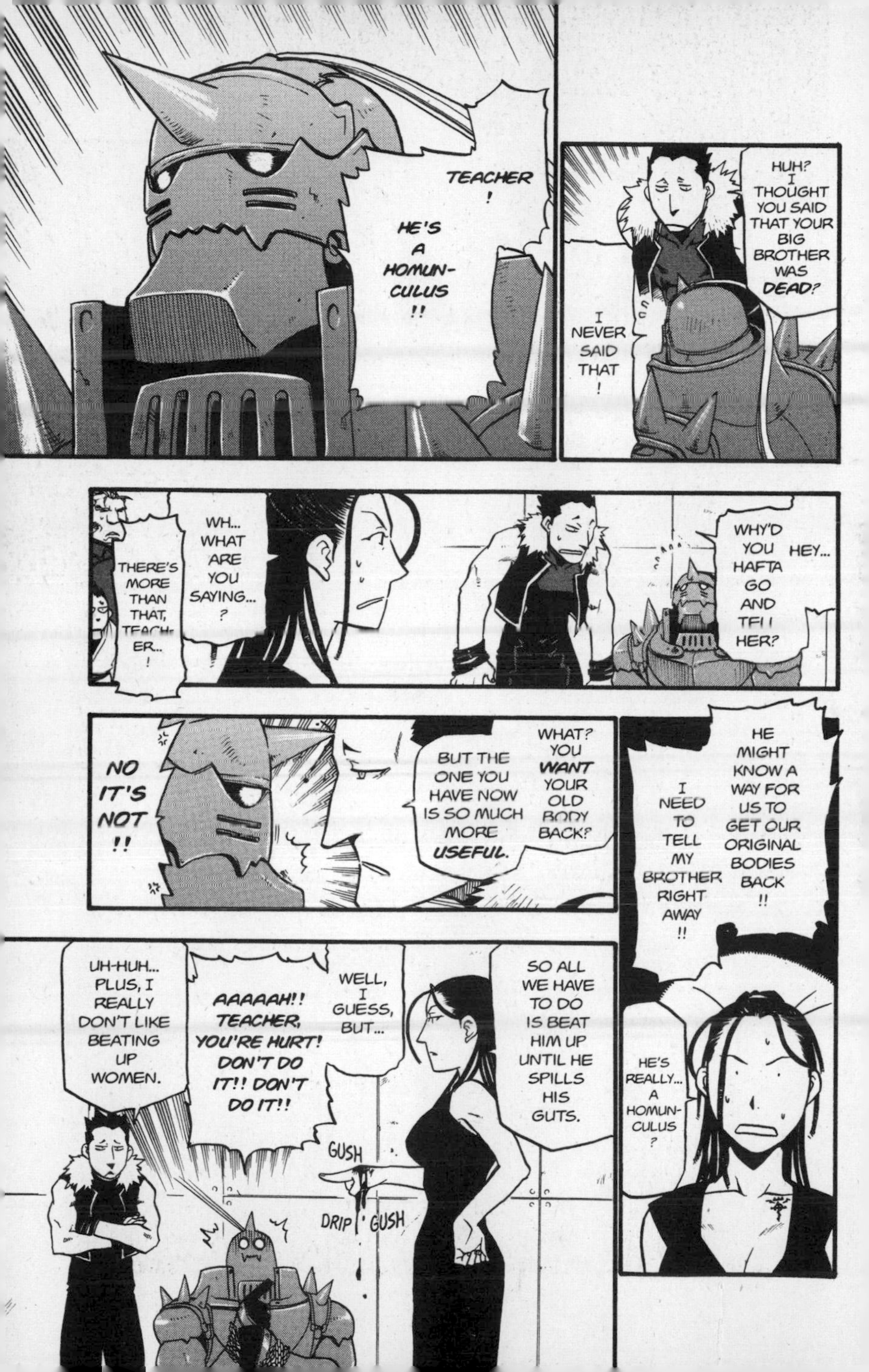
HUH? I THOUGHT YOU SAID THAT YOUR BIG BROTHER WAS DEAD?
I NEVER SAID THAT!
TEACHER!
HE'S A HOMUNCULUS!!
HEY...
WHY'D YOU HAFTA GO AND TELL HER?
WH... WHAT ARE YOU SAYING...?
THERE'S MORE THAN THAT, TEACHER...!
HE MIGHT KNOW A WAY FOR US TO GET OUR ORIGINAL BODIES BACK!!
I NEED TO TELL MY BROTHER RIGHT AWAY!!
HE'S REALLY... A HOMUNCULUS?
WHAT? YOU WANT YOUR OLD BODY BACK?
BUT THE ONE YOU HAVE NOW IS SO MUCH MORE USEFUL.
NO IT'S NOT!!
SO ALL WE HAVE TO DO IS BEAT HIM UP UNTIL HE SPILLS HIS GUTS.
WELL, I GUESS, BUT...
AAAAAH!! TEACHER, YOU'RE HURT! DON'T DO IT!! DON'T DO IT!!
UH-HUH... PLUS, I REALLY DON'T LIKE BEATING UP WOMEN.
GUSH
DRIP
GUSH

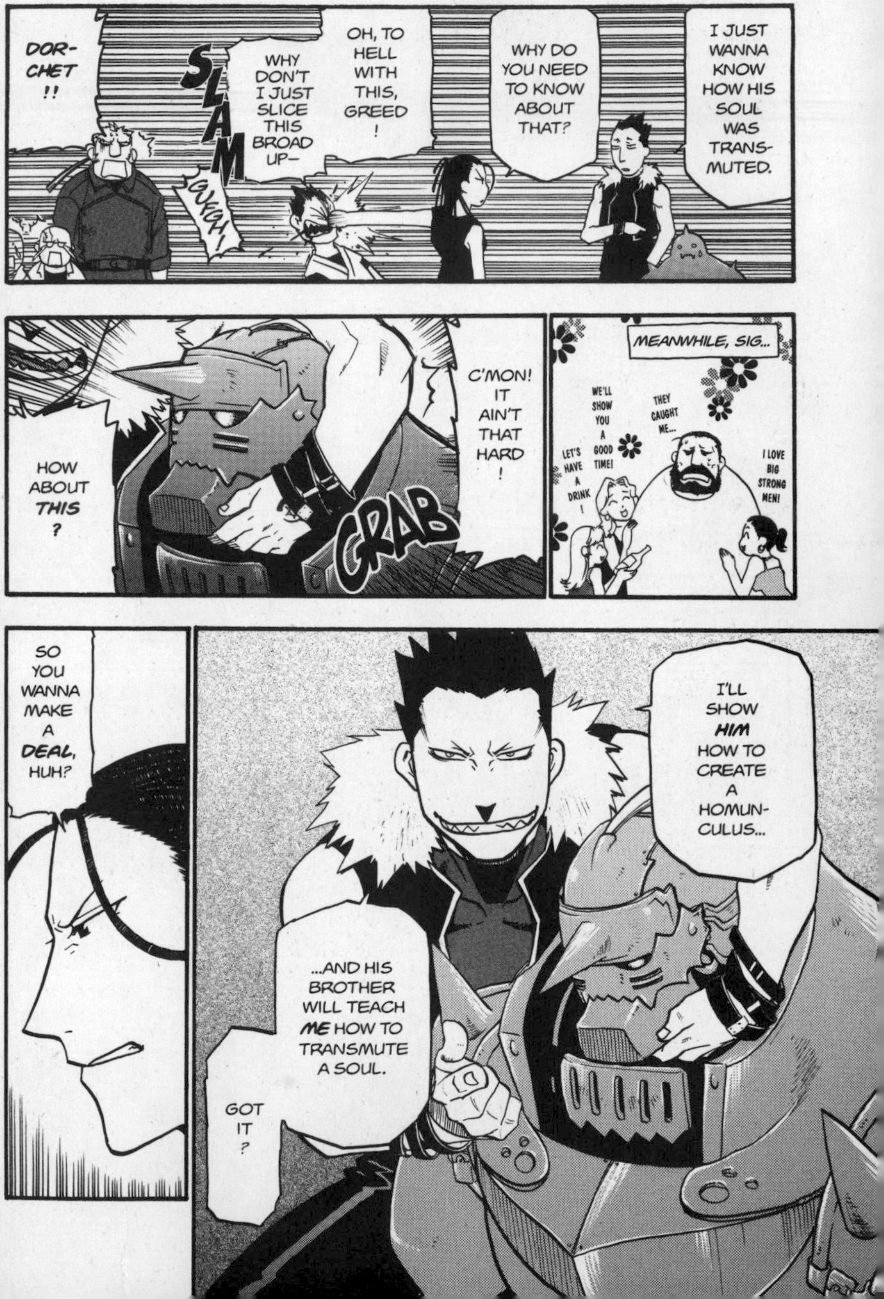
I JUST WANNA KNOW HOW HIS SOUL WAS TRANSMUTED.
WHY DO YOU NEED TO KNOW ABOUT THAT?
OH, TO HELL WITH THIS, GREED!
WHY DON'T I JUST SLICE THIS BROAD UP–
SLAM
GUKGH!
DORCHET!!
MEANWHILE, SIG...
THEY CAUGHT ME...
I LOVE BIG STRONG MEN!
WE'LL SHOW YOU A GOOD TIME!
LET'S HAVE A DRINK!
C'MON! IT AIN'T THAT HARD!
GRAB
HOW ABOUT THIS?
I'LL SHOW HIM HOW TO CREATE A HOMUNCULUS...
...AND HIS BROTHER WILL TEACH ME HOW TO TRANSMUTE A SOUL.
GOT IT?
SO YOU WANNA MAKE A DEAL, HUH?

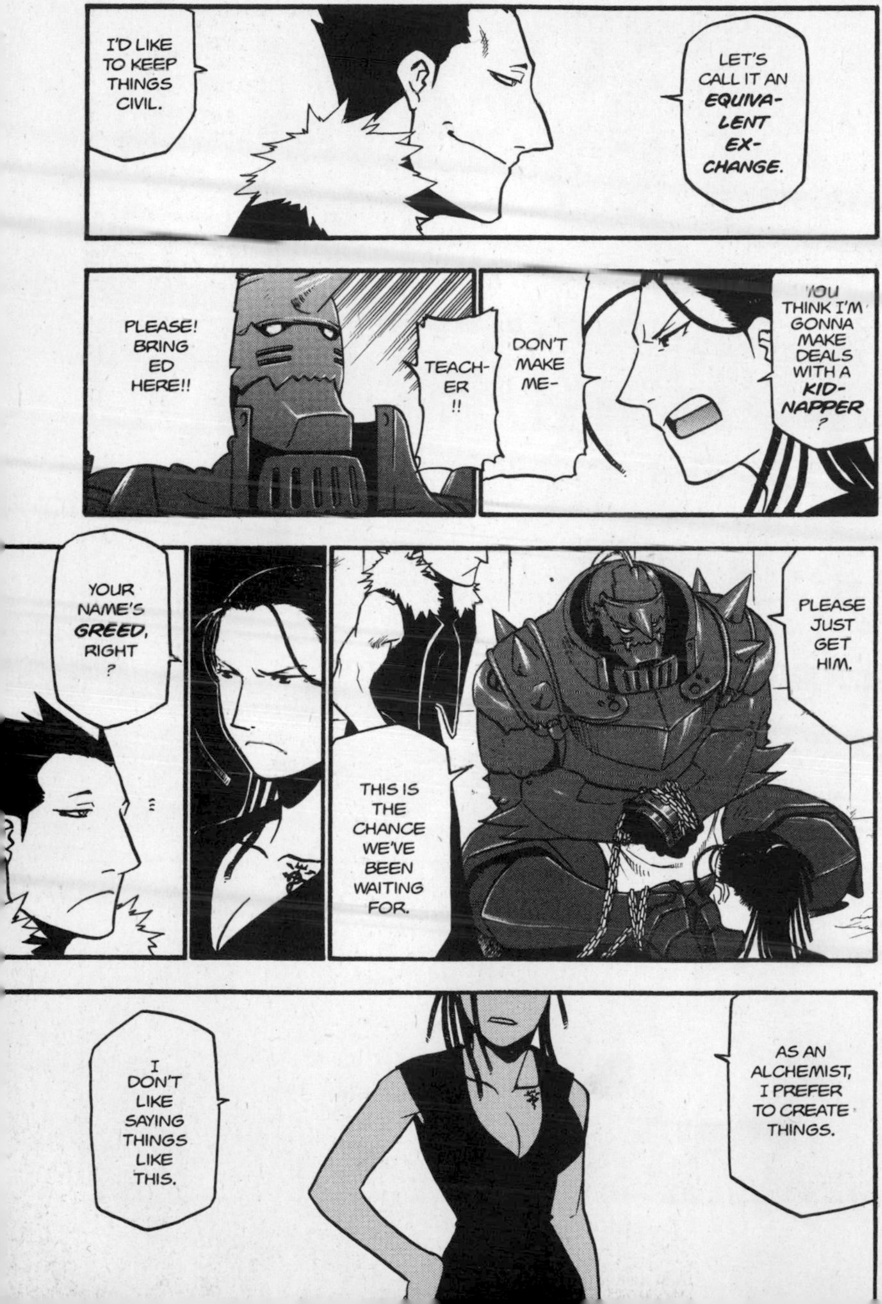
LET'S CALL IT AN EQUIVALENT EXCHANGE.
I'D LIKE TO KEEP THINGS CIVIL.
YOU THINK I'M GONNA MAKE DEALS WITH A KIDNAPPER?
DON'T MAKE ME-
TEACHER!!
PLEASE! BRING ED HERE!!
PLEASE JUST GET HIM.
THIS IS THE CHANCE WE'VE BEEN WAITING FOR.
YOUR NAME'S GREED, RIGHT?
AS AN ALCHEMIST, I PREFER TO CREATE THINGS.
I DON'T LIKE SAYING THINGS LIKE THIS.

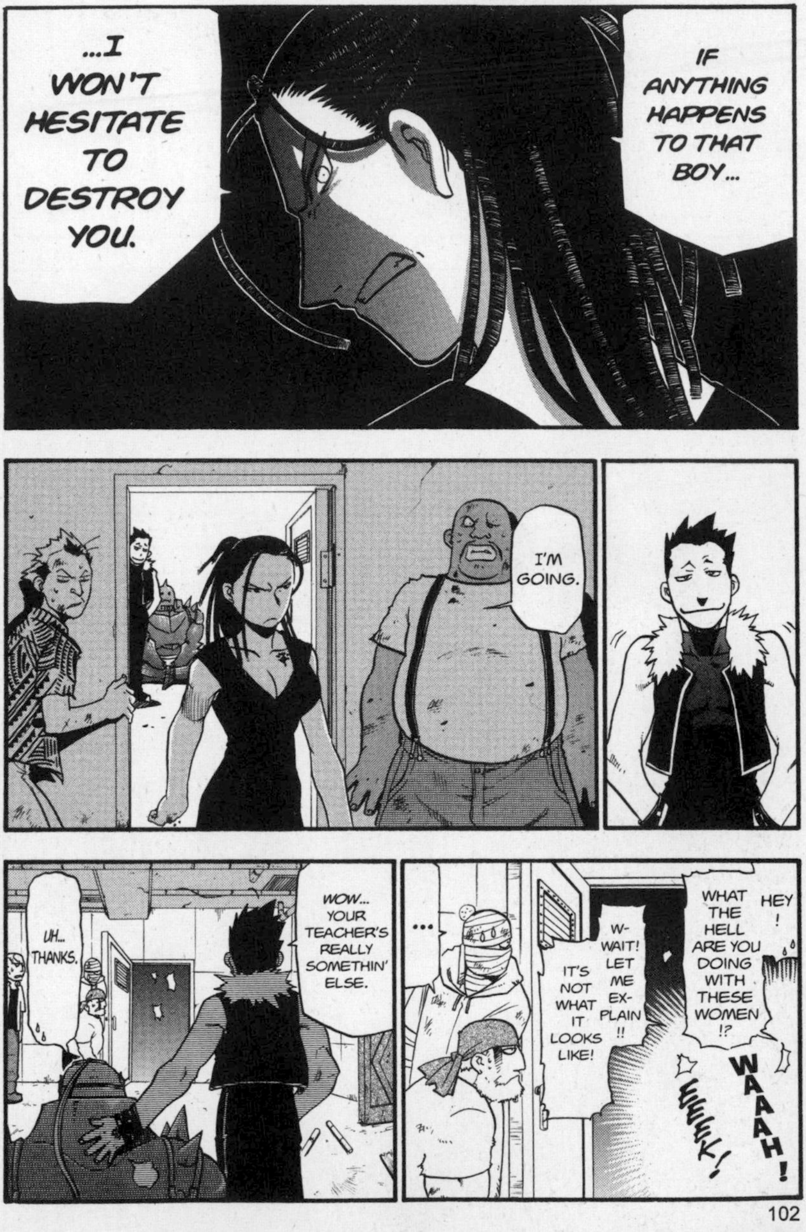
IF ANYTHING HAPPENS TO THAT BOY...
...I WON'T HESITATE TO DESTROY YOU.
I'M GOING.
HEY!
WHAT THE HELL ARE YOU DOING WITH THESE WOMEN!?
WAAAH!
EEEEK!
W-WAIT! LET ME EX-PLAIN!!
IT'S NOT WHAT IT LOOKS LIKE!
...
WOW... YOUR TEACHER'S REALLY SOMETHIN' ELSE.
UH... THANKS.

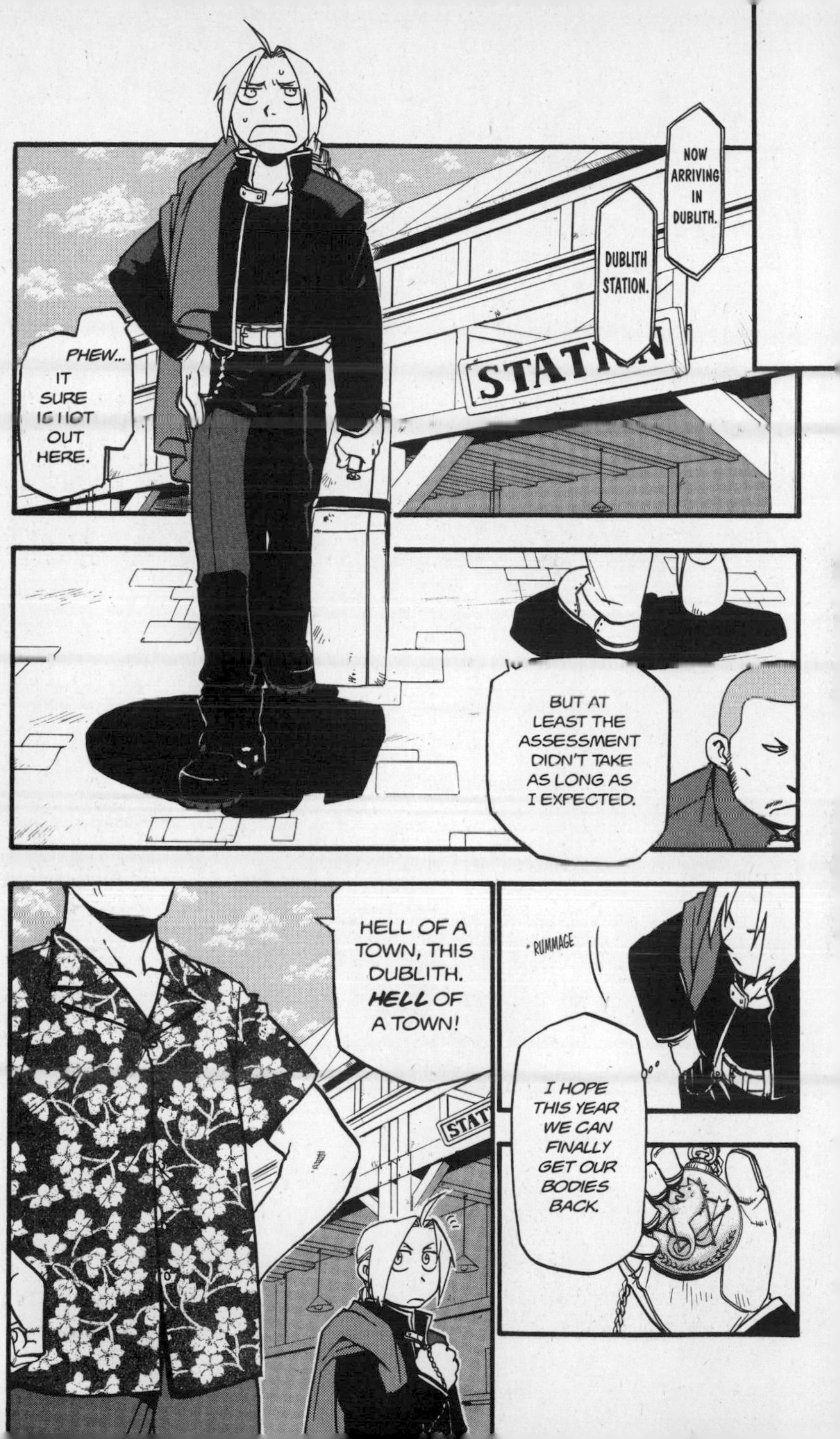

NOW ARRIVING IN DUBLITH.
DUBLITH STATION.
PHEW... IT SURE IS HOT OUT HERE.
BUT AT LEAST THE ASSESSMENT DIDN'T TAKE AS LONG AS I EXPECTED.
RUMMAGE
I HOPE THIS YEAR WE CAN FINALLY GET OUR BODIES BACK.
HELL OF A TOWN, THIS DUBLITH. **HELL** OF A TOWN!

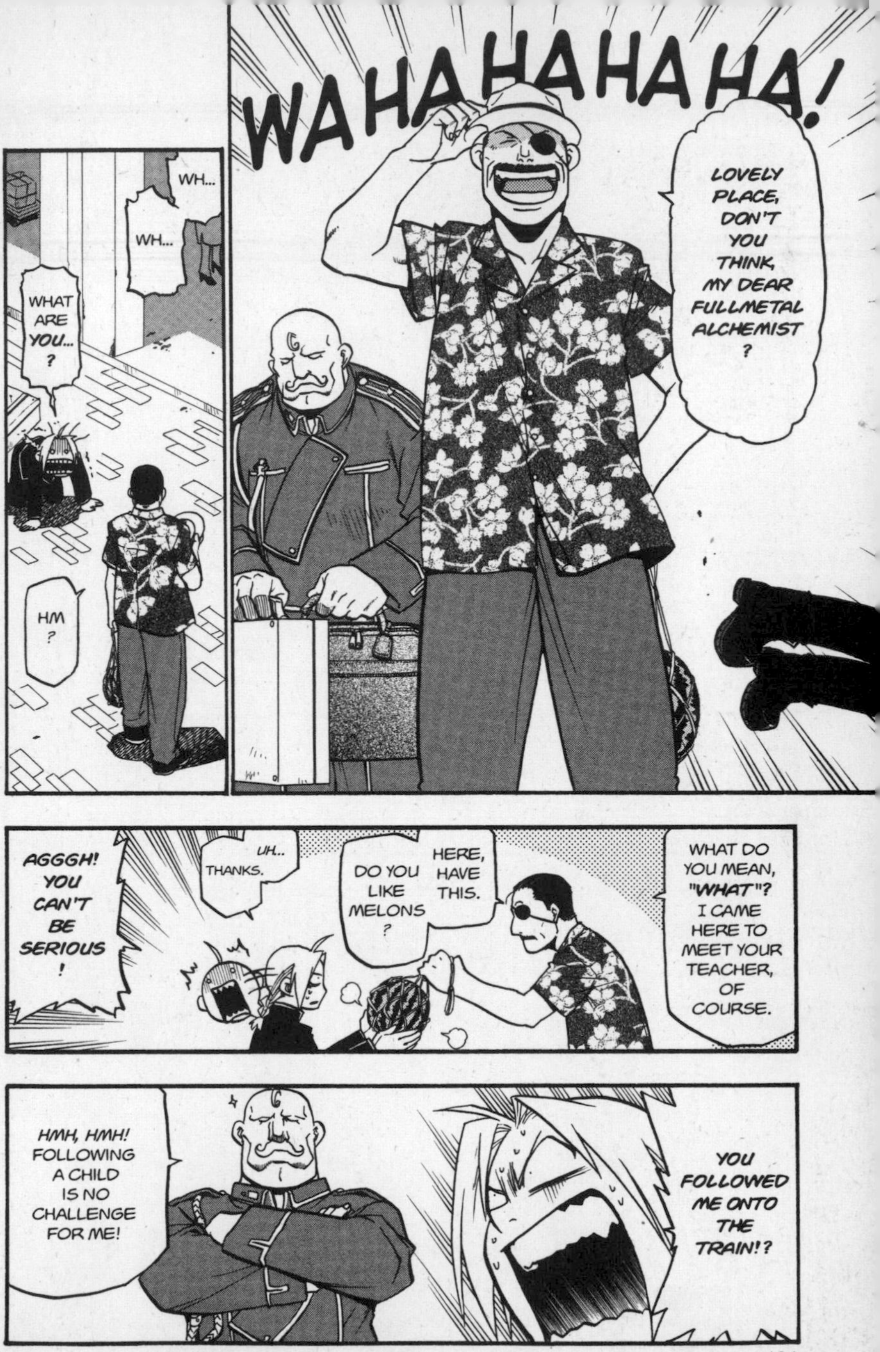
WAHAHAHAHAHA!
LOVELY PLACE, DON'T YOU THINK, MY DEAR FULLMETAL ALCHEMIST?
WH...
WH...
WHAT ARE YOU...?
HM?
WHAT DO YOU MEAN, "WHAT"? I CAME HERE TO MEET YOUR TEACHER, OF COURSE.
HERE, HAVE THIS.
DO YOU LIKE MELONS?
UH.. THANKS.
AGGGH! YOU CAN'T BE SERIOUS!
YOU FOLLOWED ME ONTO THE TRAIN!?
HMH, HMH! FOLLOWING A CHILD IS NO CHALLENGE FOR ME!

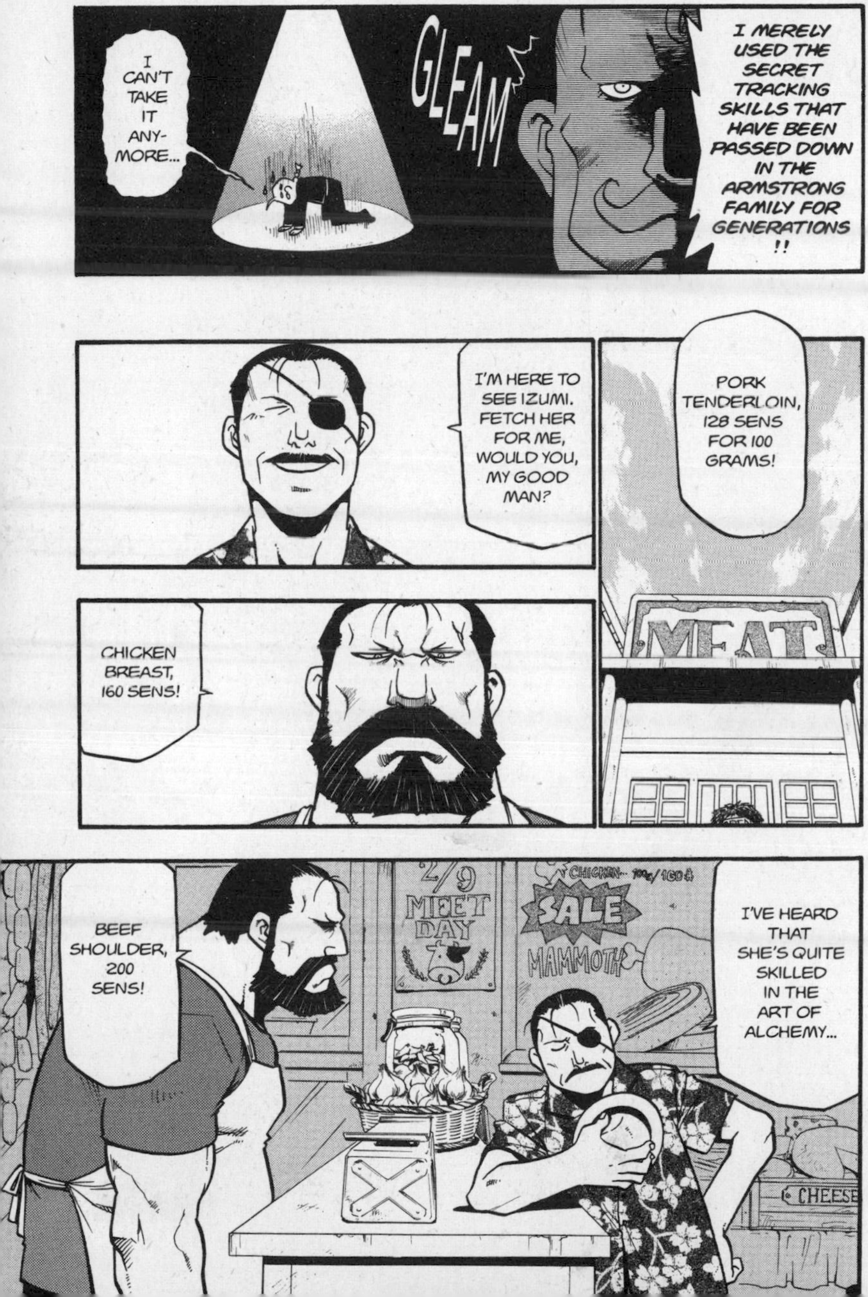
I MERELY USED THE SECRET TRACKING SKILLS THAT HAVE BEEN PASSED DOWN IN THE ARMSTRONG FAMILY FOR GENERATIONS !!
GLEAM
I CAN'T TAKE IT ANY-MORE...
PORK TENDERLOIN, 128 SENS FOR 100 GRAMS!
MEAT
I'M HERE TO SEE IZUMI. FETCH HER FOR ME, WOULD YOU, MY GOOD MAN?
CHICKEN BREAST, 160 SENS!
I'VE HEARD THAT SHE'S QUITE SKILLED IN THE ART OF ALCHEMY...
CHICKEN... 100g/160¢
SALE
MAMMOTH
2/9 MEET DAY
CHEESE
BEEF SHOULDER, 200 SENS!

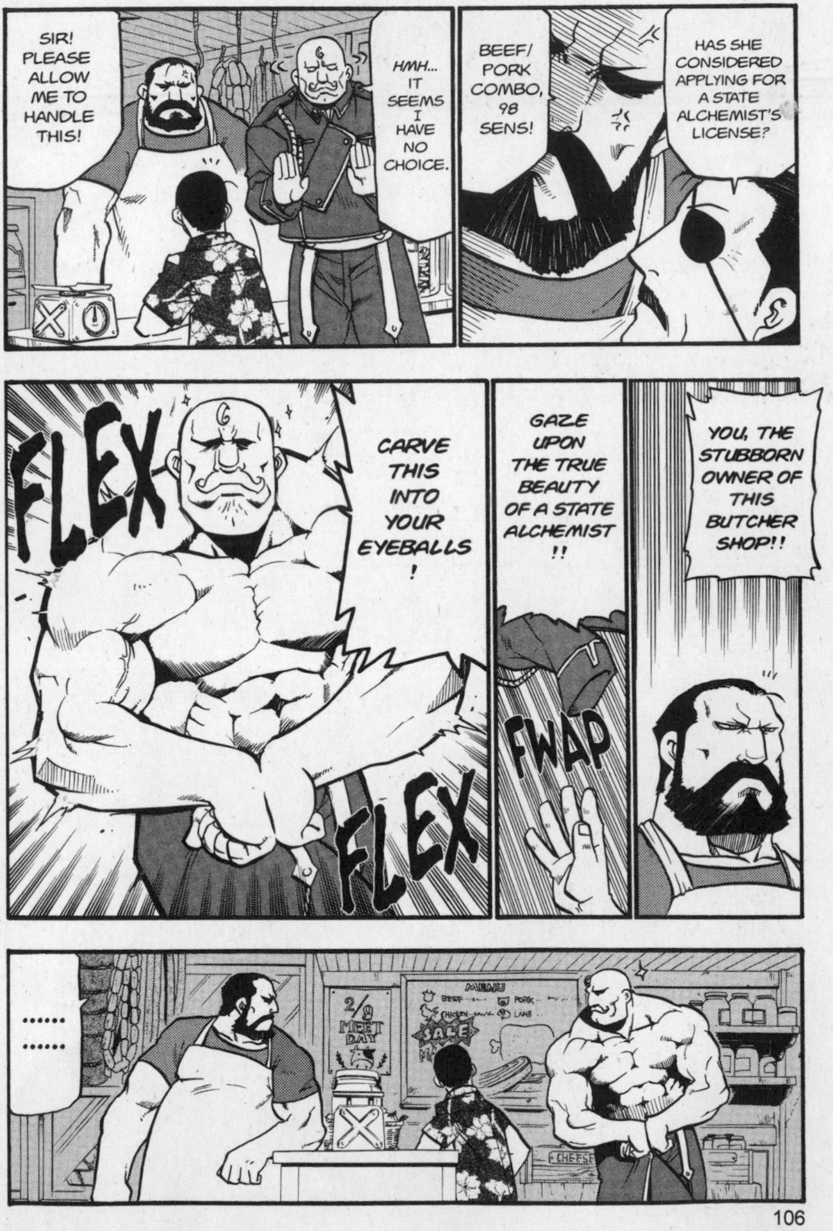
HAS SHE CONSIDERED APPLYING FOR A STATE ALCHEMIST'S LICENSE?
BEEF/ PORK COMBO, 98 SENS!
HMH... IT SEEMS I HAVE NO CHOICE.
SIR! PLEASE ALLOW ME TO HANDLE THIS!
YOU, THE STUBBORN OWNER OF THIS BUTCHER SHOP!!
GAZE UPON THE TRUE BEAUTY OF A STATE ALCHEMIST!!
FWAP
CARVE THIS INTO YOUR EYEBALLS!
FLEX
FLEX
MENU
SALE
2/9 MEET DAY
CHEESE
......
......

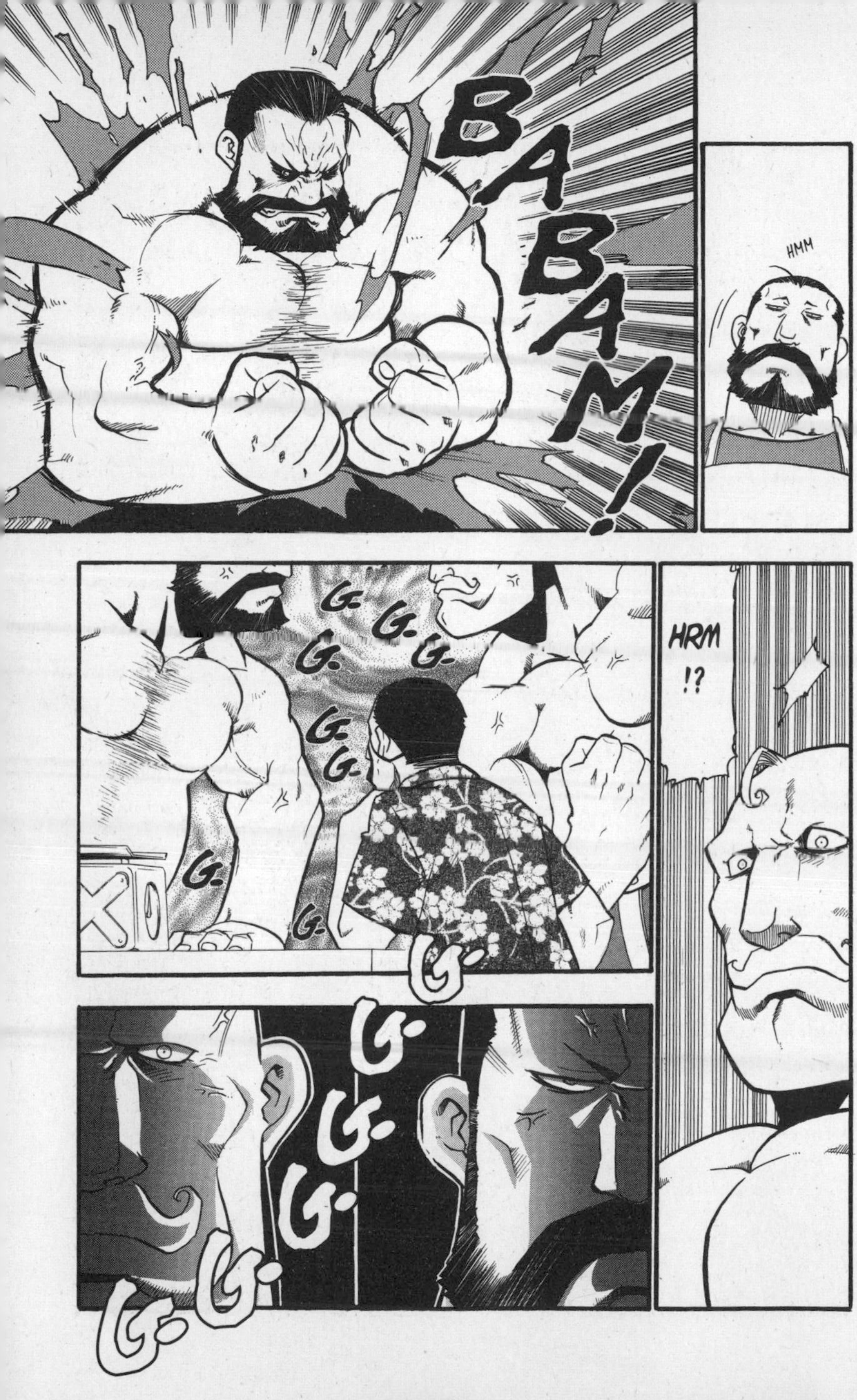
HMM
BABAM!
HRM
!?
G- G- G- G- G- G- G- G- G-
G- G- G- G- G- G-

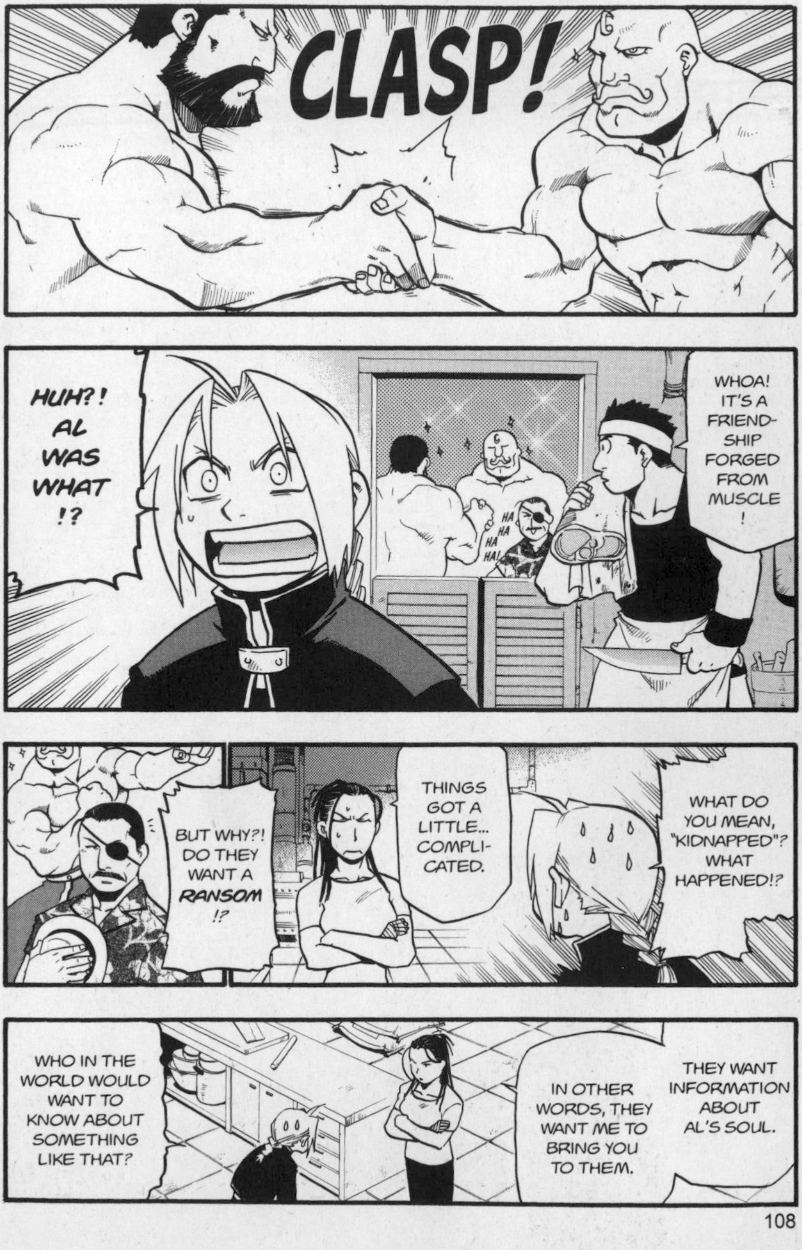
CLASP!
WHOA! IT'S A FRIEND-SHIP FORGED FROM MUSCLE!
HA HA HA HA!
HUH?! AL WAS WHAT!?
WHAT DO YOU MEAN, "KIDNAPPED"? WHAT HAPPENED!?
THINGS GOT A LITTLE... COMPLI-CATED.
BUT WHY?! DO THEY WANT A RANSOM!?
THEY WANT INFORMATION ABOUT AL'S SOUL.
IN OTHER WORDS, THEY WANT ME TO BRING YOU TO THEM.
WHO IN THE WORLD WOULD WANT TO KNOW ABOUT SOMETHING LIKE THAT?

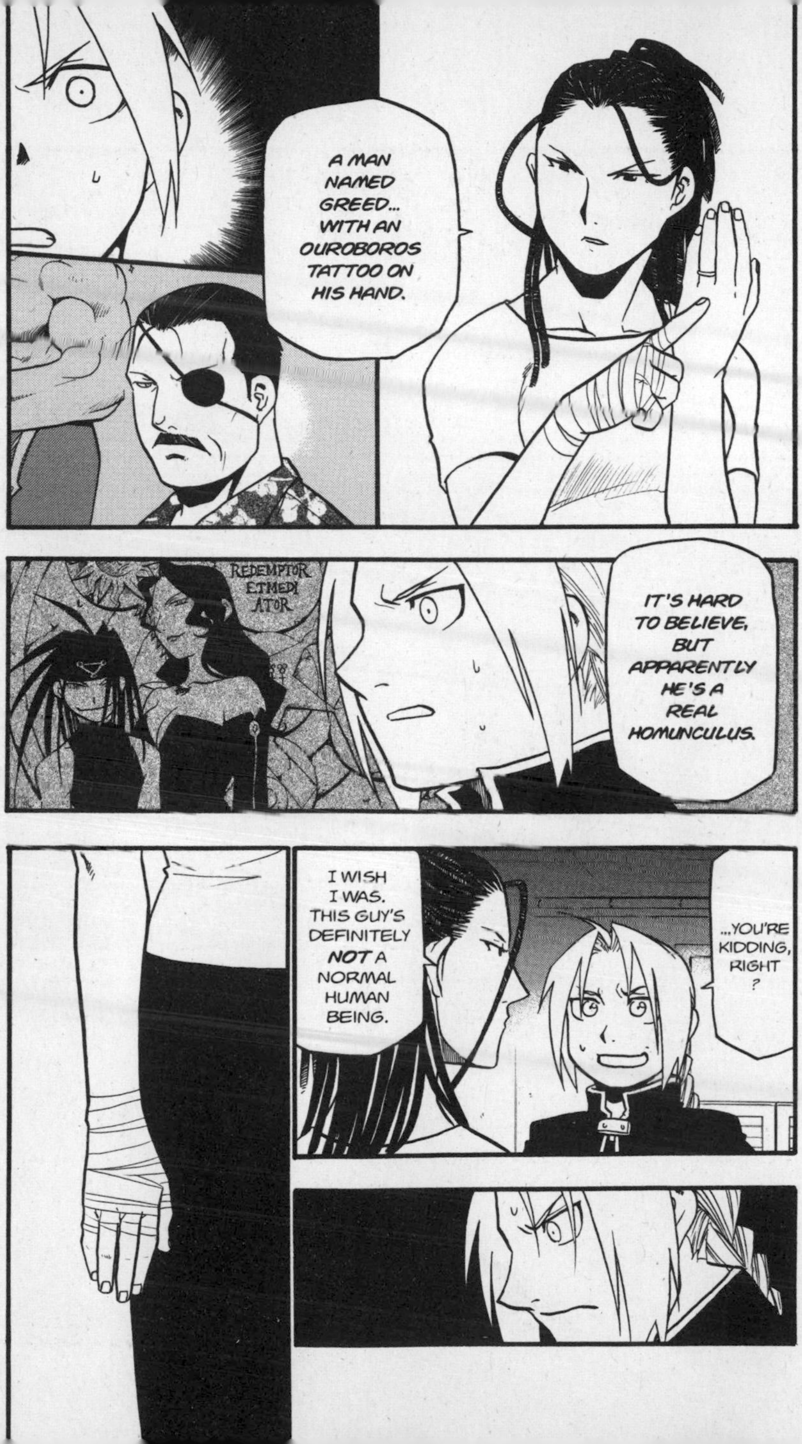
A MAN NAMED GREED... WITH AN OUROBOROS TATTOO ON HIS HAND.
IT'S HARD TO BELIEVE, BUT APPARENTLY HE'S A REAL HOMUNCULUS.
REDEMPTOR ET MEDI ATOR
...YOU'RE KIDDING, RIGHT?
I WISH I WAS. THIS GUY'S DEFINITELY NOT A NORMAL HUMAN BEING.

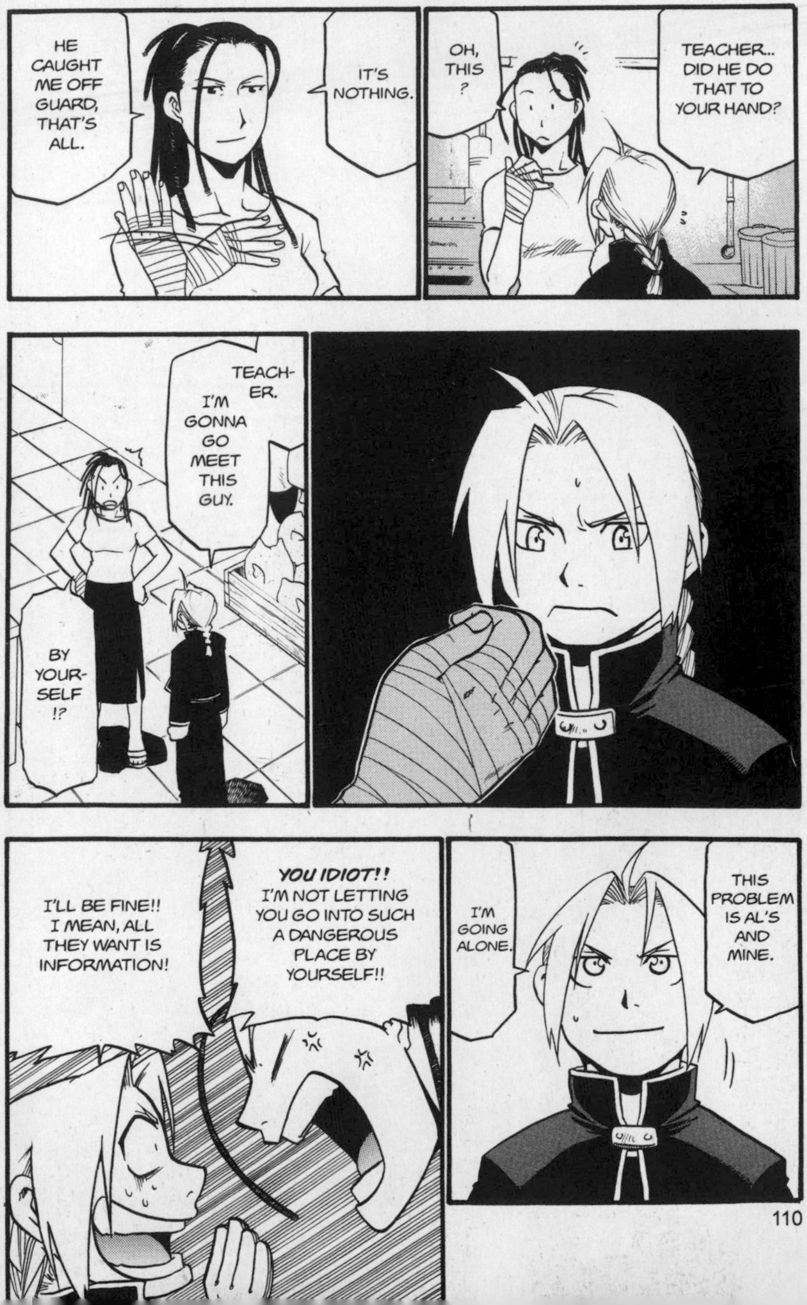
TEACHER... DID HE DO THAT TO YOUR HAND?
OH, THIS ?
IT'S NOTHING.
HE CAUGHT ME OFF GUARD, THAT'S ALL.
TEACHER. I'M GONNA GO MEET THIS GUY.
BY YOURSELF !?
THIS PROBLEM IS AL'S AND MINE.
I'M GOING ALONE.
YOU IDIOT!! I'M NOT LETTING YOU GO INTO SUCH A DANGEROUS PLACE BY YOURSELF!!
I'LL BE FINE!! I MEAN, ALL THEY WANT IS INFORMATION!

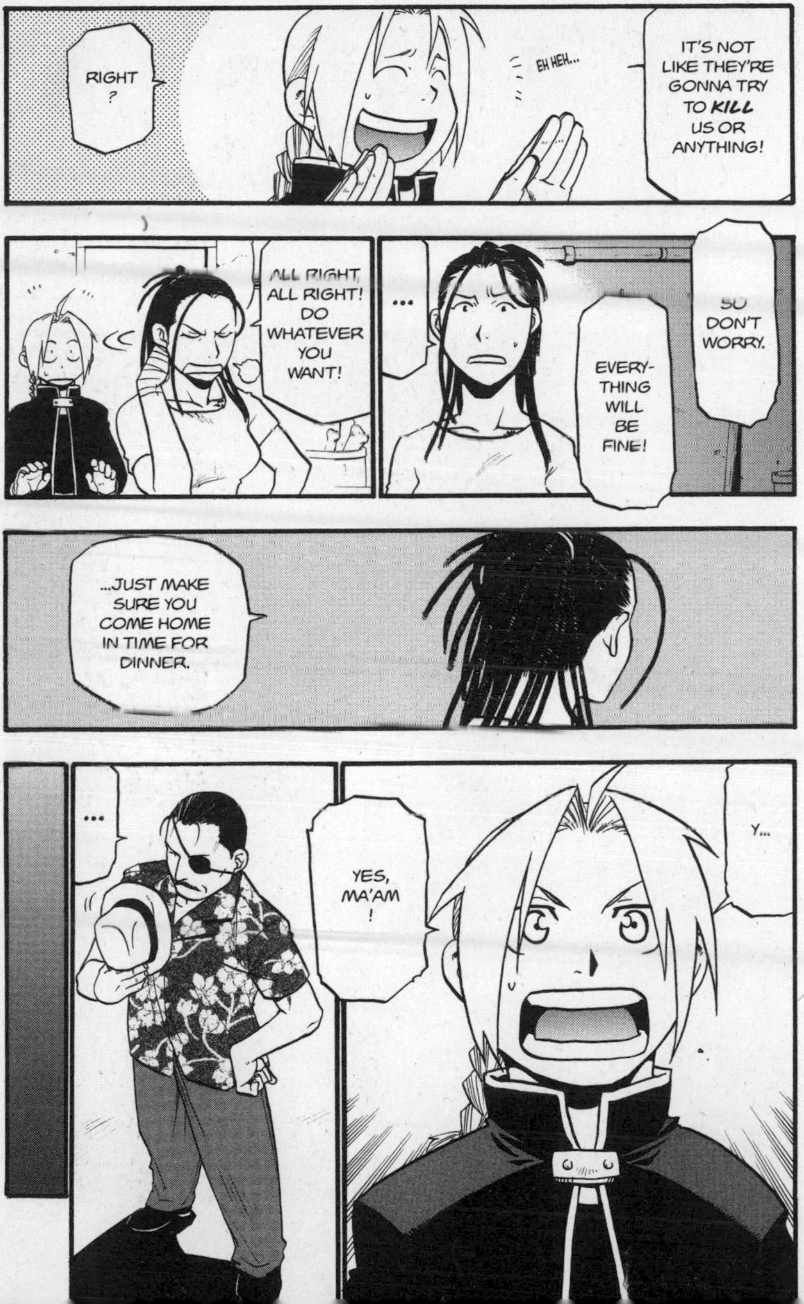
IT'S NOT LIKE THEY'RE GONNA TRY TO **KILL** US OR ANYTHING!
EH HEH...
RIGHT?
SO DON'T WORRY.
EVERYTHING WILL BE FINE!
...
ALL RIGHT, ALL RIGHT! DO WHATEVER YOU WANT!
...JUST MAKE SURE YOU COME HOME IN TIME FOR DINNER.
Y...
YES, MA'AM!
...

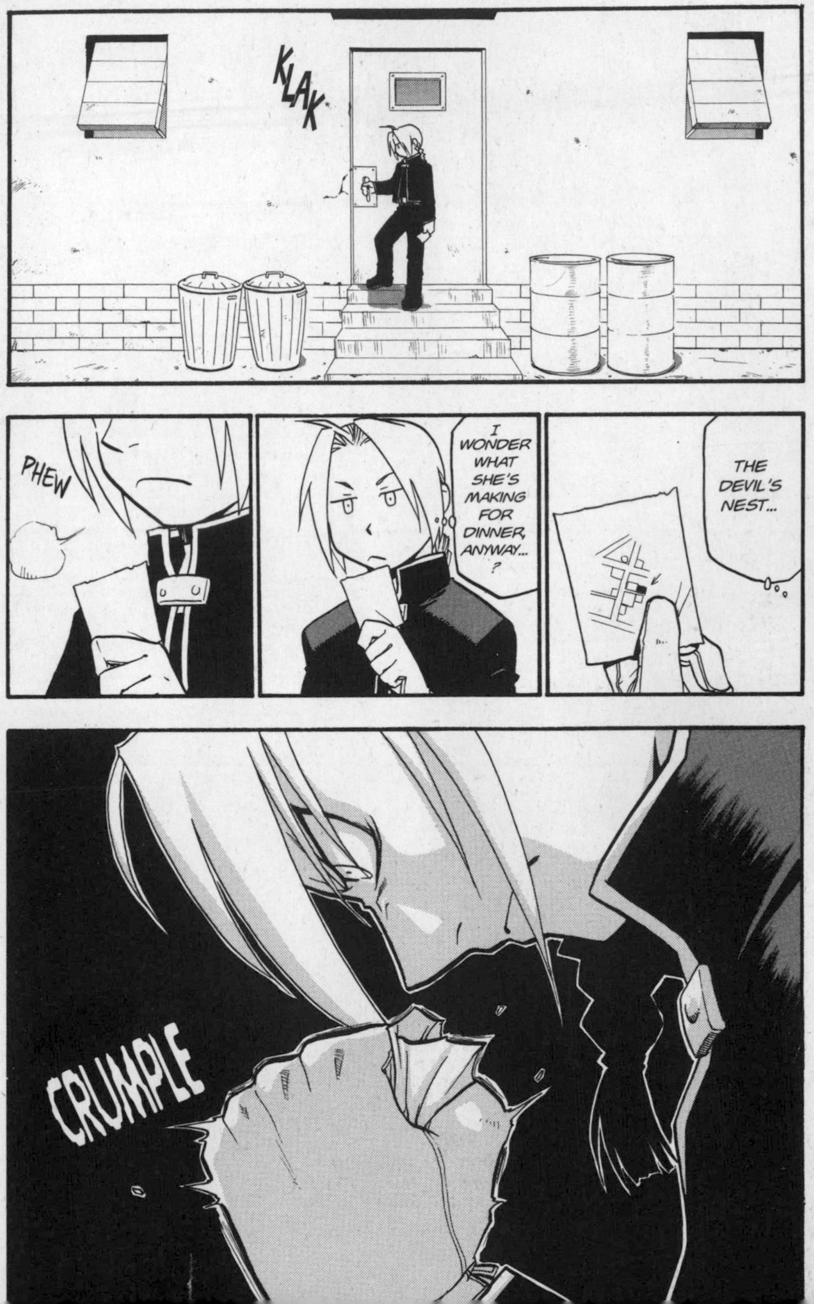
KLAK
THE DEVIL'S NEST...
I WONDER WHAT SHE'S MAKING FOR DINNER, ANYWAY...?
PHEW
CRUMPLE

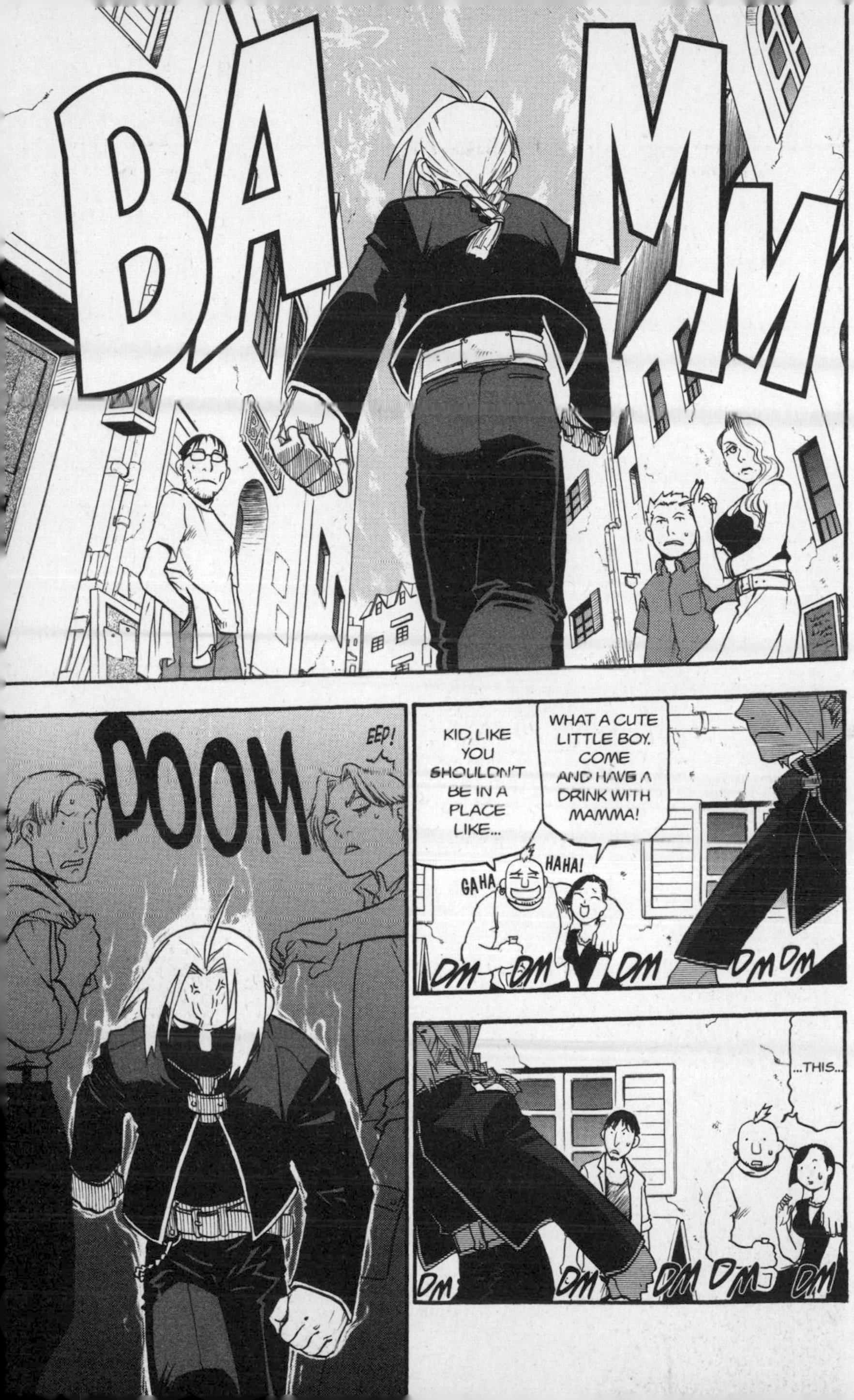
BAMM
WHAT A CUTE LITTLE BOY. COME AND HAVE A DRINK WITH MAMMA!
KID LIKE YOU SHOULDN'T BE IN A PLACE LIKE...
HAHA!
GAHA
DM DM DM DM DM
...THIS...
DM DM DM DM DM
EEP!
DOOM

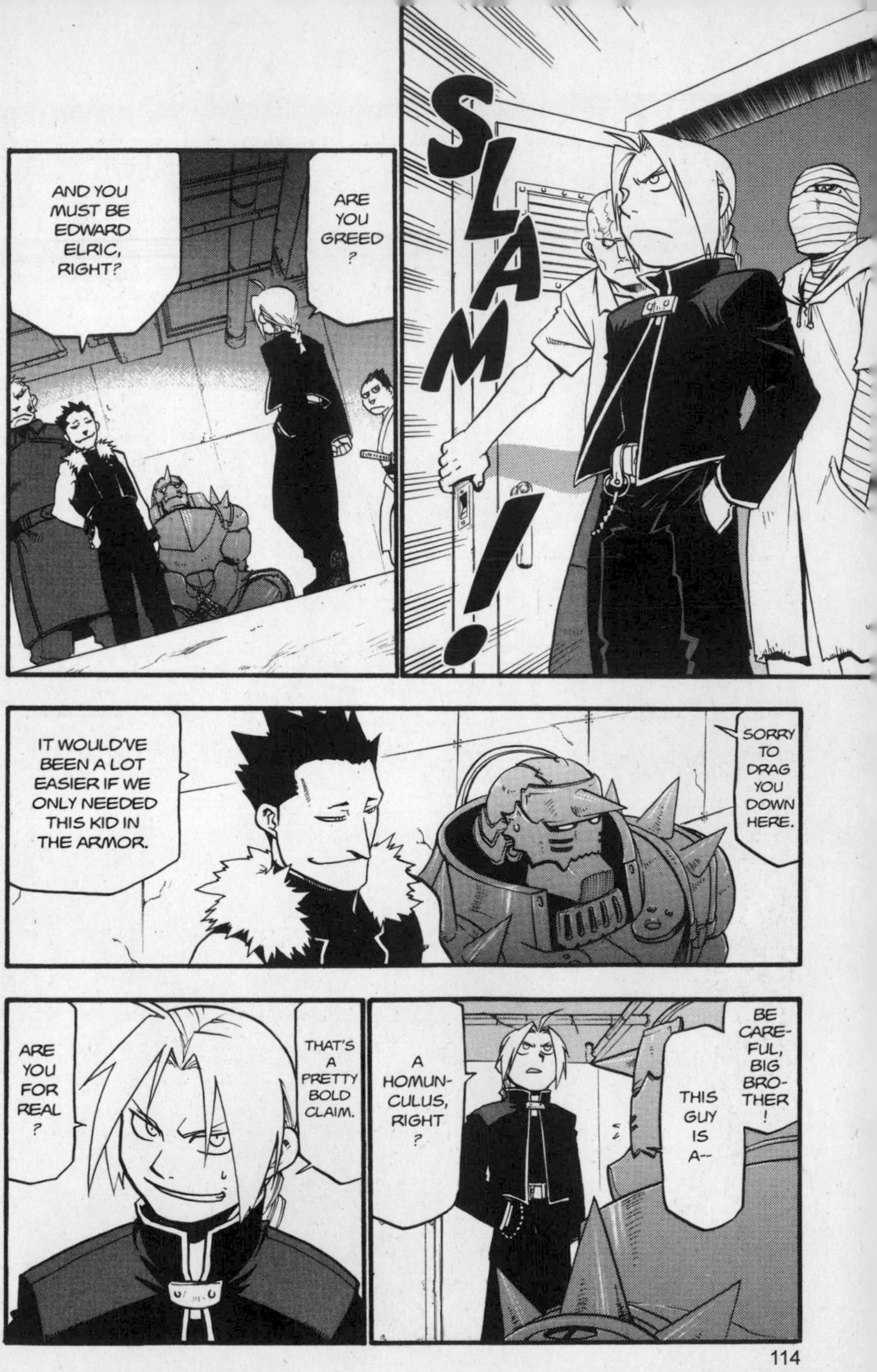
SLAM!
ARE YOU GREED?
AND YOU MUST BE EDWARD ELRIC, RIGHT?
SORRY TO DRAG YOU DOWN HERE.
IT WOULD'VE BEEN A LOT EASIER IF WE ONLY NEEDED THIS KID IN THE ARMOR.
BE CAREFUL, BIG BROTHER!
THIS GUY IS A--
A HOMUNCULUS, RIGHT?
THAT'S A PRETTY BOLD CLAIM.
ARE YOU FOR REAL?

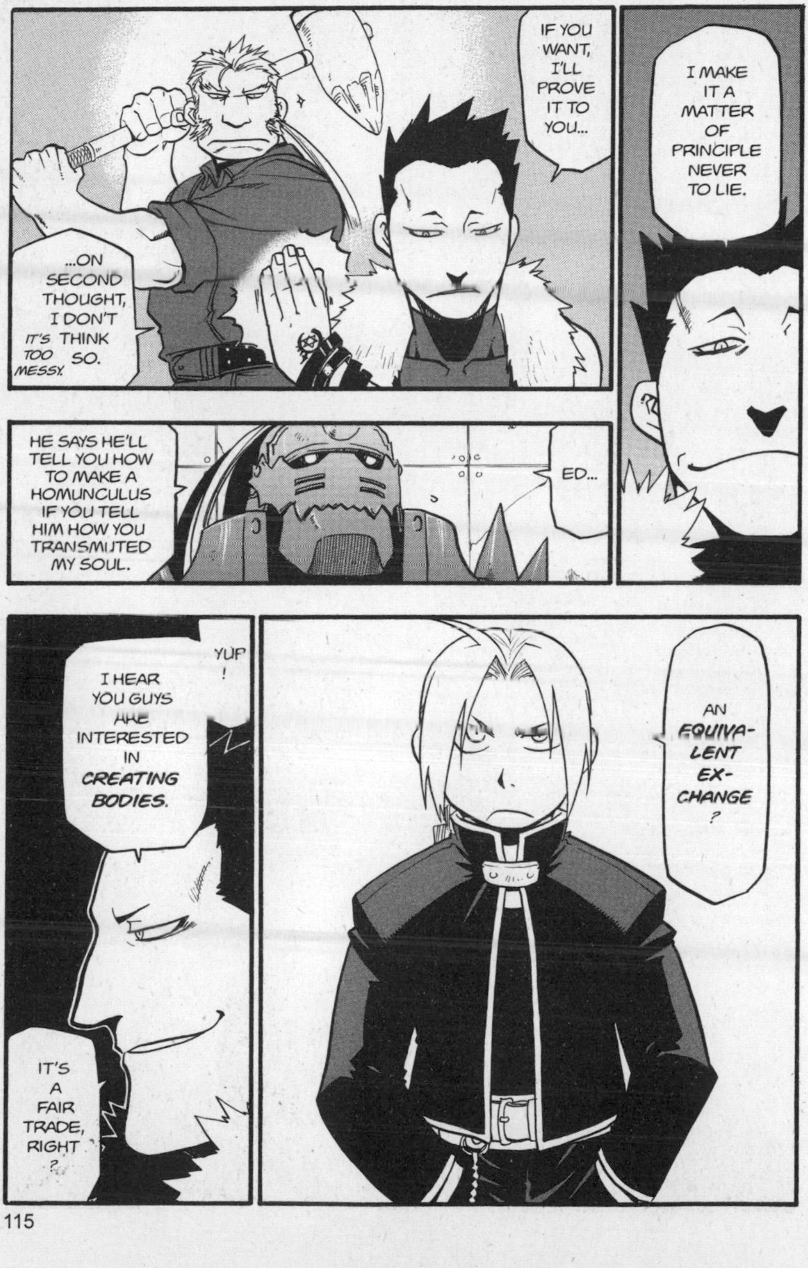
I MAKE IT A MATTER OF PRINCIPLE NEVER TO LIE.
IF YOU WANT, I'LL PROVE IT TO YOU...
...ON SECOND THOUGHT, I DON'T THINK SO.
IT'S TOO MESSY.
ED...
HE SAYS HE'LL TELL YOU HOW TO MAKE A HOMUNCULUS IF YOU TELL HIM HOW YOU TRANSMUTED MY SOUL.
AN EQUIVALENT EXCHANGE?
YUP!
I HEAR YOU GUYS ARE INTERESTED IN CREATING BODIES.
IT'S A FAIR TRADE, RIGHT?

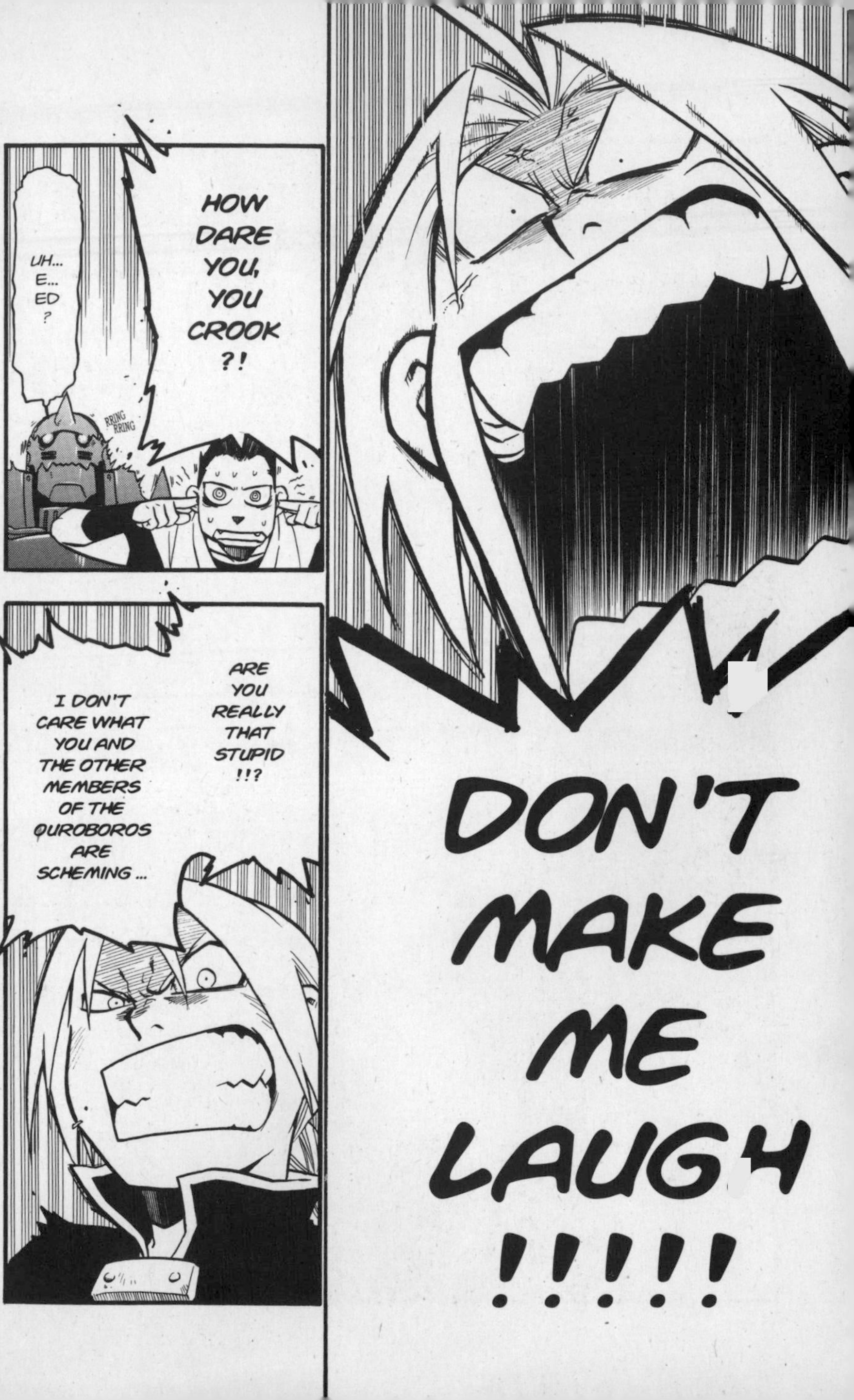
DON'T MAKE ME LAUGH !!!!!
HOW DARE YOU, YOU CROOK ?!
UH... E... ED ?
RRING RRING
ARE YOU REALLY THAT STUPID !!?
I DON'T CARE WHAT YOU AND THE OTHER MEMBERS OF THE OUROBOROS ARE SCHEMING ...

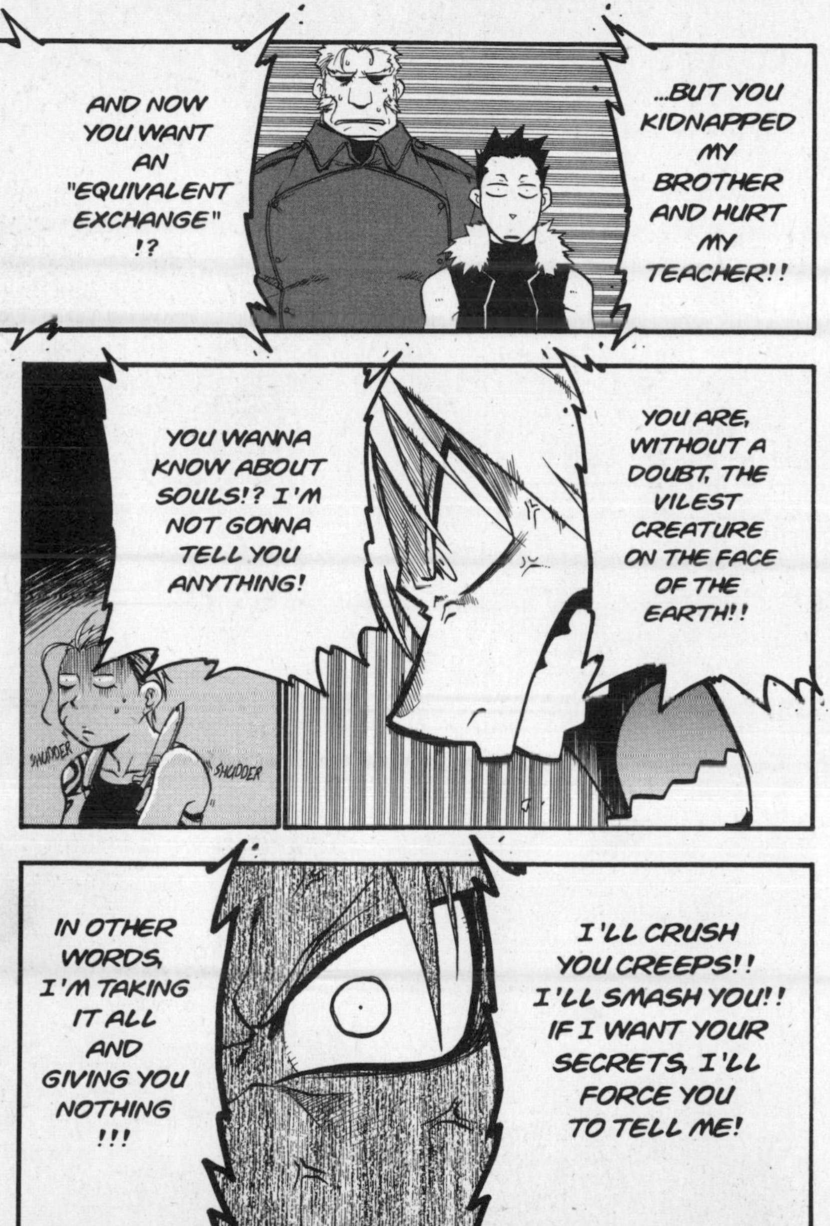
...BUT YOU KIDNAPPED MY BROTHER AND HURT MY TEACHER!!
AND NOW YOU WANT AN "EQUIVALENT EXCHANGE" !?
YOU ARE, WITHOUT A DOUBT, THE VILEST CREATURE ON THE FACE OF THE EARTH!!
YOU WANNA KNOW ABOUT SOULS!? I'M NOT GONNA TELL YOU ANYTHING!
SHUDDER
SHUDDER
I'LL CRUSH YOU CREEPS!! I'LL SMASH YOU!! IF I WANT YOUR SECRETS, I'LL FORCE YOU TO TELL ME!
IN OTHER WORDS, I'M TAKING IT ALL AND GIVING YOU NOTHING !!!

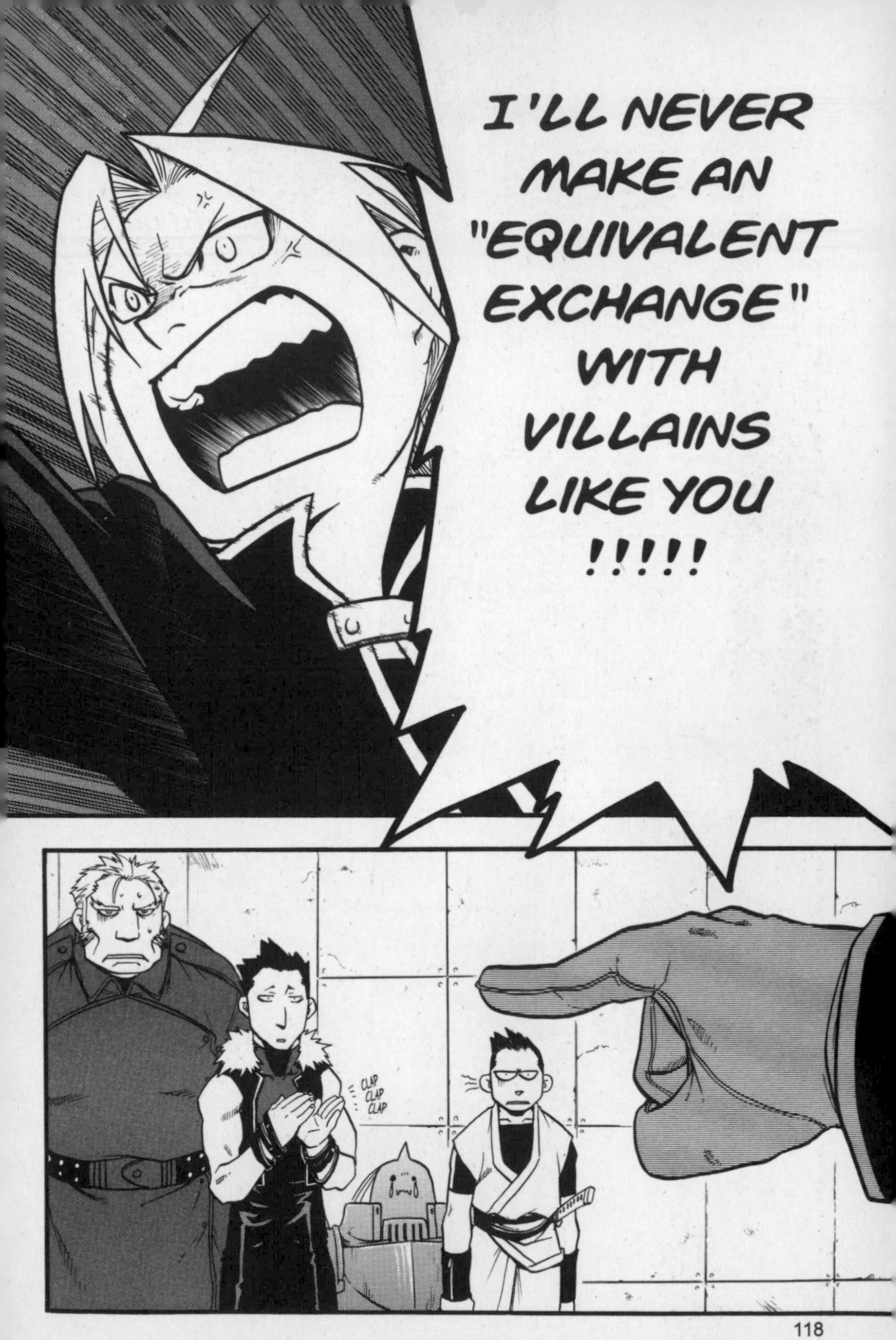
I'LL NEVER MAKE AN "EQUIVALENT EXCHANGE" WITH VILLAINS LIKE YOU !!!!!
CLAP CLAP CLAP

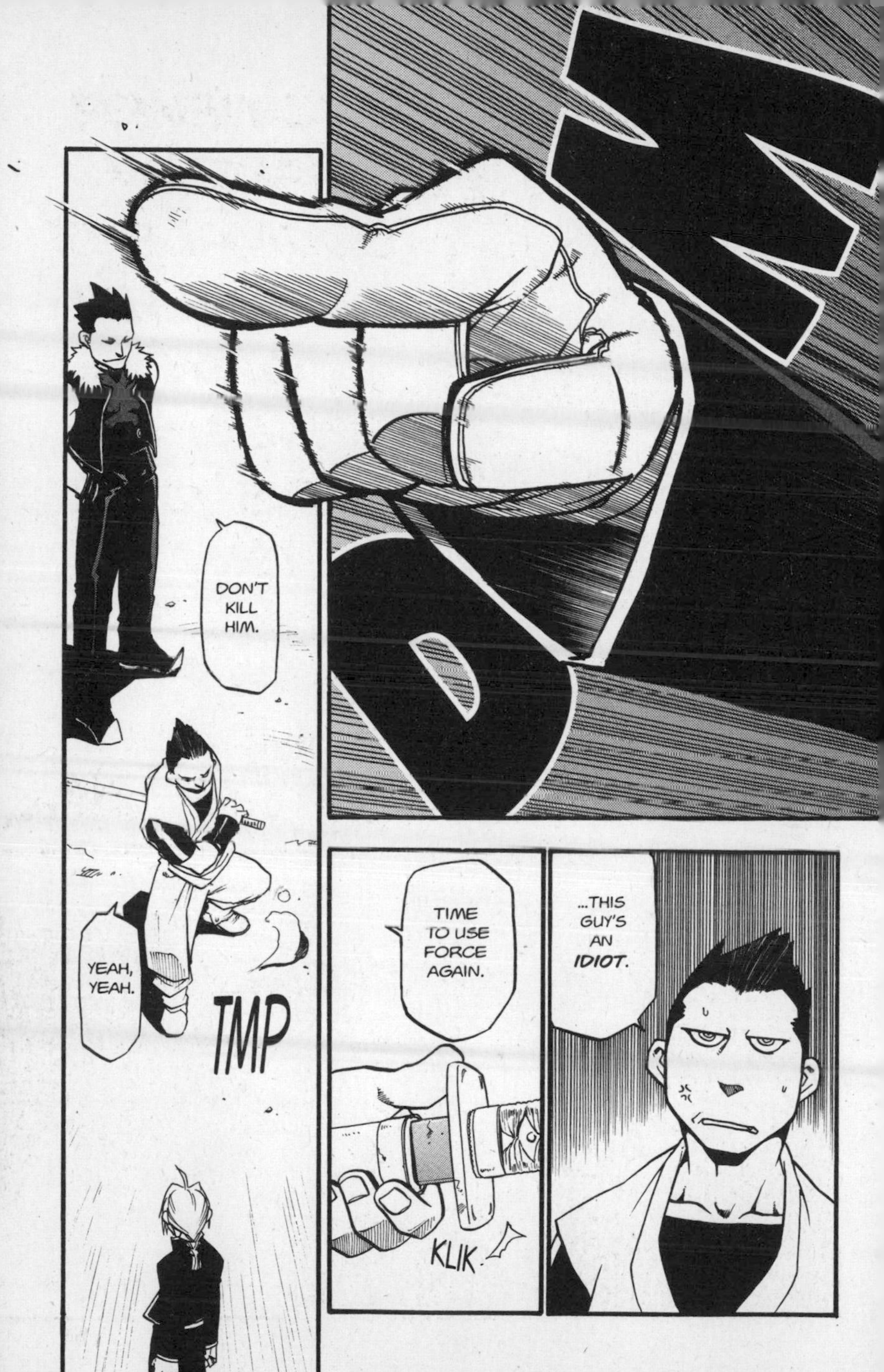
...THIS GUY'S AN IDIOT.
TIME TO USE FORCE AGAIN.
KLIK
DON'T KILL HIM.
YEAH, YEAH.
TMP

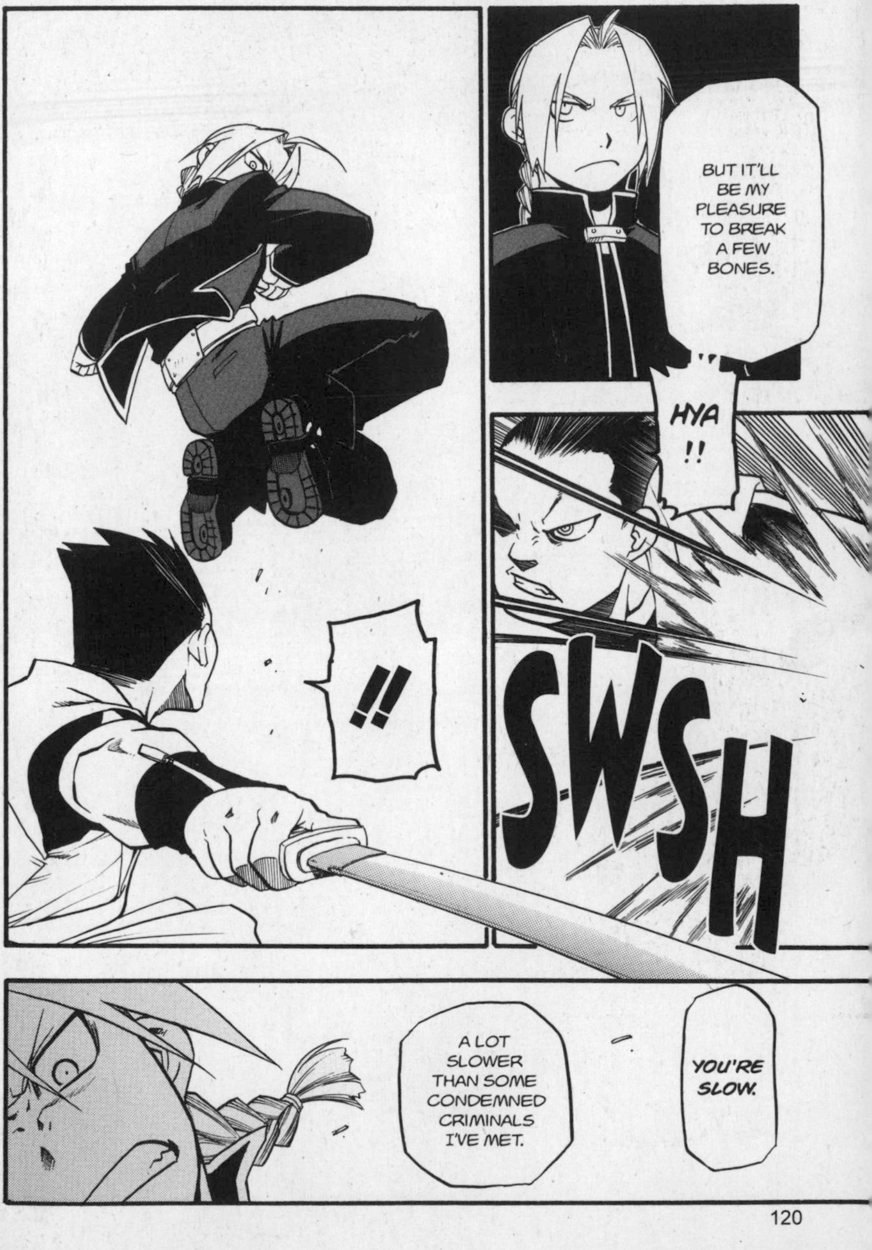
BUT IT'LL BE MY PLEASURE TO BREAK A FEW BONES.
HYA !!
SWSH
!!
YOU'RE SLOW.
A LOT SLOWER THAN SOME CONDEMNED CRIMINALS I'VE MET.

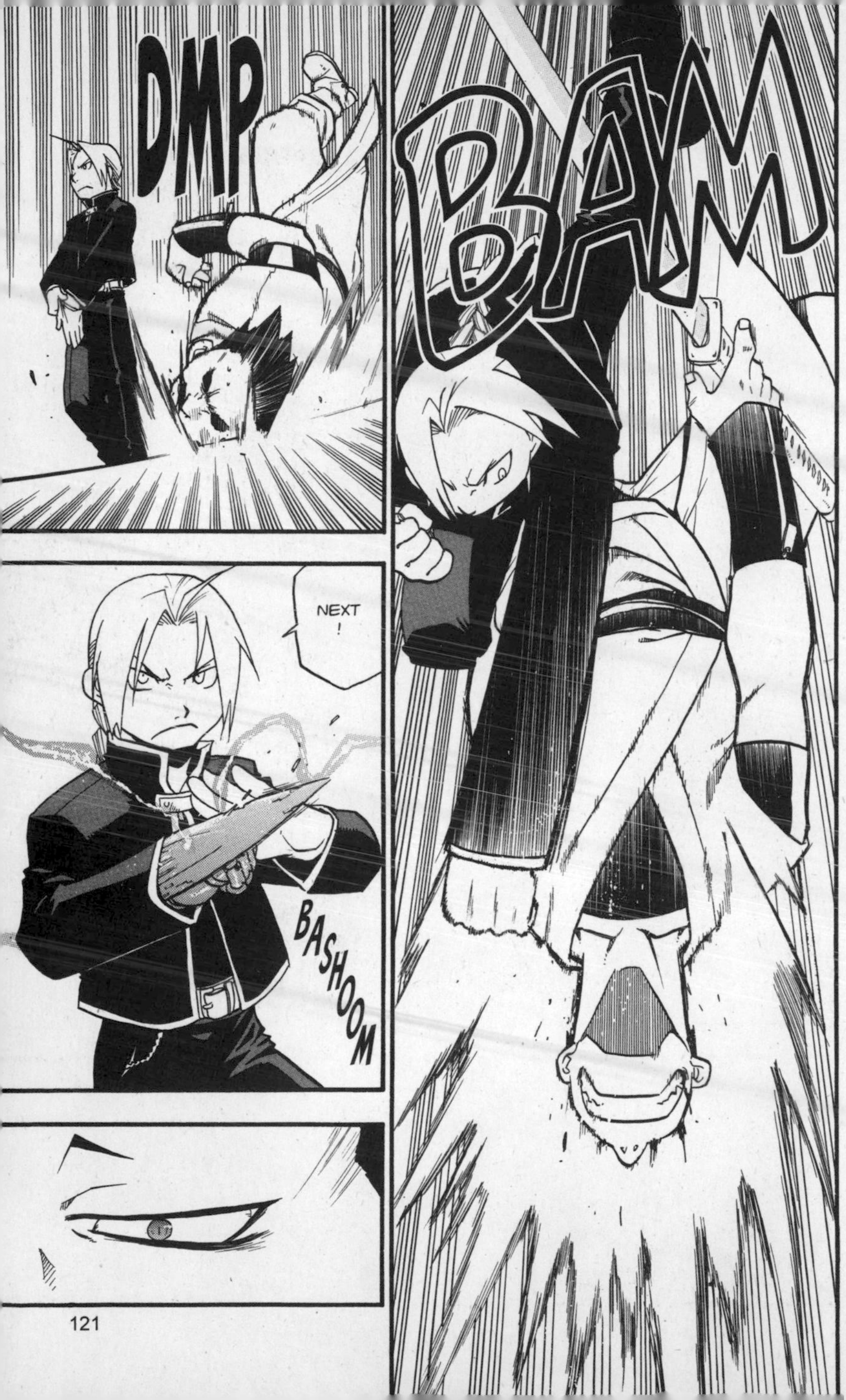
BAM
BAM
DMP
NEXT!
BASHOOM

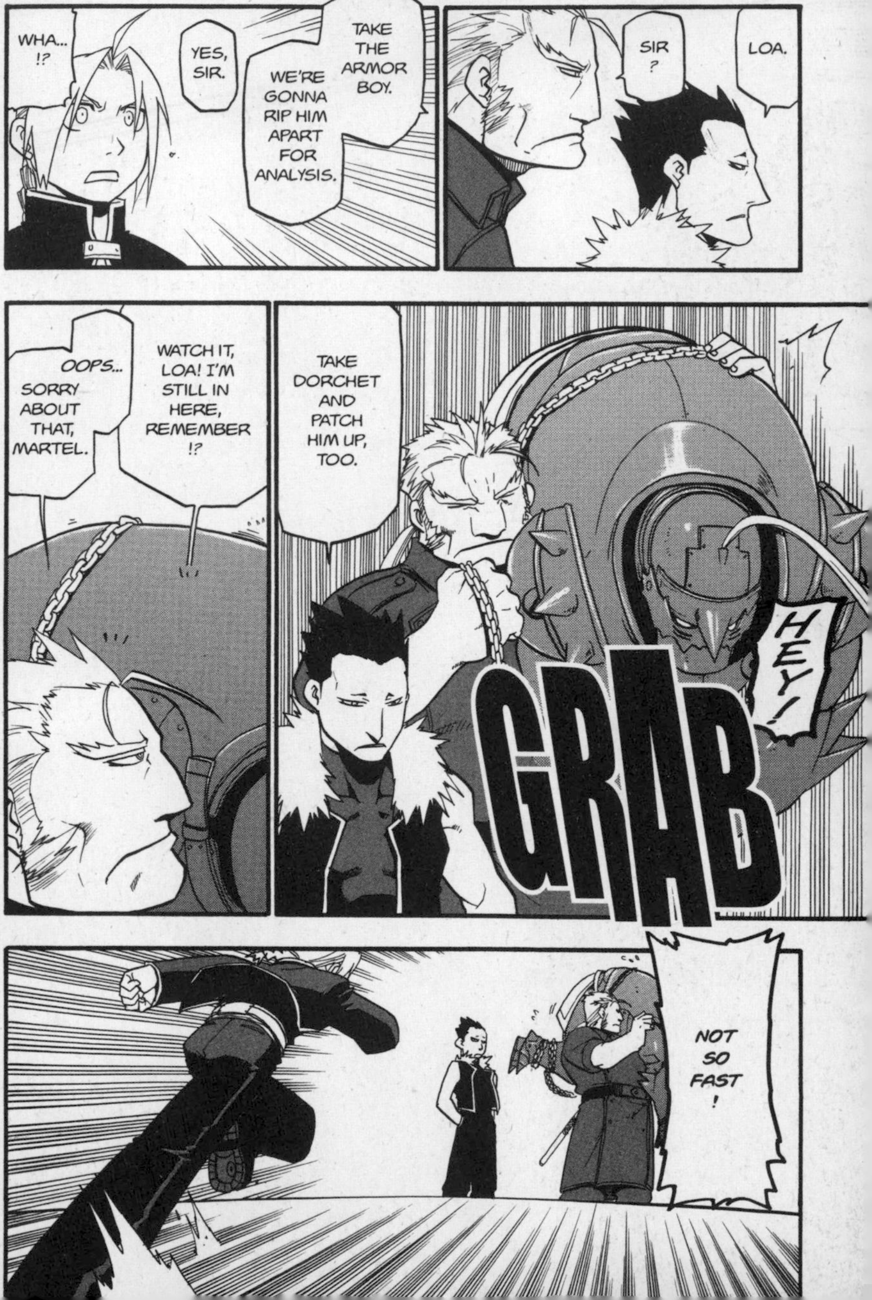
LOA.
SIR?
TAKE THE ARMOR BOY.
WE'RE GONNA RIP HIM APART FOR ANALYSIS.
YES, SIR.
WHA...!?
TAKE DORCHET AND PATCH HIM UP, TOO.
HEY!
GRAB
WATCH IT, LOA! I'M STILL IN HERE, REMEMBER!?
OOPS... SORRY ABOUT THAT, MARTEL.
NOT SO FAST!

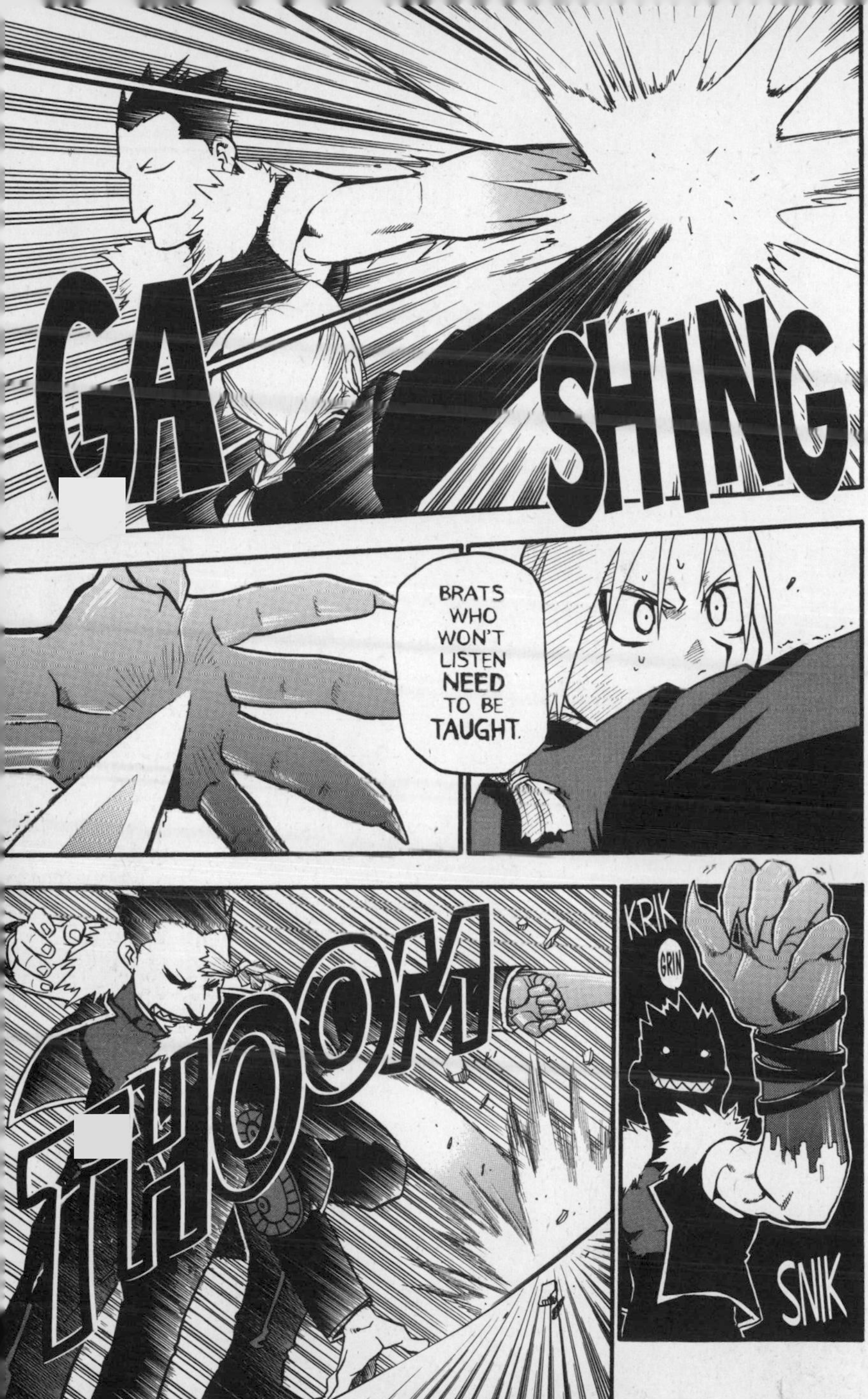
GA SHING
BRATS WHO WON'T LISTEN NEED TO BE TAUGHT.
KRIK
GRIN
SNIK
THOOM

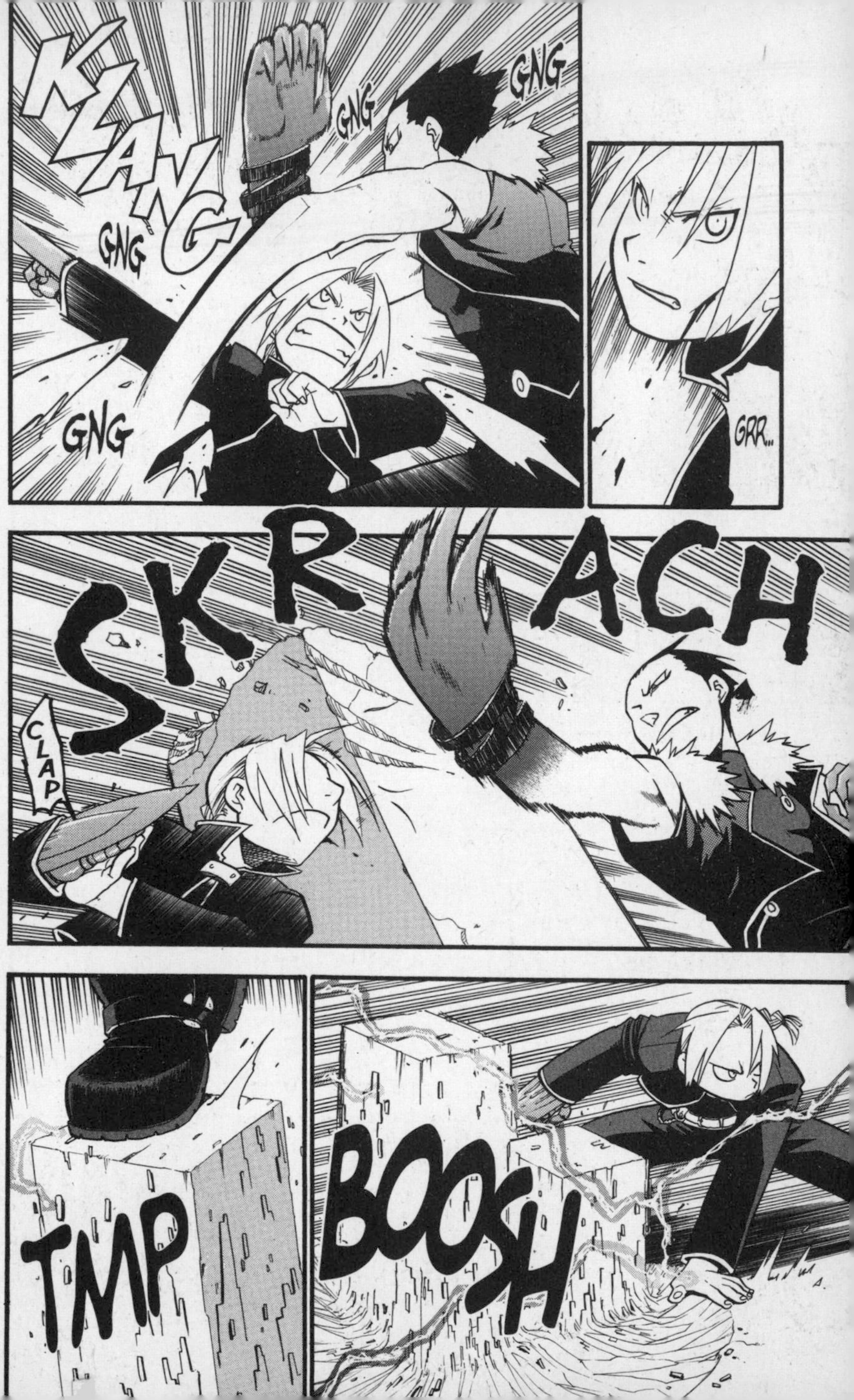
GRR...
GNG
GNG
KLANG
GNG
GNG
SKRACH
CLAP
BOOSH
TMP

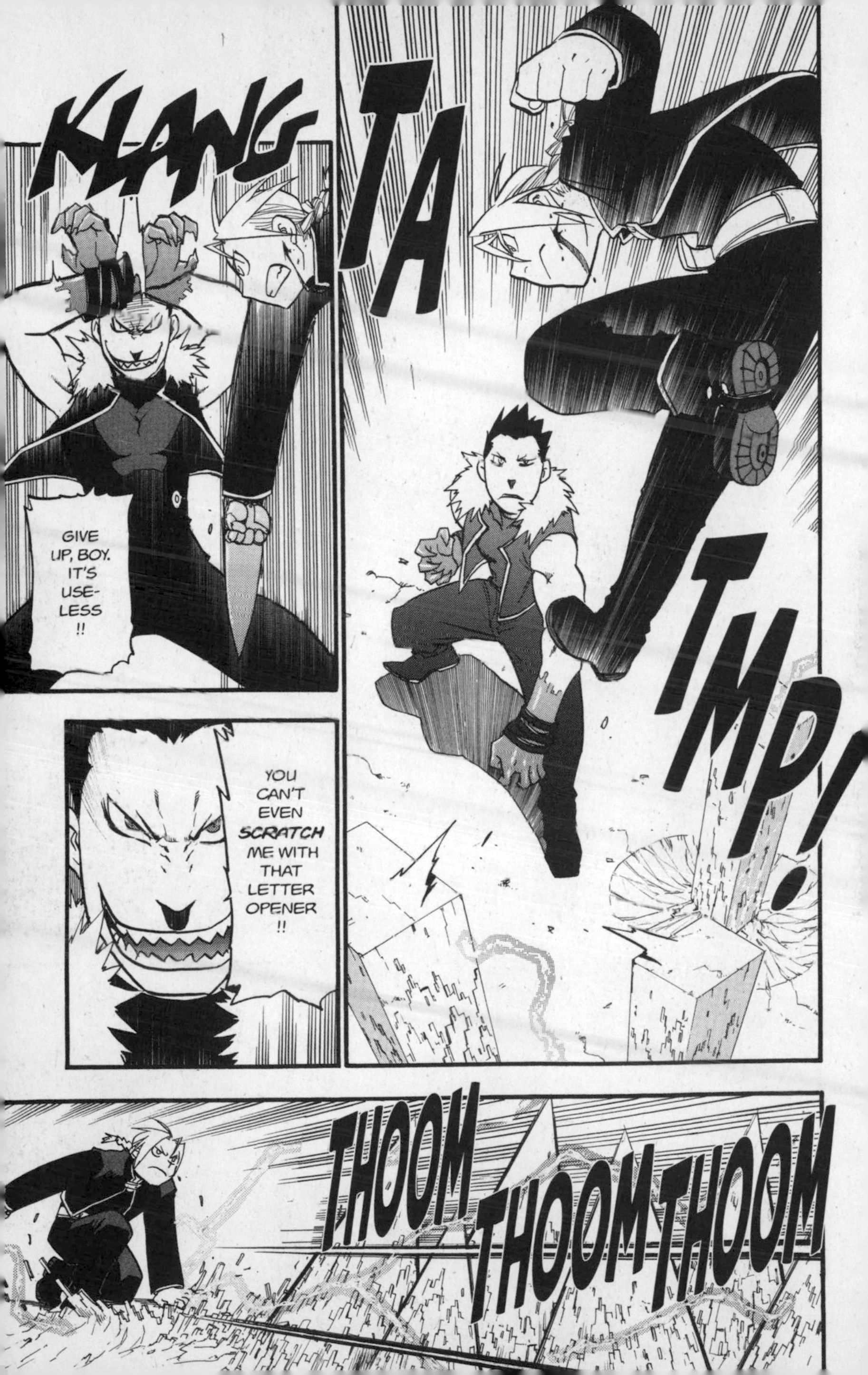
TA
TMP!
KLANG
GIVE UP, BOY. IT'S USELESS!!
YOU CAN'T EVEN *SCRATCH* ME WITH THAT LETTER OPENER!!
THOOM THOOM THOOM

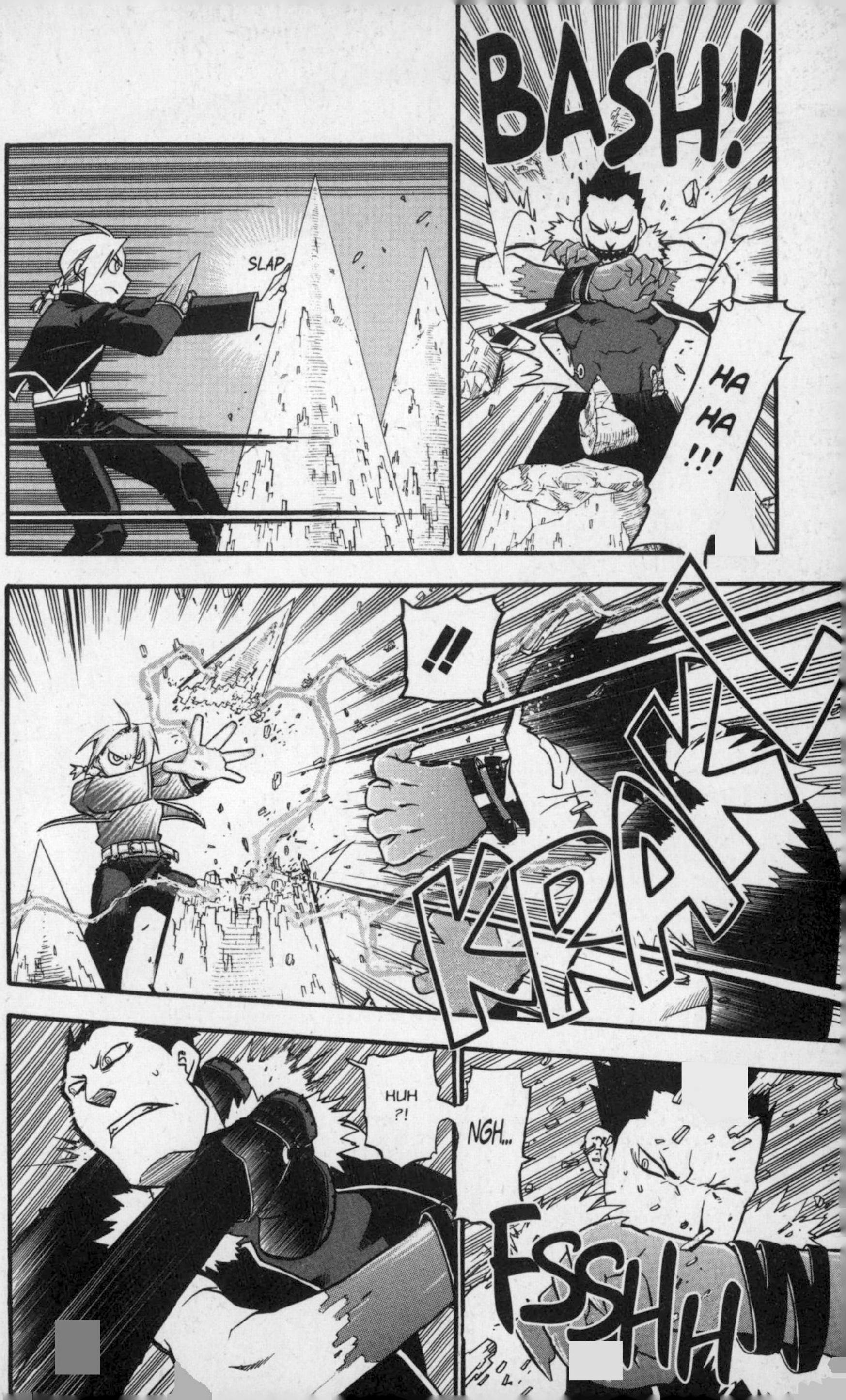
BASH!
HA HA !!!
SLAP
!!
KRAK
NGH...
FSSHH
HUH ?!

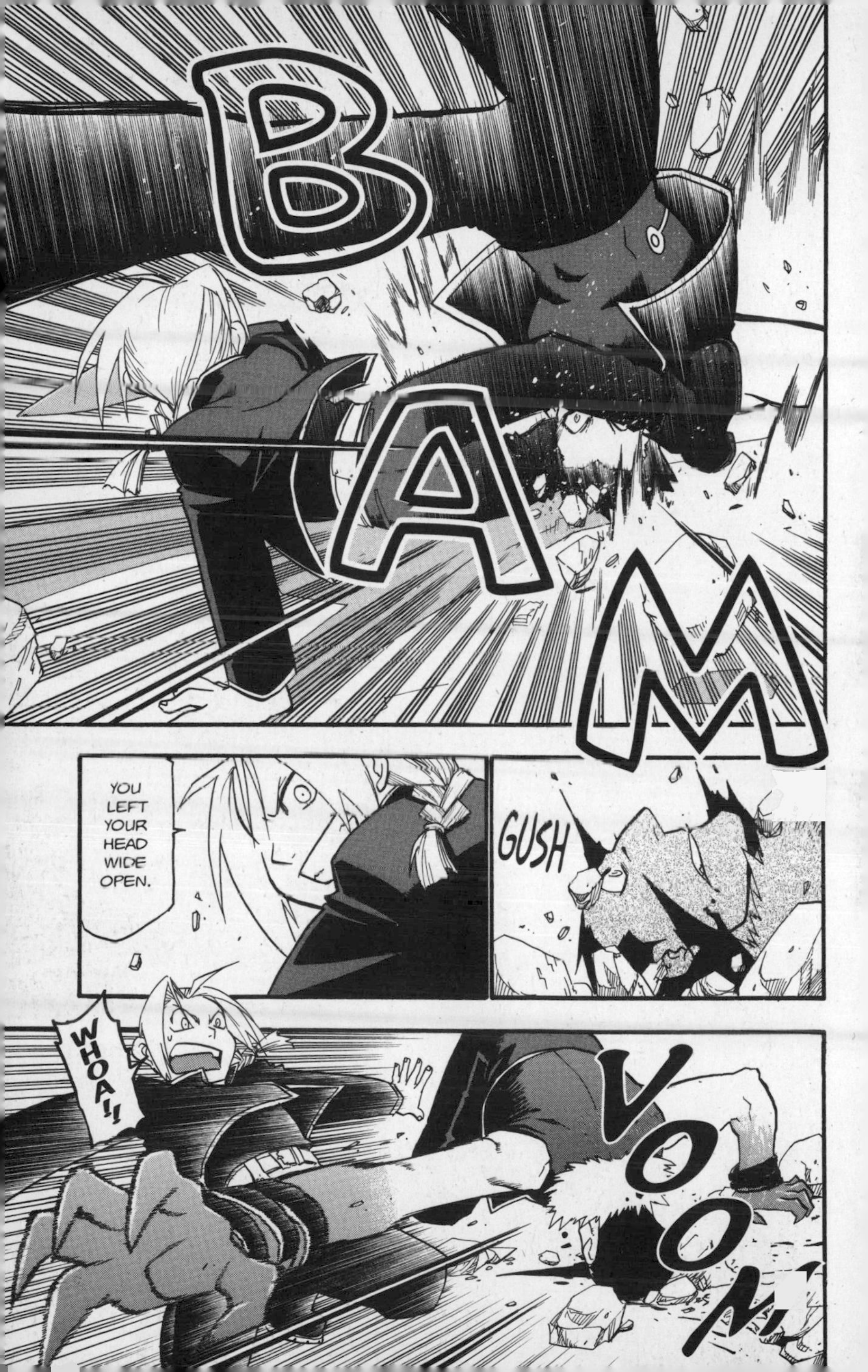
BAM
GUSH
YOU LEFT YOUR HEAD WIDE OPEN.
VOOM
WHOA!!

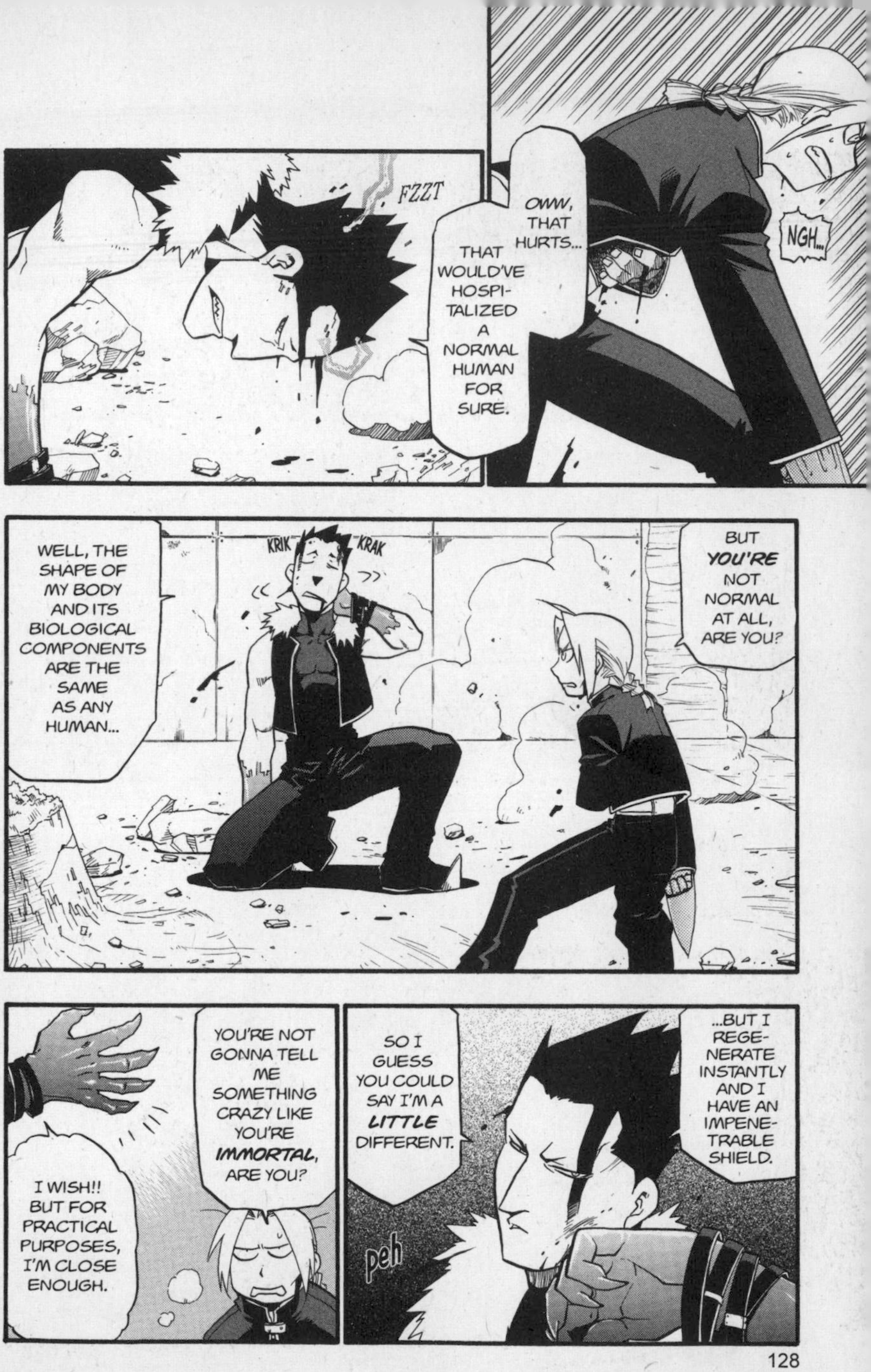
NGH...
FZZT
OWW, THAT HURTS... THAT WOULD'VE HOSPITALIZED A NORMAL HUMAN FOR SURE.
BUT *YOU'RE* NOT NORMAL AT ALL, ARE YOU?
KRIK
KRAK
WELL, THE SHAPE OF MY BODY AND ITS BIOLOGICAL COMPONENTS ARE THE SAME AS ANY HUMAN...
...BUT I REGENERATE INSTANTLY AND I HAVE AN IMPENETRABLE SHIELD.
SO I GUESS YOU COULD SAY I'M A *LITTLE* DIFFERENT.
peh
YOU'RE NOT GONNA TELL ME SOMETHING CRAZY LIKE YOU'RE *IMMORTAL*, ARE YOU?
I WISH!! BUT FOR PRACTICAL PURPOSES, I'M CLOSE ENOUGH.

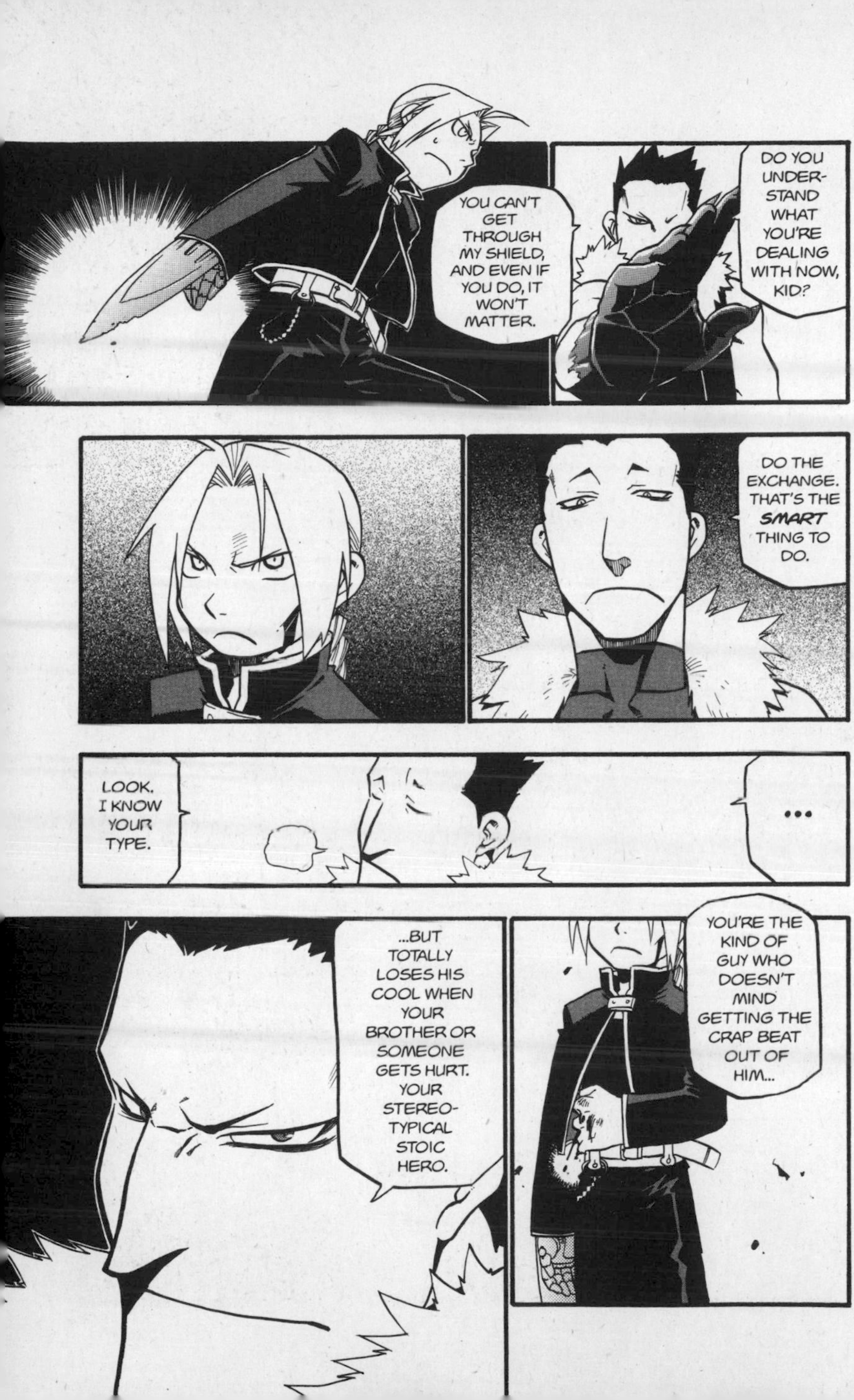
DO YOU UNDERSTAND WHAT YOU'RE DEALING WITH NOW, KID?
YOU CAN'T GET THROUGH MY SHIELD, AND EVEN IF YOU DO, IT WON'T MATTER.
DO THE EXCHANGE. THAT'S THE **SMART** THING TO DO.
...
LOOK. I KNOW YOUR TYPE.
YOU'RE THE KIND OF GUY WHO DOESN'T MIND GETTING THE CRAP BEAT OUT OF HIM...
...BUT TOTALLY LOSES HIS COOL WHEN YOUR BROTHER OR SOMEONE GETS HURT. YOUR STEREOTYPICAL STOIC HERO.

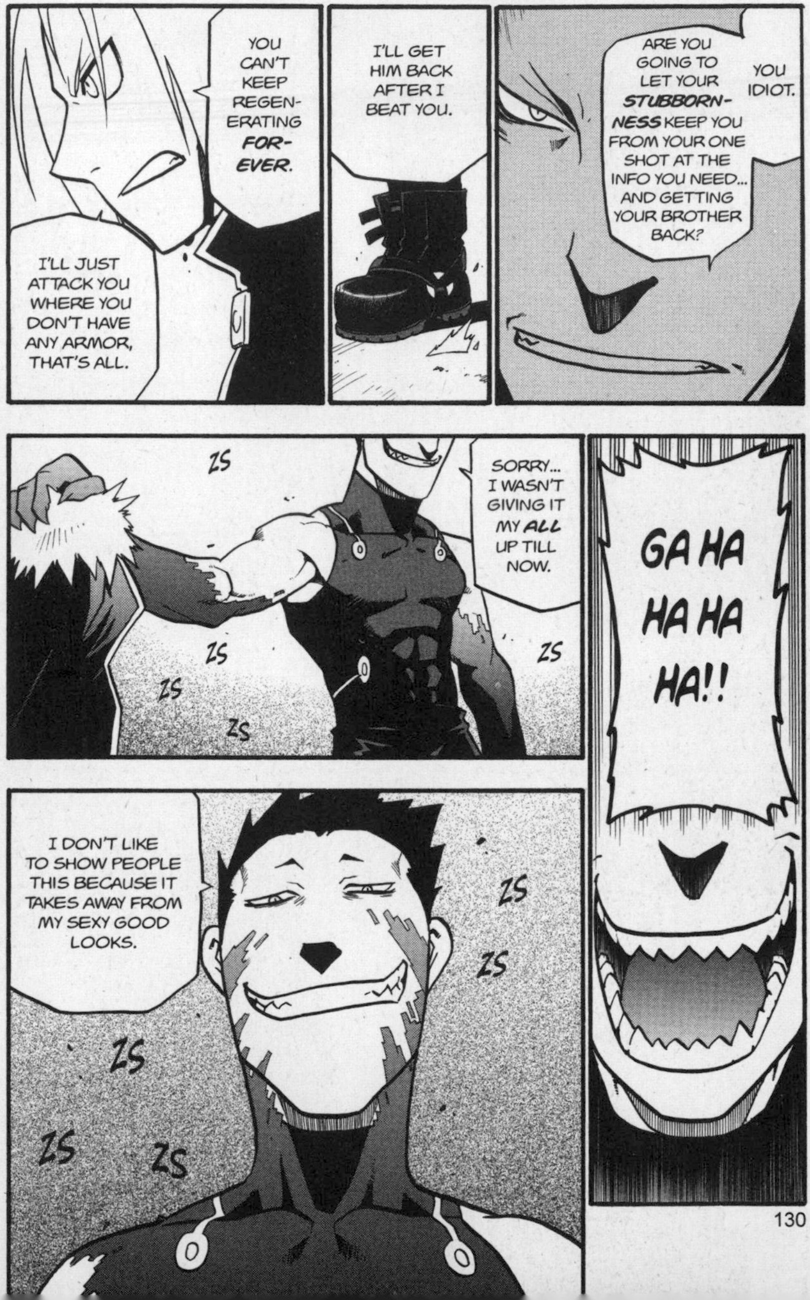
ARE YOU GOING TO LET YOUR STUBBORNNESS KEEP YOU FROM YOUR ONE SHOT AT THE INFO YOU NEED... AND GETTING YOUR BROTHER BACK?
YOU IDIOT.
I'LL GET HIM BACK AFTER I BEAT YOU.
YOU CAN'T KEEP REGENERATING FOREVER.
I'LL JUST ATTACK YOU WHERE YOU DON'T HAVE ANY ARMOR, THAT'S ALL.
GA HA HA HA HA!!
SORRY... I WASN'T GIVING IT MY ALL UP TILL NOW.
ZS
ZS
ZS
ZS
ZS
I DON'T LIKE TO SHOW PEOPLE THIS BECAUSE IT TAKES AWAY FROM MY SEXY GOOD LOOKS.
ZS
ZS
ZS
ZS
ZS

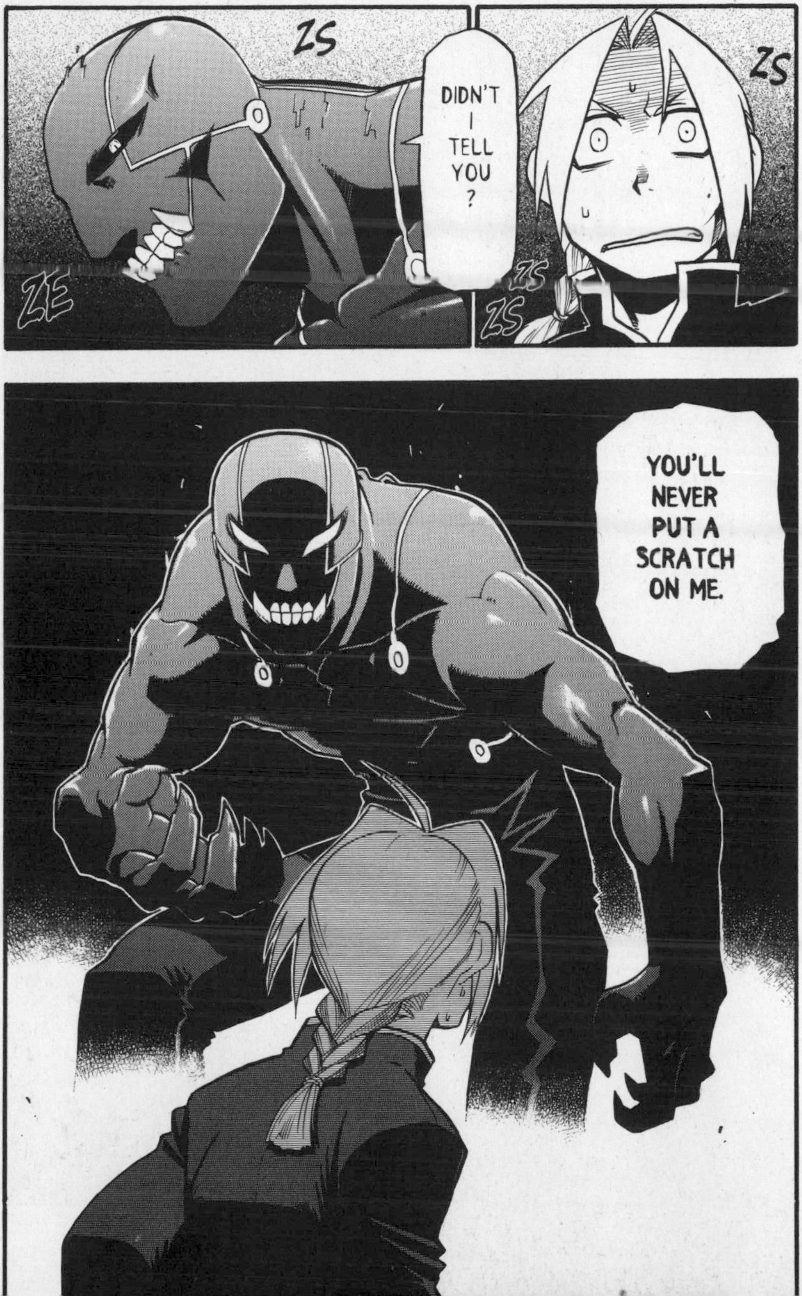
ZS
ZS
ZS
ZS
DIDN'T I TELL YOU?
ZE
YOU'LL NEVER PUT A SCRATCH ON ME.

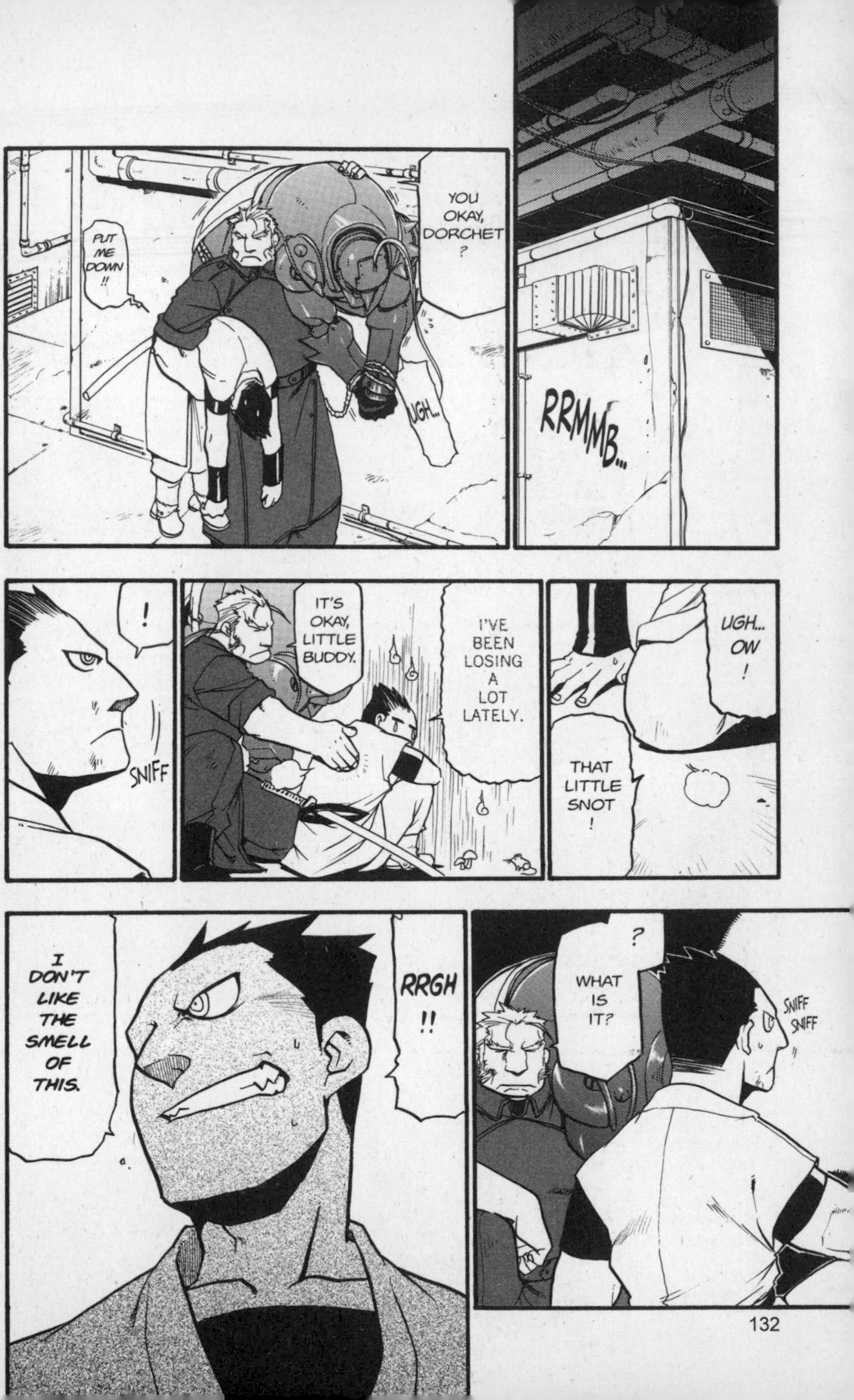
RRMMB...
YOU OKAY, DORCHET?
PUT ME DOWN!!
UGH...
UGH... OW!
THAT LITTLE SNOT!
I'VE BEEN LOSING A LOT LATELY.
IT'S OKAY, LITTLE BUDDY.
!
SNIFF
?
WHAT IS IT?
SNIFF SNIFF
RRGH!!
I DON'T LIKE THE SMELL OF THIS.

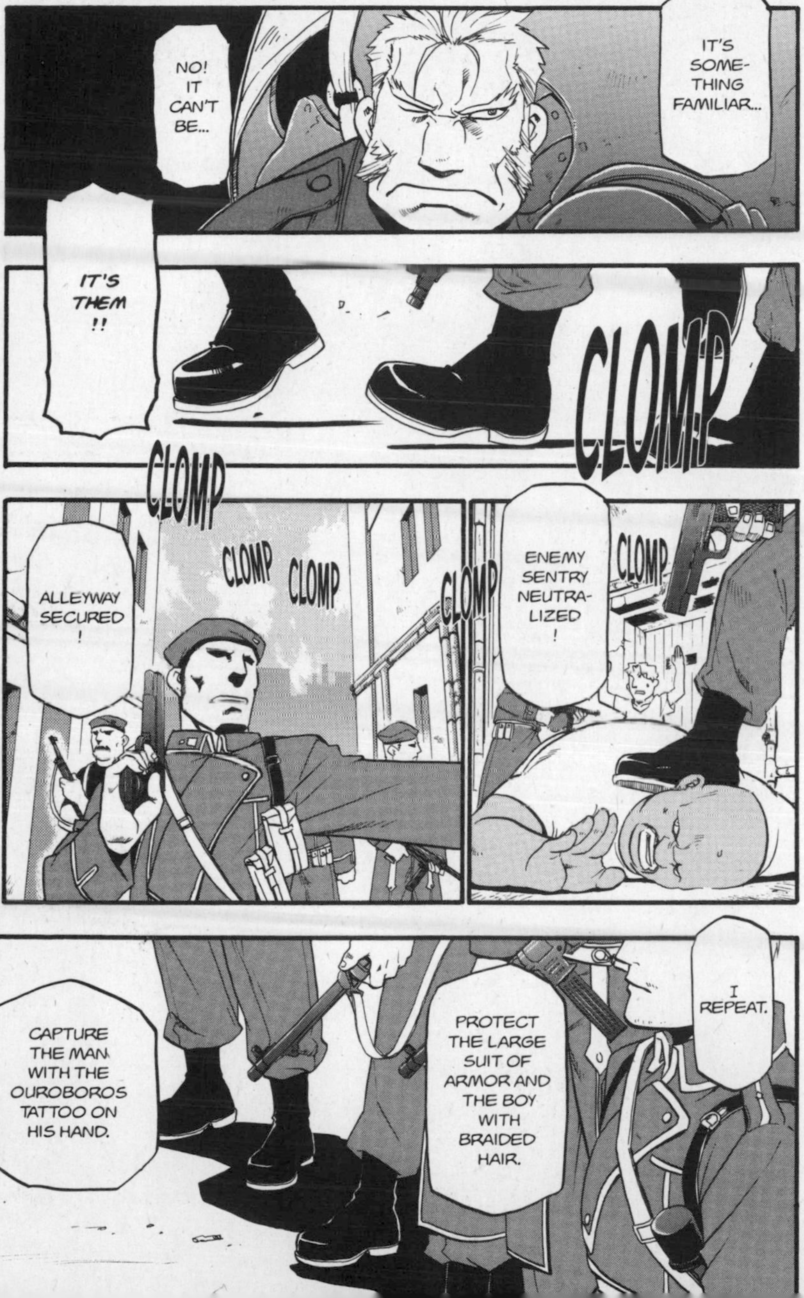
IT'S SOME-THING FAMILIAR...
NO! IT CAN'T BE...
IT'S THEM!!
CLOMP
CLOMP
CLOMP
ENEMY SENTRY NEUTRA-LIZED!
CLOMP
CLOMP
CLOMP
ALLEYWAY SECURED!
I REPEAT.
PROTECT THE LARGE SUIT OF ARMOR AND THE BOY WITH BRAIDED HAIR.
CAPTURE THE MAN WITH THE OUROBOROS TATTOO ON HIS HAND.

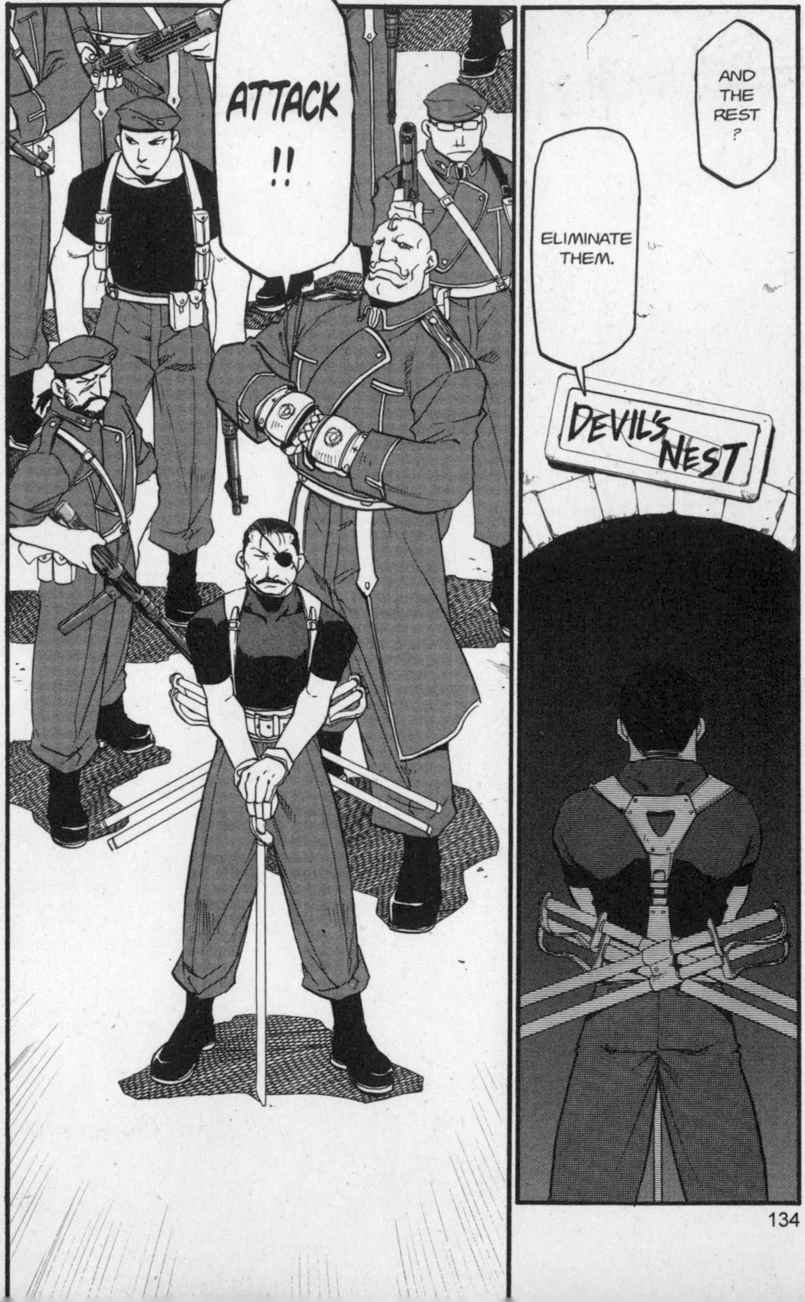
AND THE REST?
ELIMINATE THEM.
DEVIL'S NEST
ATTACK!!

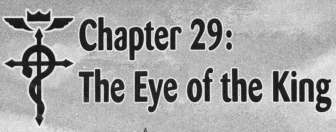

Chapter 29:
The Eye of the King

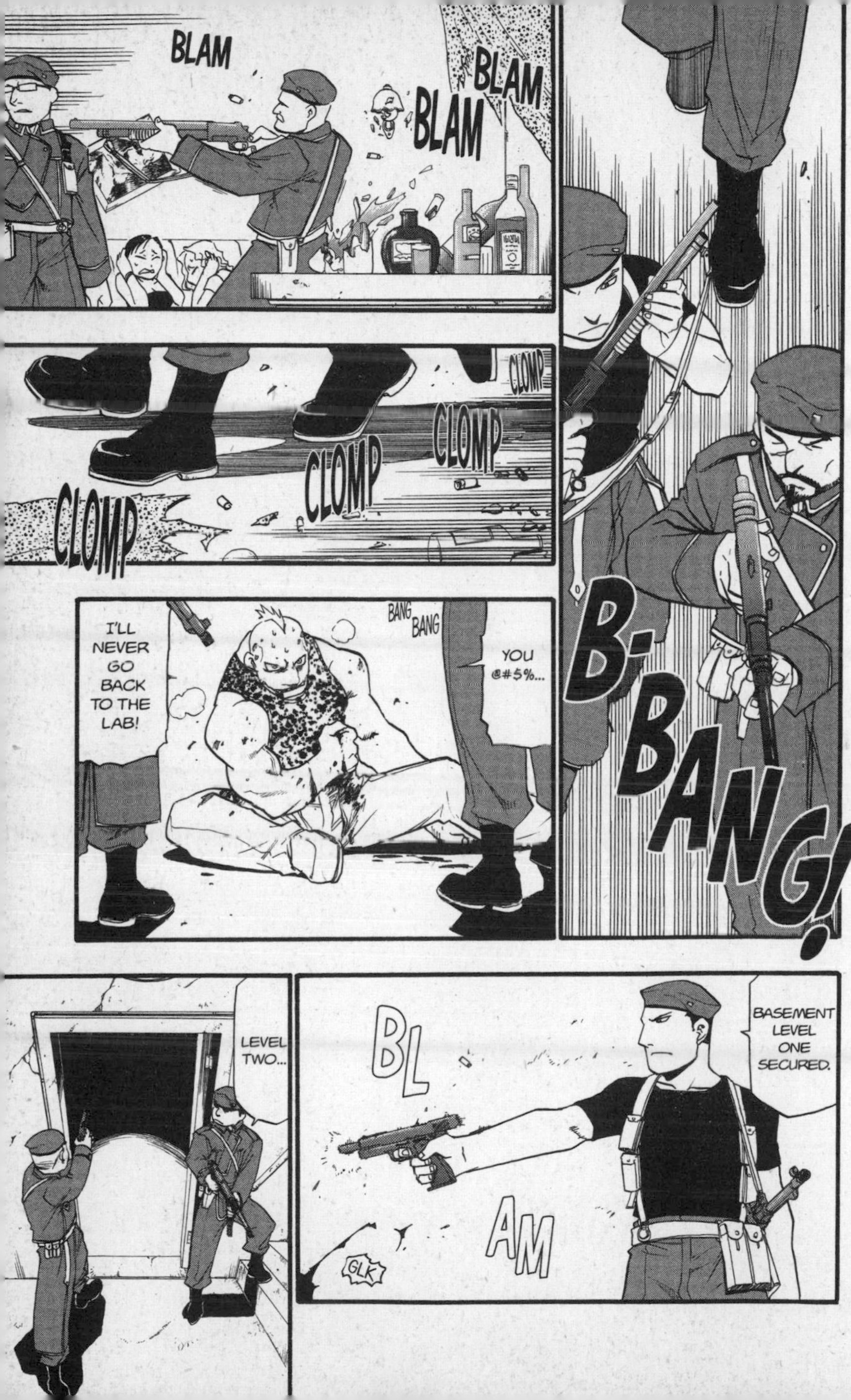
B-BANG!
BLAM
BLAM
BLAM
CLOMP
CLOMP
CLOMP
CLOMP
BANG BANG
YOU @#$%...
I'LL NEVER GO BACK TO THE LAB!
BASEMENT LEVEL ONE SECURED.
BLAM
GLK
LEVEL TWO...

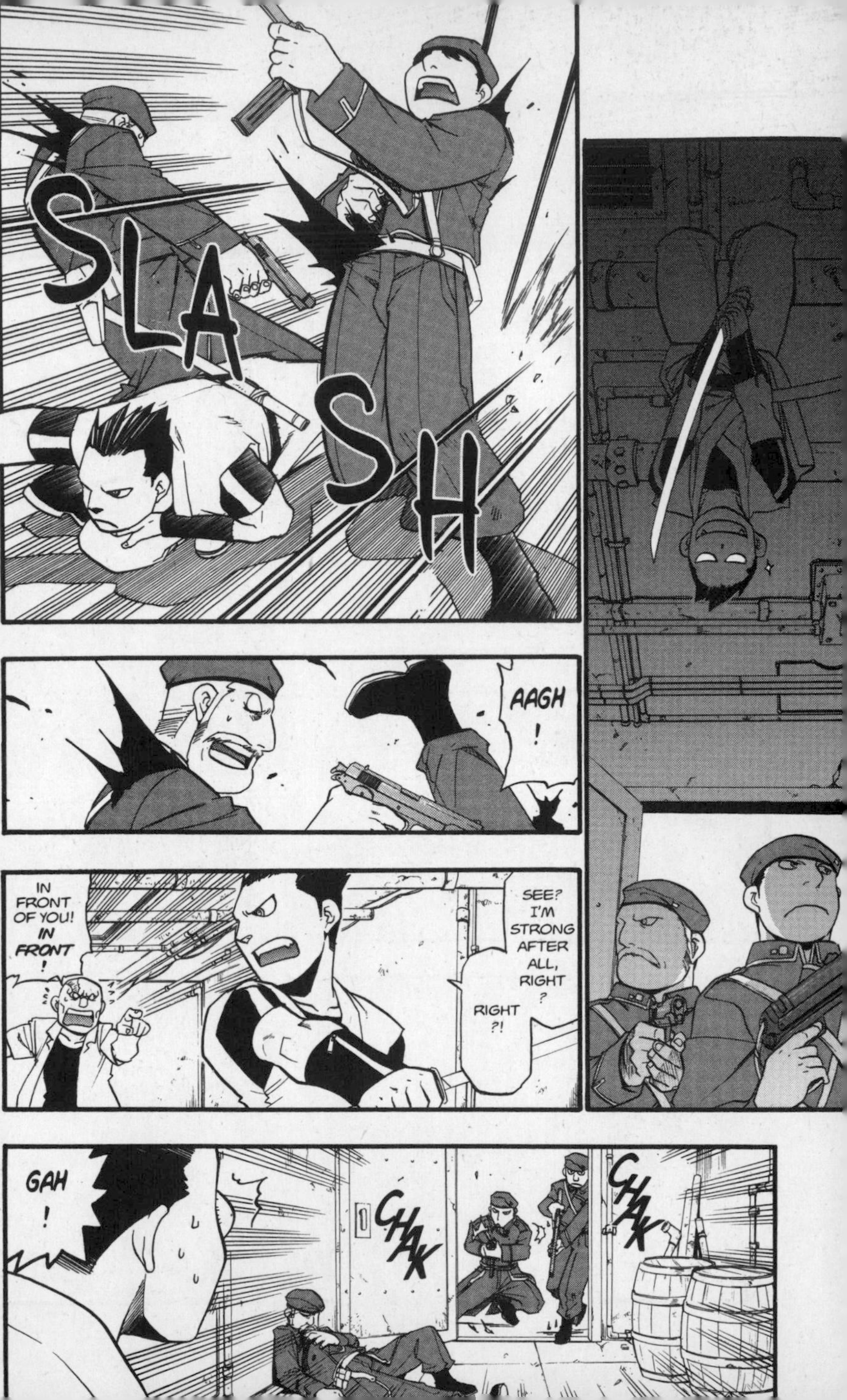
SLASH
AAGH!
SEE? I'M STRONG AFTER ALL, RIGHT?
RIGHT?!
IN FRONT OF YOU! IN FRONT!
CHAK
CHAK
GAH!

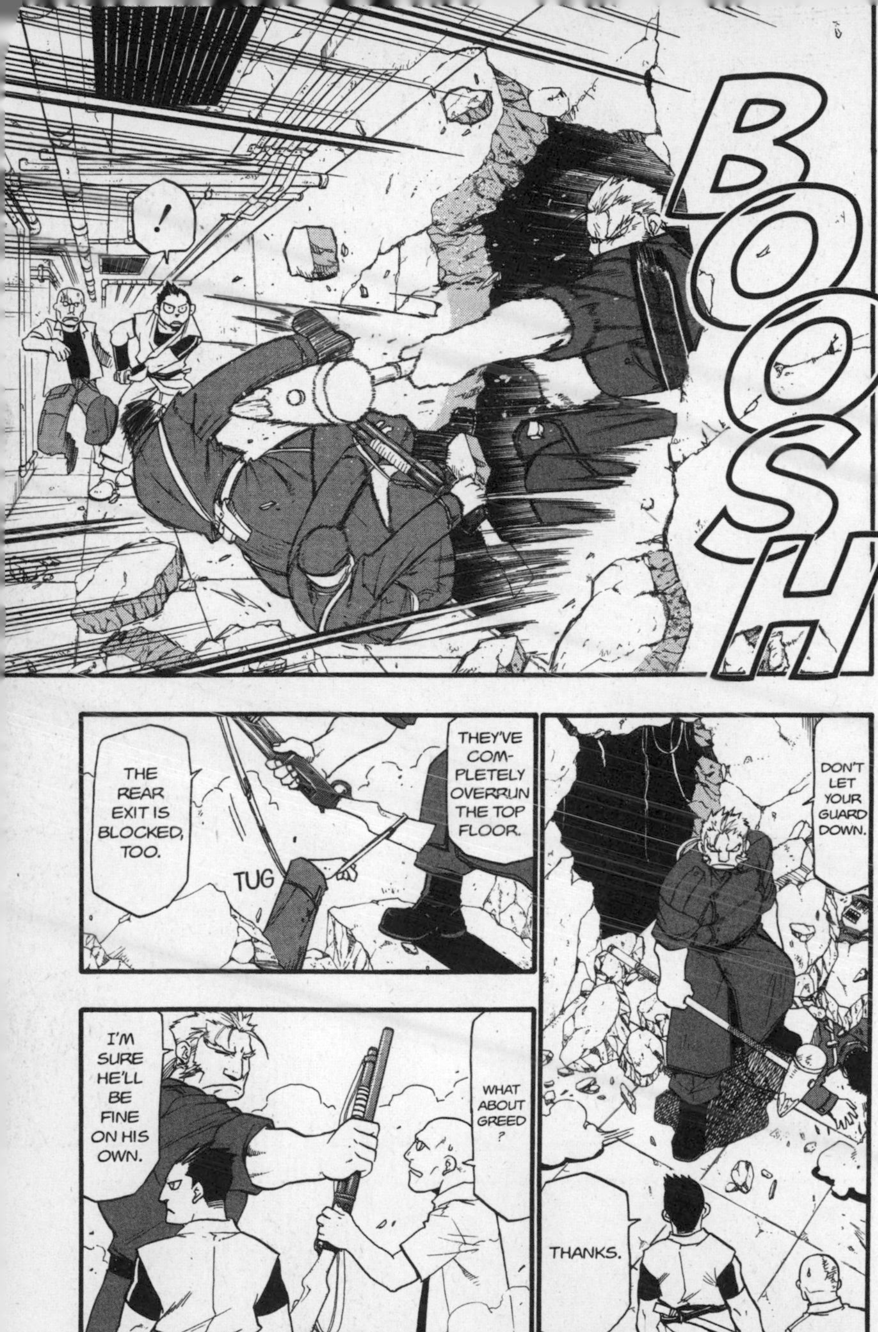
BOOOSH
!
DON'T LET YOUR GUARD DOWN.
THANKS.
THEY'VE COM-PLETELY OVERRUN THE TOP FLOOR.
THE REAR EXIT IS BLOCKED, TOO.
TUG
WHAT ABOUT GREED?
I'M SURE HE'LL BE FINE ON HIS OWN.

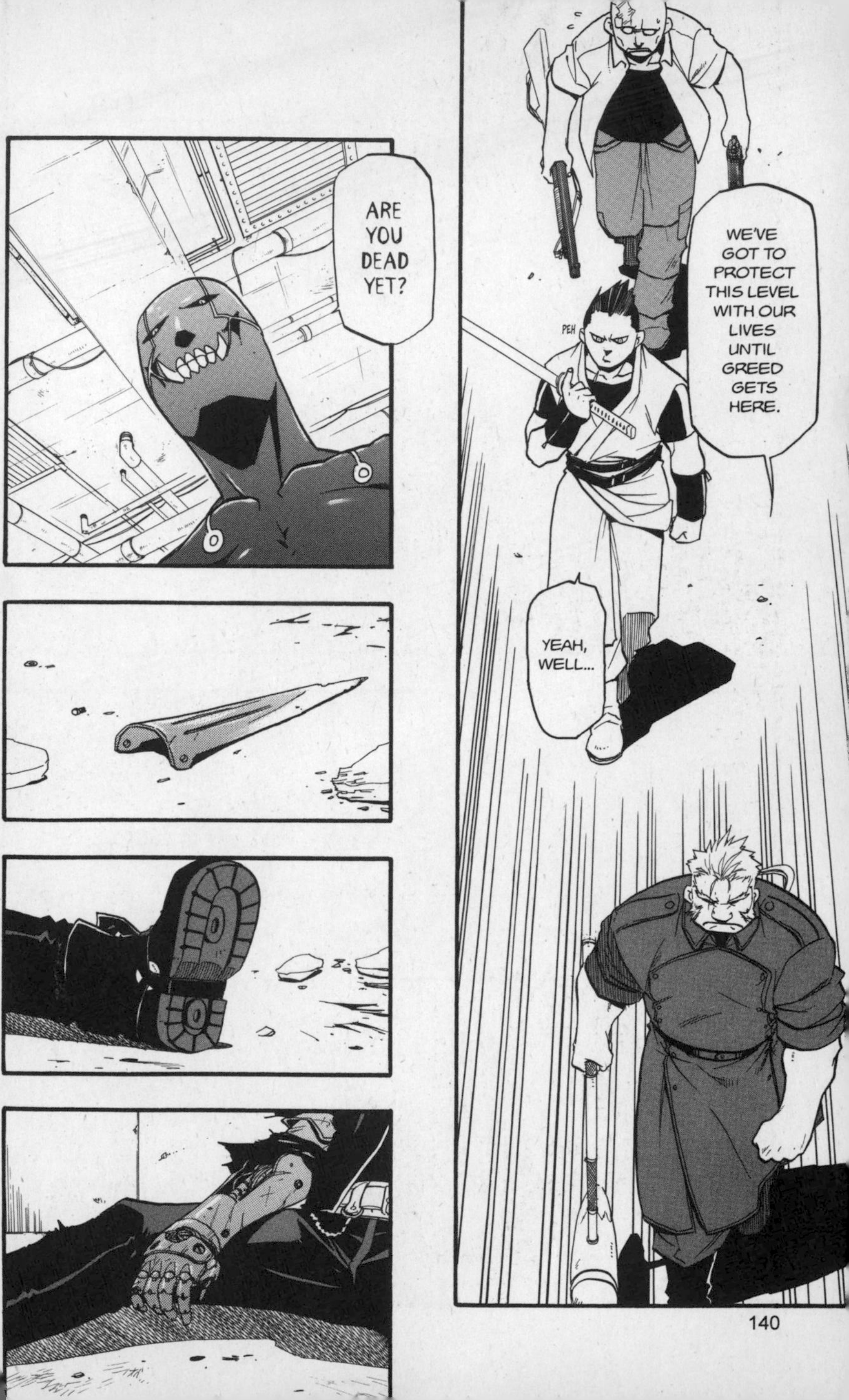
WE'VE GOT TO PROTECT THIS LEVEL WITH OUR LIVES UNTIL GREED GETS HERE.
PEH
YEAH, WELL...
ARE YOU DEAD YET?

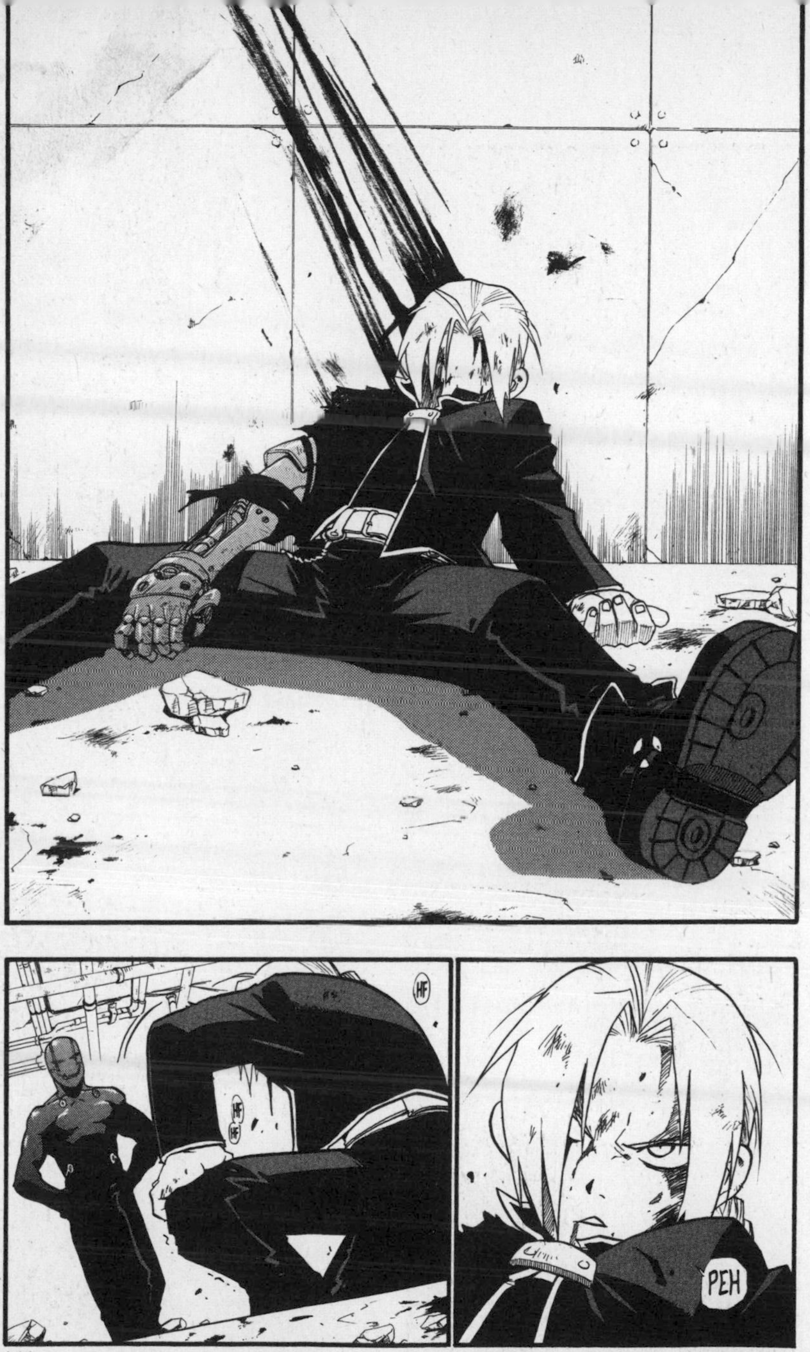
PEH
HF
HF
HF

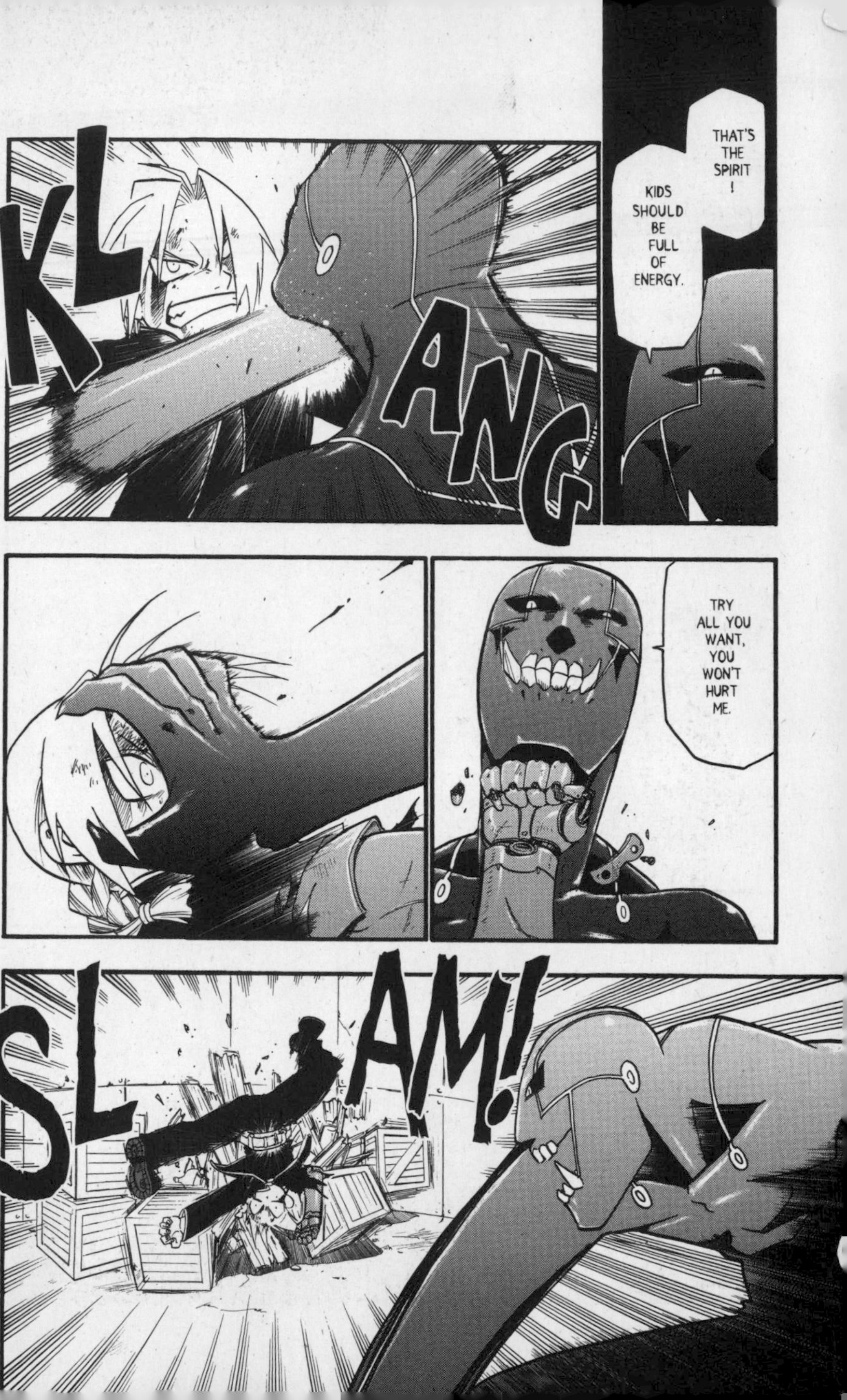
THAT'S THE SPIRIT!
KIDS SHOULD BE FULL OF ENERGY.
KLANG
TRY ALL YOU WANT, YOU WON'T HURT ME.
SLAM!

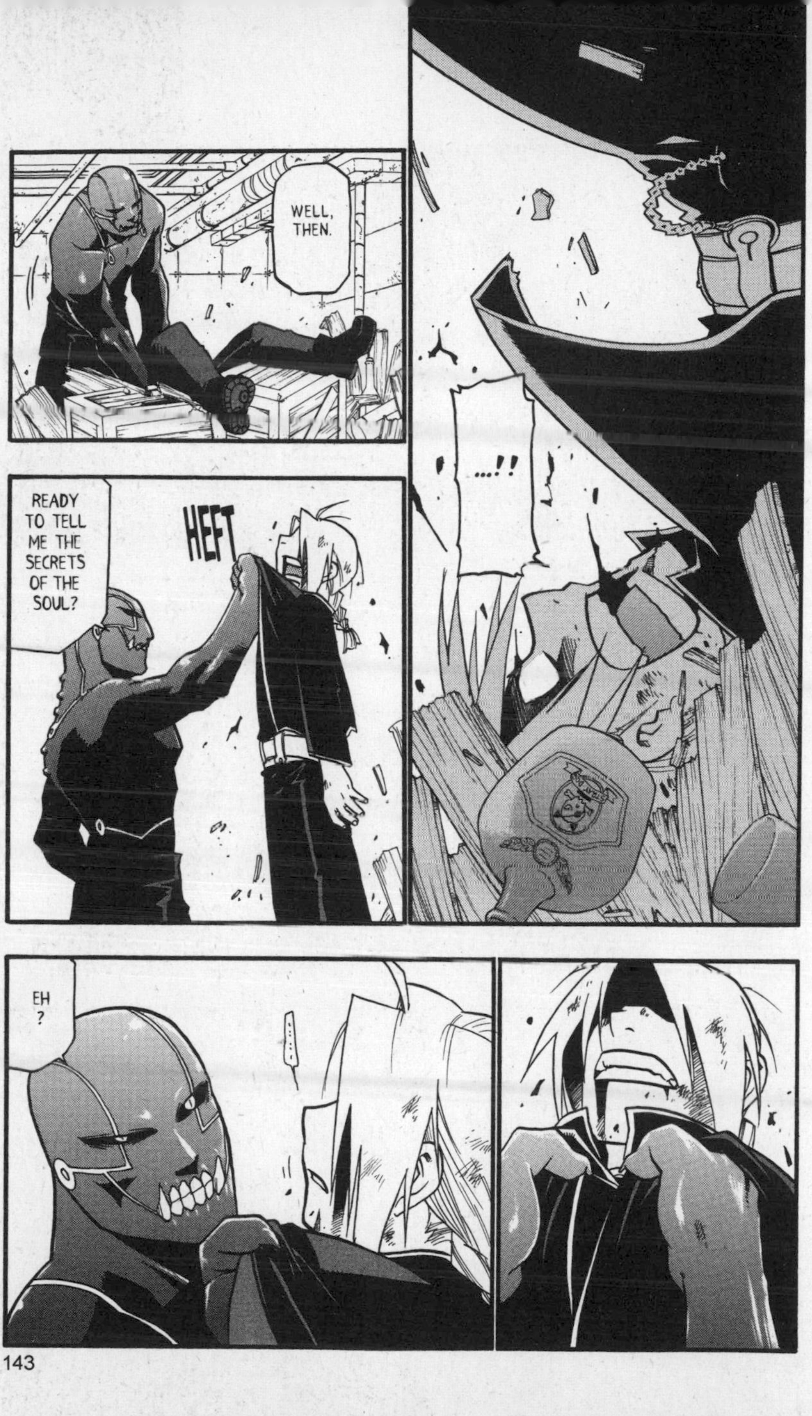
...!!
WELL, THEN.
HEFT
READY TO TELL ME THE SECRETS OF THE SOUL?
EH ?
...!

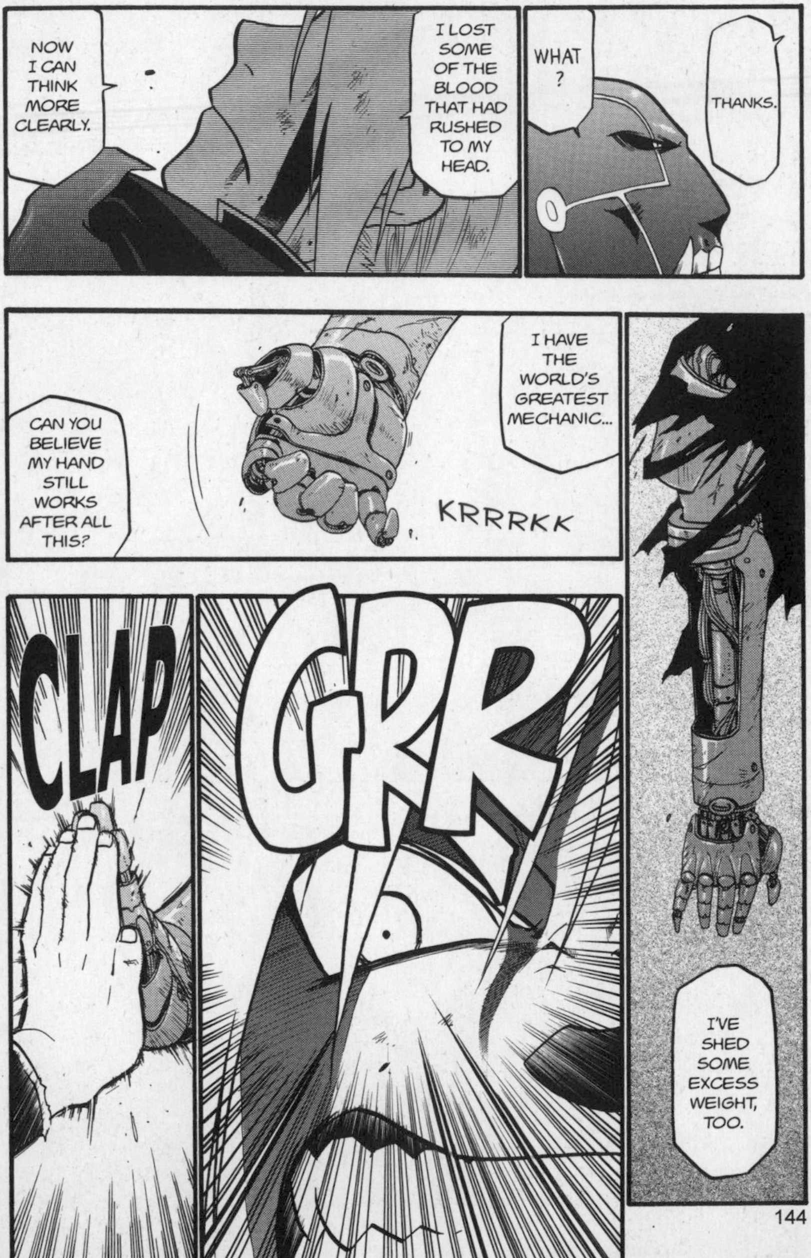
THANKS.
WHAT ?
I LOST SOME OF THE BLOOD THAT HAD RUSHED TO MY HEAD.
NOW I CAN THINK MORE CLEARLY.
I'VE SHED SOME EXCESS WEIGHT, TOO.
I HAVE THE WORLD'S GREATEST MECHANIC...
KRRRKK
CAN YOU BELIEVE MY HAND STILL WORKS AFTER ALL THIS?
GRR
CLAP

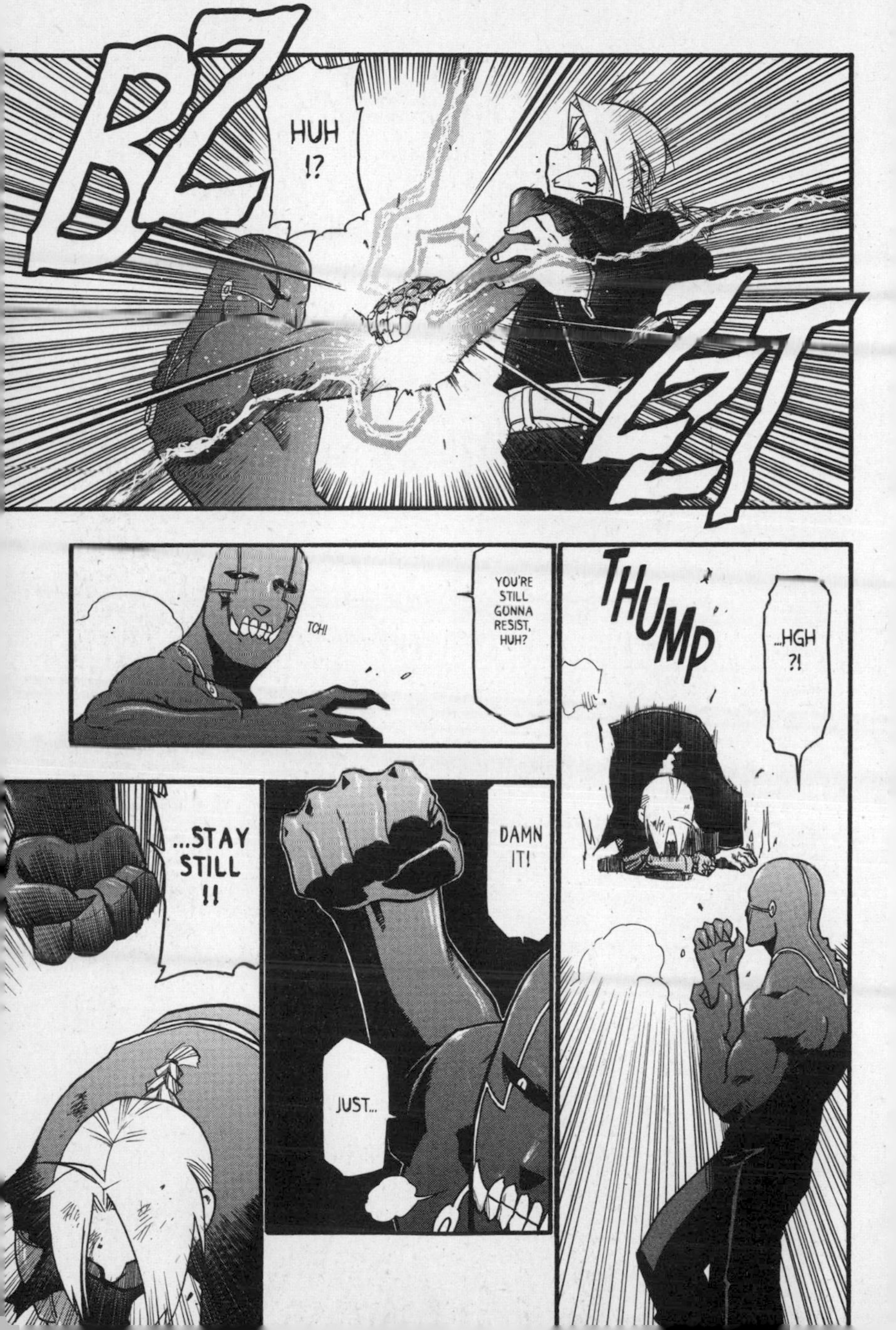
BZ
HUH !?
ZZT
THUMP
...HGH ?!
YOU'RE STILL GONNA RESIST, HUH?
TCH!
DAMN IT!
JUST...
...STAY STILL !!

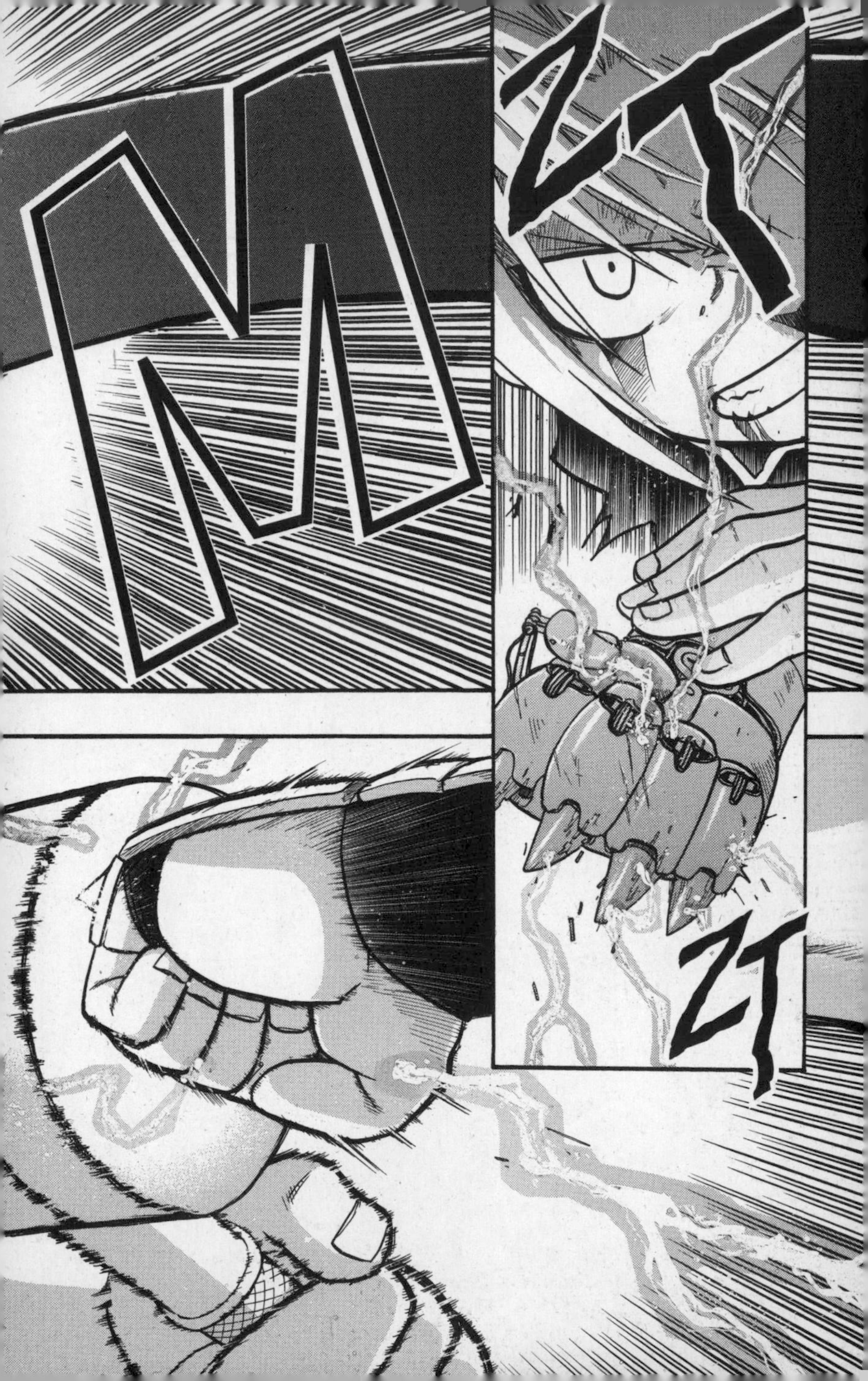
ZT
ZT
M

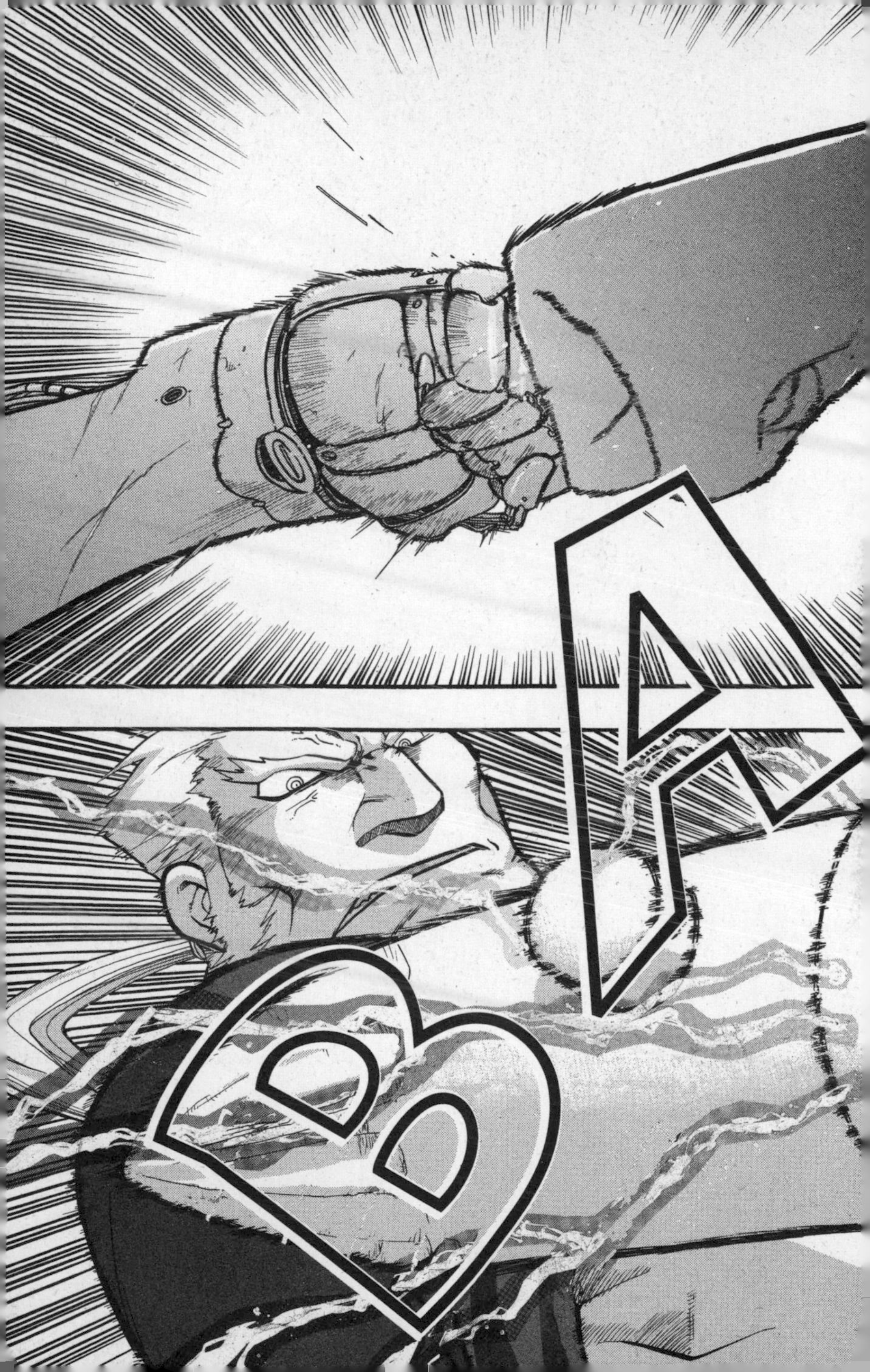
BA

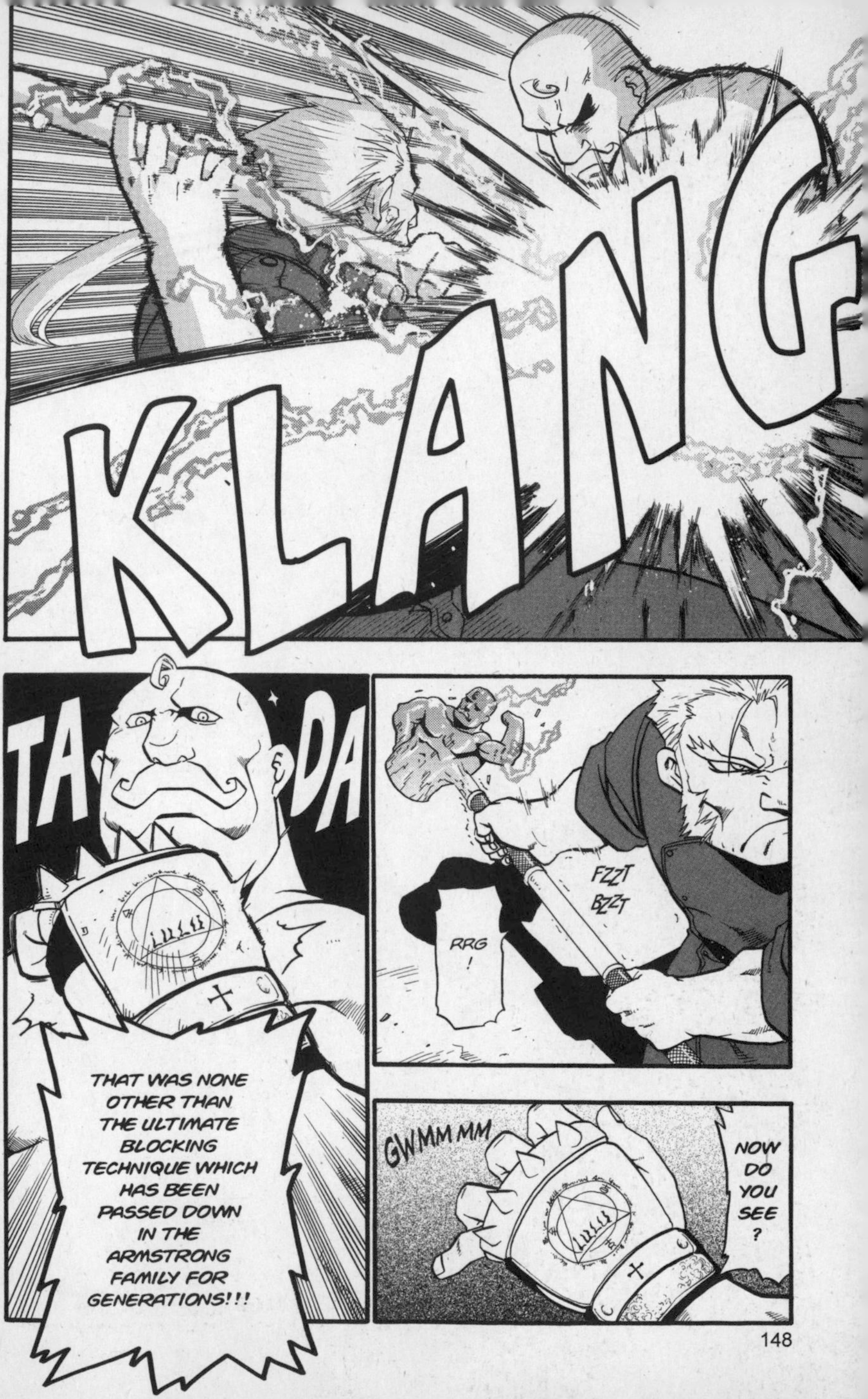
KLANG
FZZT
BZZT
RRG!
GWMM MM
NOW DO YOU SEE?
TA
DA
...
THAT WAS NONE OTHER THAN THE ULTIMATE BLOCKING TECHNIQUE WHICH HAS BEEN PASSED DOWN IN THE ARMSTRONG FAMILY FOR GENERATIONS!!!

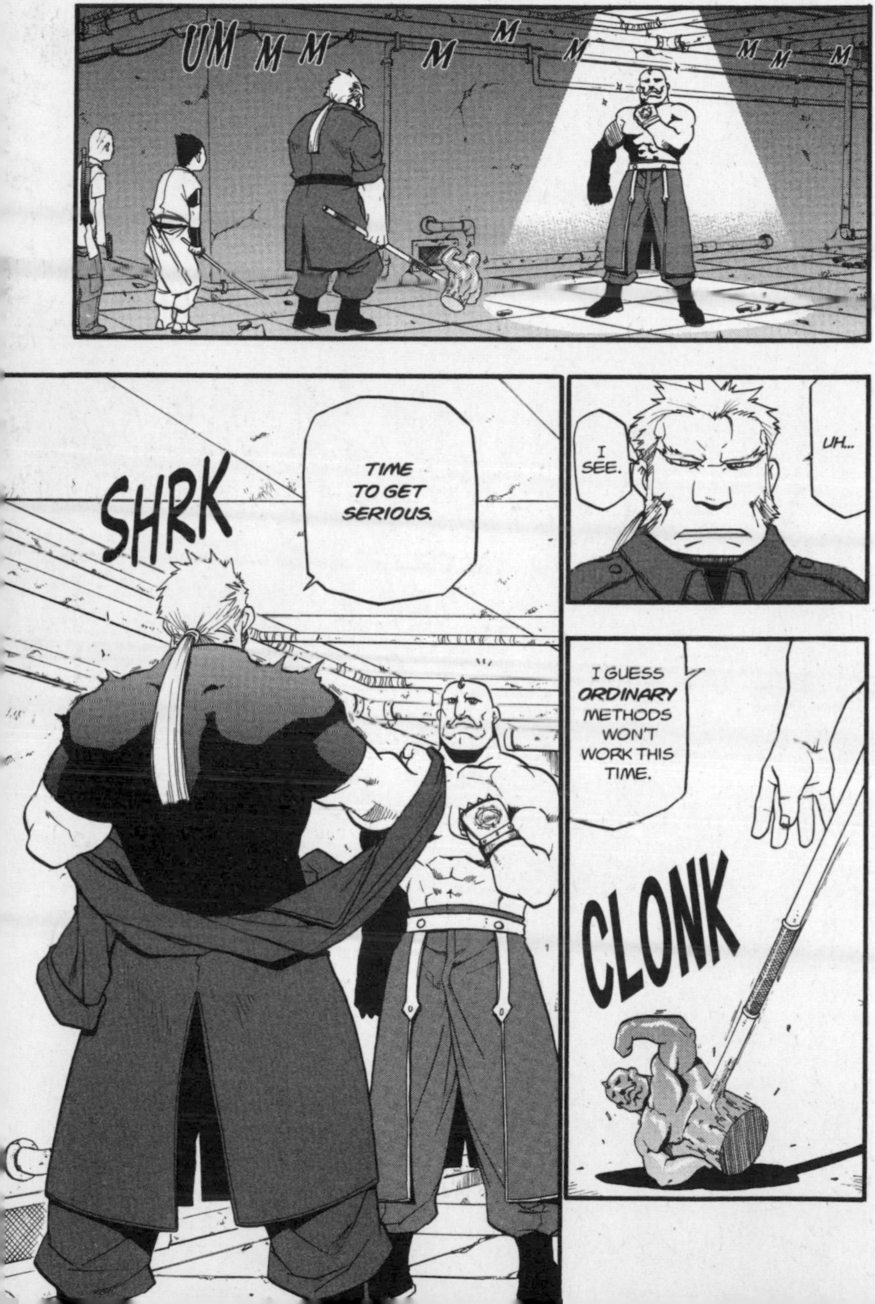
UMMMMMMMMM
UH...
I SEE.
I GUESS ORDINARY METHODS WON'T WORK THIS TIME.
CLONK
TIME TO GET SERIOUS.
SHRK

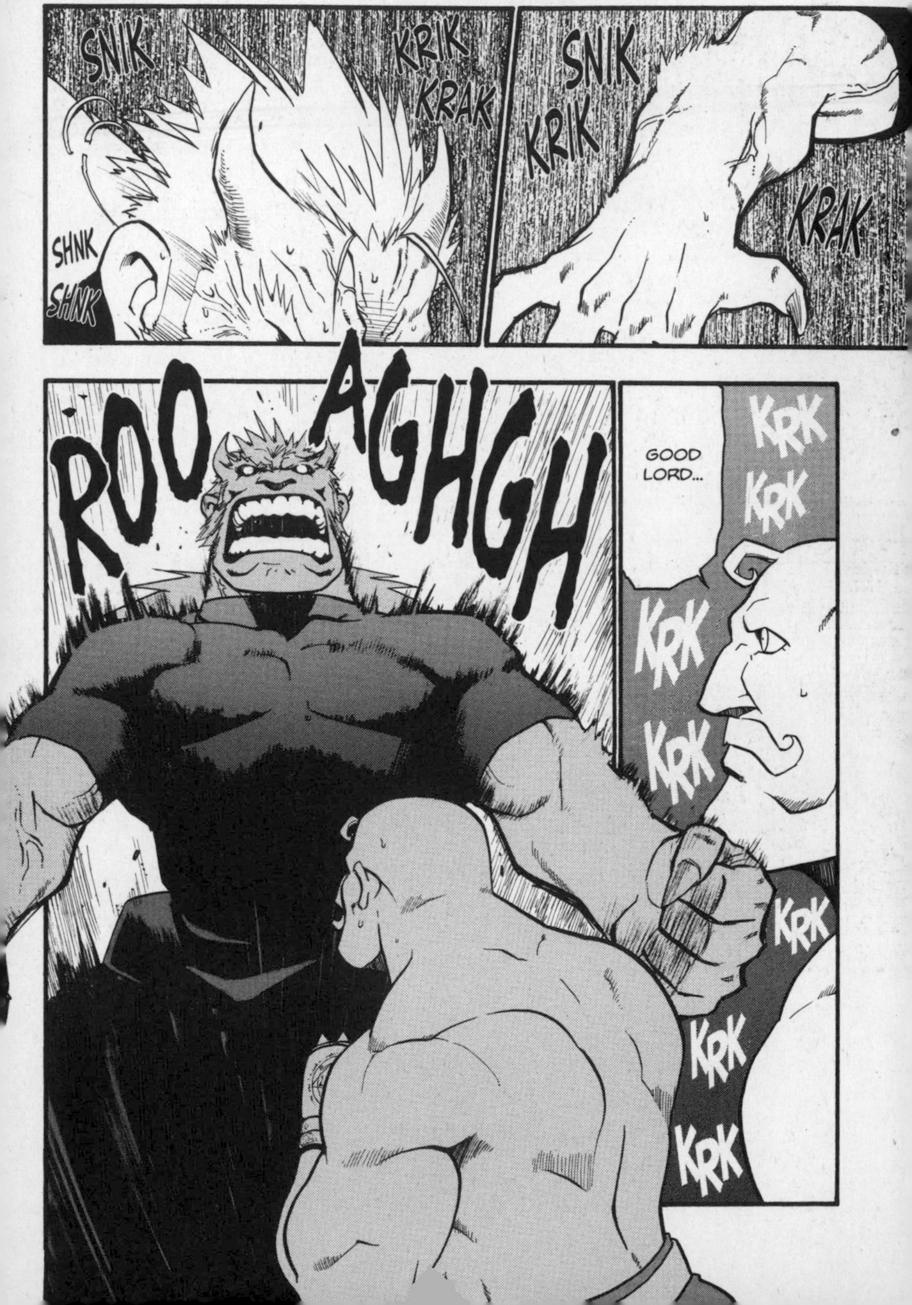
SNIK
KRIK
KRAK
SNIK
KRIK
KRAK
SHNK
SHNK
GOOD LORD...
KRK
KRK
KRK
KRK
KRK
KRK
KRK
ROOAGHGH

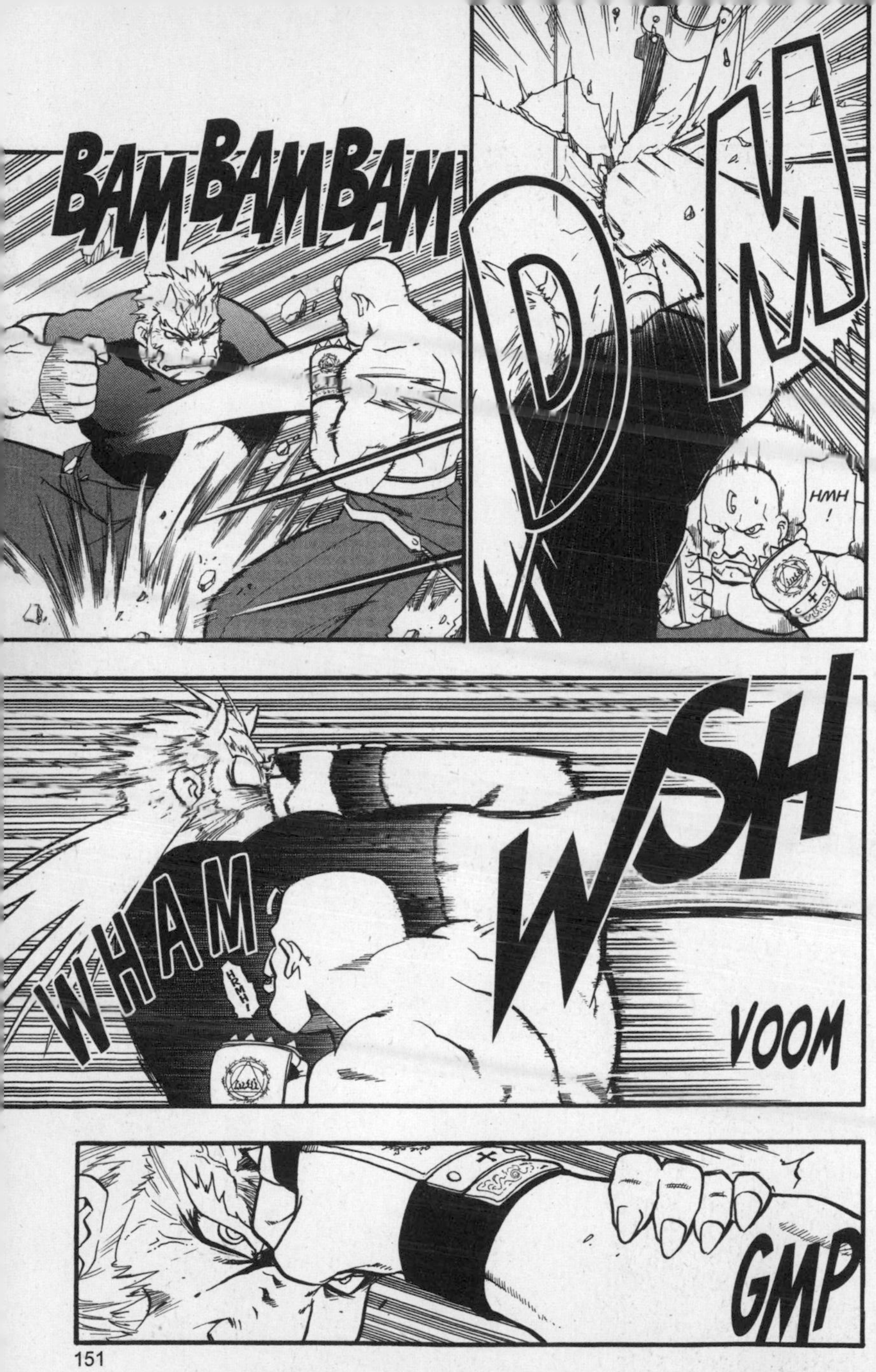
DM
HMH!
BAM BAM BAM
WSH
VOOM
WHAM
HRMH!
GMP

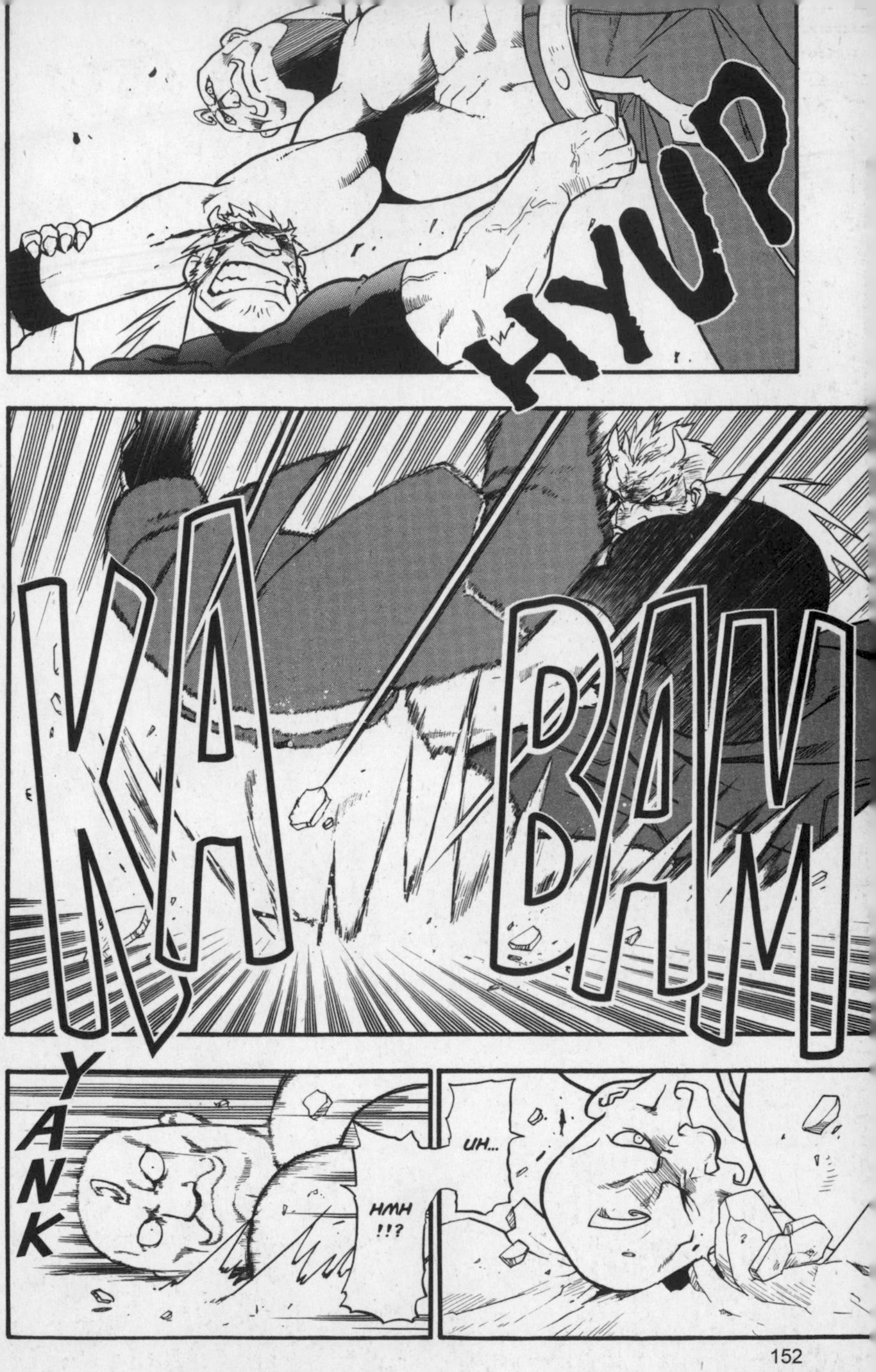
HYUP
KA
BAM
UH...
YANK
HMH !!?

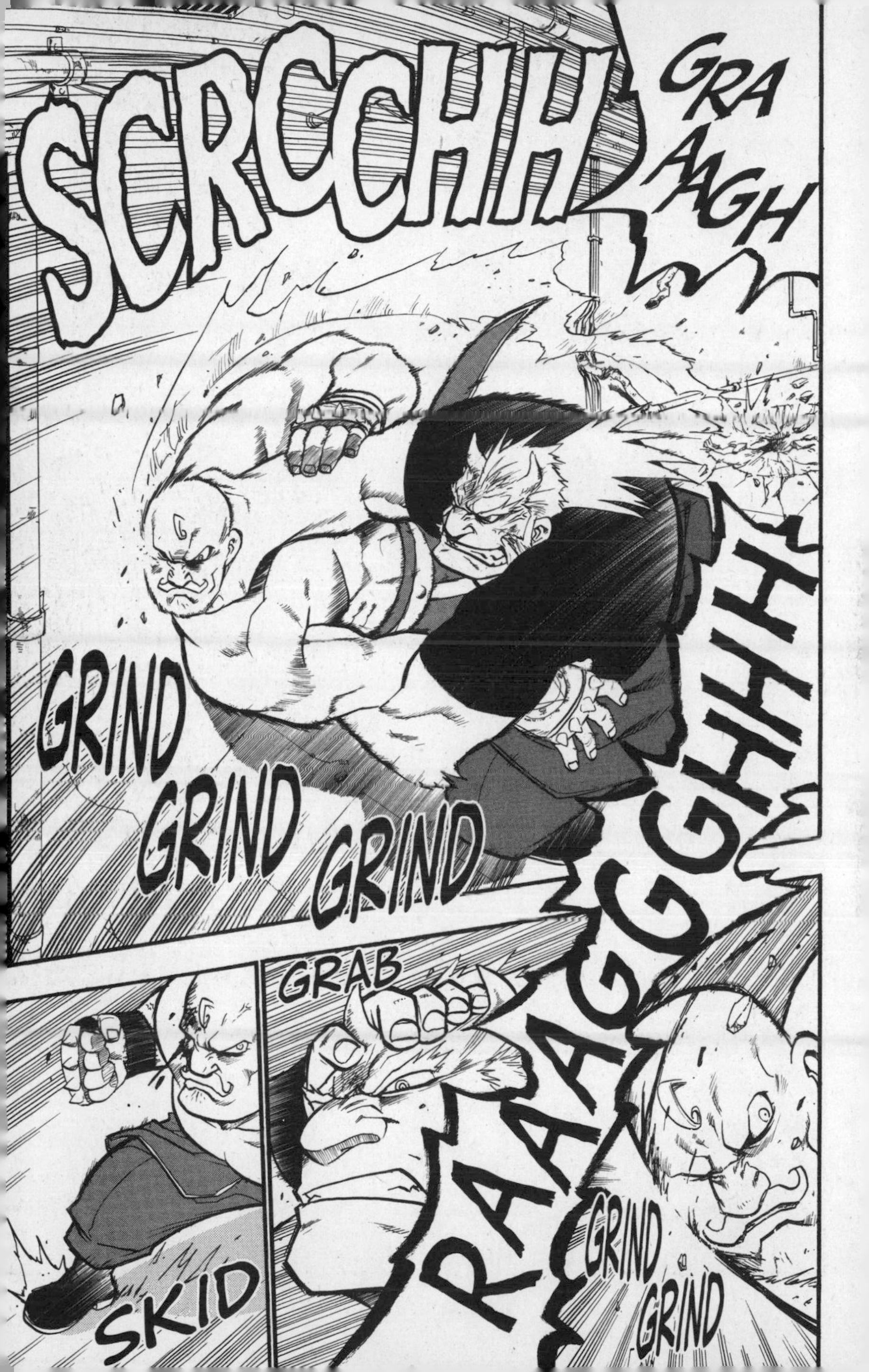
GRAAAGH
SCRCCHH
GRIND
GRIND
GRIND
RAAAGGGHHH
GRIND
GRIND
GRAB
SKID

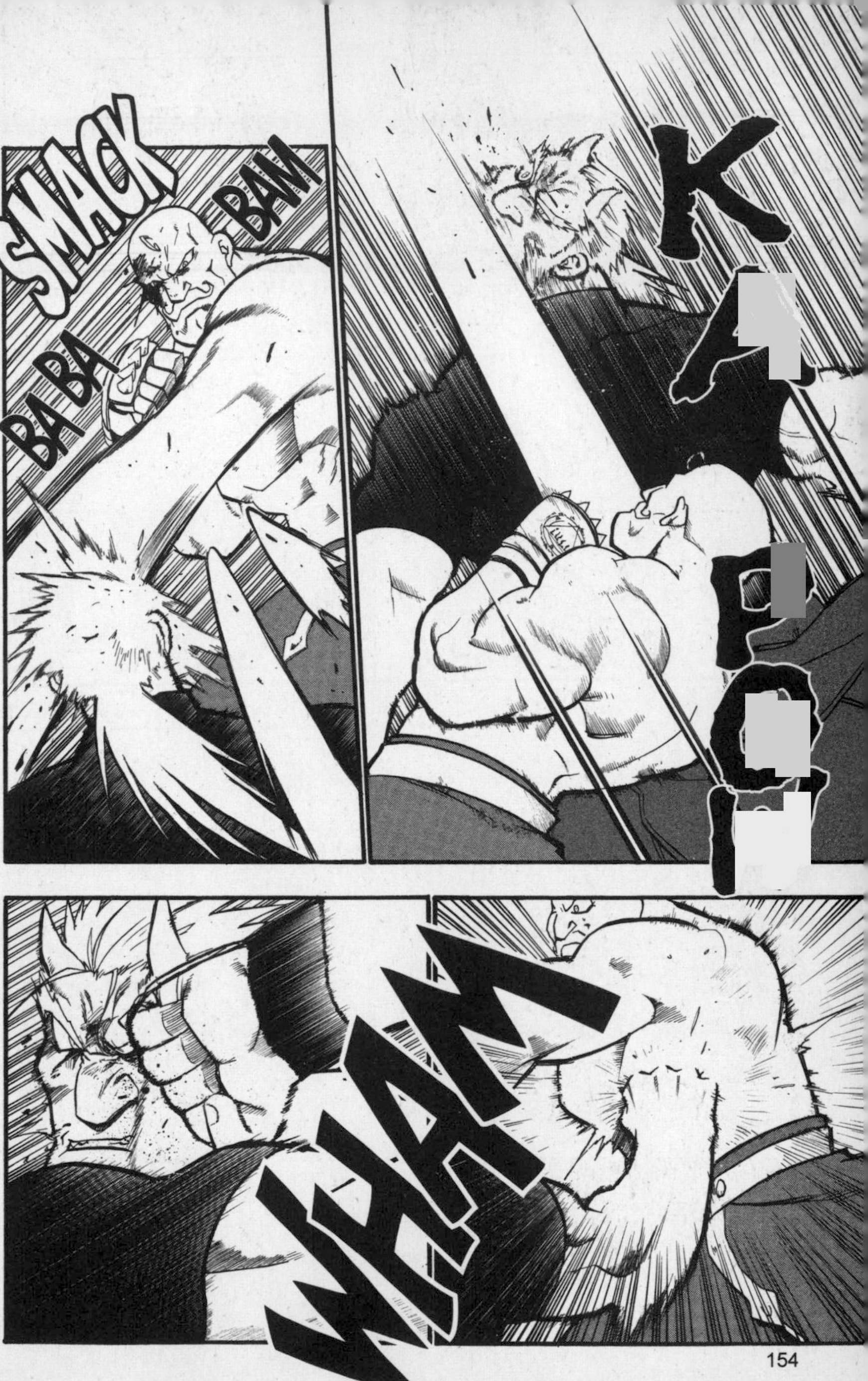
SMACK
BAM
BA BA
WHAM

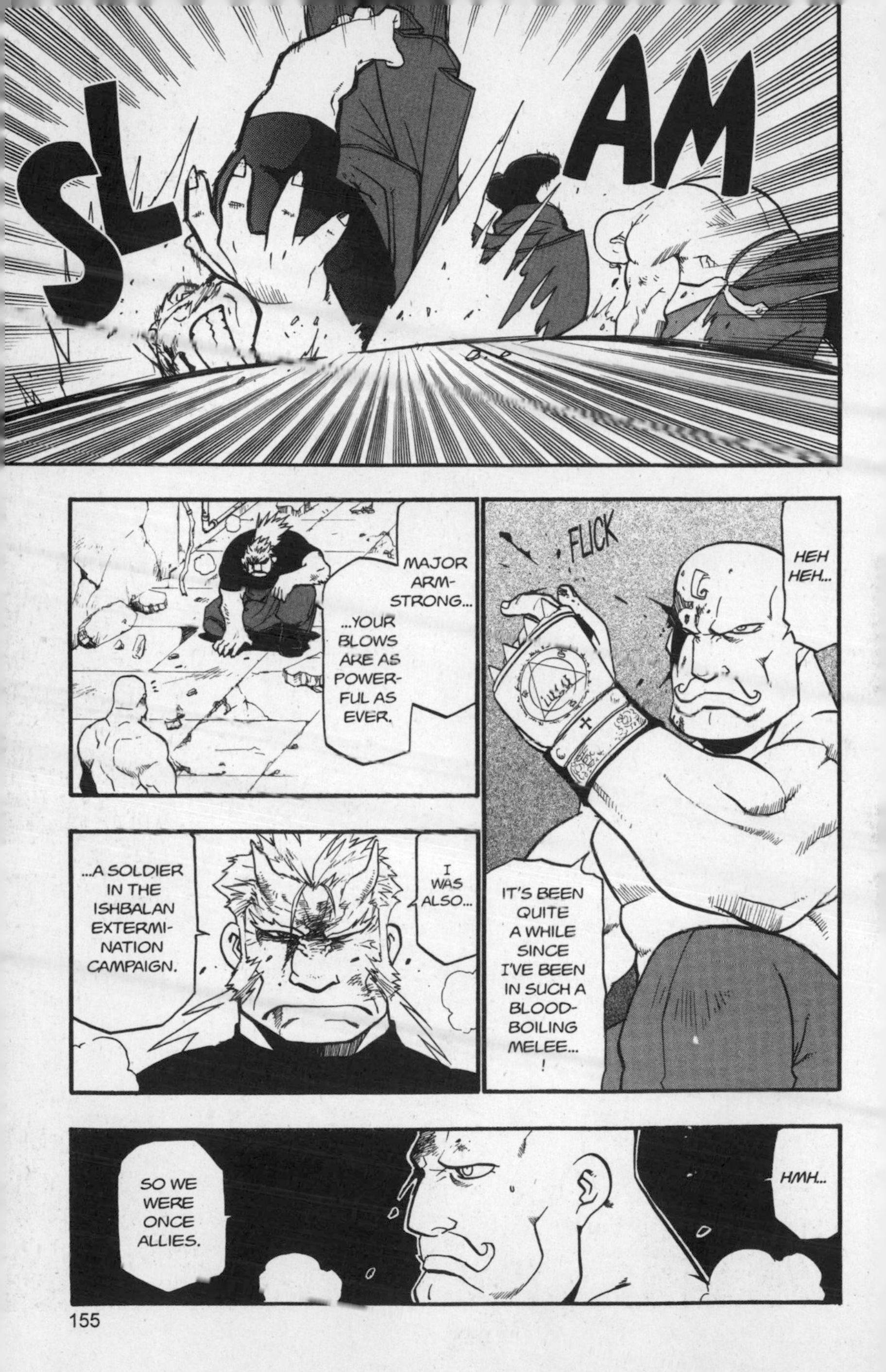
SLAM
FLICK
HEH HEH...
IT'S BEEN QUITE A WHILE SINCE I'VE BEEN IN SUCH A BLOOD-BOILING MELEE...!
MAJOR ARM-STRONG...
...YOUR BLOWS ARE AS POWERFUL AS EVER.
I WAS ALSO...
...A SOLDIER IN THE ISHBALAN EXTERMINATION CAMPAIGN.
HMH...
SO WE WERE ONCE ALLIES.

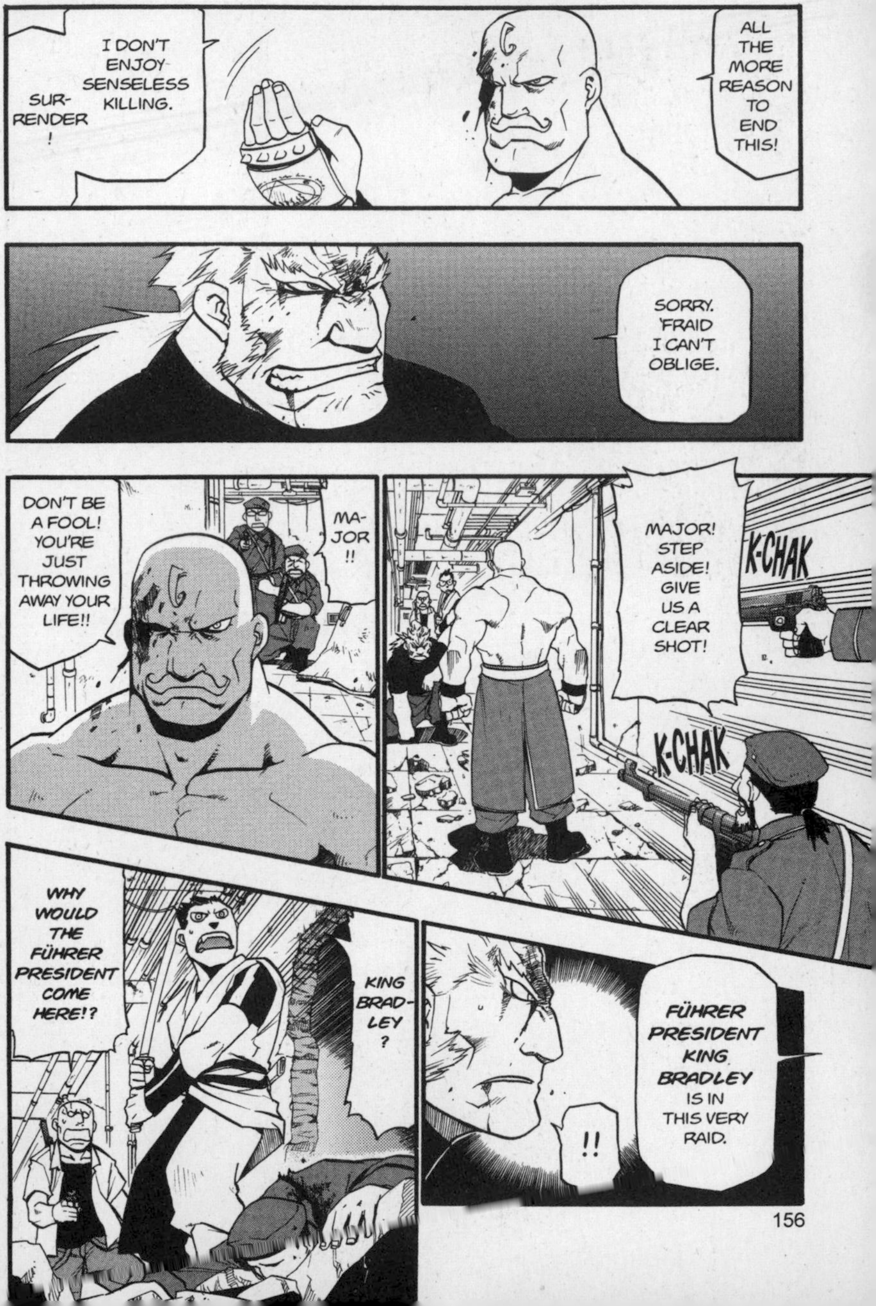
ALL THE MORE REASON TO END THIS!
I DON'T ENJOY SENSELESS KILLING.
SURRENDER!
SORRY. 'FRAID I CAN'T OBLIGE.
MAJOR! STEP ASIDE! GIVE US A CLEAR SHOT!
K-CHAK
K-CHAK
MAJOR!!
DON'T BE A FOOL! YOU'RE JUST THROWING AWAY YOUR LIFE!!
FÜHRER PRESIDENT KING BRADLEY IS IN THIS VERY RAID.
!!
KING BRADLEY?
WHY WOULD THE FÜHRER PRESIDENT COME HERE!?

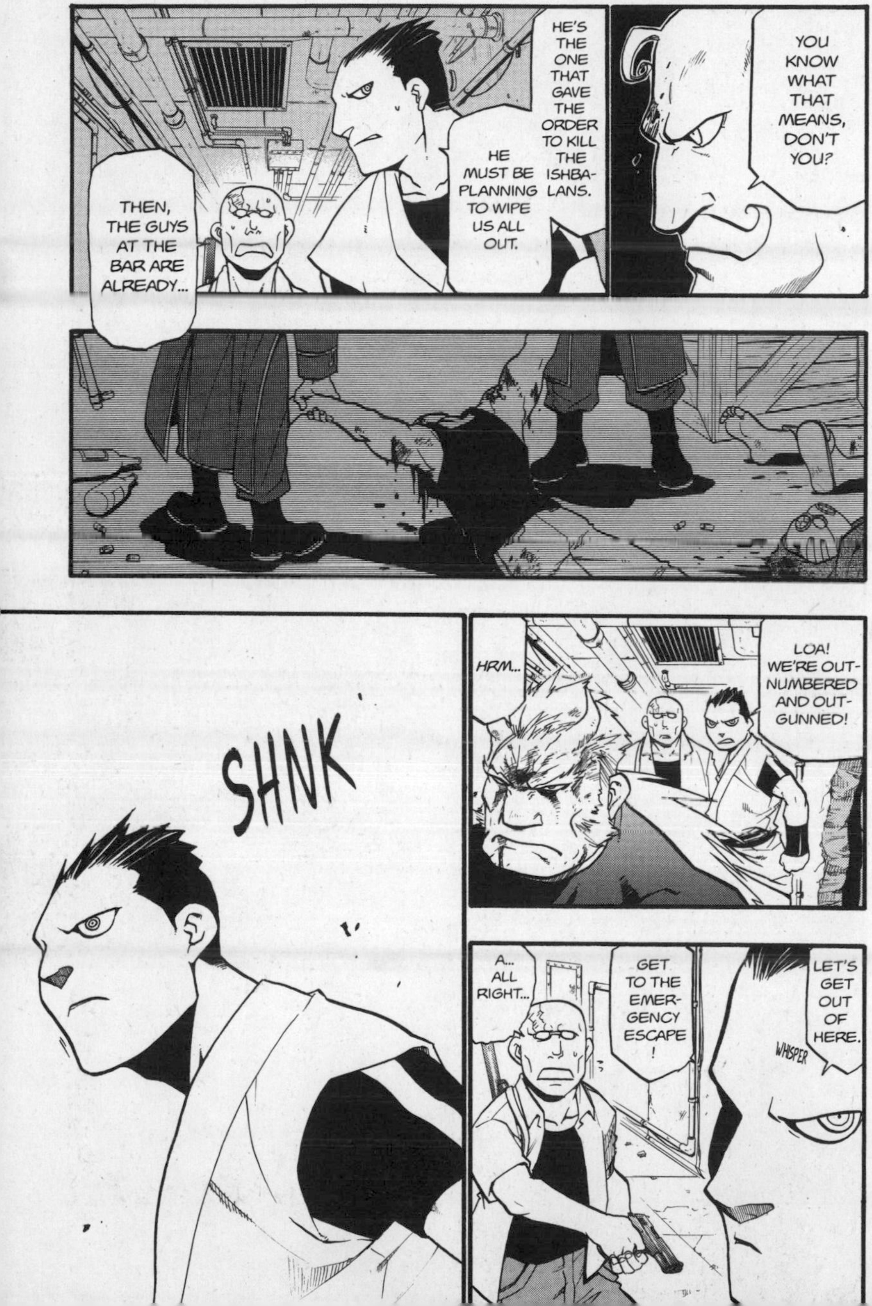
YOU KNOW WHAT THAT MEANS, DON'T YOU?
HE'S THE ONE THAT GAVE THE ORDER TO KILL THE ISHBALANS.
HE MUST BE PLANNING TO WIPE US ALL OUT.
THEN, THE GUYS AT THE BAR ARE ALREADY...
LOA! WE'RE OUTNUMBERED AND OUTGUNNED!
HRM...
LET'S GET OUT OF HERE.
WHISPER
GET TO THE EMERGENCY ESCAPE!
A... ALL RIGHT...
SHNK

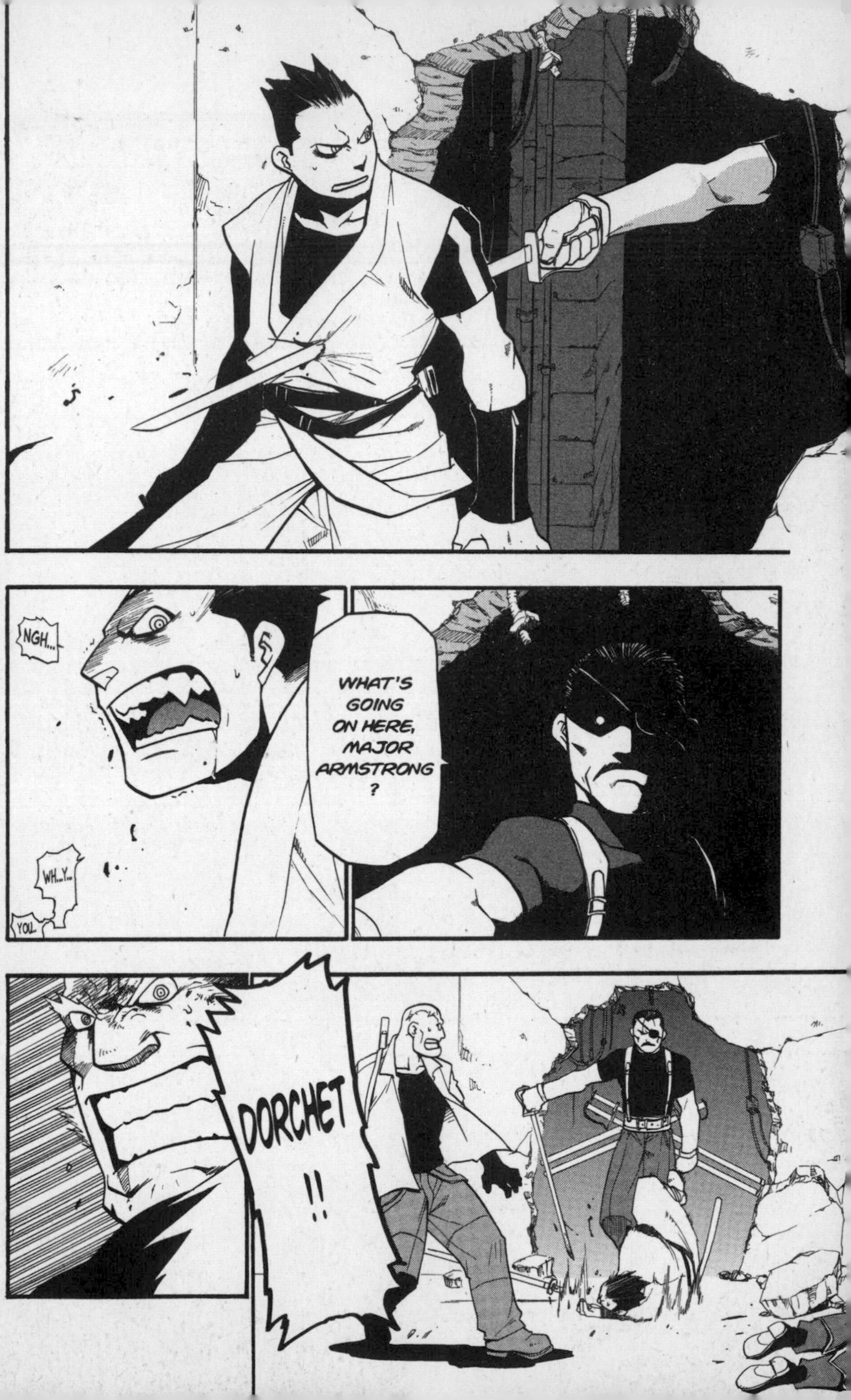
WHAT'S GOING ON HERE, MAJOR ARMSTRONG ?
NGH...
WH...Y...
YOU...
DORCHET !!

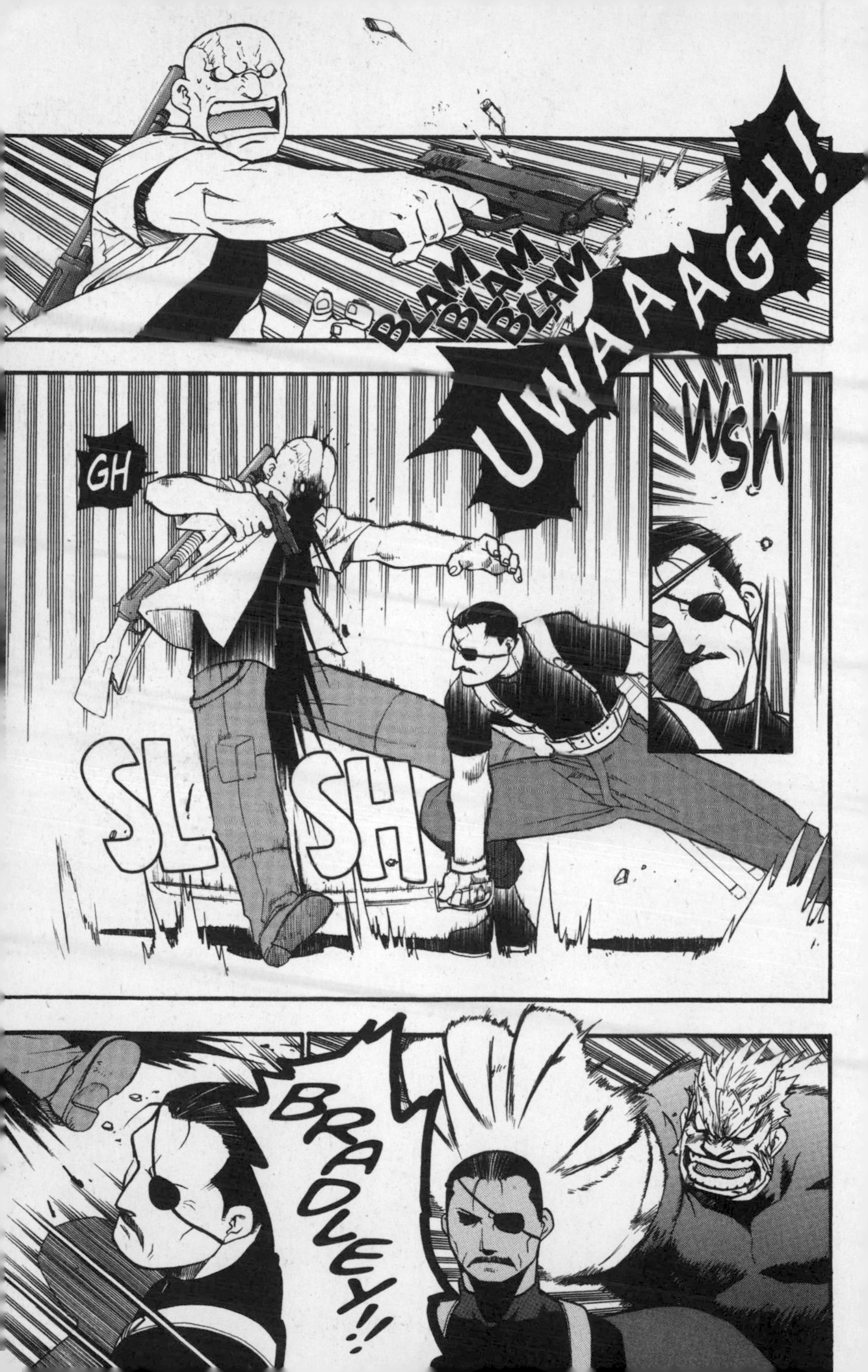
BLAM BLAM BLAM
UWAAAGH!!
Wsh
GH
SLSH
BRADOVEY!!

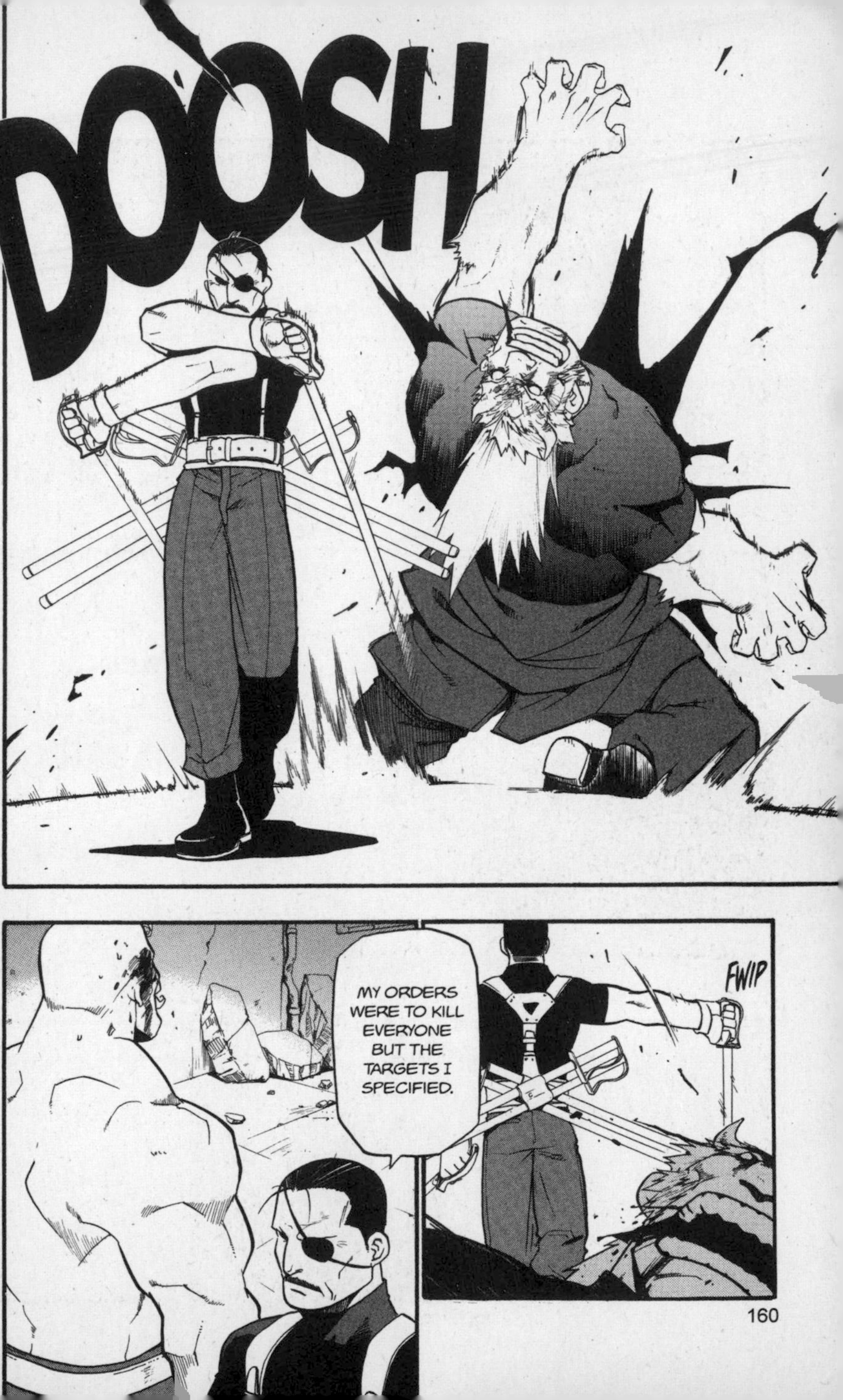
DOOSH
FWIP
MY ORDERS WERE TO KILL EVERYONE BUT THE TARGETS I SPECIFIED.

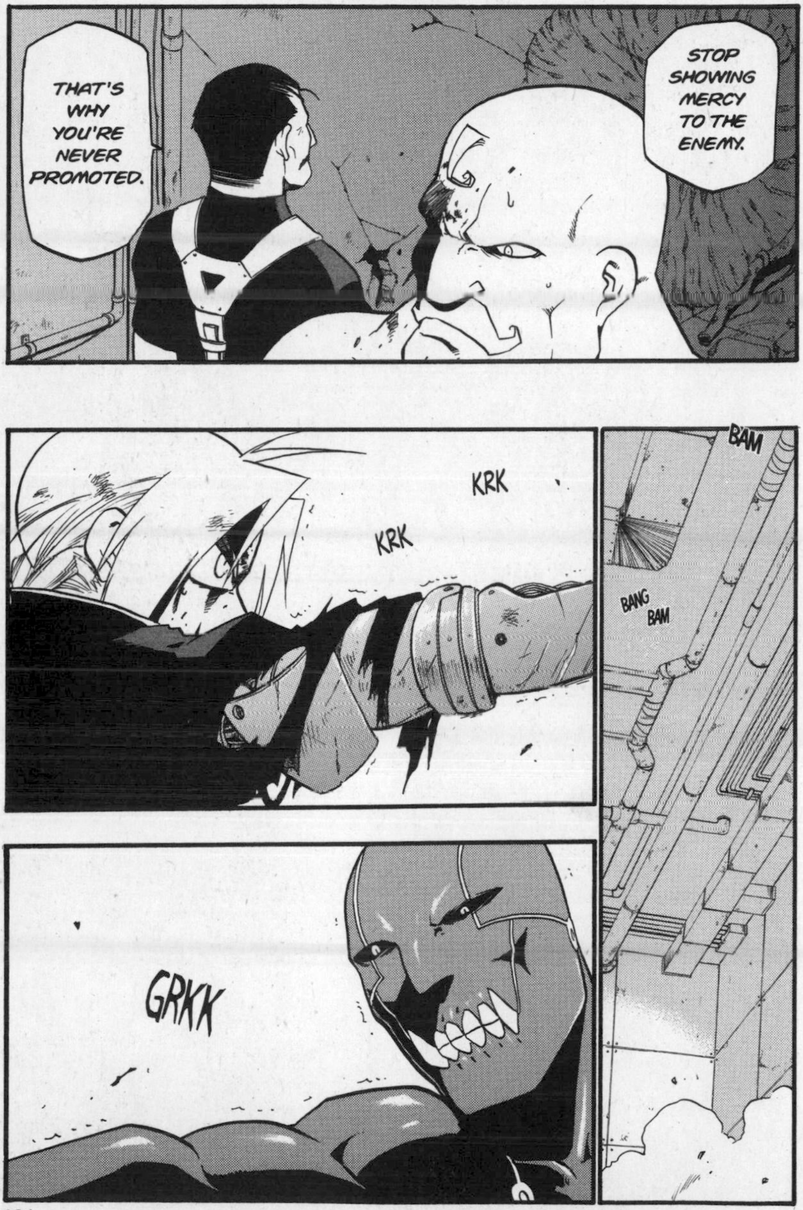
STOP SHOWING MERCY TO THE ENEMY.
THAT'S WHY YOU'RE NEVER PROMOTED.
BAM
BANG
BAM
KRK
KRK
GRKK

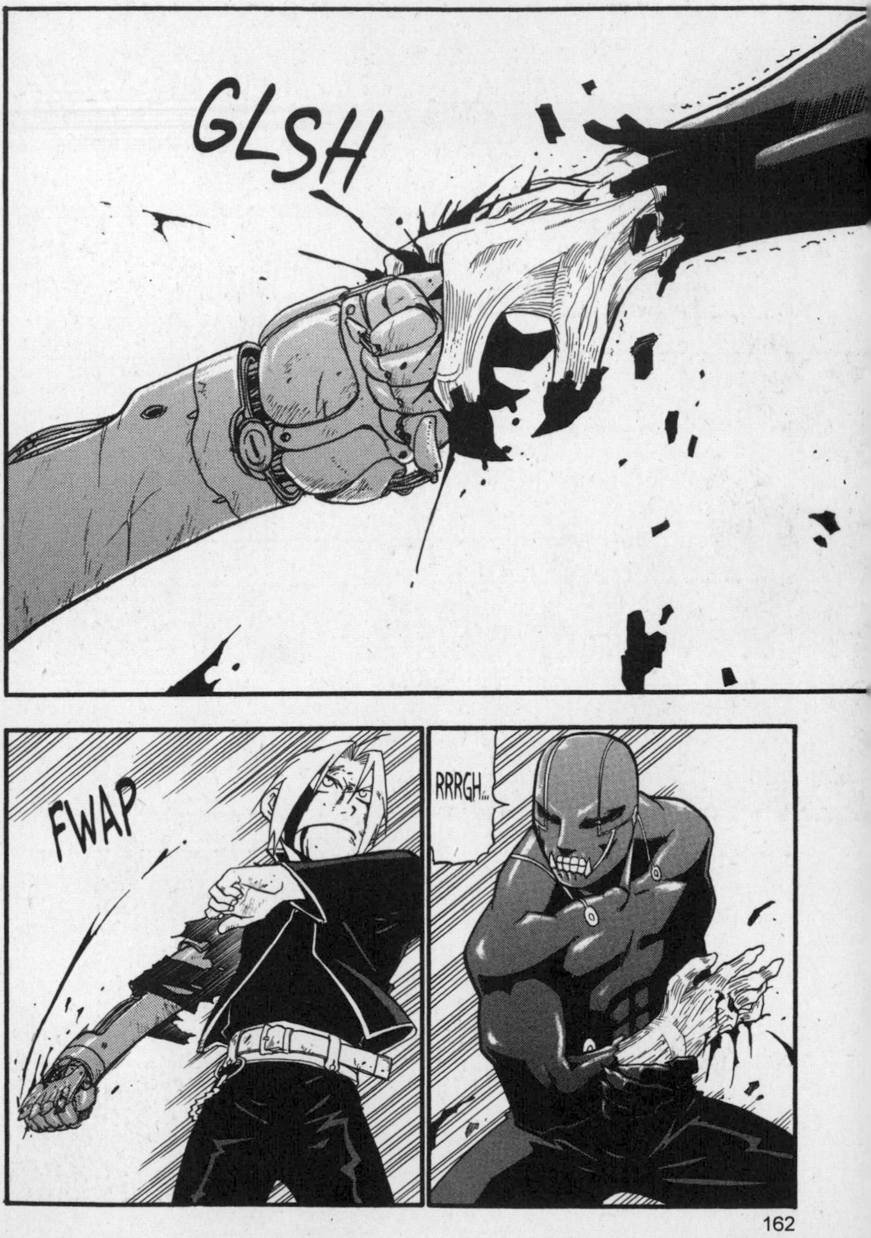
GLSH
RRRGH...
FWAP

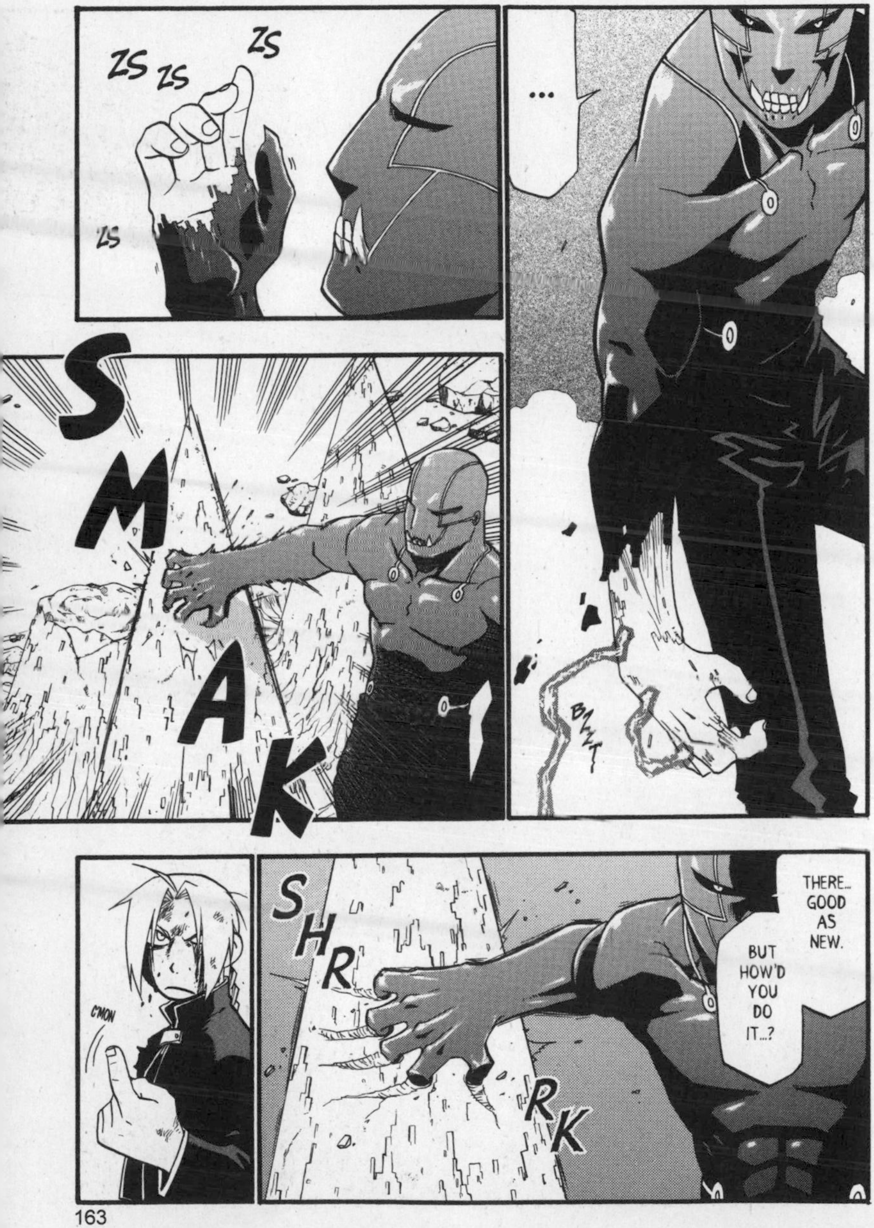
...
BZZT
ZS
ZS
ZS
ZS
SMAK
SHRRK
THERE... GOOD AS NEW.
BUT HOW'D YOU DO IT...?
C'MON

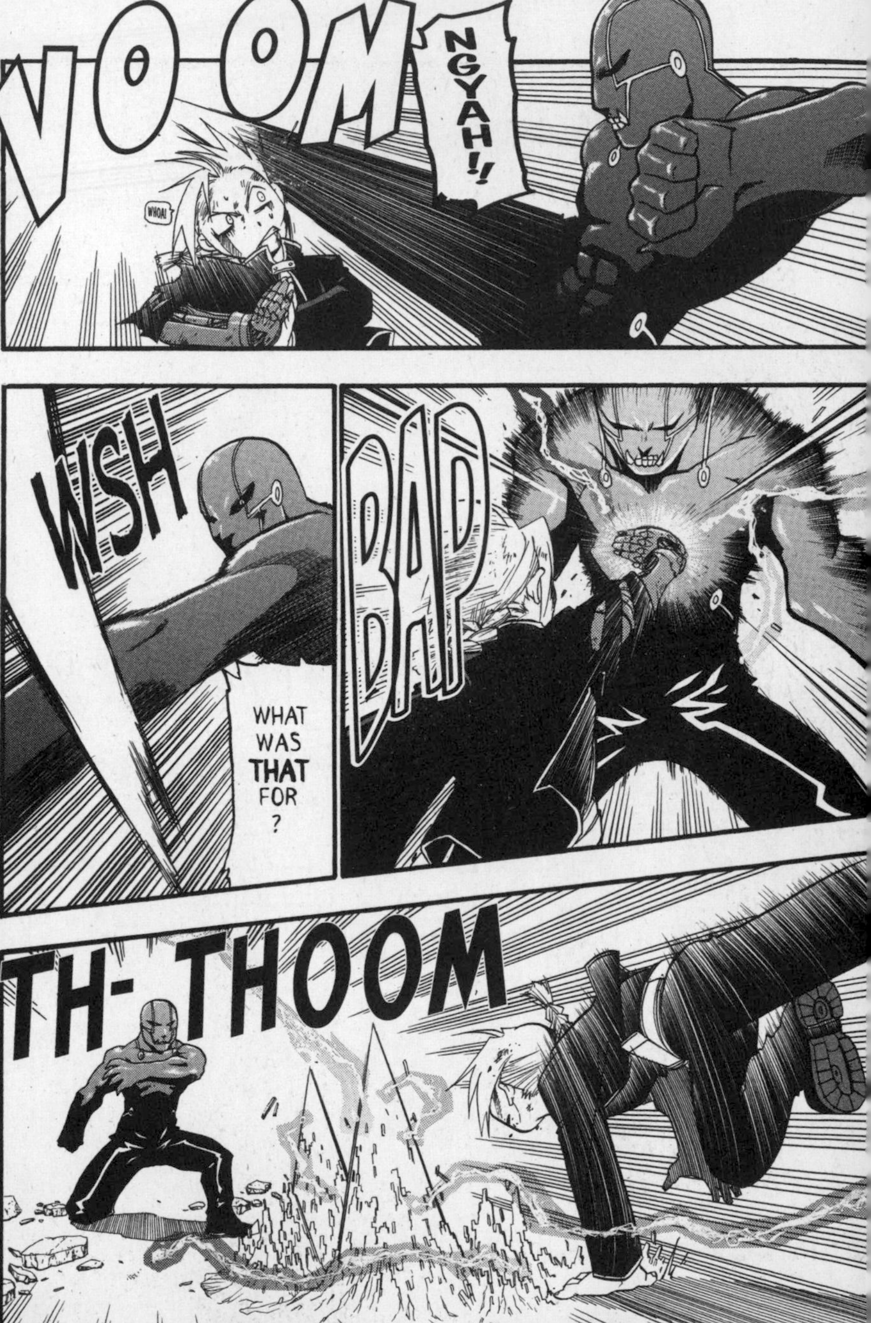
NGYAH!!
VOOM
WHOA!
BAP
WSH
WHAT WAS THAT FOR?
TH-THOOM

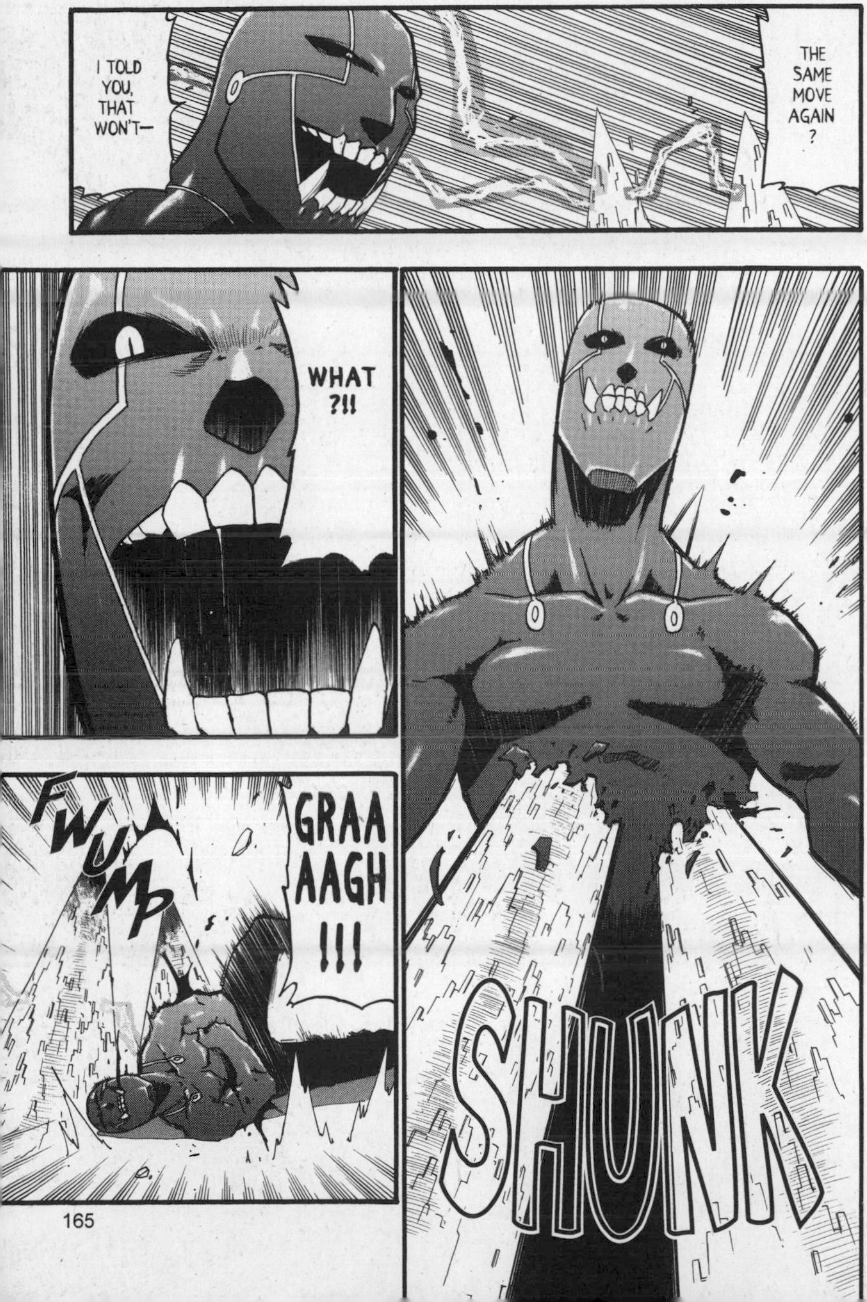
THE SAME MOVE AGAIN ?
I TOLD YOU, THAT WON'T—
SHUNK
WHAT ?!!
GRAA AAGH !!!
FWUMP

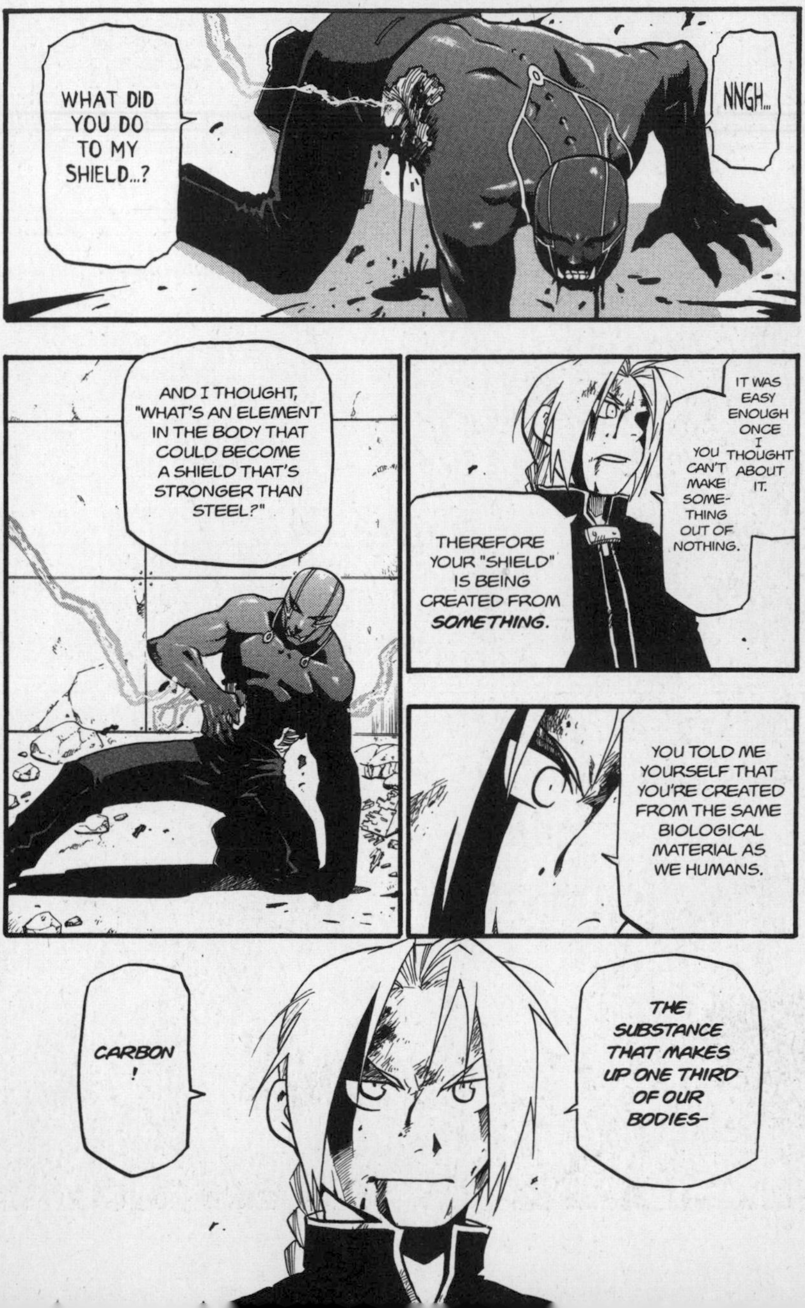
NNGH...
WHAT DID YOU DO TO MY SHIELD...?
IT WAS EASY ENOUGH ONCE I THOUGHT ABOUT IT.
YOU CAN'T MAKE SOME-THING OUT OF NOTHING.
THEREFORE YOUR "SHIELD" IS BEING CREATED FROM *SOMETHING*.
YOU TOLD ME YOURSELF THAT YOU'RE CREATED FROM THE SAME BIOLOGICAL MATERIAL AS WE HUMANS.
AND I THOUGHT, "WHAT'S AN ELEMENT IN THE BODY THAT COULD BECOME A SHIELD THAT'S STRONGER THAN STEEL?"
THE SUBSTANCE THAT MAKES UP ONE THIRD OF OUR BODIES-
CARBON!

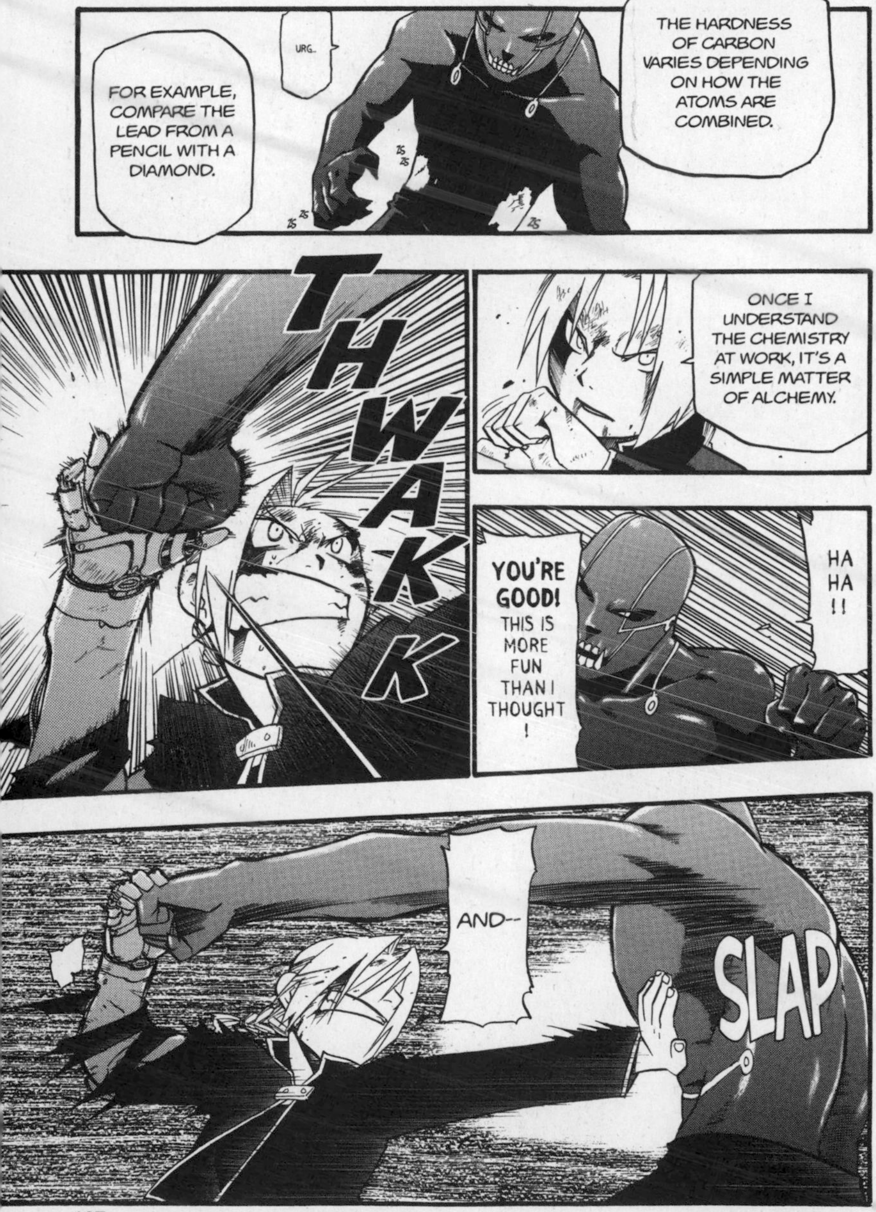
THE HARDNESS OF CARBON VARIES DEPENDING ON HOW THE ATOMS ARE COMBINED.
URG...
FOR EXAMPLE, COMPARE THE LEAD FROM A PENCIL WITH A DIAMOND.
ONCE I UNDERSTAND THE CHEMISTRY AT WORK, IT'S A SIMPLE MATTER OF ALCHEMY.
HA HA!!
YOU'RE GOOD! THIS IS MORE FUN THAN I THOUGHT!
THWAKK
AND--
SLAP

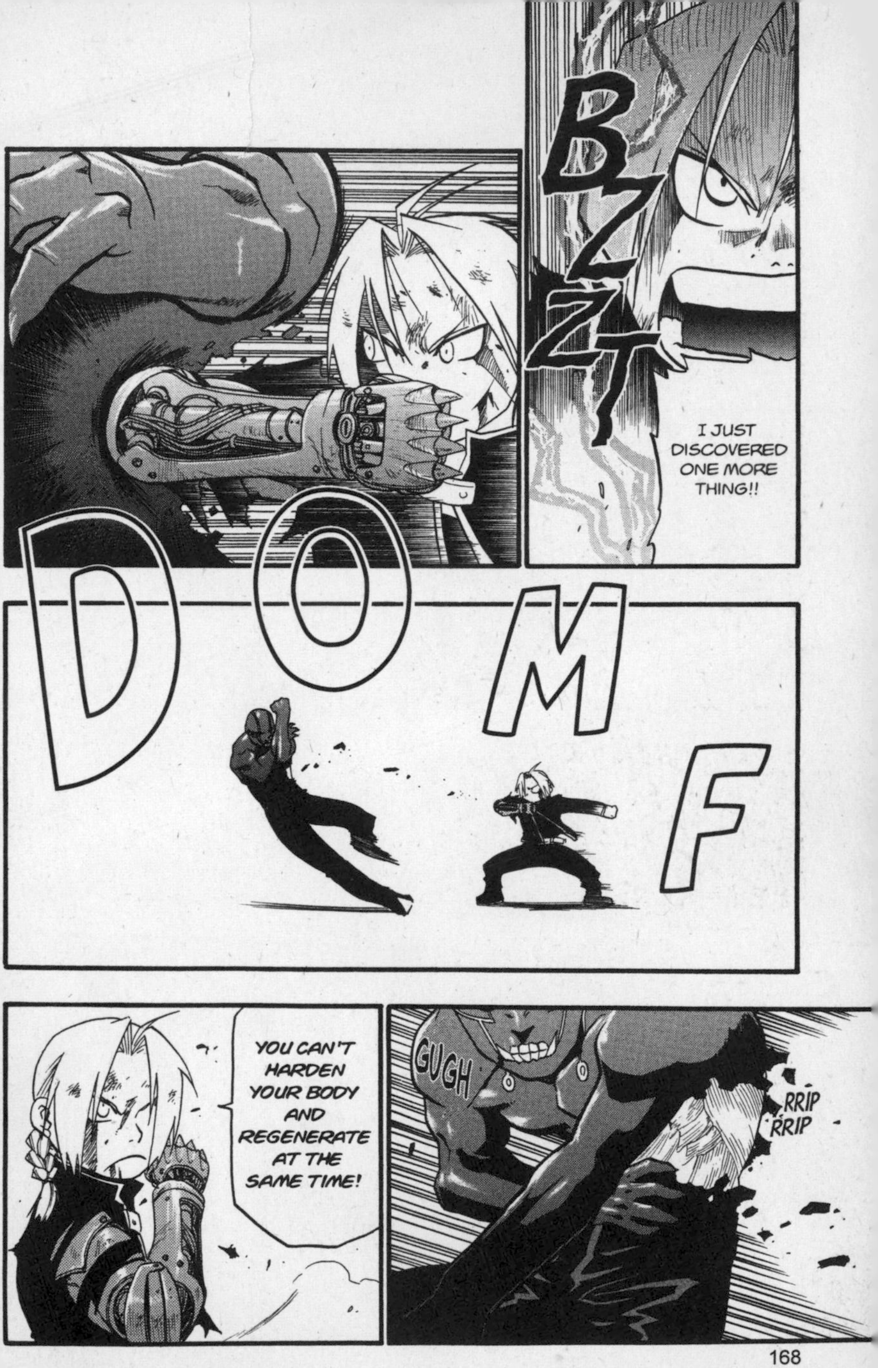
BZZT
I JUST DISCOVERED ONE MORE THING!!
DOMF
GUGH
RRIP RRIP
YOU CAN'T HARDEN YOUR BODY AND REGENERATE AT THE SAME TIME!

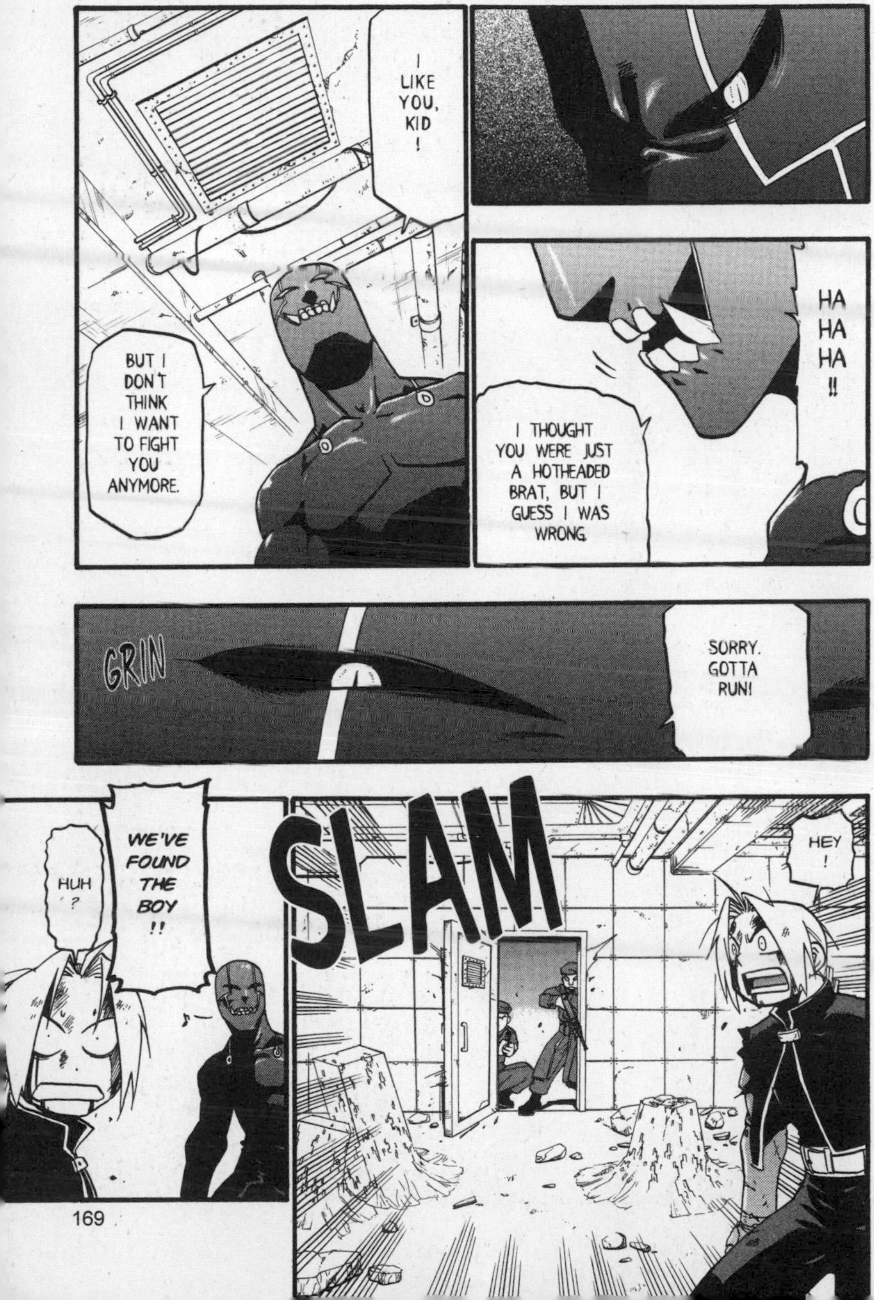
HA HA HA !!
I THOUGHT YOU WERE JUST A HOTHEADED BRAT, BUT I GUESS I WAS WRONG.
I LIKE YOU, KID!
BUT I DON'T THINK I WANT TO FIGHT YOU ANYMORE.
SORRY. GOTTA RUN!
GRIN
HEY!
SLAM
WE'VE FOUND THE BOY!!
HUH?

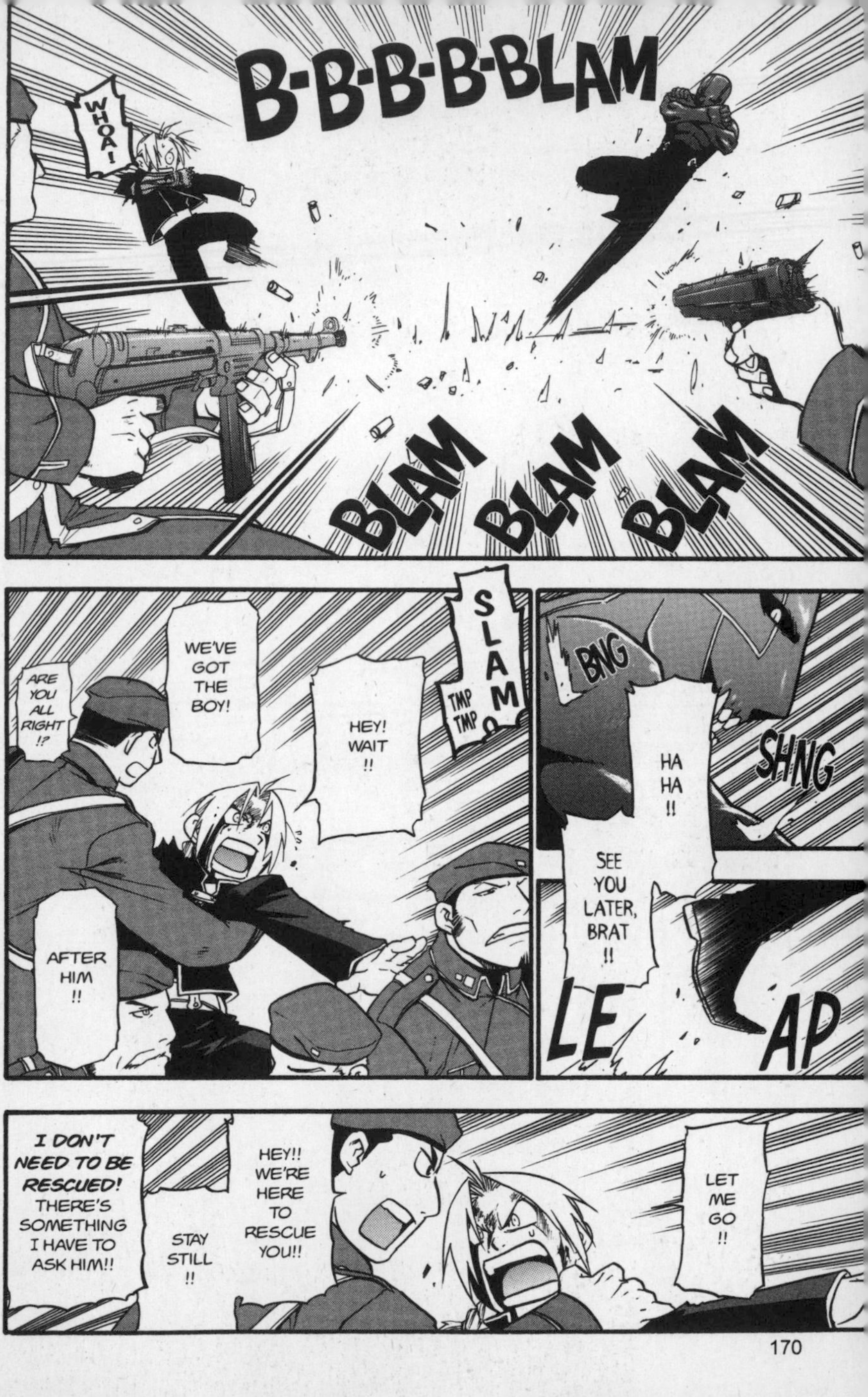
B-B-B-B-BLAM
WHOA!
BLAM BLAM BLAM
BNG
SHNG
HA HA !!
SEE YOU LATER, BRAT !!
LEAP
SLAM
TMP TMP
HEY! WAIT !!
WE'VE GOT THE BOY!
ARE YOU ALL RIGHT !?
AFTER HIM !!
LET ME GO !!
HEY!! WE'RE HERE TO RESCUE YOU!!
STAY STILL !!
I DON'T NEED TO BE RESCUED! THERE'S SOMETHING I HAVE TO ASK HIM!!

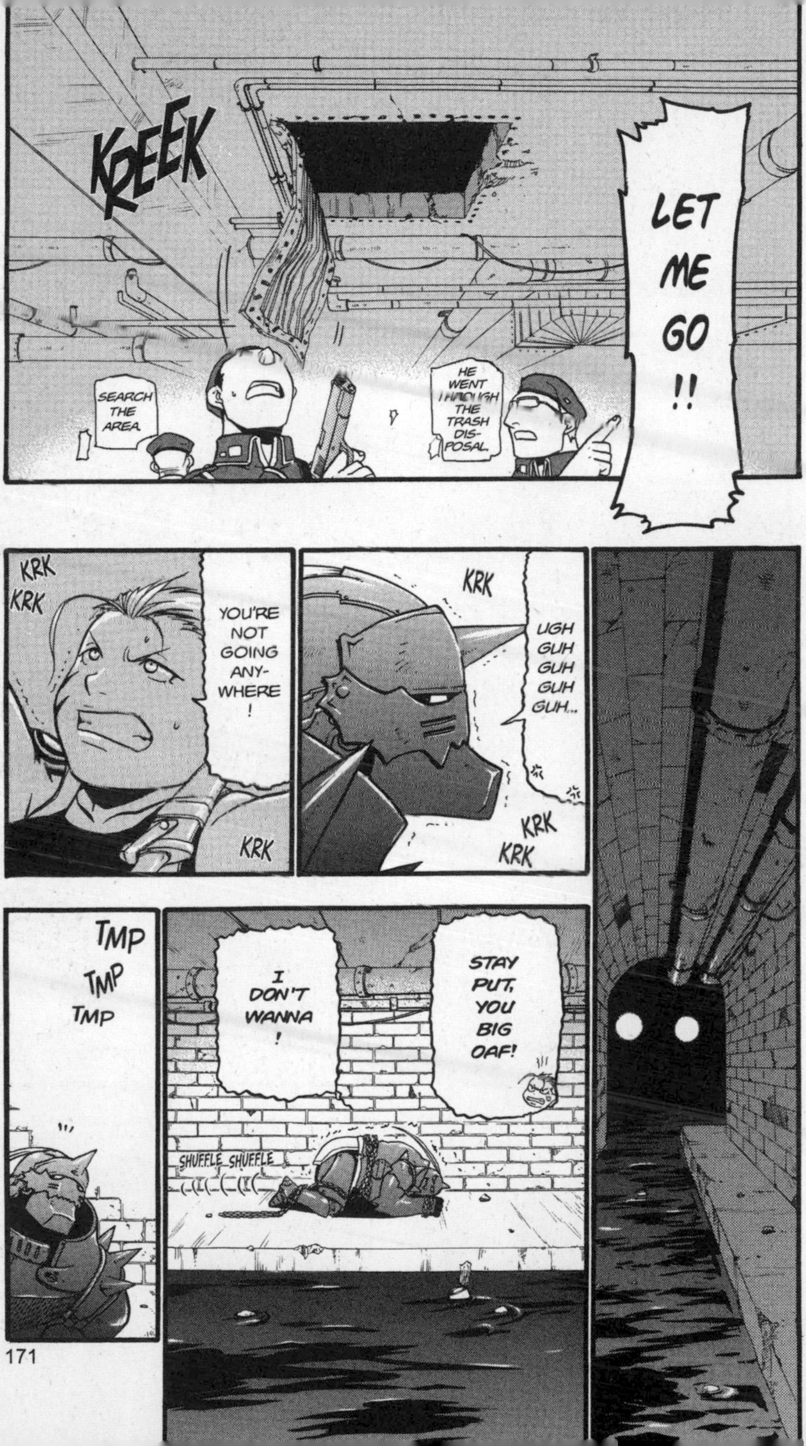
LET ME GO!!
KREEK
HE WENT THROUGH THE TRASH DISPOSAL.
SEARCH THE AREA.
KRK
UGH GUH GUH GUH GUH...
KRK KRK
KRK KRK
YOU'RE NOT GOING ANYWHERE!
KRK
STAY PUT, YOU BIG OAF!
I DON'T WANNA!
SHUFFLE SHUFFLE
TMP TMP TMP

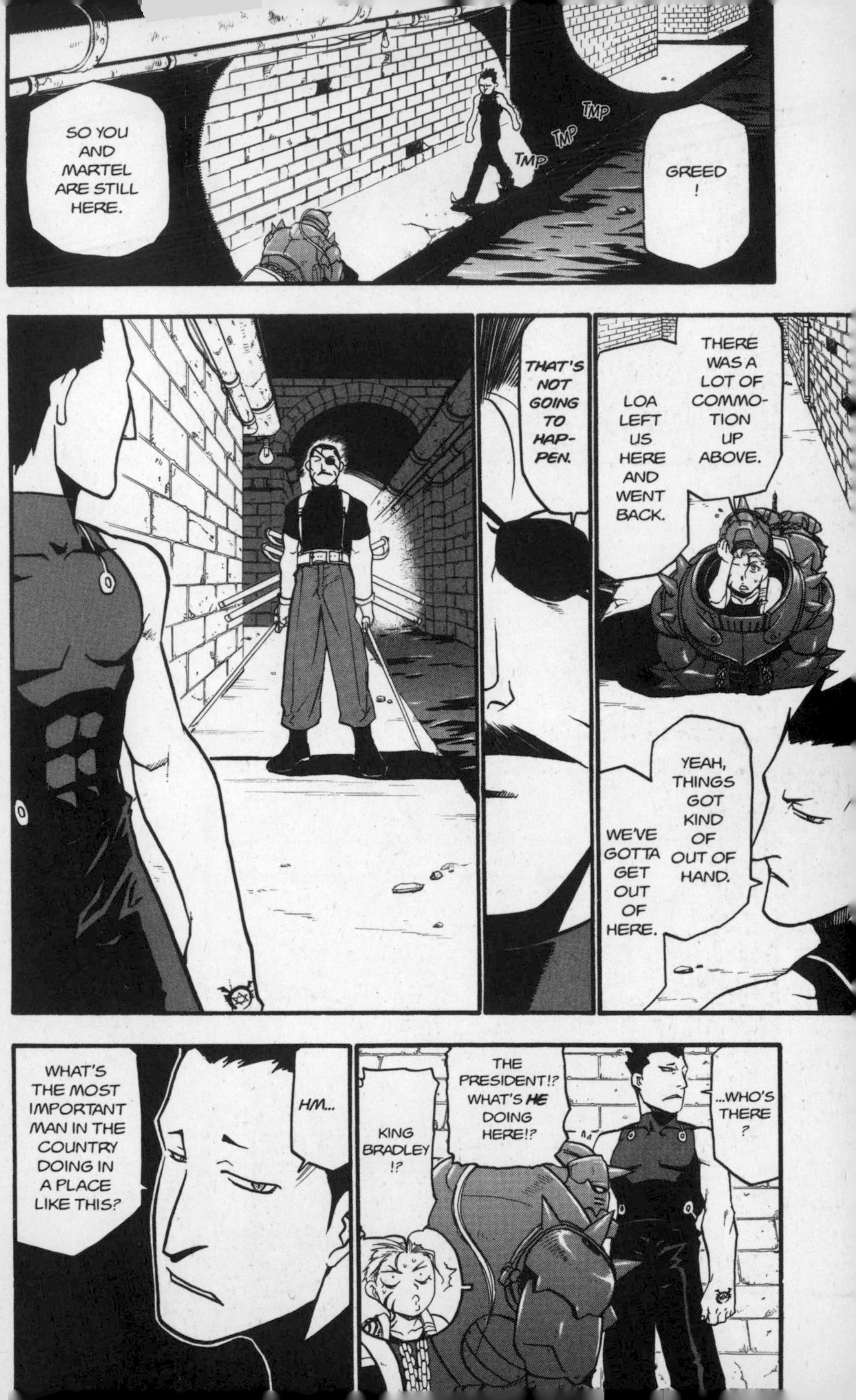
TMP TMP TMP
GREED!
SO YOU AND MARTEL ARE STILL HERE.
THERE WAS A LOT OF COMMOTION UP ABOVE.
LOA LEFT US HERE AND WENT BACK.
YEAH, THINGS GOT KIND OF OUT OF HAND.
WE'VE GOTTA GET OUT OF HERE.
THAT'S NOT GOING TO HAPPEN.
...WHO'S THERE?
THE PRESIDENT!? WHAT'S *HE* DOING HERE!?
KING BRADLEY!?
HM...
WHAT'S THE MOST IMPORTANT MAN IN THE COUNTRY DOING IN A PLACE LIKE THIS?

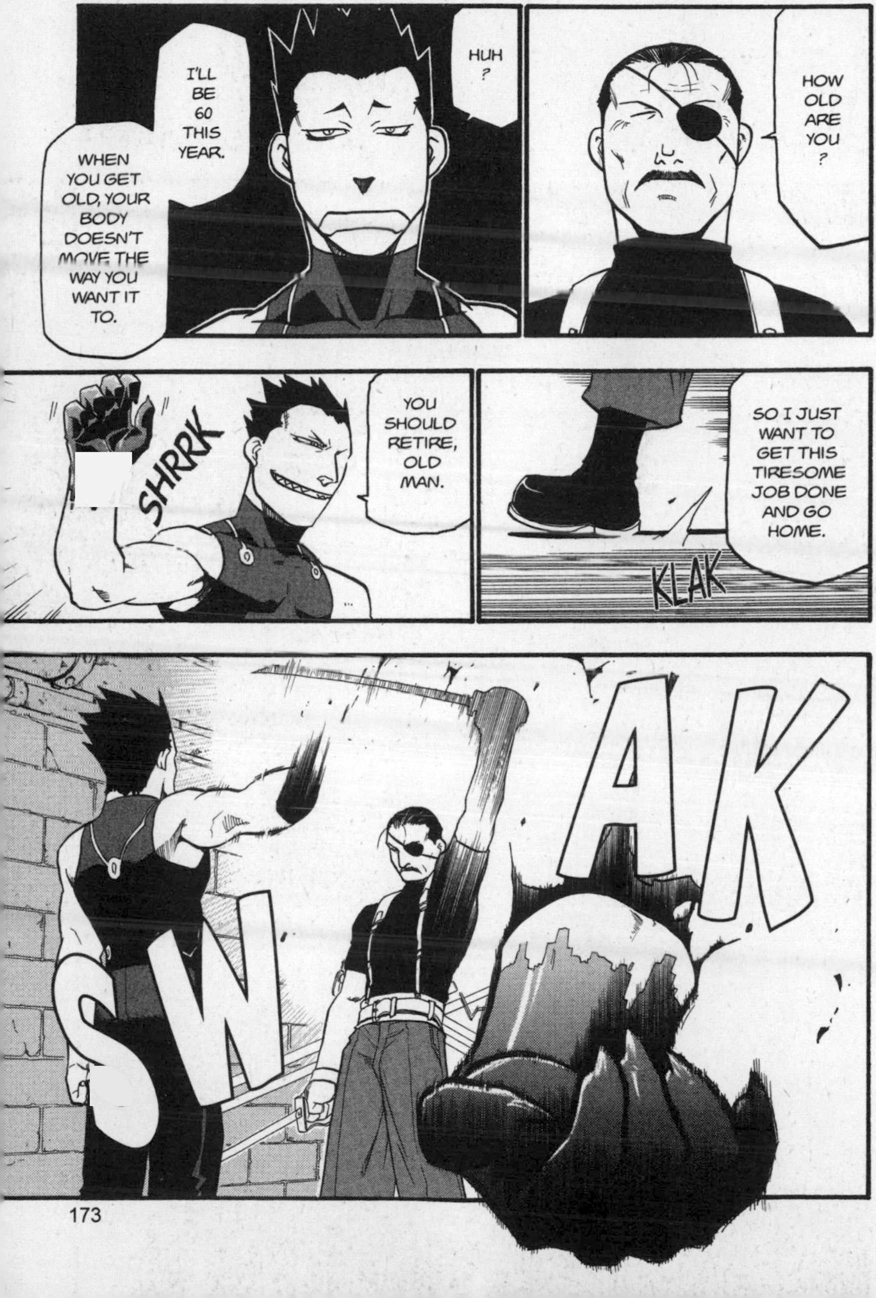
HOW OLD ARE YOU?
HUH?
I'LL BE 60 THIS YEAR.
WHEN YOU GET OLD, YOUR BODY DOESN'T MOVE THE WAY YOU WANT IT TO.
SO I JUST WANT TO GET THIS TIRESOME JOB DONE AND GO HOME.
KLAK
SHRRK
YOU SHOULD RETIRE, OLD MAN.
SWAK

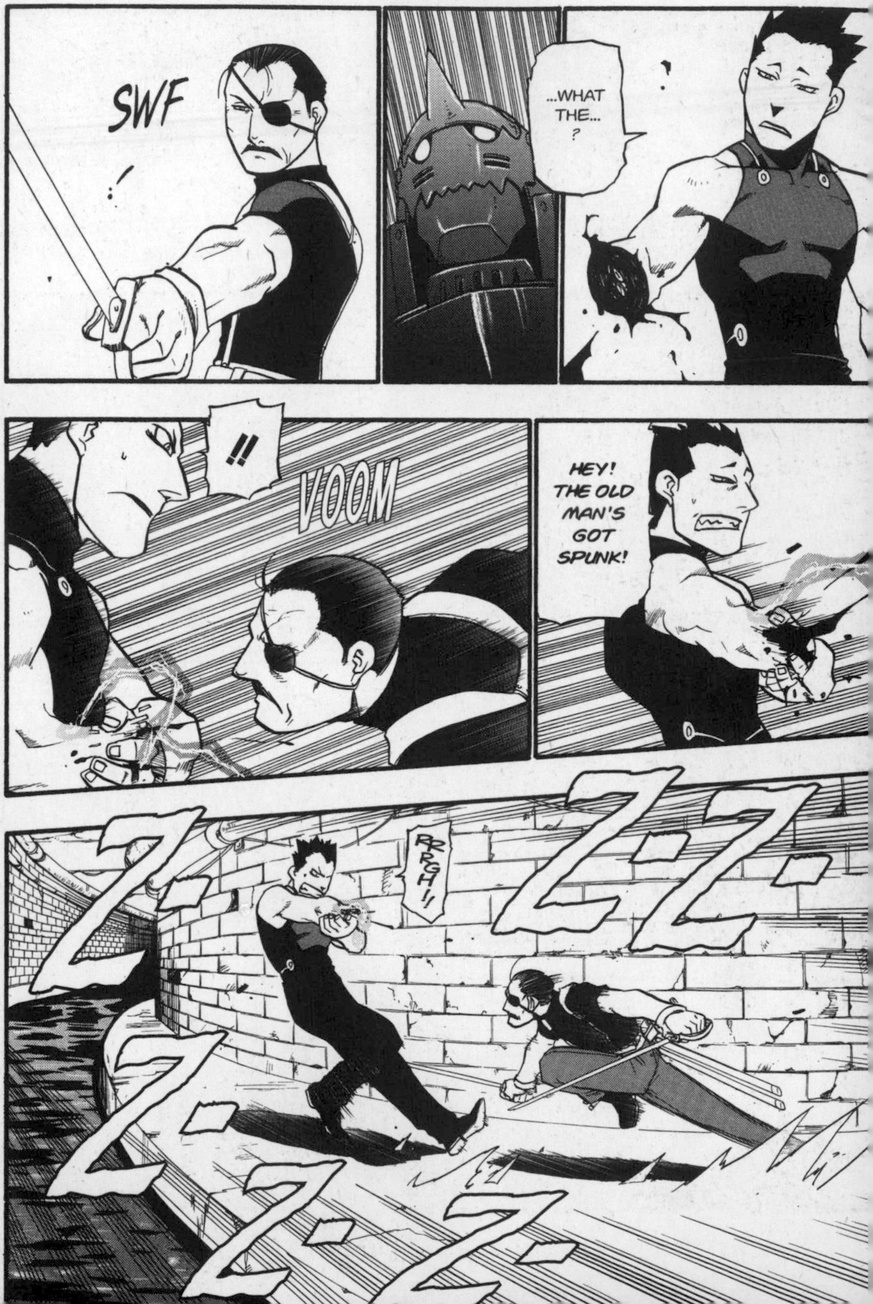
...WHAT THE...?
SWF
HEY! THE OLD MAN'S GOT SPUNK!
!!
VOOM
RRRGH!!

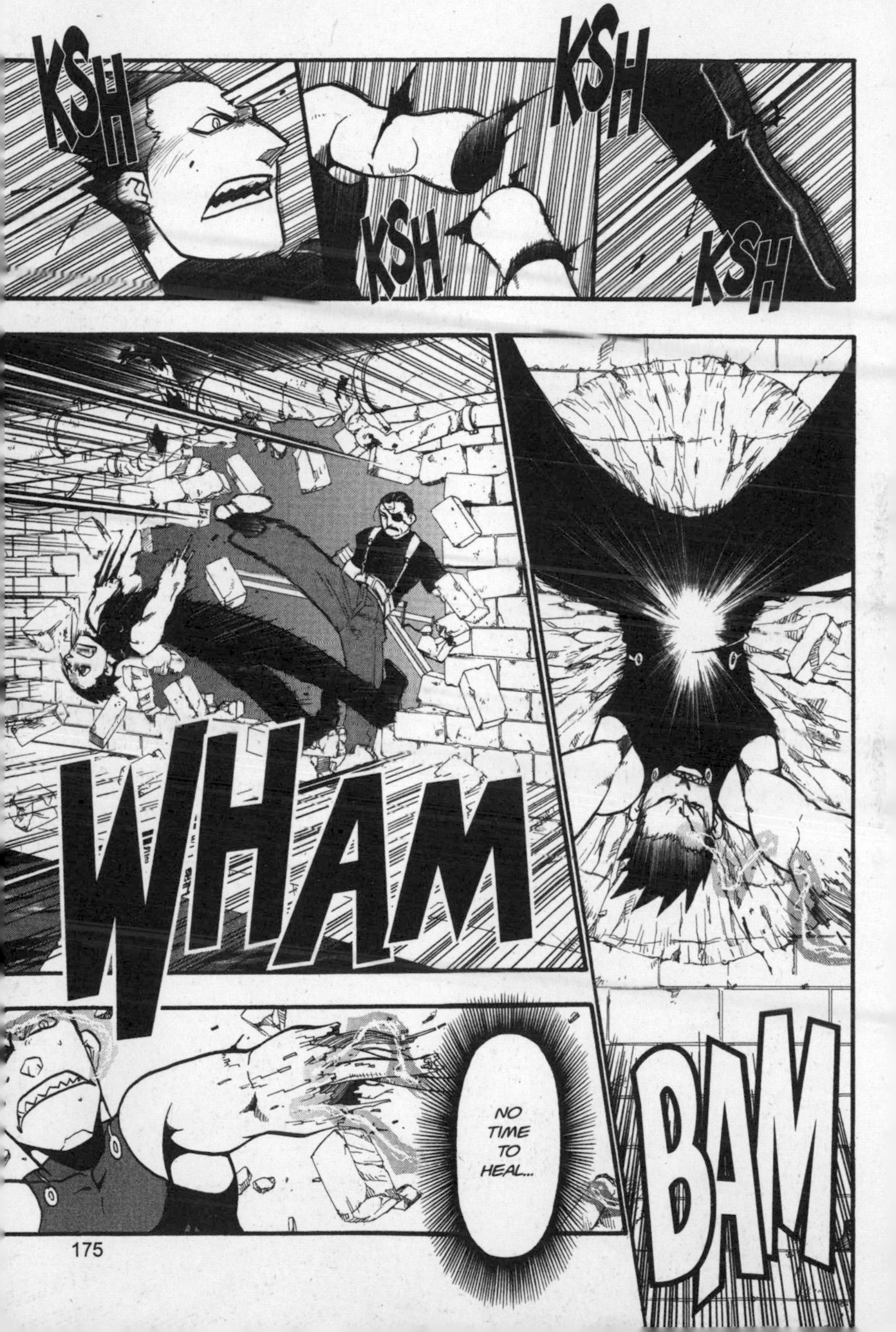
KSH
KSH
KSH
KSH
BAM
WHAM
NO TIME TO HEAL...

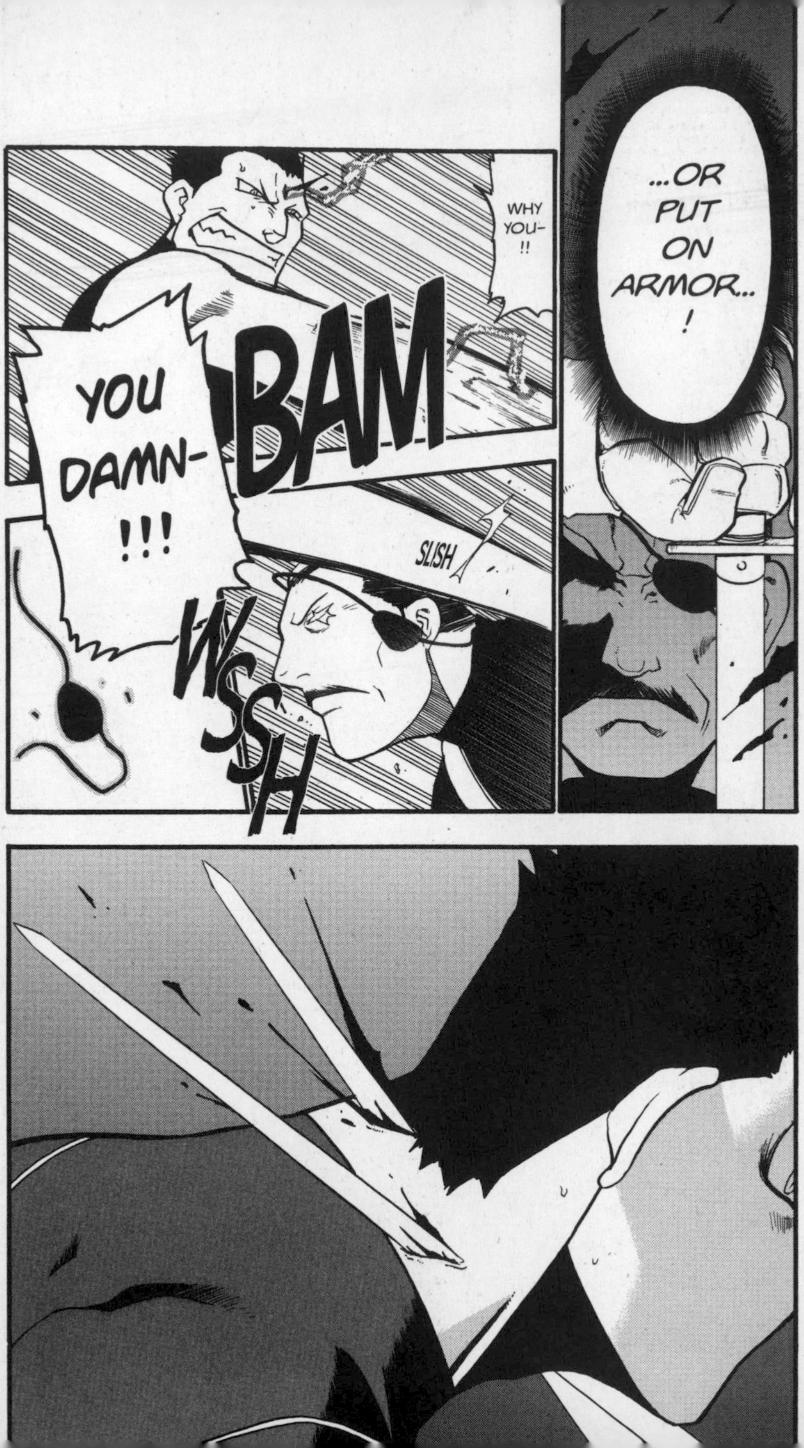
...OR PUT ON ARMOR...!
WHY YOU-!!
BAM
YOU DAMN-!!!
SLISH
WSSH

THIS MANGA WAS ORIGINALLY PRINTED IN MONTHLY **SHONEN GANGAN**, SEPTEMBER THROUGH DECEMBER 2003.

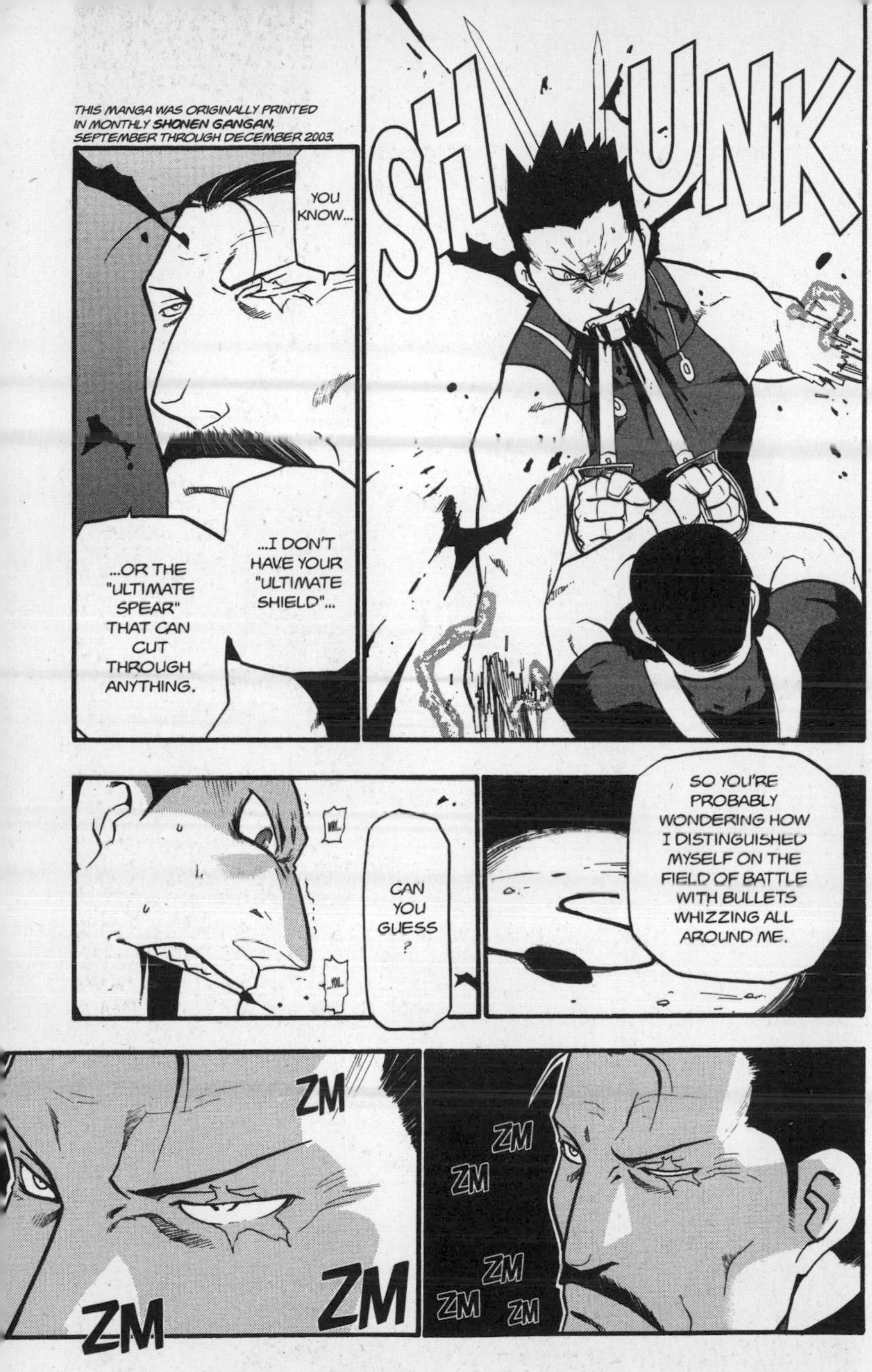
SHUNK
YOU KNOW...
...I DON'T HAVE YOUR "ULTIMATE SHIELD"...
...OR THE "ULTIMATE SPEAR" THAT CAN CUT THROUGH ANYTHING.
SO YOU'RE PROBABLY WONDERING HOW I DISTINGUISHED MYSELF ON THE FIELD OF BATTLE WITH BULLETS WHIZZING ALL AROUND ME.
CAN YOU GUESS?
WHY...
...YOU...
ZM
ZM
ZM
ZM
ZM
ZM
ZM
ZM

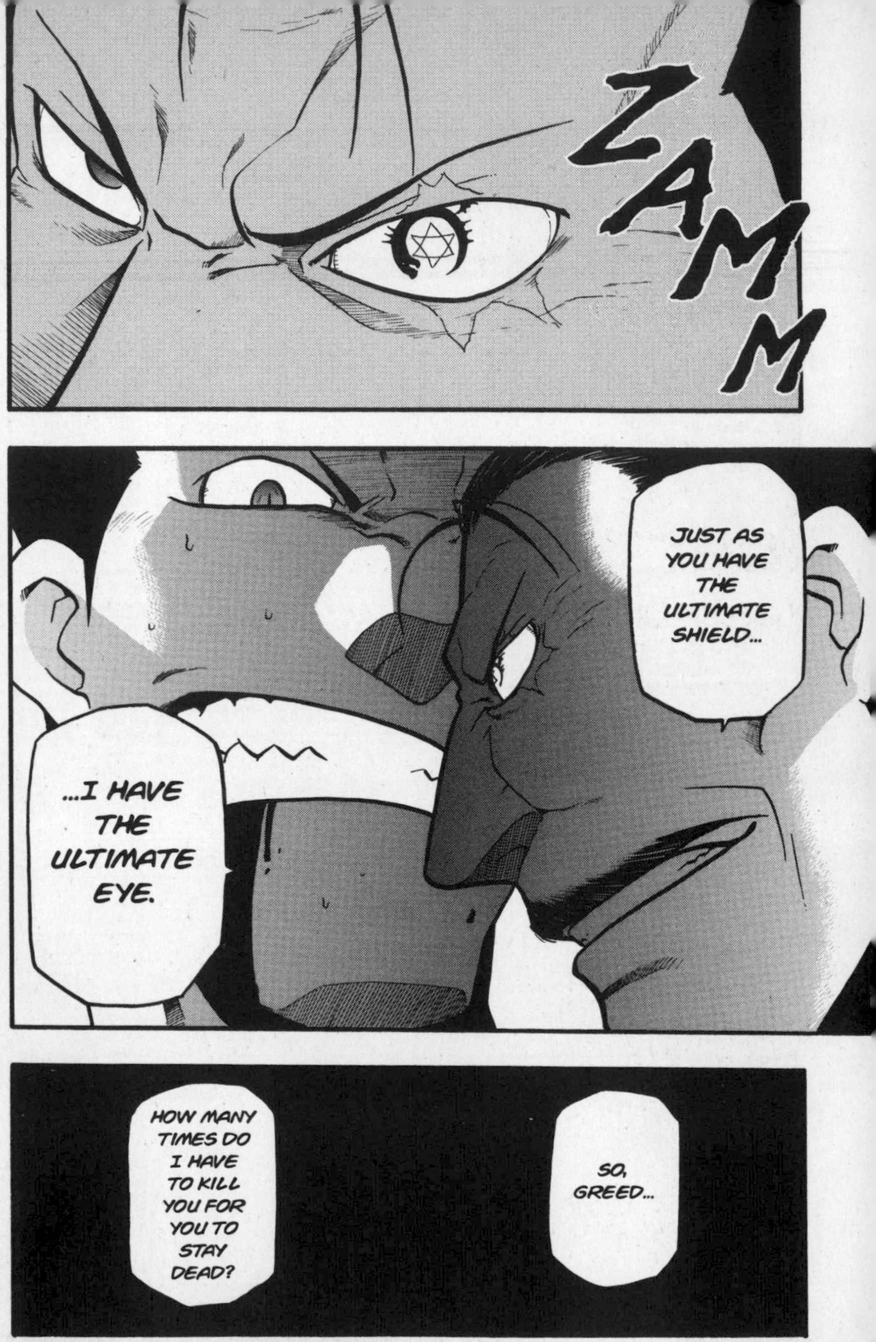
ZAMM
JUST AS YOU HAVE THE ULTIMATE SHIELD...
...I HAVE THE ULTIMATE EYE.
SO, GREED...
HOW MANY TIMES DO I HAVE TO KILL YOU FOR YOU TO STAY DEAD?

To be Continued…

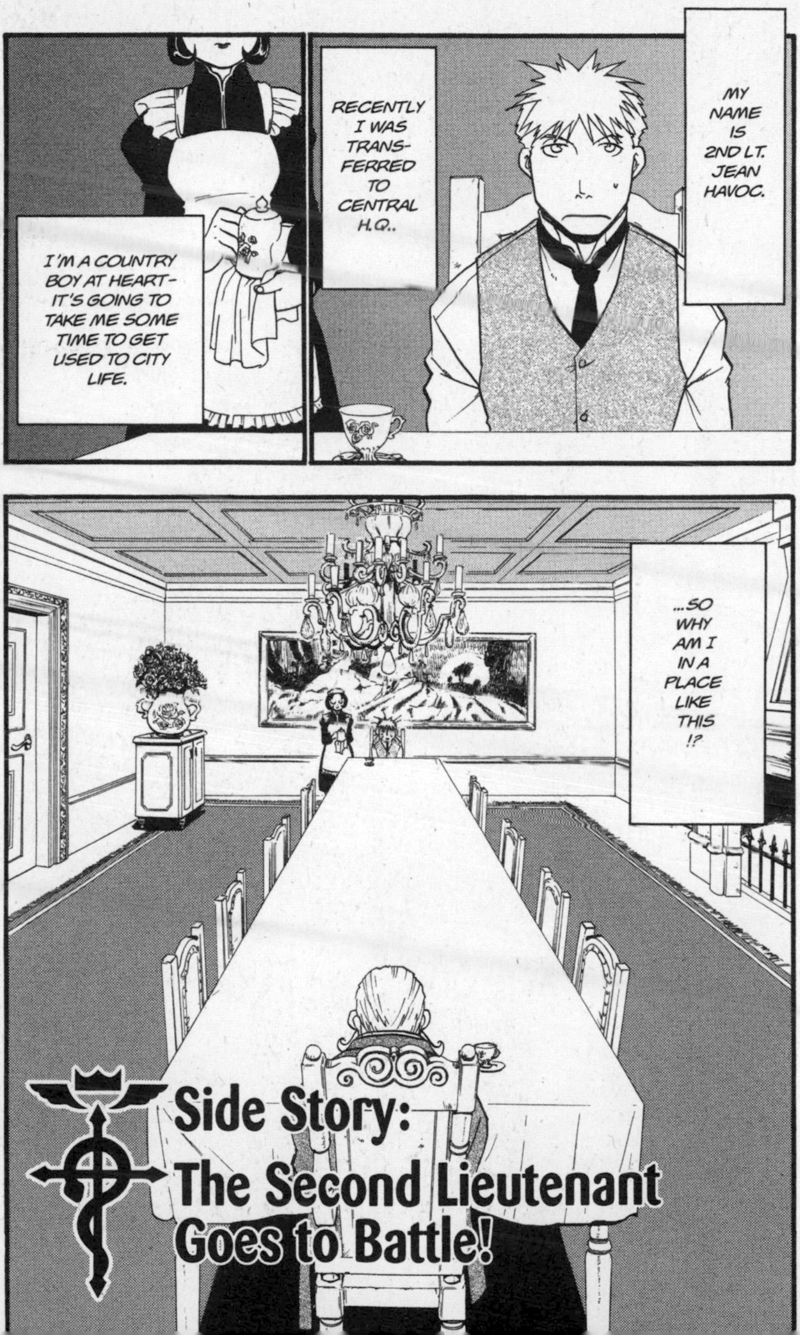
MY NAME IS 2ND LT. JEAN HAVOC.
RECENTLY I WAS TRANS-FERRED TO CENTRAL H.Q..
I'M A COUNTRY BOY AT HEART-IT'S GOING TO TAKE ME SOME TIME TO GET USED TO CITY LIFE.
...SO WHY AM I IN A PLACE LIKE THIS!?
Side Story:
The Second Lieutenant Goes to Battle!

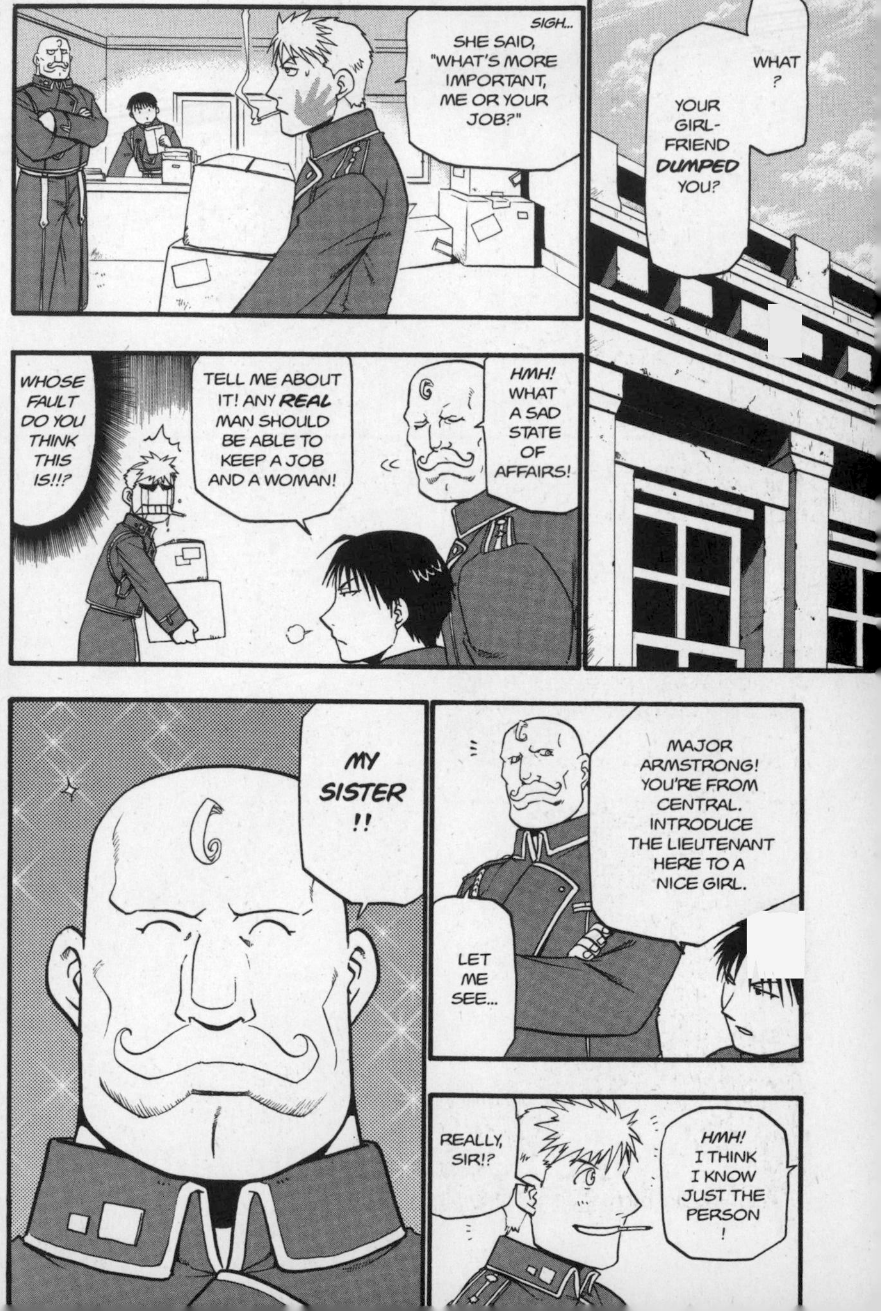
WHAT?
YOUR GIRLFRIEND DUMPED YOU?
SIGH... SHE SAID, "WHAT'S MORE IMPORTANT, ME OR YOUR JOB?"
HMH! WHAT A SAD STATE OF AFFAIRS!
TELL ME ABOUT IT! ANY REAL MAN SHOULD BE ABLE TO KEEP A JOB AND A WOMAN!
WHOSE FAULT DO YOU THINK THIS IS!!?
MAJOR ARMSTRONG! YOU'RE FROM CENTRAL. INTRODUCE THE LIEUTENANT HERE TO A NICE GIRL.
LET ME SEE...
HMH! I THINK I KNOW JUST THE PERSON!
REALLY, SIR!?
MY SISTER!!

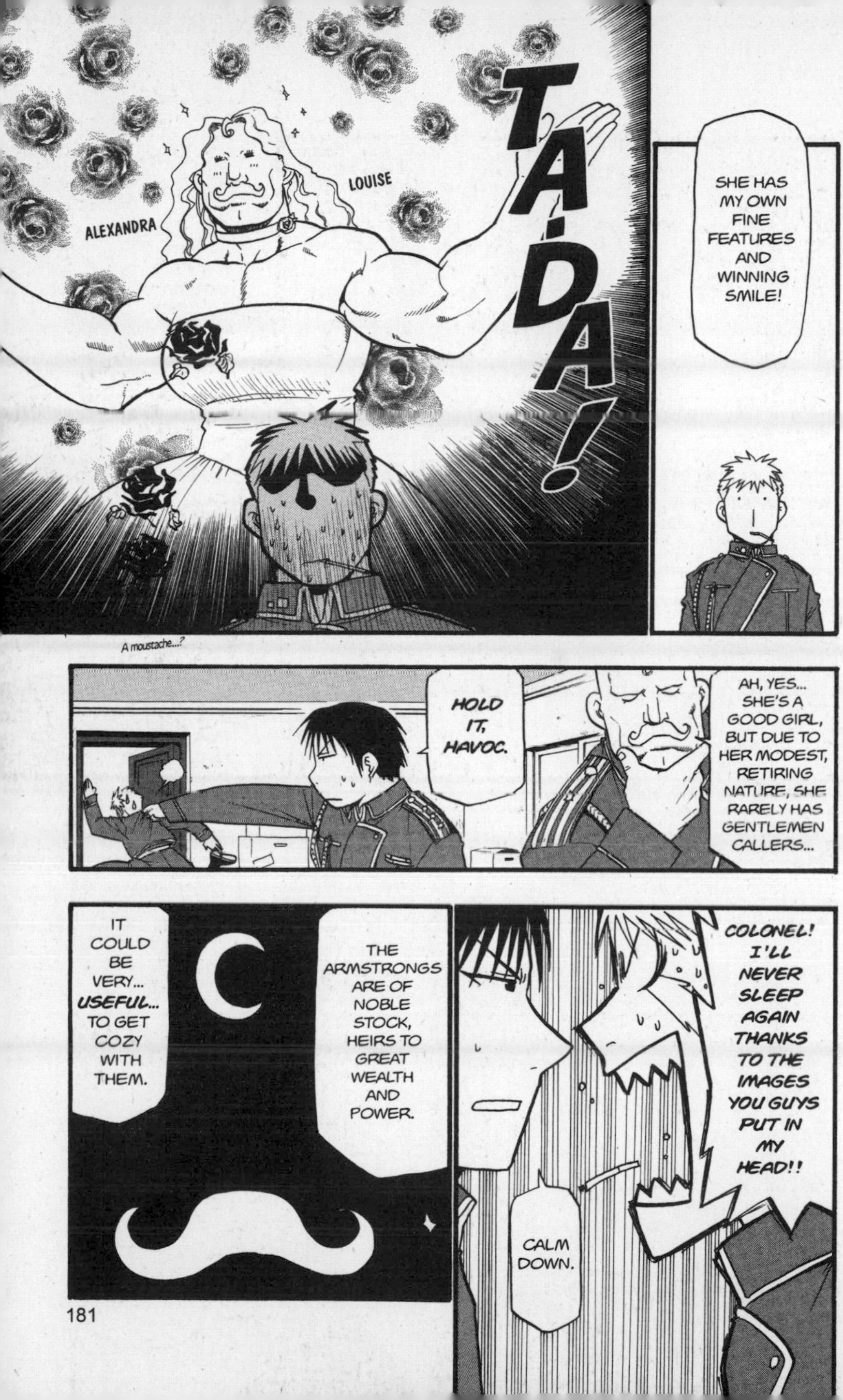
SHE HAS MY OWN FINE FEATURES AND WINNING SMILE!
TA-DA!
LOUISE
ALEXANDRA
A moustache...?
AH, YES... SHE'S A GOOD GIRL, BUT DUE TO HER MODEST, RETIRING NATURE, SHE RARELY HAS GENTLEMEN CALLERS...
HOLD IT, HAVOC.
COLONEL! I'LL NEVER SLEEP AGAIN THANKS TO THE IMAGES YOU GUYS PUT IN MY HEAD!!
CALM DOWN.
THE ARMSTRONGS ARE OF NOBLE STOCK, HEIRS TO GREAT WEALTH AND POWER.
IT COULD BE VERY... USEFUL... TO GET COZY WITH THEM.

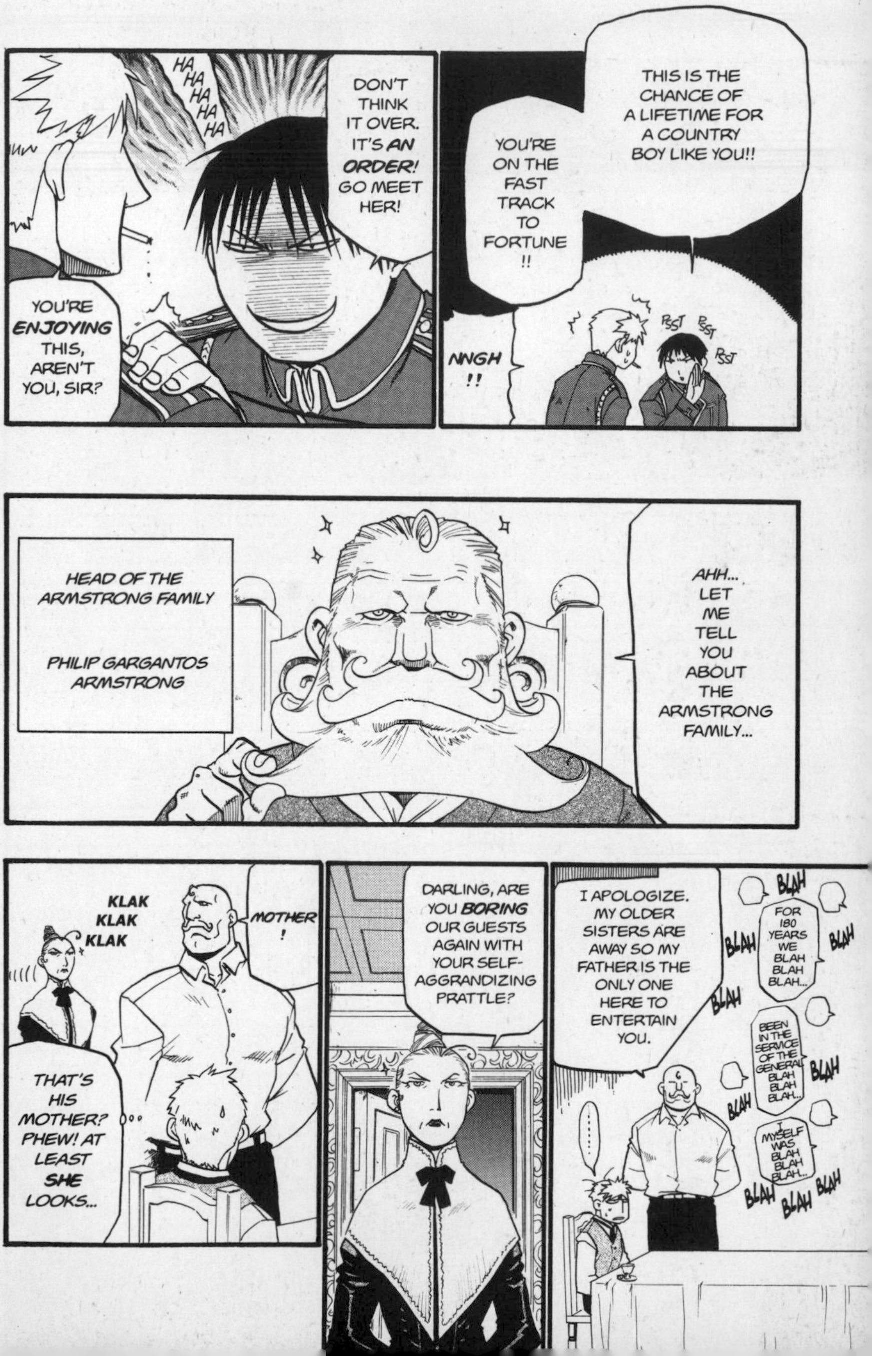
THIS IS THE CHANCE OF A LIFETIME FOR A COUNTRY BOY LIKE YOU!!
YOU'RE ON THE FAST TRACK TO FORTUNE !!
PSST PSST PSST
NNGH !!
HA HA HA HA HA
DON'T THINK IT OVER. IT'S AN ORDER! GO MEET HER!
YOU'RE ENJOYING THIS, AREN'T YOU, SIR?
AHH... LET ME TELL YOU ABOUT THE ARMSTRONG FAMILY...
HEAD OF THE ARMSTRONG FAMILY
PHILIP GARGANTOS ARMSTRONG
I APOLOGIZE. MY OLDER SISTERS ARE AWAY SO MY FATHER IS THE ONLY ONE HERE TO ENTERTAIN YOU.
BLAH
FOR 180 YEARS WE BLAH BLAH BLAH...
BLAH
BLAH
BLAH
BEEN IN THE SERVICE OF THE GENERAL BLAH BLAH BLAH...
BLAH
BLAH
I MYSELF WAS BLAH BLAH BLAH...
BLAH
BLAH
BLAH
......
DARLING, ARE YOU BORING OUR GUESTS AGAIN WITH YOUR SELF-AGGRANDIZING PRATTLE?
MOTHER!
KLAK KLAK KLAK
THAT'S HIS MOTHER? PHEW! AT LEAST SHE LOOKS...

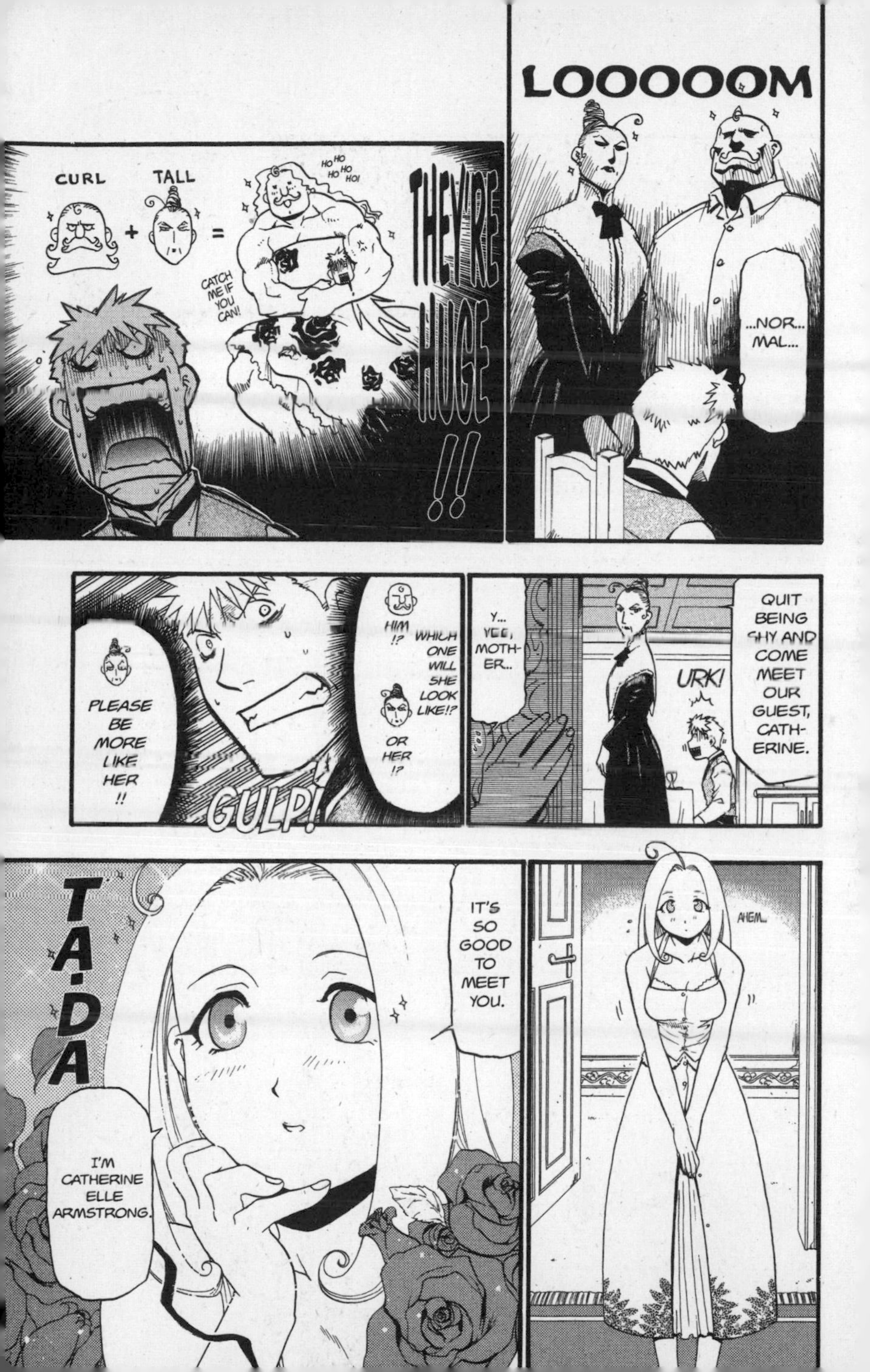
LOOOOOM
...NOR... MAL...
CURL
TALL
HO HO HO HO HO!
CATCH ME IF YOU CAN!
THEY'RE HUGE!!
QUIT BEING SHY AND COME MEET OUR GUEST, CATHERINE.
URK!
Y... YEE, MOTHER..
WHICH ONE WILL SHE LOOK LIKE!?
HIM!?
OR HER!?
PLEASE BE MORE LIKE HER!!
GULP!
AHEM...
TA-DA
IT'S SO GOOD TO MEET YOU.
I'M CATHERINE ELLE ARMSTRONG.

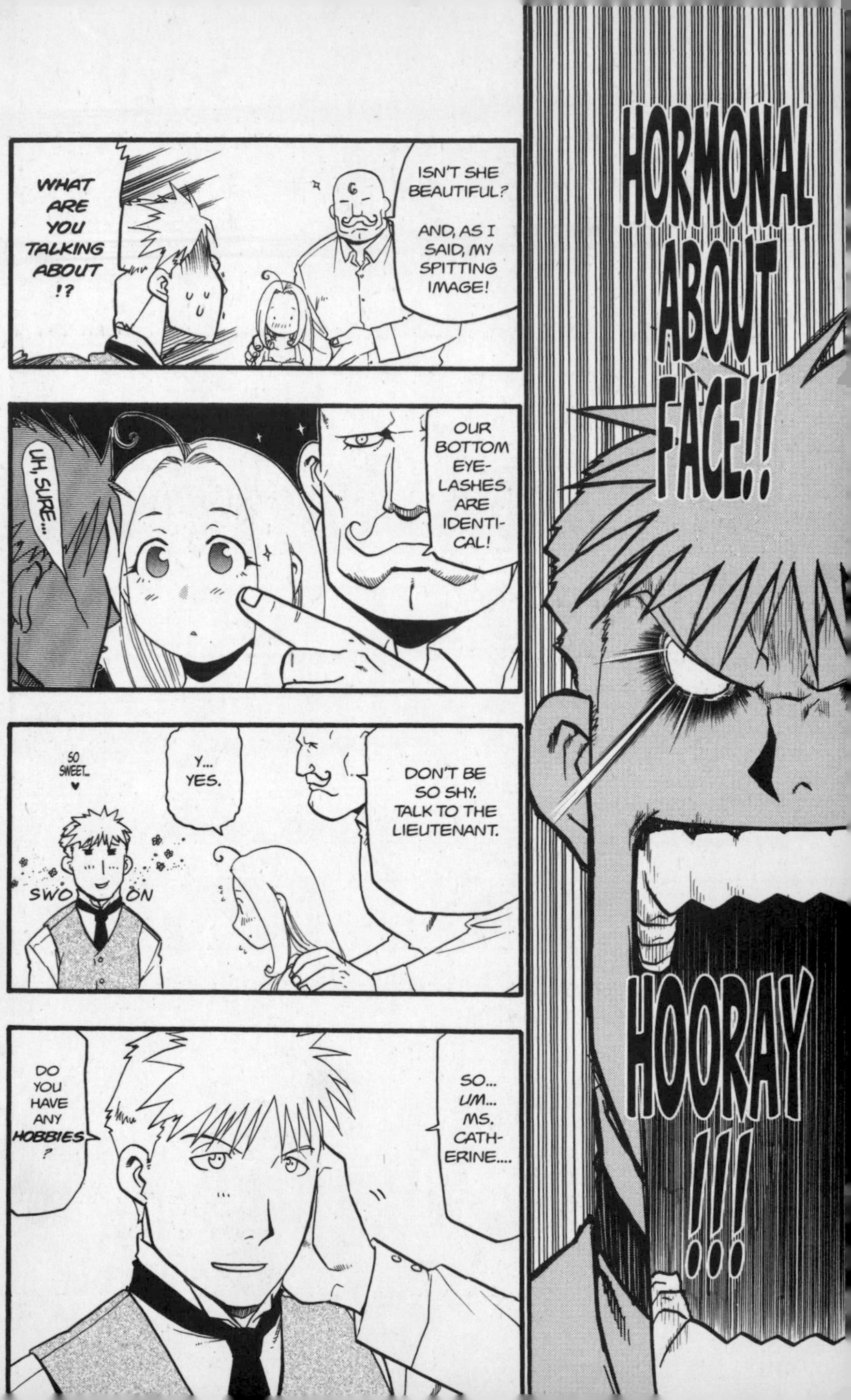
HORMONAL ABOUT FACE!!
HOORAY!!!
ISN'T SHE BEAUTIFUL?
AND, AS I SAID, MY SPITTING IMAGE!
WHAT ARE YOU TALKING ABOUT!?
OUR BOTTOM EYE-LASHES ARE IDENTI-CAL!
UH, SURE...
DON'T BE SO SHY. TALK TO THE LIEUTENANT.
Y... YES.
SO SWEET... ♥
SWOON
SO... UM... MS. CATH-ERINE....
DO YOU HAVE ANY HOBBIES?

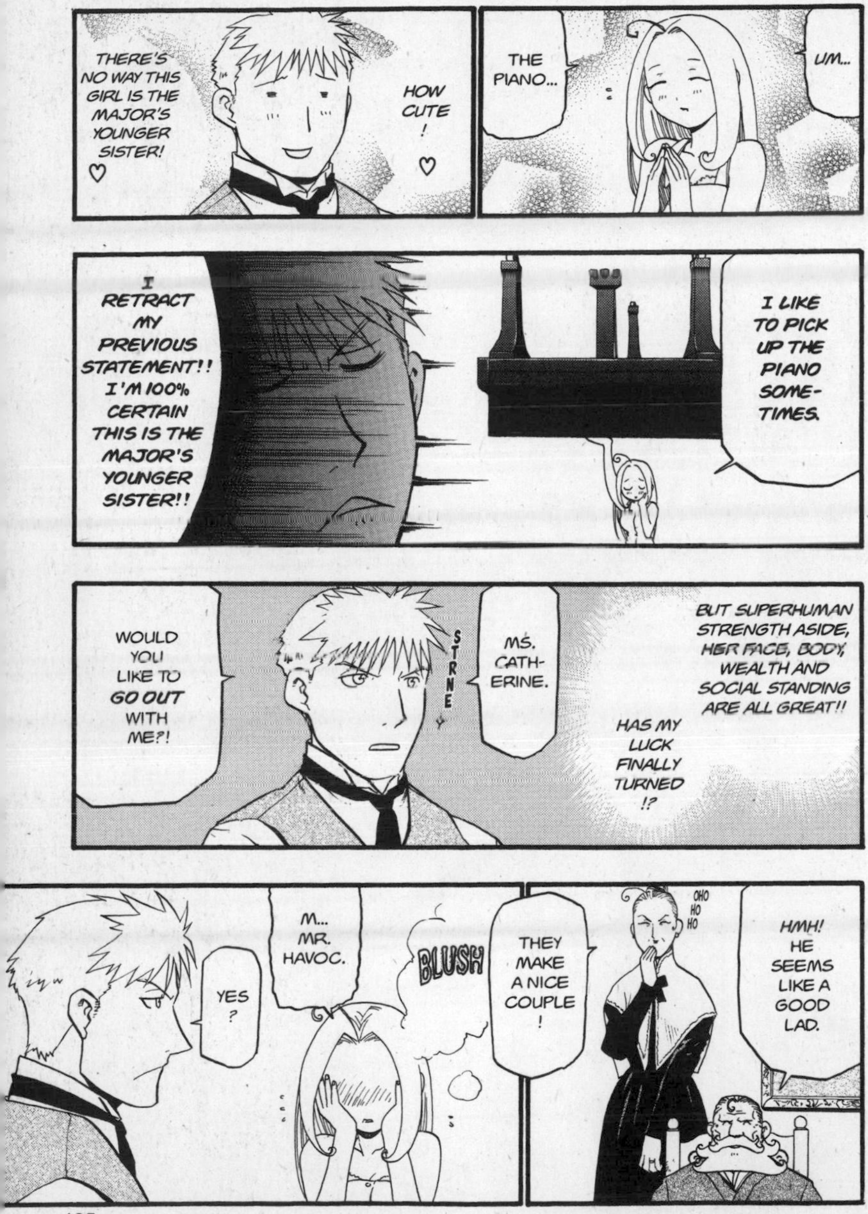
UM...
THE PIANO...
HOW CUTE!
THERE'S NO WAY THIS GIRL IS THE MAJOR'S YOUNGER SISTER!
I LIKE TO PICK UP THE PIANO SOME-TIMES.
I RETRACT MY PREVIOUS STATEMENT!! I'M 100% CERTAIN THIS IS THE MAJOR'S YOUNGER SISTER!!
BUT SUPERHUMAN STRENGTH ASIDE, HER FACE, BODY, WEALTH AND SOCIAL STANDING ARE ALL GREAT!!
HAS MY LUCK FINALLY TURNED!?
MS. CATH-ERINE.
STRNE
WOULD YOU LIKE TO GO OUT WITH ME?!
HMH! HE SEEMS LIKE A GOOD LAD.
OHO HO HO
THEY MAKE A NICE COUPLE!
M... MR. HAVOC.
BLUSH
YES?

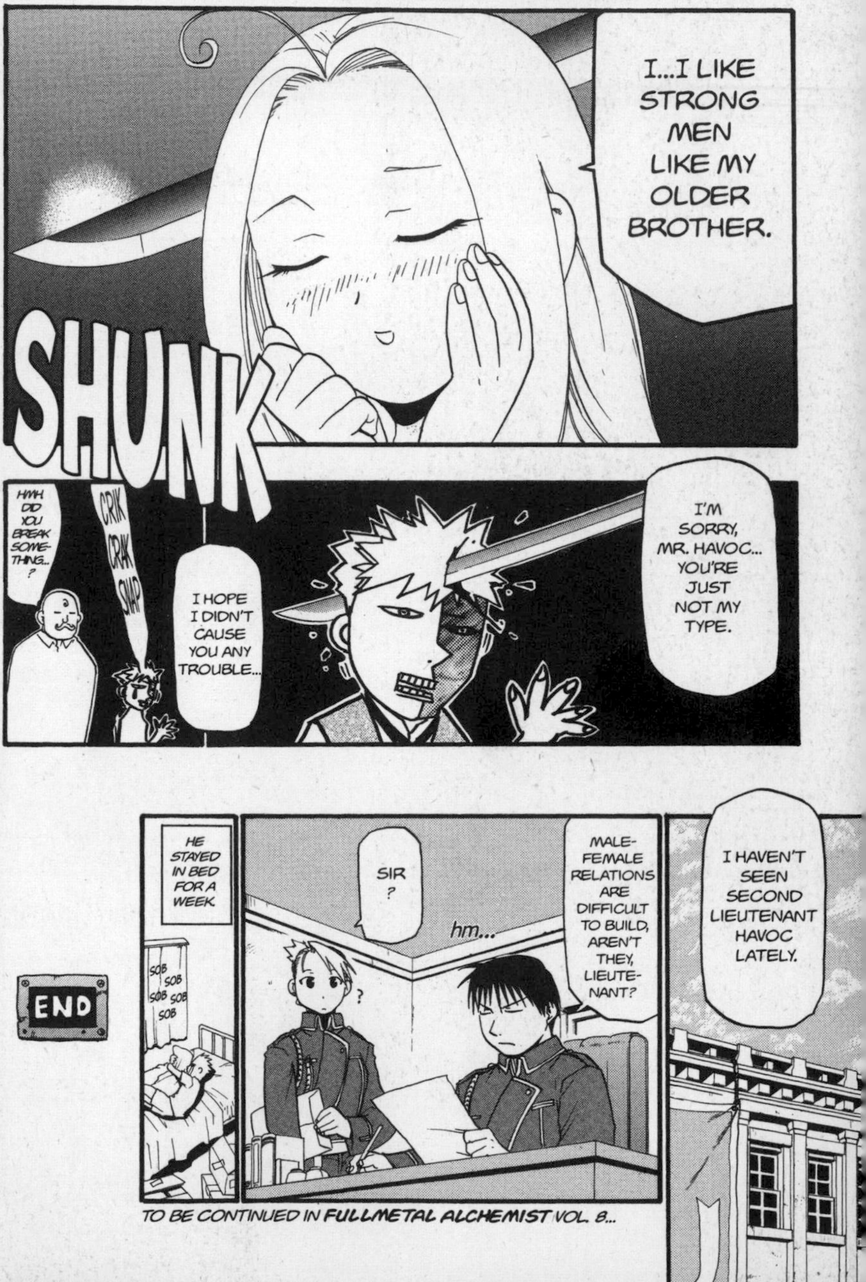
I...I LIKE STRONG MEN LIKE MY OLDER BROTHER.
SHUNK
I'M SORRY, MR. HAVOC... YOU'RE JUST NOT MY TYPE.
I HOPE I DIDN'T CAUSE YOU ANY TROUBLE...
CRIK CRAK SNAP
HMH. DID YOU BREAK SOME-THING... ?
I HAVEN'T SEEN SECOND LIEUTENANT HAVOC LATELY.
MALE-FEMALE RELATIONS ARE DIFFICULT TO BUILD, AREN'T THEY, LIEUTE-NANT?
hm...
SIR ?
?
HE STAYED IN BED FOR A WEEK.
SOB SOB SOB SOB SOB
END

TO BE CONTINUED IN **FULLMETAL ALCHEMIST** VOL. 8...

CRUEL GIRL

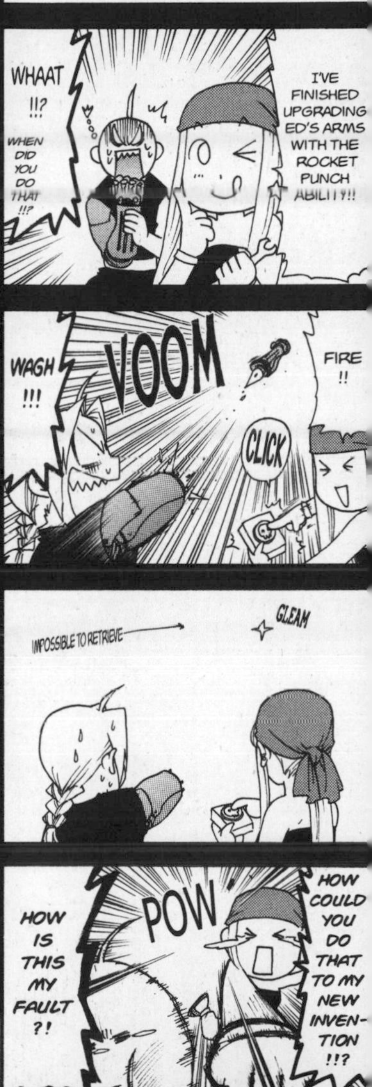
I'VE FINISHED UPGRADING ED'S ARMS WITH THE ROCKET PUNCH ABILITY!!
WHAAT!!?
WHEN DID YOU DO THAT!!?
FIRE!!
VOOM
CLICK
WAGH!!!
GLEAM
IMPOSSIBLE TO RETRIEVE
HOW COULD YOU DO THAT TO MY NEW INVENTION!!?
POW
HOW IS THIS MY FAULT?!

FULLMETAL ALCHEMIST 7

SPECIAL THANKS TO...

KEISUI TAKAEDA-SAN
SANKICHI HINODEYA-SAN
MASANARI YUBEKA-SAN
JUNSHI BABA-SAN
AIYAABALL-SAN
JUN TOKO-SAN
YOICHI SHIMOMURA-SHI (MANAGER)

AND YOU!!

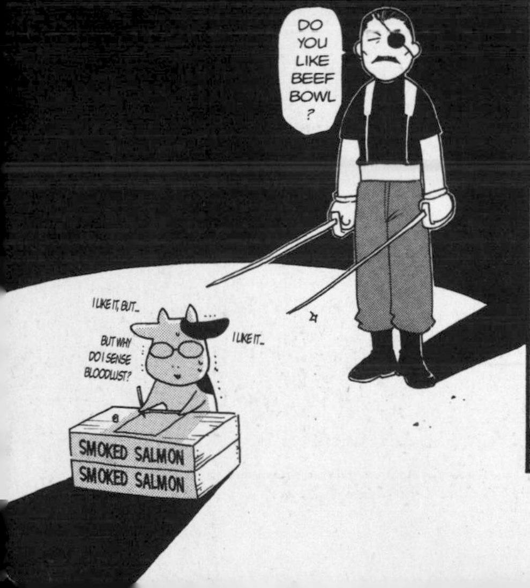
DO YOU LIKE BEEF BOWL?
I LIKE IT...
I LIKE IT, BUT...
BUT WHY DO I SENSE BLOODLUST?
SMOKED SALMON
SMOKED SALMON

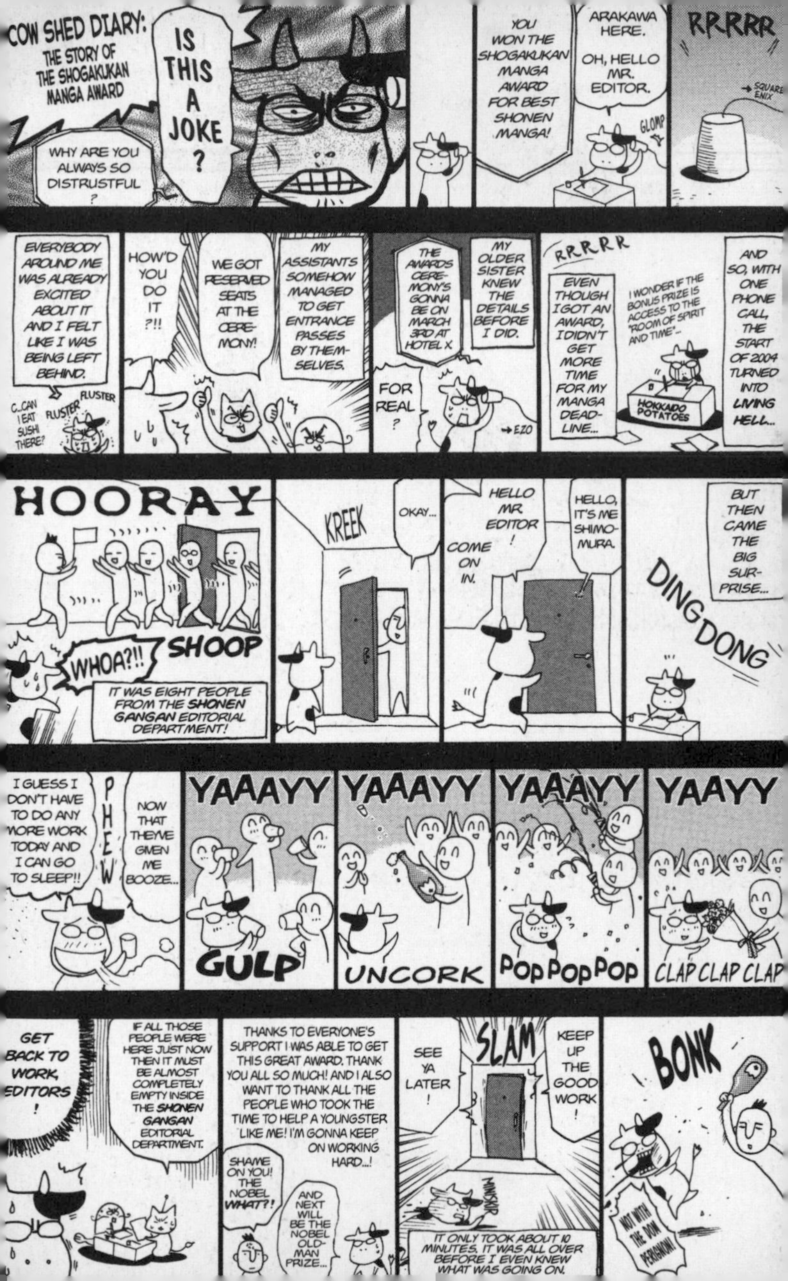
RRRRR
→SQUARE ENIX
ARAKAWA HERE.
OH, HELLO MR. EDITOR.
GLOMP
YOU WON THE SHOGAKUKAN MANGA AWARD FOR BEST SHONEN MANGA!
COW SHED DIARY: THE STORY OF THE SHOGAKUKAN MANGA AWARD
IS THIS A JOKE?
WHY ARE YOU ALWAYS SO DISTRUSTFUL?
AND SO, WITH ONE PHONE CALL, THE START OF 2004 TURNED INTO LIVING HELL...
RRRRR
EVEN THOUGH I GOT AN AWARD, I DIDN'T GET MORE TIME FOR MY MANGA DEADLINE...
I WONDER IF THE BONUS PRIZE IS ACCESS TO THE "ROOM OF SPIRIT AND TIME"...
HOKKAIDO POTATOES
MY OLDER SISTER KNEW THE DETAILS BEFORE I DID.
THE AWARDS CEREMONY'S GONNA BE ON MARCH 3RD AT HOTEL X
FOR REAL?
→EZO
MY ASSISTANTS SOMEHOW MANAGED TO GET ENTRANCE PASSES BY THEMSELVES.
WE GOT RESERVED SEATS AT THE CEREMONY!
HOW'D YOU DO IT?!!
EVERYBODY AROUND ME WAS ALREADY EXCITED ABOUT IT AND I FELT LIKE I WAS BEING LEFT BEHIND.
FLUSTER FLUSTER
C...CAN I EAT SUSHI THERE?
BUT THEN CAME THE BIG SURPRISE...
DING DONG
HELLO, IT'S ME SHIMOMURA.
HELLO MR. EDITOR!
COME ON IN.
OKAY...
KREEK
HOORAY
SHOOP
WHOA?!!
IT WAS EIGHT PEOPLE FROM THE SHONEN GANGAN EDITORIAL DEPARTMENT!
YAAYY
CLAP CLAP CLAP
YAAAYY
POP POP POP
YAAAYY
UNCORK
YAAAYY
GULP
NOW THAT THEY'VE GIVEN ME BOOZE...
PHEW
I GUESS I DON'T HAVE TO DO ANY MORE WORK TODAY AND I CAN GO TO SLEEP!!
BONK
NOT WITH THE DOM PERIGNON!
KEEP UP THE GOOD WORK!
SLAM
SEE YA LATER!
IT ONLY TOOK ABOUT 10 MINUTES. IT WAS ALL OVER BEFORE I EVEN KNEW WHAT WAS GOING ON.
THANKS TO EVERYONE'S SUPPORT I WAS ABLE TO GET THIS GREAT AWARD. THANK YOU ALL SO MUCH! AND I ALSO WANT TO THANK ALL THE PEOPLE WHO TOOK THE TIME TO HELP A YOUNGSTER LIKE ME! I'M GONNA KEEP ON WORKING HARD...!
AND NEXT WILL BE THE NOBEL OLD-MAN PRIZE...
SHAME ON YOU! THE NOBEL WHAT?!
IF ALL THOSE PEOPLE WERE HERE JUST NOW THEN IT MUST BE ALMOST COMPLETELY EMPTY INSIDE THE SHONEN GANGAN EDITORIAL DEPARTMENT.
GET BACK TO WORK, EDITORS!

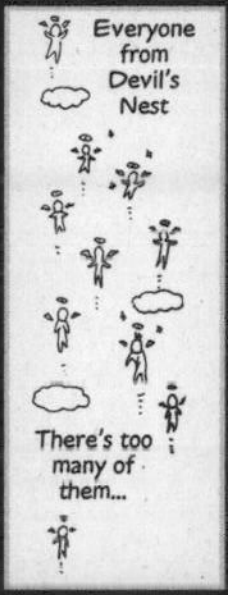
Everyone from Devil's Nest
There's too many of them...
In Memoriam

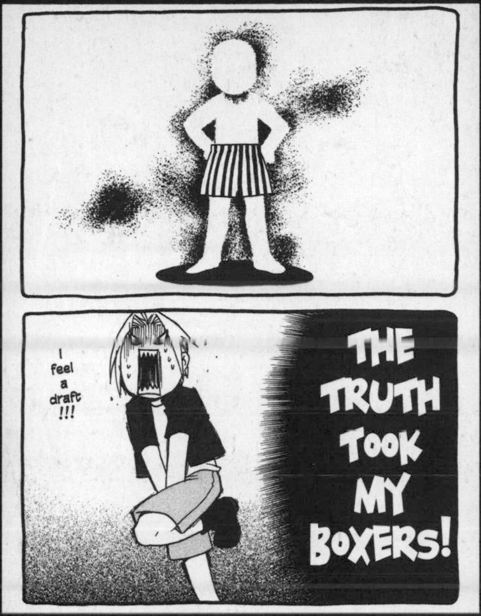
I feel a draft !!!
THE TRUTH TOOK MY BOXERS!

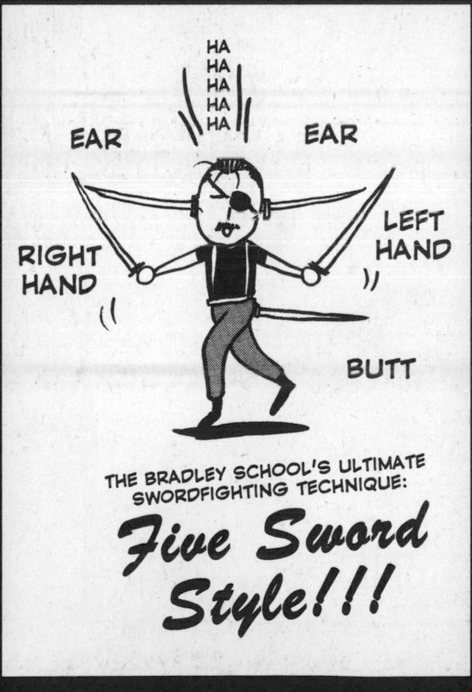
HA HA HA HA HA
EAR
EAR
LEFT HAND
RIGHT HAND
BUTT
THE BRADLEY SCHOOL'S ULTIMATE SWORDFIGHTING TECHNIQUE:
Five Sword Style!!!

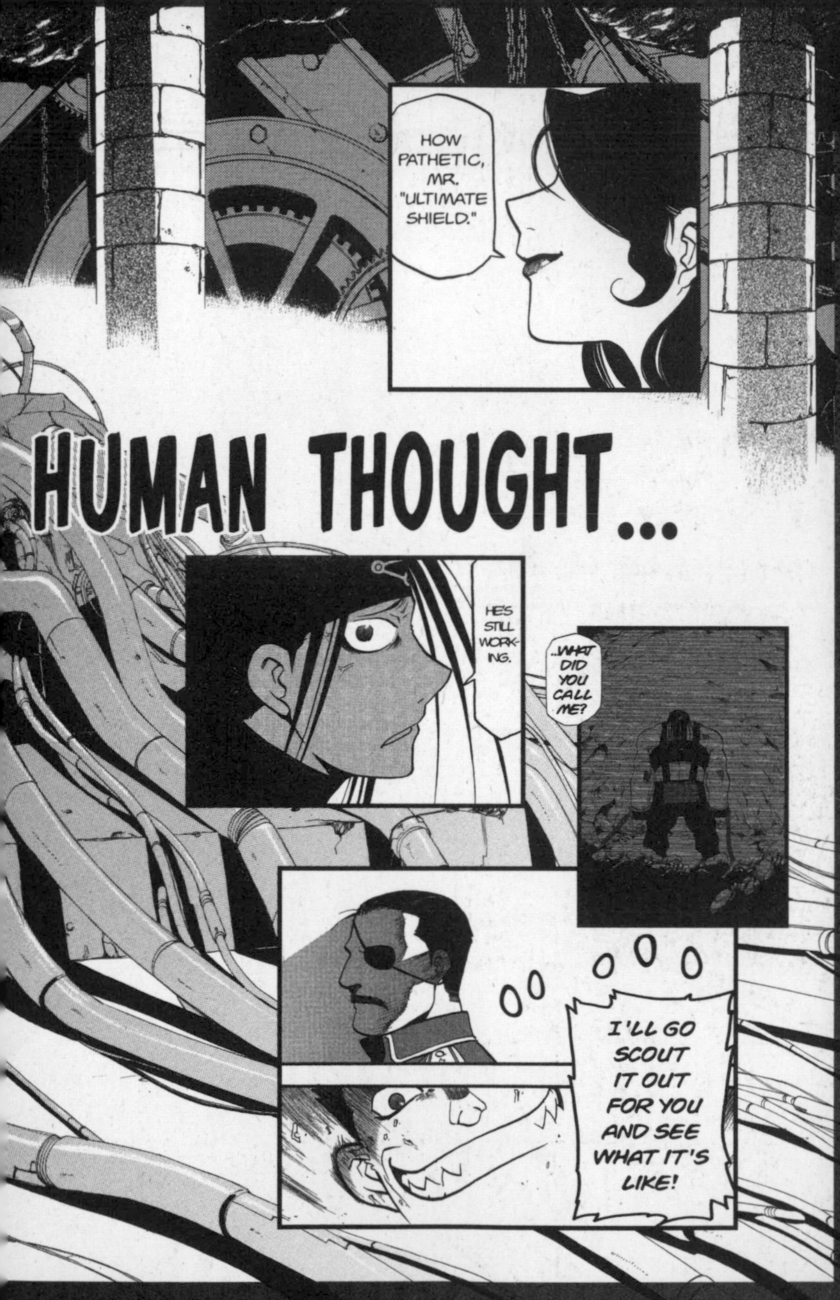
HOW PATHETIC, MR. "ULTIMATE SHIELD."
HUMAN THOUGHT...
...WHAT DID YOU CALL ME?
HE'S STILL WORKING.
I'LL GO SCOUT IT OUT FOR YOU AND SEE WHAT IT'S LIKE!

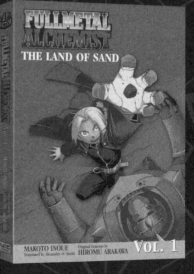
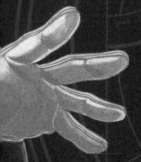

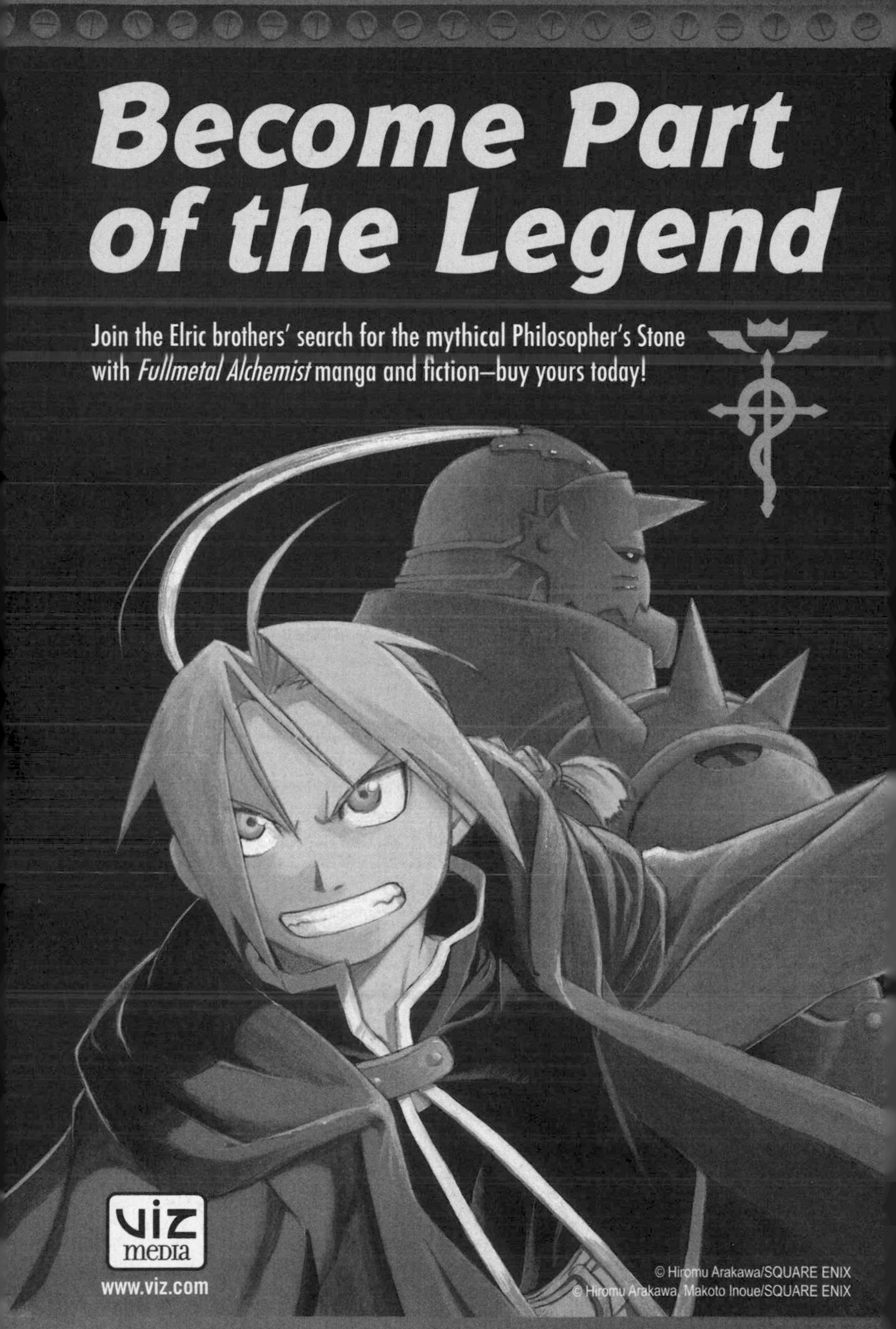
Become Part of the Legend
Join the Elric brothers' search for the mythical Philosopher's Stone with Fullmetal Alchemist manga and fiction—buy yours today!
viz media
www.viz.com
© Hiromu Arakawa/SQUARE ENIX
© Hiromu Arakawa, Makoto Inoue/SQUARE ENIX

Fullmetal Alchemist Profiles

Get the background story and world history of the manga, plus:

- Character bios
- New, original artwork
- Interview with creator Hiromu Arakawa
- Bonus manga episode only available in this book

Fullmetal Alchemist Anime Profiles

Stay on top of your favorite episodes and characters with:

- Actual cel artwork from the TV series
- Summaries of all 51 TV episodes
- Definitive cast biographies
- Exclusive poster for your wall

FULLMETAL ALCHEMIST™

Everything You Need to Get Up to
Fullmetal Speed

Get the who's who and what's what in Edward and Alphonse's world—buy these *Fullmetal Alchemist* profile books today at store.viz.com!

The Art of Fullmetal Alchemist

Contains all the manga artwork from 2001 to 2003!
- Gorgeously painted illustrations
- Color title pages, Japanese tankobon and promotional artwork
- Main character portraits and character designs from the video games

And a special two-page message from series creator Hiromu Arakawa!

Hardcover
$19⁹⁹

The Art of Fullmetal Alchemist: The Anime

Includes art inspired by the popular anime series!
- Initial character designs
- Cel art
- Production notes

Plus, an interview with Yoshiyuki Ito, character designer for the anime!

Hardcover
$19⁹⁹

FULLMETAL ALCHEMIST

ART OF

viz media

www.viz.com
store.viz.com

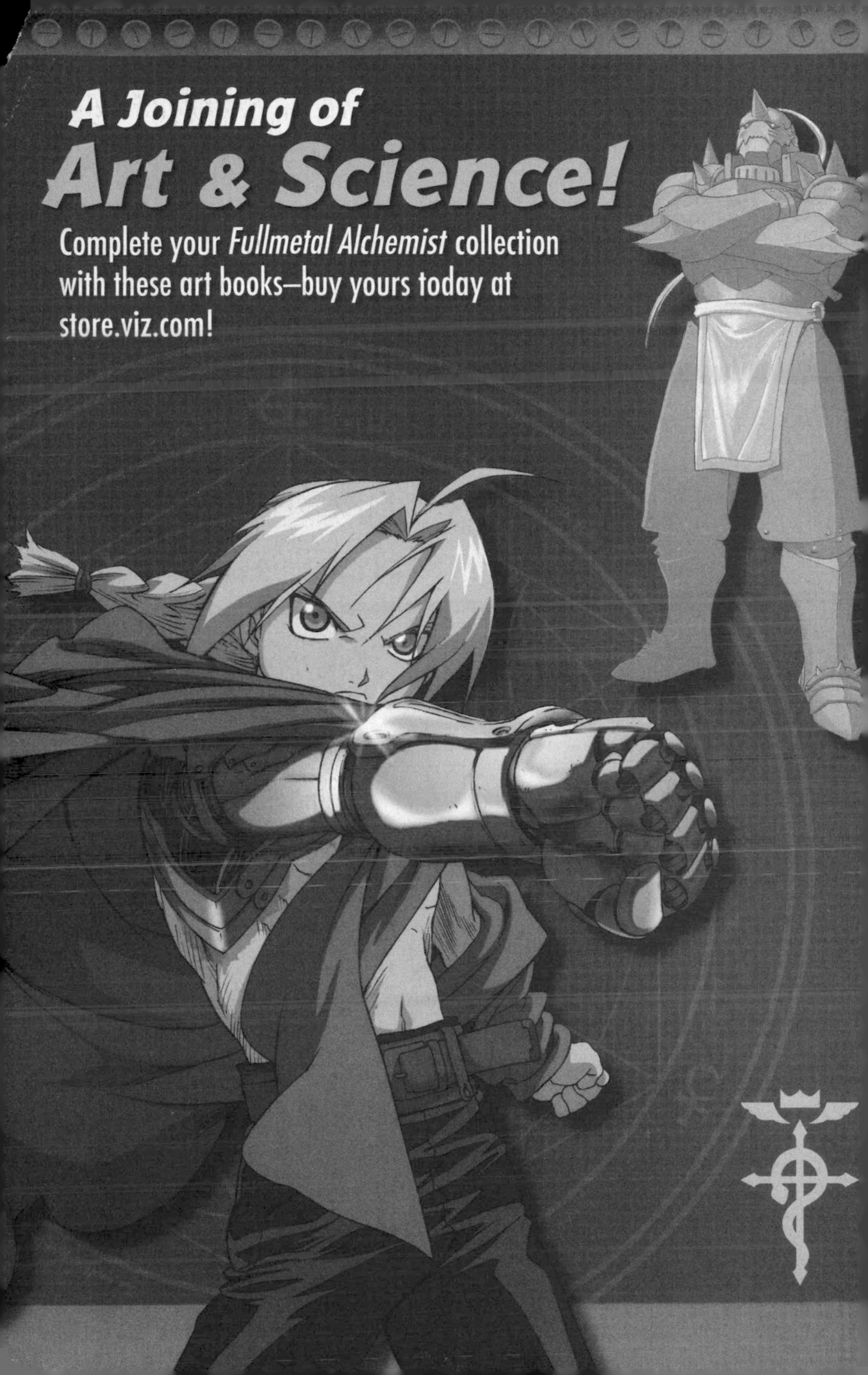
A Joining of
Art & Science!
Complete your Fullmetal Alchemist collection with these art books—buy yours today at store.viz.com!

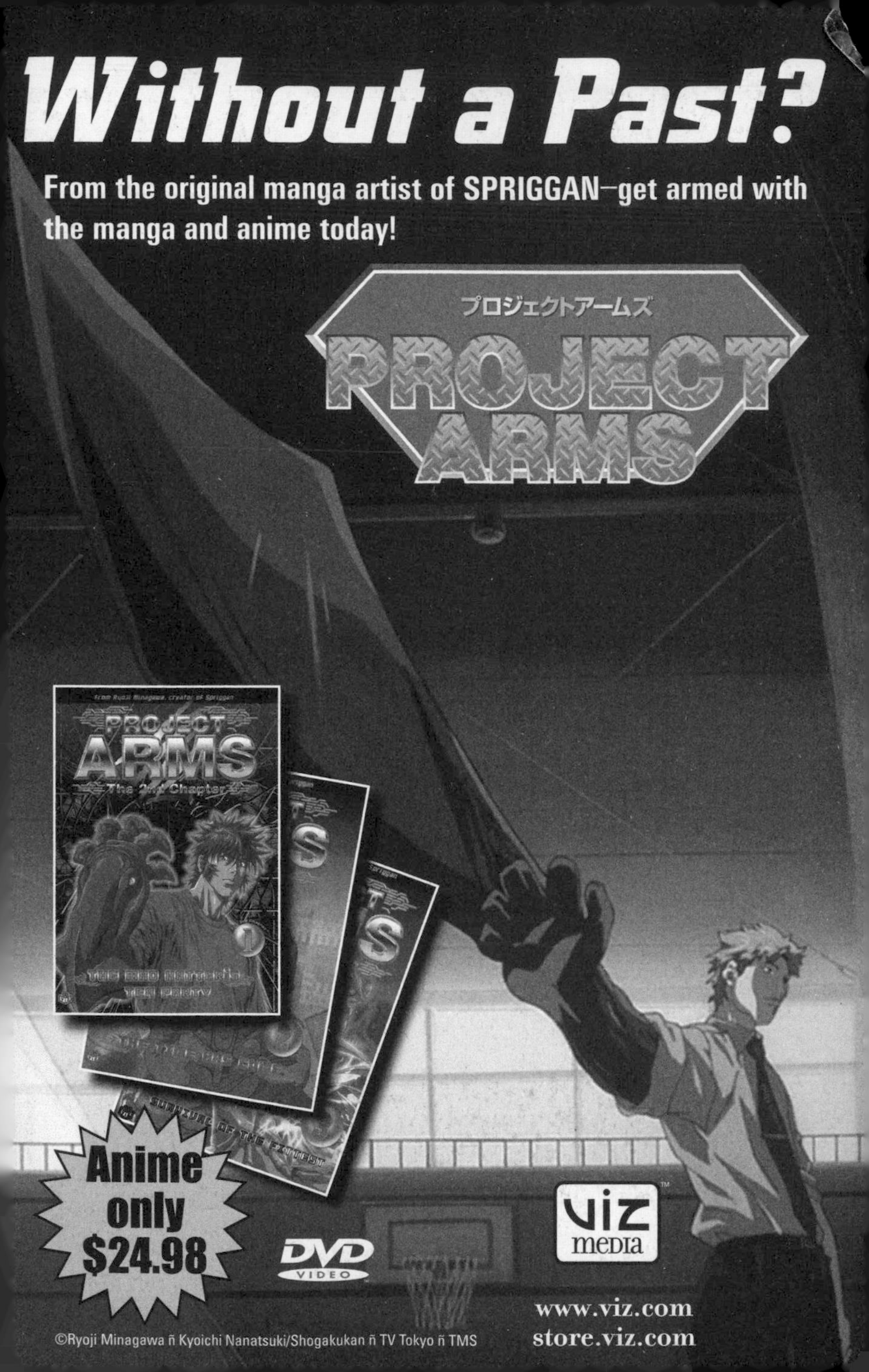
Without a Past?
From the original manga artist of SPRIGGAN—get armed with the manga and anime today!
プロジェクトアームズ
PROJECT ARMS
PROJECT ARMS
The 2nd Chapter
Anime only $24.98
DVD VIDEO
viz media
www.viz.com
store.viz.com
©Ryoji Minagawa ñ Kyoichi Nanatsuki/Shogakukan ñ TV Tokyo ñ TMS